A PORTRAIT OF SAMUEL HARTLIB

Rembrandt, Scholar in his Study, etching, with drypoint and burin, c.1652, Elizabeth Harvey-Lee, Image Conscious (North Aston, Oxon, 2024), No.12.

A Portrait of Samuel Hartlib

In Search of Universal Betterment

Charles Webster

https://www.openbookpublishers.com

© 2025 Charles Webster

This work is licensed under a Creative Commons Attribution-NonCommercial 4.0 International (CC BY-NC 4.0). This license allows you to share, copy, distribute and transmit the text; to adapt the text for non-commercial purposes of the text providing attribution is made to the author (but not in any way that suggests that they endorse you or your use of the work). Attribution should include the following information:

Charles Webster, *A Portrait of Samuel Hartlib: In Search of Universal Betterment*, Cambridge, UK: Open Book Publishers, 2025, https://doi.org/10.11647/OBP.0486

In order to access detailed and updated information on the license, please visit https://doi.org/10.11647/OBP.0486

Further details about CC BY-NC 4.0 licenses are available at http://creativecommons.org/licenses/by-nc/4.0/

All external links were active at the time of publication unless otherwise stated and have been archived via the Internet Archive Wayback Machine at https://archive.org/web

Any digital material and resources associated with this volume are available at https://doi.org/10.11647/OBP.0486#resources

Every effort has been made to identify and contact copyright holders and any omission or error will be corrected if notification is made to the publisher.

ISBN Paperback: 978-1-80511-691-2
ISBN Hardback: 978-1-80511-692-9
ISBN Digital (PDF): 978-1-80511-693-6
ISBN Digital ebook (html): 978-1-80511-695-0
ISBN Digital ebook (epub): 978-1-80511-694-3

DOI: 10.11647/OBP.0486

Cover image: After Ernst Barlach, Die Vertriebenen, 1918, woodcut, in E. Laur, *Ernst Barlach. Die Druckgraphik* (Leipzig: E.A.Seeman, 2001), No. 57, p. 116.

Cover design by Jeevanjot Nagpal

To Carol

Contents

List of Illustrations	xi
Preface	xiii
Acknowledgements	xv
List of Abbreviations	xvii
Introduction	1
1. The Young Hartlib	11
1.1 Elbing	11
1.2 Brieg and Silesia	13
1.3 Cambridge	19
1.4 Elbing: The Antilian Adventure	21
1.5 John Dury	25
2. Communion of Saints	29
2.1 Academies and Educational Debate	32
2.2 Puritan Orientation	35
2.3 Communications and Status	36
2.4 Introducing Jan Amos Komenský	39
2.5 Evaluating Comenius	48
2.6 Diversification	57
2.7 Comenius in London	59
2.8 Israel's Call	71
3. The Hartlibian Resurgence	79
3.1 Stabilisation	82
3.2 Active Reconstruction	88
3.3 Benjamin Worsley, Robert Boyle and William Petty	92
3.4 John Hall	96

3.5 William Rand	104
3.6 Apocalypticism	115
4. Man of the Moment	131
4.1 Changing Times	131
4.2 The Hartlib Partnership Continued	135
4.3 Education and Training	137
4.4 The Thirst for Betterment	165
4.5 Husbandry Revolution	179
5. *Phosphore Redde Diem!*	195
5.1 Family Affairs	195
5.2 Oppressive Pain	199
5.3 Hard Times	203
5.4 'Not Without Dust and Heat'	208
5.5 From Pomiculture to the Good Old Cause	211
5.6 Address: The Hartlibian Panacea	214
5.7 Loose Ends	225
5.8 Extinction of the Ephemerides	232
5.9 Being of the Spirit	238
Epilogue	249
Bibliography	259
Primary Sources: Publications by Samuel Hartlib	259
Other Primary Sources	261
Secondary Sources	263
Index	279

List of Illustrations

Frontispiece	Rembrandt, *Scholar in his Study*, etching, with drypoint and burin, c.1652, Elizabeth Harvey-Lee, *Image Conscious* (North Aston, Oxon, 2024), No. 12.	p. ii
1	Ludwig Richter, *Einwandrung protestantischer Böhmen in Sachsen*, 1834, copper engraving. Leaf of a calendar. https://commons.wikimedia.org/wiki/File:Die_Dezembernacht_1653_von_Ludwig_Richter.jpg	p. 10
2	Engraved title page of Jan Amos Komenský (Comenius) *Opera didactica omnia. Variis hucusque occasionibus scripta, diversisque locis edita: nunc autem non tantùm in unum, ut simul sint, collecta, sed & ultimô conatu in systema unum mechanicè constructum, redacta* (Amsterdam: Laurens de Geer, printed by Christoffel Cunrad and Gabriel de Roy, with engraved title page executed by Crisijn van der Passe the younger, assisted by David Loggan.	p. 28
3	Title page of Samuel Hartlib, *Clavis apocalyptica, or, A prophetical key by which the great mysteries in the revelation of St. John and the prophet Daniel are opened: it beeing made apparent that the prophetical numbers com to an end with the year of our Lord, 1655: in two treatises: 1. Shewing what in these our times hath been fulfilled, 2. At this present is effectually brought to pass, 3. And henceforth is to bee expected in the year neer at hand* (London: Printed by William Du-Gard for Thomas Matthewes, and sold by Giles Calvert), Thomason E.1260[2], dated by Thomason Feb 27 1650; Wing H979.	p. 78
4	Title page of Iacopo Aconcio, *Darkness discovered. Or the Devils secret statagems laid open...* [translated by William Rand] (London: printed by John Macock for William Ley, 1651), Thomason E.634[2], dated by Thomason 7 July; Wing A442.	p. 130

5 Engraved title page of *Biblia święta: to jest, księgi pisma* p. 194
   swietego starego y nowego przymierza (Amsterdam:
   Christophel Cunrad, 1660).

Preface

My investigations into the Hartlib Papers began in 1962, but since then the realities of my various employment situations gave only limited opportunities for this work. However, I was able to produce a relevant small book in 1970 and a much larger one in 1975. This present study, one of my main long-term objectives, only became practicable during my retirement, when I was surprised that the opportunity to generate a study specifically devoted to Hartlib had not already been grasped. However, in 2018 there appeared an outstanding French monograph composed by Stéphane Haffemayer. Since my own plan was significantly different, I pressed on, confident that both studies would prove their value. Fortuitously, the miserably slow pace of my own work occasioned some major advantages, such as the emergence of the digitised edition of the Hartlib Papers and the publications of a swelling band of scholars who recognised both the importance of Hartlib and the remarkable opportunities offered by the Hartlib Papers. The final stages of work on this book have therefore coincided with what amounts to a Hartlib renaissance.

Concerning the technicalities of presentation: I follow standard practice by applying a small degree of regularisation of spelling in quotations. On place and proper names, I generally follow the practice of Hartlib and his correspondents. For dates, in most cases I opt for the Gregorian 'New Style' alternative, and also use January as the starting point for the year. The chronological chapter divisions adopted seem to work reasonably well, but it will be observed that, unavoidably, many of the case studies breach the chapter boundaries, a few of them to a substantial extent.

During the early stages of this project I was deeply indebted to the late Professor W.H.G. Armytage, who encouraged me to continue the work of his predecessor, Professor George Turnbull, who had died in 1961. Also invaluable at this early stage was the assistance given by Joan Gilham of the Archive Department of the Sheffield University Library. Since my arrival in Oxford I have enjoyed the companionship of a growing band of colleagues who have become users, indeed experts, on the Hartlib Papers. Alas, those no longer here include Pamela Barnett, John Cooper, Christopher Hill, Vivian Salmon, Joan Thirsk and Hugh Trevor-Roper. Those still active include Toby Barnard, Philip Beeley, Michael Braddick, David Cram, Peter Elmer, Howard Hotson, Colin Kidd, Rhodri Lewis, Noel Malcolm, Scott Mandelbrote, Adam Parr, William Poole and Emil Wohl. My greatest debt in the academic sphere is to Mark Greengrass, whom I have known for more than fifty years, who is rightly regarded as the architect of Hartlib Studies, and whose contributions relate to every sphere of this particular field of research and information technology.

With respect to the final stages of this project I am also grateful to Professor Henrike Laehnemann for her general help and encouragement, above all for introducing me to Open Book Publishers, who are a delight to work with in every department of their operations. In this context I must thank their three referees for their invaluable and penetrating reporting, which has been a major asset to me during this last phase of my work. I must also thank many neighbours and friends for their forbearance during my long spells spent at the treadmill. Crucial at this final stage of the project has been the acute editorial assistance of Margaret Pelling, which represents an input of definitive importance. Also fundamental at this final stage has been the many facets of technical assistance contributed by Helena Webster, my daughter, who has patiently compensated for my incompetence regarding everything connected with the computer. Finally, all of this would not have been possible without the support of my family as a whole, above all, Carol. Without her, none of this would have been remotely possible.

Acknowledgements

For his generosity during the early years of this project I owe deep gratitude to the late Thomas Cholmondeley, the fourth Baron Delamere, for allowing my unrestricted use of the Hartlib Papers, of which his family are the owners. Latterly, I owe a similar debt to Hartlib Papers Project of the University of Sheffield, which generated their CD-ROM edition of the Hartlib Papers and prepared the ground for the digitised version of 2013, which is now the standard source of reference.

With respect to the illustrations: I am the source of the cover illustration, but Ernst Barlach is the inspiration. The Rembrandt Frontispiece is reproduced with the kind permission of Elizabeth Harvey-Lee, as illustrated and listed in her December 2024 Catalogue, *Image Conscious*, No. 12. Illustration 1, the leaf of a calendar produced in 1834, designed by Ludwig Richter, comes from my own print collection. Illustration 2, The Comenius title page, originates from the All Souls College Library, S.R. 134 g. 80/3, and is reproduced with the permission of the Warden and Fellows of All Souls College, Oxford. Illustrations 3 and 4, the title pages of *Clavis Apocalyptica* and *Darkness Discovered*, derive from the Thomason Collection E.1260[22] and E.634[2] respectively, and are reproduced by courtesy of the British Library. Illustration 5, the title page of *Biblia Święta* 1660, is reproduced by the kind permission of the National Library of Poland, Warsaw, *SD xvii.3.1803*.

List of Abbreviations

Akkerman *Elizabeth*	N. Akkerman, *Elizabeth Stuart, Queen of Hearts* (Oxford: Oxford University Press, 2021).
Barnett *Haak*	P. R. Barnett, *Theodore Haak F.R.S. The first German Translator of Paradise Lost* ('S Gravenhage: Mouton & Co., 1962).
BL	British Library.
Blekastad *Comenius*	M. Blekastad, *Comenius. Versuch eines Umrisses von Leben, Werk und Schicksal des Jan Amos Komenský* (Oslo: Universitetsforlaget/Prague: Akademia, 1969).
Boyle *Correspondence*	M. Hunter, A. Clericuzio and L.M. Principe (eds.), *The Correspondence of Robert Boyle 1636-1661*, volume I (London: Pickering & Chatto, 2001).
CPW II	E. Sirluck (ed.), *John Milton, The Complete Prose Works, volume 2, 1643-1648* (New Haven, Connecticut: Yale University Press, 1959).
Comenius *Korespondence 26/1*	*Dílo Jana Amose Komenského 26/I Korespondence Část I, 1628-1638* (Prague: Academia, 2018).
Crossley	J. Crossley (ed.), *The Diary and Correspondence of John Worthington* (Manchester: Chetham Society Remains, XIII (Vol. 1), XXXVI (Vol. 2, Part 1) and CXIV (Vol. 2, Part 2) (1847-1886).

Culpeper *Letters*	M.J. Braddick and M. Greengrass (eds.), *The Letters of Sir Cheney Culpeper (1641–1657)*, Camden Miscellany XXXIII, Camden Fifth Series, volume 7 (Cambridge: Cambridge University Press, 1996).
Dickson *Tessera of Antilia*	D.R. Dickson, *The Tessera of Antilia. Utopian Brotherhoods & Secret Societies in the Early Seventeenth Century* (Leiden: Brill, 1998).
DJAK	*Dílo Jana Amose Komenského*.
EMLO	Early Modern Letters Online—Samuel Hartlib. University of Oxford. 2015.
Gewalt sei ferne den Dingen	W. Goris, M. A. Meyer and V. Urbánek (eds.), *Gewalt sei ferne den Dingen! Contemporary Perspectives on the Works of John Amos Comenius* (Wiesbaden: Springer, 2016).
Greengrass, *Samuel Hartlib and Universal Reformation*	M. Greengrass, M. Leslie and T. Raylor (eds.), *Samuel Hartlib and Universal Reformation. Studies in Intellectual Communication* (Cambridge: Cambridge University Press, 1994).
Haffemeyer, *Les Lumières radicales*	S. Haffemeyer, *Les Lumières radicales de la Révolution Anglaise. Samuel Hartlib et les réseaux de l' Intelligence (1600–1660)* (Paris: Classiques Garnier, 2018).
HP	Hartlib Papers, University of Sheffield Library.
KK	Ján Kvačala, *Korrespondence Jana Amosa Komenského. Listy Komenského a vrstevníků jeho*, 2 vols. (Prague: České akademie císaře Františka Josefa, 1898-1902).
Léchot *Dury*	P.-O. Léchot, *Un christianisme "sans partialitié" Irénisme et méthod chez John Dury (v.1600-1680)* (Paris: Honoré Champion, 2011).
Leng *Worsley*	T. Leng, *Benjamin Worsley (1618-1673) Trade, Interest and the Spirit in Revolutionary England* (Woodbridge: Royal Historical Society/Boydell & Brewer, 2008).

Malcolm/Stedall *Pell*	N. Malcolm and J. Stedall, *John Pell (1611-1685) and his Correspondence with Sir Charles Cavendish* (Oxford: Oxford University Press, 2005).
MGP	Ján Kvačala (ed.), *Die pädagogische Reform des Comenius in Deutschland bis zum Ausgange des XVII Jahrhunderts* (Berlin: A. Hofmann 1903) (Monumenta Germaniae Paedagogica, Band 26).
Patera *Korrespondence*	A. Patera, *Komenského korrespondence* (Prague: České akademie císaře Františka Josefa, 1892).
Slack *Invention of Improvement*	P. Slack, *The Invention of Improvement. Information and Material Progress in Seventeenth-Century England* (Oxford: Oxford University Press).
Turnbull *Hartlib*	G.H. Turnbull, *Samuel Hartlib: A Sketch of his Life and his Relations to J.A. Comenius* (London: Oxford University Press/Humphrey Milford, 1920).
Turnbull *HDC*	G. H. Turnbull, *Hartlib, Dury and Comenius: Gleanings from Hartlib's Papers* (Liverpool: Liverpool University Press, 1947).
Vaughan *Protectorate*	R. Vaughan, *The Protectorate of Oliver Cromwell, and the State of Europe during the Early Part of the Reign of Louis XIV*, 2 vols. (London: H. Colburn, 1839).
Webster *Instauration*	C. Webster, *The Great Instauration: Science, Medicine and Reform 1626–1660* (London: Duckworth, 1975).
Young *Comenius in London*	R.F. Young, *Comenius in England: The Visit of Jan Amos Komenský (Comenius) to London in 1641–1642* (London: Oxford University Press/Humphrey Milford, 1932).
Young *Moriaen*	J.T. Young, *Faith, Medical Alchemy and Natural Philosophy: Johann Moriaen, Reformed Intelligencer and the Hartlib Circle* (Farnham: Ashgate, 1998).

Introduction

As an immigrant without professional status or recognised employment, and with no settled income, it is perhaps no surprise that, after his death, Samuel Hartlib (c.1600–1662) sank into oblivion. Eventually, during the Victorian period, such factors as his friendship with John Pym and John Milton, editions of his correspondence with Robert Boyle, John Pell and John Worthington and his reputation as a friend of technical innovation served to increase familiarity with his activities and even earned him a modest entry in the *Dictionary of National Biography*.

Further progress was hampered by lack of evidence, but the position was transformed in 1933 with the discovery of Hartlib's personal papers. These were fortunate to become the subject of the amazing labours of George Turnbull, whose publications still form the bedrock of all work in this field. After the death of Turnbull, the Hartlib Papers were transferred to Sheffield, and soon to the University of Sheffield Library, which, for the first time, made this archive accessible to scholars. The situation was again transformed when, just over ten years ago, the Hartlib Papers became available in a digitised form.

Owing to many obstacles and the scale of the challenge, the forces of modern scholarship have still made only limited incursions into the Hartlib Papers. However, in recent years, as noted in the Preface, the pace has greatly accelerated, which has been a great asset to my own project, which aims to inspire yet further work in this rich field of investigation.

The full collection of Hartlib's papers in their original wrappers, housed in their domed travel trunk chest, as Turnbull and I experienced them, amounted to no fewer than seventy bundles, many of which contained hundreds of separate items. Considering the chaotic circumstances after his death, it is remarkable that Hartlib's archive survived in such good order, which we owe to Hartlib himself and then Worthington and his coworkers operating at Brereton Hall in Cheshire.

Indicative of the scale of the problems facing editors and users, the largest generator of papers, apart from Hartlib himself, was John Dury, who was responsible for more than a thousand letters and hundreds of related items. Hartlib is calculated to have generated more than five thousand letters, while the letters addressed to him total at least twice that amount.[1] The Hartlib-Worthington correspondence, which is the only major case where both sides of the exchange are preserved, we owe to James Crossley. His fine Chetham Society edition conveys a unique insight into Hartlib's capacities as a correspondent, the scale and quality of which, almost without remission, he maintained until the eve of his death.

Arguably the most important single item in Hartlib's archive is his daybook, or Ephemerides for the years 1634-1660, which occupies some 1,200 sheets, and constitutes a major source of reference in itself.[2] The impressive range of additional material takes the Hartlib Papers to about thirty thousand sheets. The single-handed accumulation and ordering of this massive archive were in themselves a remarkable, indeed almost heroic, achievement. As the opening sections of chapter 5 indicate, Hartlib's achievement was all the greater considering the extreme ill-health that afflicted him during the last decade of his life, which rendered him house-bound and often bed-ridden.

The only major correspondence so far published in its entirety in modern times is that relating to Sir Cheney Culpeper, an excellent edition which illustrates the wide range of Hartlib's interests, and the depth of the involvement of Culpeper and Hartlib in the political affairs of the day. John Young and Thomas Leng have ably complemented the Culpeper edition with their exhaustive surveys of the letters and papers relating to Johann Moriaen and Benjamin Worsley. The other segment of the Hartlib papers that has been extensively explored and edited is the important archive comprising the letters and writings of Comenius. Hartlib was one of the most active correspondents of Comenius: there

---

[1] M. Greengrass and L.T.I. Penman, 'L'ombre des archives dans les cultures du savoir du XVIIe siècle: les papiers de Samuel Hartlib (v. 1600-1662)', *Bibliothèque de l'Ecole des Chartes*, 171:1 (2013), 51–64 (pp. 58–60).

[2] S. Clucas, 'Samuel Hartlib's *Ephemerides*, 1635-59, and the Pursuit of Scientific and Philosophical Manuscripts: The Religious Ethos of an Intelligencer', *The Seventeenth Century*, 6 (1991), 33–55; M. Greengrass, 'An "Intelligencer's Workshop": Samuel Hartlib's *Ephemerides*', *Studia Comeniana et Historica*, 26 (1996), 48–62.

survive about seventy letters of Comenius to Hartlib, but only one from Hartlib to Comenius. In such cases, assessment of the contribution of Hartlib is therefore to a large degree an exercise of inference based on a modicum of evidence.

It is also important to remember that Hartlib played a significant role as a publisher. He was directly responsible for more than seventy publications during the period 1638–1660. Many of these works and the projects relating to them are reviewed in the following chapters. Sometimes, as in the case of William Rand's translation of Aconcio's *Satans Stratagems*, it is doubtful whether such major and influential publications would have materialised without Hartlib's intervention. As is evident from the following survey, his record as a publisher was very uneven. Therefore, in some unexpected fields he excelled, but his record was weaker in areas such as education, which was supposed to be his greatest strength. It is also a shock that Hartlib, who was a prolific correspondent, was reticent to compose anything for publication. The few examples of his writings that have survived confirm his lack of confidence and the poor quality of many of these products. On the other hand, he was fanatically active as an editor. The Hartlib Papers contain hundreds of draft documents that were meticulously prepared for publication by him personally. These included many dozens of sensitive personal letters. On occasion, as with the *Praeludium* of Comenius, the *Brabant Husbandry* of Weston, or deeply personal letters of Dorothy Dury, Hartlib opened himself up to embarrassment by rushing into publication without seeking the author's permission.[3] On the positive side, as in the case of such seminal documents as Benjamin Worsley's 'Proffits humbly presented', which have only recently appeared in print, the editions upon which we now rely are the product of the sensitive and skilful editorial handling by Hartlib.[4]

---

3   Two letters from Dorothy Moore (and three from Dury) to Lady Ranelagh, were published by Hartlib without authorisation in 1645, earning him a stern rebuke. For details, L. Hunter, *Letters of Dorothy Moore*, p. 63, n.111 and 79–81.

4   M. Greengrass, 'Archive Refractions: Hartlib's Papers and the Workings of an Intelligencer', in *Archives of the Scientific Revolution: The Formation and Exchange of Ideas in Seventeenth-Century Europe*, ed. by M. Hunter (Woodbridge: Boydell Press, 1998), pp. 35–48; idem, 'Samuel Hartlib and the Commonwealth of Learning', in *The Cambridge History of the Book in Britain*, vol. 4, ed. by J. Barnard et al. (Cambridge: Cambridge University Press, 2002), pp. 304–22.

Still neglected as an area of study is Hartlib's role in the field of scribal transmission. As the case of Dorothy Dury reminds us, anything that came into his hands was likely to find its way to anyone designated by Hartlib. This study touches upon dozens of such cases. In the case of four important and highly personal letters that he received from Lady Ranelagh, Hartlib even had these translated into German for transmission to his friends in the Netherlands. Perhaps the most important example of this practice of scribal transmission occurred in the late 1590's when, as further discussed in chapter 4, Hartlib was the avenue of communication for exchanges on economic affairs that are becoming recognised as fundamental documents in the evolution of economic thinking.[5]

As John Coffey exclaimed with respect to the extraordinary range of work undertaken by Hartlib and his coworkers: 'the Hartlib Papers reveal the breathtaking extent of their ambition. Those associated with the reformer drafted countless schemes for the advancement of chemistry, agriculture, technology, medicine, law, mathematics, social welfare, Protestant ecumenism, education and commerce.'[6] A good number of the elements within this remarkable repertoire of subject-matter are now the subject of active research, and many of them find their place in the present study.

Quite correctly, as Coffey points out, almost all of Hartlib's interventions involved to some degree his partnership with coworkers. Often projects initiated by Hartlib took on a life of their own, with the result that Hartlib virtually disappeared from the scene. The case studies investigated in the following chapters exhibit every level of participation by Hartlib. Even when he played a limited role, he remained an important common denominator, and was sought out by an unending succession

---

5   On scribal communication in general, the classic: Harold Love, *The Culture and Commerce of Texts. Scribal Publication in Seventeenth-Century England* (Oxford: Clarendon Press, 1993), and for Hartlib, the pioneering M. Greengrass, 'Samuel Hartlib and Scribal Communication', *Acta Comeniana*, 12 (1997), 47–62.

6   John Coffey, 'The Impact of Apocalypticism during the Puritan Revolutions', *Perichoresis*, 4:2 (2006), 117–48 (p. 127). For a lively assessment of the Hartlib network, see Carol Pal, 'The Early Modern Information Factory. How Samuel Hartlib Turned Correspondence into Knowledge', in *Empires of Knowledge. Scientific Networks in the Early Modern World*, ed. by P. Finden (London: Routledge, 2018), pp. 166–58.

of thinkers and innovators as their very best means of facilitating the furtherance of their specialities.

In view of his ubiquitous presence and recognised role of leadership, it is entirely appropriate to build this study around the biography of Hartlib, which is an urgent desideratum, and should not have been so long delayed. The case studies that comprise the major part of this volume are therefore built around his biographical record, but the fit between the biography and case studies tends to be approximate. For instance, the section on apocalypticism located in chapter 3, and the one on the Office of Address in chapter 5, both chronologically relate to the scope of the whole volume, but these are an exception.

Naturally, the following expositions bring to the fore the multitude of coworkers of Hartlib. These range from his closest personal friends to humble artisans occupying just a limited niche. With respect to the closest of Hartlib's many associates, this study is almost a collective biography of the whole group. As implied above, John Dury was the dominant figure in Hartlib's professional life and therefore features prominently in most chapters. I point out that the nature of their relationship was not always to the advantage of Hartlib. Worthington, Culpeper and other long-term associates from Britain and elsewhere in Europe were also central to his life and work. Among these feature two women, Dorothy Dury and her niece, Katherine Boyle, Viscountess Ranelagh, both of whom came into Hartlib's life in the early 1640s, and remained important to him thereafter, both as personal friends and correspondents. An extensive literature has developed concerning the nature and dynamics of Hartlib's 'circle' or 'network'. This literature, with its strong quantitative emphasis, has developed a life of its own. It is important to bear this sphere of research in mind, but for the present purposes, it is mostly of marginal relevance. With respect to terminology, I apply terms like 'circle' and 'network' very sparingly, and many others according to the situation under review, therefore in a non-prescriptive sense, in fact reflecting the loose usage adopted by Hartlib and his contemporaries.

As a biographically organised study, no attempt is made to iron out the weaknesses in Hartlib's character, which were numerous. However, his positive qualities were so many that he captured and maintained the admiration and confidence of members of every generation among his contemporaries, many of whom judged him to have achieved the status of a national, indeed, international institution, so much so that, among those who knew him best, he seemed to be irreplaceable. Therefore, to all of these he was a man well worth knowing. It is hoped that this study will contribute to repairing the neglect of ages and demonstrate that many classes of historian still stand to benefit from the treasures of the archive bequeathed by Samuel Hartlib. It is certain that such further work will bolster the case to regard Hartlib as a figure at the very forefront of his generation in his importance.

Concerning the ordering of this study, chapter 1 briefly considers Hartlib's early life and education. Important were his six years at the academy at Brieg in Silesia, which delivered a sound classical education in an environment which witnessed the transition from Lutheranism to Calvinism. Silesia at this date was home to a remarkably sophisticated and pluralistic culture. Additional depth was given to Hartlib's education by the seven years spent as a private student at the University of Cambridge, which introduced him to the Puritan intelligentsia, establishing links which served him well when he settled in London and indeed in later life. A final short stay at Elbing was important on account of his affiliation with the Antilian utopian fraternity. Here also was his first acquaintance with John Dury, and the start of their lifetime partnership.

Chapter 2 considers the first phase of Hartlib's life in London, where he remained resident for the rest of his life: first, a false start with failed Academy projects in Chichester and Hackney. However, he was firmly committed to education, as exemplified by his immersion in the exchanges between William Brookes and Joseph Webb. There soon followed Hartlib's discovery of Comenius, which launched another of his partnerships of a lifetime. This raised the possibility of the relocation of Comenius to London, though circumstances intervened to make this a short but eventful interlude. This chapter also considers the role of Hartlib in the Puritan community, among whom he emerged as a prized source of international intelligence and technical information. Thereby, Hartlib established himself as a practical asset, and also as an established figure within the perceived Communion of Saints and architects of the New Jerusalem.

Chapter 3 deals with the years from 1642 to 1648, but spreads to later dates with respect to its case studies. It begins with the catastrophic decline in the fortunes of Hartlib and his associates during the first years of the civil war. But the ground was quickly prepared for the emergence of a new team of patrons and coworkers. Especially important was his new friendships with Dorothy Moore, soon the wife of John Dury, and Katherine Boyle, Viscountess Ranelagh. These two cemented Hartlib's involvement with Ireland and Katherine introduced him to Robert Boyle, her younger brother. The return of John Dury to England, and especially his appointment at Winchester, promoted a flood of innovatory ideas from Hartlib relating to the organisation and institutionalisation of intellectual labour. This coincided with the general reconstruction and rejuvenation of his team of associates and the move to a much higher plane of ambition. This transition is illustrated with reference to Benjamin Worsley, William Petty, Robert Boyle and in greater detail with respect to John Hall and William Rand, who well illustrate the productivity and versatility of Hartlib's new recruits.

Chapter 4 covers the period from 1648 to 1658, when Hartlib reached the height of his influence and activism, all catalysed by the continuing diversification in his spectrum of coworkers and correspondents. The chapter is dominated by two major case studies, the first being education in its many dimensions. The educational activists under review range from the famous John Milton and William Petty to the obscure Samuel Harmar, George Snel and Ezerel Tong. In some respects, Hartlib and Dury emerge from this survey in a less positive light than is usually indicated. The second major case study relates to technical, chemical and agricultural innovation, areas which ranked among the major obsessions of this period. Many of Hartlib's most active coworkers were engaged in the drive for economic expansion. Hartlib was already curious about technical innovation through his patronage of figures such as Gabriel Plattes and other technicians, but in this period these areas of innovation became his obsession, which was, among other things, expressed by his unexpected emergence as an important publisher in the sphere of husbandry.

Chapter 5 is diverse in its subject matter, and inescapably preoccupied by the instabilities and reorientations that characterised the period from the death of Oliver Cromwell in 1658 to the death of Hartlib himself in

1662. It begins with a brief overview of Hartlib's life as a husband and father and the impact of chronic ill-health on his later work. There follows a review of the Office of Address, in which great hopes were invested. The concept was intrinsically sound, but the attempts at realisation were confused and incompetent. Then, with the collapse of the republic, the outcome for the whole of Hartlib's programme became jeopardised. The Restoration brought about the challenge of readjustment. Among Hartlib's associates there emerged marked divergence in their fortunes. Hartlib himself faced personal ruin and escalating ill-health. But these hardships were hardly reflected in the intellectual sphere. The nucleus of his team of coworkers remained intact and his correspondence network continued to flourish. His interest in innovation and scientific organisation was unabated. He opened up new fronts of activism in such arcane fields as biblical translation and Oriental studies, all complicated undertakings, most of which were still incomplete when Hartlib's participation ended with his sudden death in March 1662.

Regarding the employment of the term 'Betterment' in the subtitle and when relevant, the text, some readers may believe that this is anachronistic. However, by the time of Hartlib, it was in standard use. Hence, in the context of husbandry it is found in Walter Blith and Sir Kenelm Digby. In other contexts, it is present in the works of Sir Thomas Browne, John Bunyan and Henry Burton, the Puritan controversialist and rector of St. Matthew, Friday Street, Cheapside, who was well-known to Hartlib. In 1628, in his *Israels Fast*, Burton conveyed the assurance that, as fundamental to the love of Christ, 'he seeth us through to our betterment'.

Finally: a note concerning the illustrations to this study. Most refer to some definite element in the relevant chapter. The illustration for the first chapter bears a general relationship with the first two chapters and also with the study as whole. This touching memorial to the expelled Czech Protestant exiles is rooted in events in which Comenius was directly involved. One of the main destinations of the dispossessed exiles was Leszno, where Comenius and the leadership of the Unitas Fratrum settled, before they were again exiled in 1657. The cover illustration was inspired by Ernst Barlach's woodcut, *Die Vertriebenen*, which was typical of the work that he produced just after World War I. It was a pioneer effort with the woodcut, consciously produced in the manner of a much earlier date, and portraying figures in a timeless mode. This image therefore constituted a general memorial to the dispossessed and their will to survive regardless of the scale of their suffering. This theme connects with Hartlib, who left his homeland owing to the depredations of war and occupation, and in England experienced the most turbulent of times, but managed to make a remarkable contribution to human betterment, notwithstanding the harshness of his personal circumstances. It is generally agreed that the iconography of the frontispiece copper engraving by Rembrandt was indebted to the artist's partnership with Menasseh ben Israel who, at the date of execution of this Scholar image, was in London, immersed in negotiations serving the interests of his people. These events feature in chapter 3. They were of the utmost interest to Hartlib and Dury, and they directly involved some of Hartlib's nearest allies. The interpretation of this image is a matter of ongoing debate, but it is agreed that its symbolism draws on both Christian and Jewish sources, representing a synergy which probably reflects the standpoint of Hartlib himself.

Fig. 1 Ludwig Richter, *Einwandrung protestantischer Böhmen in Sachsen*, 1834, copper engraving. Leaf of a calendar.

1. The Young Hartlib

There is little about Samuel Hartlib's early life that foreshadows the man of public affairs that he later became in London. It was nevertheless evident that, as a young man, he aspired to much greater things than were possible to achieve in the little port of Elbing where he was born.

1.1 Elbing

Samuel Hartlib's father, Georg Hartlib (Hartlieb) (c.1552–1627), represented the branch of his family that sought betterment by moving East. They settled in Poland at the start of the sixteenth century. Their first stop was Szprotawa (Sprottau), not too far from the Brandenburg border. There they succeeded in both trade and the professions. As a young man, Georg Hartlieb followed his own father into manufacture and trade. He moved some 200km north-east to Posnań (Posen), at that date a thriving trading centre with a population of 30,000.[1] Protestants were at the heart of this economic boom. However, their economic and civic supremacy was rapidly reversed in final decades of the sixteenth century. Establishment of the Jesuit College in 1571 was a key turning point. With encouragement from their superiors, Jesuit students mounted increasingly violent attacks on Protestant property, including places of worship. One small indicator of this changing mood may well be Georg Hartlieb's difficulty in securing rights of citizenship. Nevertheless, by the late 1570s he was a churchwarden and was ranked among the most prosperous and generous members of the Lutheran community. Yet, in 1579 he and his wife vacated Posen which, in light of the mounting

---

1   Both Szprotawa (Sprottau) and Posnań (Posen) were equidistant from Leszno (Lissa), which became the stronghold of the exiled Bohemian Brethren and therefore played a fundamental role in the career of Comenius.

©2025 Charles Webster, CC BY-NC 4.0   https://doi.org/10.11647/OBP.0486.01

distress of the Protestant community, was a wise decision. The last hopes of the Protestants were extinguished in August 1592 with the death of Stanisław Górka, the Lutheran voivode [chief administrator] of Poznań.[2]

Hartlieb and his wife moved north to the Baltic coast, first to Danzig (Gdańsk) and then in 1589 to nearby Elbing (Elbląg). The latter was, at this date, an attractive commercial option, partly owing to its recently introduced trading arrangements with foreign trading companies such as the British Eastland Company. This made Elbing for a short period something of a boom town and attractive centre for immigrants. Georg Hartlieb successfully exploited this opportunity. He became one of the most successful businessmen in Elbing, where he was known as both merchant and banker. Shortly after the death of Regina, his second wife, and soon after his arrival in Elbing, Georg married his third wife, Elizabeth Langton (c.1570–c.1660), who was the second child of John Langton, a prosperous mercer, who was a founder and the Deputy of the Eastland Company.[3] Of their children, most relevant to this study are Georg, born c.1590 and Samuel, c.1600.

Their father Georg's expectations of stability were eventually disappointed. Tension between Danzig and Elbing worsened. In 1620, Elbing took the risk of withdrawing from the Hanseatic League. This decision was calculated to strengthen trading relations with Britain. However, the Polish authorities instituted punitive measures against Elbing, culminating in 1625, which effectively terminated the Eastland Company's viability in this sphere of its operations. At this very moment the town was also hit by a violent outbreak of the plague which claimed more than 3,000 lives out of a population of about 10,000. Just a year later Elbing was occupied and plundered by the Swedish army. Direct Swedish rule extended until 1635 and again from 1655 to 1660. Axel Oxenstierna, Governor-General for the new Swedish possessions,

---

2   Tomasz Kempa, 'Religious Relations and the Issue of Religious Tolerance in Poland and Lithuania in the 16th and 17th Centuries', *Sarmatia Europaea. Polish Review of Early Modern History*, 1 (2010), 31–66; T. Wotschke, 'Der posener Kirchenpfleger Georg Hartlieb', *Historische Monatsblätter für die Provinz Posen*, 11:1 (1910), 1–5; idem, *Die Reformation in Lande Posen* (Leszno: Oskar Gulitz, 1913), pp. 81–99.
    At Posen the Bohemian Brethren congregation was attacked earlier and more vigorously that were the Lutherans.
3   For Langton, H. Zins, *England and the Baltic in the Elizabethan Era* (Manchester: Manchester University Press, 1972), pp. 69, 102–04, 124, 131, 175.

adopted Elbing as his headquarters for Sweden's operations in that region in the course of the Thirty Years' War.[4]

The later education of Georg and Samuel therefore took place against the backdrop of instability, war and economic turmoil. However, their early education occurred in a more clement atmosphere. Both could anticipate a leisurely pace of schooling without any pressure to earn their living.

In 1598 Georg entered one of the lower grades of the Elbing Gymnasium. In 1608 he transferred to the Danzig Gymnasium. Both of these institutions were at that date prospering.[5] In 1612 Georg matriculated at Heidelberg University as a student of theology. In view of observations made by Comenius, cited below, it is quite possible that the acquaintance of the two began at this date. Georg remained there until at least 1620, at which point he had reached the age of 30.[6]

1.2 Brieg and Silesia

The details of the education of Samuel are more difficult to establish. It is likely that he followed Georg into the Elbing Gymnasium and at a similar age, which would suggest a date of about 1608. It is usually assumed, based on the detective work of George Turnbull in 1920, that Samuel then went on to the University of Königsberg. This would have been an understandable course of action, but this idea, although much repeated, is not supported by convincing evidence. However,

---

4   M. North, 'Elbings Außen- und Binnenhandel im 16. und 17. Jahrhundert', in *Elbing 1237–1987: Beiträge zum Elbing-Kolloquium im November 1987 in Berlin*, ed. by B. Jähnig and H.-J. Schuch (Münster, Westf.: Nicolaus-Copernicus Verlag, 1991), pp. 129–44; J.K. Fedorowics, *England's Baltic Trade in the Early Seventeenth Century* (Cambridge: Cambridge University Press, 2011).

5   Georg Hartlib entered the Elbing gymnasium at the point when Jan Mylius, the new Rector, was undertaking major improvements. Samuel Hartlib would then have benefitted from these changes.

6   Among Georg's fellow students was Comenius, who matriculated at Heidelberg in 1613 and left the following year. H. Röhrs, 'Die Studentzeit des Comenius in Heidelberg', in *Semper Apertus*, 1, ed. by W. Doerr and P.A. Riedl (Berlin: Springer Verlag, 1985), pp. 399–413. For the importance of Heidelberg as an irenicist centre, see H. Hotson, 'A Previously Unknown Early Work by Comenius: *Disputatio de S. Domini Coena, sive Eucharistia* under David Pareus, Heidelberg, 19 March 1614', *Studia Comeniana et Historica*, 24 (1994), 129–44 and idem, 'Irenicism and Dogmatics in the Confessional Age: Pareus and Comenius in Heidelberg, 1614', *The Journal of Ecclesiastical History*, 46:3 (1995), 432–53.

there is both direct and circumstantial evidence that Samuel attended the Academy at Brieg (Brzeg) in Silesia, likely from about 1615, which would have allowed him to reach the highest grade in 1618, a date for which there is incontrovertible evidence of his presence.[7] While it is certain that he remained in Brieg until 1618, it is also reasonable to conclude that he was there at least until 1620, and perhaps until 1621.[8] Contrary to the speculation currently circulating, there is no evidence that his brother Georg ever attended the Brieg academy.

At this date, in northern Europe it was by no means uncommon to select academies rather than universities for higher education. As already indicated by the case of John Dury at Leiden, an academy could be the ideal choice. Apart from Königsberg there was no university within easy reach of Elbing or Danzig. For complex political reasons Silesia was also entirely without a university. This vacuum was filled by a number of academies, many of which were well-endowed and in a flourishing state until the outbreak of the Thirty Years' War.[9] One of these was the academy at Brieg, which was a cosmopolitan institution

---

7 H.M. Barycz, 'Polacy w dawnym gimnazjum w Brzegu (w. XVI–XVIII)', Śląski Kwart. *Hist. Sobótka*, 26:2 (1974), 177–91, citing a now-destroyed inventory of students, pp. 183–87, in which appears the entry 'Samuel Hartlib Elbingensis Borussus', which relates to Class 1, the most advanced level in the academy.

8 It was customary to spend more than one year in the first Class. Friedrich von Logau, for instance, at precisely this date, spent much longer: M. Powak, *Jan Mylius (1557–1630), rektor Gimnazjum Elbląskiego w. Zasłużeni ludzie dawnego Elbląga* (Wrocław: Narodowy im. Ossolińskich, Wrocław, 1987); idem, 'Die Geschichte des Elbinger Gymnasiums in den Jahren 1535–1772', in *Kulturgeschichte Preußens königlich polnischen Anteils in der Frühen Neuzeit*, ed. by S. Beckmann and K. Garber (Tübingen: Niemeyer, 2005), pp. 371–94; Sven Tode, 'Bildung Wissenskultur der Geistlichkeit im Danzig der Frühen Neuzeit', in *Bildung und Konfession: Theologenausbildung im Zeitalter der Konfessionalisierung* ed. by H.J. Selderhuis and M. Wriedt (Tübingen: Mohr Siebeck, 2006), pp. 71–101. Generally, at Brieg final graduation took place when students were, on average, about twenty years of age. A leaving date for Hartlib of 1621 coincides with the conclusion of G.H. Turnbull, made on the basis of his evaluation of correspondence from this date, Turnbull *HDC*, pp. 12–15.

9 H.-J. Bömelburg, 'Die Kontakte der schlesischen Reformierten zum polnischen und litauischen Adel in der ersten Hälfte des 17. Jahrhundert', in *Die Reformierten in Schlesien. Vom 16. Jahrhundert bis zur Altpreußischen Union von 1817*, ed. by J. Bahlcke and I. Dingel (Göttingen: Vandenhoeck & Ruprecht, 2016), pp. 65–81; M. Holý, 'Silesia fere academica. Vergebliche Bemühungen um die Gründung einer Universität in Schlesien im 16. und 17. Jahrhundert und ihre Folgen', *Acta Universitatis Carolinae. Historia Universitatis Carolinae Pragensis*, 49:2 (2009), 243–56; G. Wąs, 'Calvinismus und Modernisierung. Ein Fallstudie zur politisch-konfessonellen Entwicklung der schesischen Fürstentümer Liegnitz und Brieg im

attracting students from a wide region, including Poland. Indeed, trade with Poland was a major source of prosperity for Silesian cities. At the same time, a lively cultural exchange took place. Thus, it came about that influences stemming from West and East, or from South and North, found their natural meeting point in Silesia.[10]

The Brieg academy was founded in 1569 by Duke Georg II consciously as an outpost of German Protestantism against the predominant Catholicism of the Habsburg territories. Under Jakob Schickfus (1574–1637), who was the rector at Brieg from 1603 until 1613, student numbers increased at times to 500. The academy was particularly praised for its high standards in Latin and Greek rhetoric, drama and poetry.[11] It is noteworthy that Schickfus resigned from the *Gymnasium illustre* at exactly the point at which the ducal estates were being divided between Johann Christian (1591–1634) of Brieg and Georg Rudolf (1589–1653) of Liegnitz and Wohlau, the sons of Duke Joachim Friedrich († 1602). In 1613 Schickfus resigned in order to enter the service of the elder of the Piast dukes. The light duties of this new post enabled him more easily to further his scholarly interests. Another sign of the instability of his age, in 1619 Schickfus converted to Catholicism. He was succeeded as Rector of the academy by the equally competent and more tenaciously Protestant Melchior Lauban (1567–1633), who was, as seen below, much admired by Samuel Hartlib.[12]

Reflecting the uncertainties of the times, in 1620 student numbers at Brieg suddenly collapsed. It seems that the immediate cause was spiralling inflation, the effect of which was the impoverishment of

---

16. und 17.Jahrhundert', in *Die Reformierten in Schlesien*, ed. by Bahlcke and Dingel, pp. 189–204.

10   M. Szyrocki, *Andreas Gryphius. Sein Leben und Werk* (Tübingen: Niemeyer, 1964), p. 9.

11   One indicator of initiative on the part of Brieg is its productions of the important drama *Susanna*, probably in the form developed by Nicodemus Frischlin in 1577. These are recorded at Brieg for 1610, 1616 and 1624, Paul F. Casey, *The Susanna Theme in German Literature* (Bonn: Bouvier Verlag, 1976), p. 245.

12   E. Pietrzak, 'Das Brieger Gymnasium und seine Rektoren in den Jahren 1604–1633', *Germanica Wratislaviensia*, 87 (1989), 29–46; R. Siedel, *Späthumanismus in Schlesien: Caspar Dornau (1577–1631). Leben und Werk* (Tübingen: Max Niemeyer Verlag, 1994), pp. 379–82. The Hartlib family may have recollected Lauban on account of his service as a classicist at the Danzig gymnasium between 1605 and 1613. At Brieg the pendulum swung yet further towards liberality with the appointment of the Socinian, Georg Vechner, as rector and superintendent of Brieg in 1646. However, he died within the year, something recounted by Kinner to Hartlib on 29 May 1648, HP 1/33/33B.

workers reliant on fixed stipends, including, of course, the teachers at the Brieg academy, who therefore neglected their duties and poached enrolled students for private gain. This crisis provoked a formal inspection of the academy. Nothing positive was achieved by this interference, but it generated hard feeling between Lauban and the eminent Caspar Dornau who was in charge of the inspection.[13]

At this date Brieg suffered its first taste of war in the form of mayhem induced by invasion of a Cossack horde. Over the next decades, indeed even after the end of the Thirty Years' War, Brieg, like much of Silesia, was afflicted by the imposition of forced quartering of Imperial soldiers, varieties of levies and taxes, the ravages of fire, epidemics of plague, mass influx of exiles, military occupation and by general gratuitous violence and destruction. Cyprian Kinner lamented the fate of the orphaned children of Brieg, who were left penniless and forced into exile, often becoming servants to Silesian noble families who had themselves been exiled at an earlier date to the Baltic area.[14]

If my conjectures about the dates of Samuel's tenure in Brieg are correct, contrary to much current supposition, he would not have overlapped with his later friend Abraham von Franckenberg, who studied there between 1608 and 1612, whereas 1615 is the earliest likely date for Hartlib's arrival. However, Hartlib would have been broadly contemporary with the poet Friedrich von Logau, the theologian Johannes Martini, and also Cyprian Kinner.[15] Kinner was close to these events. He was a native of that region, while Johannes Neomenius, his near relative and newly recruited Calvinist, was the most prominent churchman in the Brieg estates. Indicative of the incipient shift in religious alignment, in 1612 Neomenius was promoted by Duke Johann Christian to become his court preacher and then in 1614 Superintendent of the whole area. Reflecting the policy adopted by the Piast rulers since 1601, Neomenius conspicuously promoted liberty of conscience, while

---

13 T.B. Karnitscher, *Der vergessene Spiritualist Johann Theodor von Tschesch (1595–1649). Untersuchungen und Spurensicherung zu Leben und Werk eines religiösen Nonkonformisten* (Göttingen: Vandenhoeck & Ruprecht, 2015), pp. 91–92. This 1625 inspection underlined the bad feeling that had existed between the academies at Brieg and nearby Beuthen. Before emigrating to Brieg, Dornau was rector in Beuthen, which, for a short period, was immensely successful and celebrated as a home to religious toleration.

14 Kinner to Hartlib, 5 August 1648, HP 1/33/45A.

15 Kinner's letters testify that both Franckenberg and Martini were his near contemporaries at Brieg.

also encouraging Lutherans and Calvinists to engage in constructive dialogue.[16] Also, as the opportunity arose, Johann Christian packed the Brieg academy with Calvinist teachers. Kinner reminded Samuel of their keen participation in the shift to Calvinism.[17] Kinner also recalled that the learned Georg Rudolf, whom Kinner served in an advisory capacity, was a prince that 'at that time you saw and knew yourself'.[18]

It would be misleading to think that Hartlib was only preoccupied with confessional issues during his time in Brieg. Between them, the seventeen constituent parts of Silesia were a veritable hive of cultural stereotypes:

> In social, confessional, ideological, national, even cultural terms, Silesia constituted a variegated jumble. This generated tension between the individual camps, an atmosphere of debate and criticism, which was directed against a rigidity of tradition and every dogma, all of which smoothed the path for innovation...Silesia was also a refuge for numerous sects, for Anabaptists, Bohemian Brethren, Socinians, Schwenckfeldians, Paracelsians, as well as newcomers such as the Boehmists and related spiritualistic cells. In heated discussions, they fought each other, and no dogma, no sanctuary was spared, all of which constituted a spur to critical thinking among the people.[19]

Hartlib's long-term friendship with Abraham von Franckenberg from Ludwigsdorf near Oels in Lower Silesia, reminds us of his relaxed interaction with the remote fringes of spiritualism. Franckenburg and his friend Johan Theodor von Tschesch were pioneers of dialogue with Jacob Boehme of Görlitz, events that took place shortly after Hartlib's

---

16 T. Jaworski, 'Kontakty Braci czeskich i kalwinów na Dolnym Śląsku w XVI i XVII wieku', *Rocznik Lubuski*, 23:1 (1997), 69–80; J. Deventer, 'Nicht in die Ferne—nicht in die Fremde? Konfessionsmigration im schlesisch-polnischen Grenzraum im 17. Jahrhundert', in *Glaubensflüchtlinge. Ursachen, Formen und Auswirkungen frühneuzeitlicher Konfessionsmigration in Europa*, ed. by J. Bahlcke (Berlin: LIT Verlag, 2008), pp. 95–118; *Die Reformirten in Schlesien*, ed. by Bahlcke and Dingel, p. 102; T.B. Karnitscher, *Der vergessene Spiritualist Johann Theodor von Tschesch*, pp. 87–88, 114–17. For Kinner on the deaths of Neomenius and Vechner, letter to Hartlib, 28 October 1649, HP 1/83/33A-B.
17 G. Wąs, 'Calvinismus und Modernisierung', in *Die Reformierten in Schlesien*, ed. by Bahlcke and Dingel, pp. 201–04, and for Neomenius, pp. 96–99.
18 Kinner to Hartlib, 19 June 1647, HP 1/33/9A, Inprimis verò Duci Lignicensi Georgio Rudolofo, quem olim vidisti et nosti ipsemet: qui impensè favet literatis; et literarum bonarum amore ductus.
19 Szyrocki, *Andreas Gryphius*, pp. 13–14 (slightly expanded). For a comprehensive account of religious activity in Silesia, see S. Wollgast, 'Morphologie schlesischer Religiosität in der Frühen Neuzeit ', in *Kulturgeschichte Schlesiens in der Frühen Neuzeit*, vol. 1, ed. by K. Garber (Tübingen: Niemeyer, 2005), pp. 113–90.

departure from Brieg. Both Franckenberg and Tschesch, as well as others in their network, were also conversant with the writings attributed to Paracelsus, a factor which contributed to Silesia's reputation as a major centre for collecting and editing the writings of Paracelsus.[20]

Also relevant to the intellectual environment of Hartlib at Brieg were the advantages that he derived from the location of so many renowned musicians and literary figures at the Piast courts, who variously served in Liegnitz and Brieg as counsellors and court officials. Among this remarkable constellation were the literary figures Daniel Czepko, Caspar Dornau, Christian Hofmann von Hofmannswaldau, Daniel Caspar von Lohenstein, Friedrich von Logau, Bernhard Wilhelm Nüssler, Martin Opitz and Johann Theodor von Tschesch, as well as musicians such as Wencel Scherffer von Scherffenstein and Samuel Kinner.[21] Although most of these associations with the Piasts occurred after Hartlib's departure from Brieg, he would have observed that the intellectual atmosphere was conducive to this remarkable cultural flowering. He must also have known about the tendency of innovative intellectuals to agglomerate into informal and formal societies, the best known of which was the elitist *Fruchtbringende Gesellschaft* founded in Weimar in 1617, of which Duke Georg Rudolph was an early member and no doubt through him Martin Opitz was in 1629 also elected.

---

20 T.B. Karnitscher, *Der vergessene Spiritualist Johann Theodor von Tschesch*, pp. 212–47. A similar perspective was shown by other Brieg associates, as for instance Daniel Czepko, whose outlook is outlined in *Religion in Geschichte und Gegenwart* by H.-G. Roloff 'as an independent eclecticism, drawing on Jacob Boehme, Johannes Tauler, Paracelsus, Valentin Weigel, Caspar von Schwenckfeld, and Abraham von Franckenberg, which comes down to ardent worship of God'. A further Silesian adherent of both Paracelsus and Boehme (and probably also Schwenckfeld) was the Liegnitz physician and poet Balthasar Walther (c.1558–c.1630). Walther introduced Joachim Morsius to Boehme; Morsius soon was in touch with Moriaen, and the latter provided a link with the Hartlib group. L.T.I. Penman, '"Ein Liebhaber des Mysterii, und ein großer Verwandter desselben." Toward the Life of Balthasar Walther: Kabbalist, Alchemist and Wandering Paracelsian Physician', *Sudhoffs Archiv*, 94:1 (2010), 73–99. See also, Young, *Faith, Medical Alchemy*, pp. 17–20.

21 E. Pietrzak, *Literatur für den Hof: Die Piastenhöfe als kulturelle Zentren Schlesiens im 17. Jahrhundert* (Heidelberg: Universitätsverlag Winter, 2021). It is likely that Cyprian Kinner was related to one and perhaps both of these musicians; Pietrzak, 'Das kulturelle und literarische Leben im Bereich der schlesischen Piastenhöfe im 17. Jahrhundert. Bericht über ein Forschungsprojekt', *Germanica Wratislaviensia*, 85 (1989) 105–16. Kinner was also an associate of Nüssler, a lesser figure in this list, who served for a long period as secretary to the two Piast dukes. Kinner described him as an outstanding poet, philologist and Latinist, Kinner to Hartlib, 5 August 1648, HP 1/33/45A.

1.3 Cambridge

It was common for graduates of Brieg to undertake peregrinations, many of which involved periods of study at various academic centres. The precise choice depended to a large extent on their means, and sometimes they would subsist by becoming companions to richer students. The choice was also often made on the basis of confessional preference. Hence, after the Danzig academy, Georg Hartlib went on to Calvinist Heidelberg where he stayed from 1612 until at least 1620. Samuel Hartlib opted for England, and specifically Cambridge, perhaps in consequence of the widely-known Calvinist leanings within its colleges. His correspondence confirms his presence in Cambridge in 1625 and 1626, but it is also reasonable to conclude that he travelled there directly from Brieg in 1621.[22]

The preserved letters from his friends in Eastern Europe give few clues about Hartlib's activities in Cambridge, but one vital piece of information is contained in a letter from Thomas Ball to Hartlib, dated November 1638:

> Good Mr Hartlib. I went last night according to my promise to speake with Mr Jurdan who married Mrs Preston, wife and executrix to James Preston the Doctor's brother, and made that motion, that for as much as he was able to spare it, and Bourne to pay it, he would be pleased to part with it for a good worke and publick service to the church, and so acquainted him with your condition & relation to Doctor Preston in his life time. [23]

This message reminds us of Hartlib's perpetual financial difficulties. It also indicates that Ball was representing a wider group of Puritans who were supportive of both Hartlib and Dury. The said Jordan must have known that Thomas Ball and his associates were indebted to John Preston and were guardians of his memory. It would also have been no surprise to Jordan that the generous and well-connected Preston was likely to have been hospitable to the likes of Samuel Hartlib. As indicated below, Hartlib

---

22 Turnbull *HDC*, pp. 12–16, 18n.2 emphasises John Preston, for whom see also T. Webster, *Godly Clergy in Early Stuart England*, pp. 15–23; E. Davies, 'Beyond the Jesuit College: the role of Cambridge's 'Puritan' colleges in European politics and diplomacy, 1603–1625', in A. Beeton, et al. (eds), *The Mind is its Own Place? Early Modern Intellectual History in an Institutional Context* (Oxford: Oxford University Press, 2023), pp. 25–43. See also, Haffemeyer, *Les Lumières radicales*, pp. 59–65.
23 Ball to Hartlib, 28 November 1638, HP 48/3/1A-2B. Reference to this letter can be located in Turnbull *HDC*, p. 14, note 3, lines 10–14.

may have enjoyed this patronage from 1622 onwards, when Preston was Master of Emmanuel College and thereby able to further expand his already diverse range of devotees. Among these were certain foreigners. Hartlib himself testifies that Preston also 'took special care' of Johann Rülz (Rulicius, Rulice), who was soon to become a prominent member of the Dury-Hartlib community.[24] Other foreigners who perhaps trod this Cambridge path and then became associates of Hartlib were Theodore Haak and perhaps Caspar Streso.[25] In all such cases, Cambridge was the springboard to integration into the wider Puritan community.

The examples of Hartlib and his friends remind us that Cambridge habitually offered hospitality to foreign students, who were then able to avail themselves of the resources for study in accordance with their particular needs. The evidence from Hartlib's early papers suggests that he may well have benefitted from Preston himself, but also other prominent Cambridge figures such as Joseph Mede, Richard Sibbes and Samuel Ward. From the generation nearer his own, the evidence suggests that Hartlib was in close touch with the aforementioned Thomas Ball (1590–1659), who was one of the closest disciples of Preston and one of the main editors of his works. Also well-known to Hartlib from an early date were Thomas Goodwin (1600–1680) of St Catharine's College, who was another editor of Preston, and John Stoughton (1593–1639) of Emmanuel College until his departure in 1624, after which he remained in close touch with Hartlib during his tenure at the Puritan parish of St. Mary Aldermanbury. The immense respect that Hartlib harboured for these Cambridge scholars is confirmed by the frequent references to their work in the earliest pages of his working diary, the Ephemerides, which he initiated in 1634.

Although we rely mostly on supposition for assessing Hartlib's visit to Cambridge, it is likely that his experience there compared favourably with that of his contemporaries who migrated to continental universities, particularly at this date when favoured choices like Heidelberg were ruled out by wartime dislocation.

---

24 Hartlib to Worthington, October 1661, Worthington *Diary*, vol. 2, pp. 58–61. It seems that Rülz (Rulice) was recommended to Preston by the exiled Prince Friedrich of Bohemia. His arrival in Cambridge must have occurred in 1622 or later. Following a common pattern among Preston's pupils, Rulice then went on to Boston, Lincs. to serve a further apprenticeship under John Cotton.

25 P. Barnett, *Theodore Haak F.R.S.* ('S-Gravenhage: Mouton & Co. 1962), p. 13.

1.4 Elbing: The Antilian Adventure

Perhaps in the spring of 1626 Hartlib returned to Elbing. He remained there until the late summer of 1628. There he would have witnessed the ill effects of the Swedish occupation, the folding up of the Eastland Company and also in 1627, the death of his father. Such events contributed to changing the religious complexion of Elbing. Previously a stable balance had been achieved between the Lutheran and Calvinist congregations. The new situation eroded Calvinist influence and cemented Lutheran dominance: a trend not disfavoured by the new Swedish administration. For the rest of Hartlib's life, complaints about increasing intolerance towards the Elbing Calvinists regularly featured in his correspondence.

In Elbing he might well have met Nathaniel Ward, who was Dury's chaplain predecessor in Elbing and the younger brother of Samuel Ward, who is mentioned above with respect to Cambridge. Naturally, the most important event in this Elbing visit was Hartlib's first acquaintance with John Dury.[26] The first hint of their acquaintance is contained in two letters addressed to Hartlib in Elbing by Johann Fridwald, then residing in Königsberg, but from a family having close links with both Danzig and Elbing.[27] Fridwald reacted with excitement to Hartlib's reports about an *'Englischen Prediger'*, who seems to have been first mentioned in a lost letter of Hartlib to Fridwald dated 28 December 1627. Fridwald initially understood that Dury was in possession of knowledge about the occult sciences that might practically assist the work of their Antilian community. The second letter noted that this preacher was also evolving a new way of interpreting the scriptures. Hartlib expressed the hope that this scholar would enlighten the Antilians about the *Kabbalah*. This ends Fridwald's remarks about the 'English Preacher', but one further reference to Dury occurs, this time using his actual name.

The ten letters of Fridwald to Hartlib composed between 1628 and 1633 are mainly valued for the light they shed on the Antilian fraternity in which Hartlib was a key player. This aspect of Hartlib's career is

---

26 For the recent literature on Dury, P.O. Léchot, *Un christianisme 'sans partilitié' Irénisme et méthode chez John Dury (v.1600–1680)* (Paris: Honoré Champion Éditeur, 2011), and Haffemeyer, *Les Lumières radicales*, pp. 109–49 et passim.

27 Fridwald to Hartlib, 10 February and 8 March 1628, HP 27/32/1–2.

the object of much curiosity and some idle speculation. Fortunately, the most intensive study of this episode is contained in a monograph by Ronald Dickson, which is an impeccable work of scholarship.[28] As Professor Dickson observed, the Antilian fraternity was just one of many groups that were inspired by Johann Valentin Andreae's idea of Christian Societies, which he conceived as activist cells that would make a utilitarian contribution and also strengthen Protestant morale. Andreae's schemes were themselves closely related to the burgeoning Rosicrucian phenomenon, in the launch of which he himself had participated.[29] Both the Rosicrucian episode and the Andreae-inspired Christian Societies were also important in the resurgence of political and social Paracelsianism, for which the Antilian group provides yet further evidence.[30]

The direct source of the Antilian model seems to have been the flurry of little special interest groups that sprang up at the University of Rostock in the early 1620s. Central to these developments was Heinrich Hein (c.1590–1655).[31] Of the younger generation of Hein's followers, the main link with Antilia was the youthful and well-born Johann Abraham Poehmer (1604–1687) who, with respect to the Antilian project, displayed the strongest proprietorial tendency and over the longest period. Because of his direct connection with Andreae, Poehmer was held in high respect. His own base was Nuremberg, from where he set out on a variety of diplomatic missions. Throughout he preserved

---

28 D.R. Dickson, *The Tessera of Antilia: Utopian Brotherhood and Secret Societies in the Early Seventeenth Century* (Leiden: Brill, 1998). My own comments serve as modest additions and clarifications, together with some differences in emphasis. See also Dickson's 'Utopian Brotherhood and Secret Societies in the Early Seventeenth Century', *Renaissance Quarterly*, 49:4 (1996), 760–802.

29 For the various ramifications of Andreae's work and early Rosicrucianism, M. Brecht, 'Joh. Val. Andreaes Versuch einer Erneuerung der Württembergischen Kirche im 17. Jahrhundert', in idem, *Kirchenordnung und Kirchenzucht in Württemberg vom 16. bis zum 18. Jahrhundert*, ed. by Brecht (Stuttgart: Calwer Verlag, 1967), pp. 53–82; idem, 'Johann Valentin Andreae. Weg und Programm eines Reformers zwischen Reformation und Moderne', in *Theologen und Theologie an der Universität Tübingen*, ed. by Brecht (Tubingen, Mohr Verlag, 1977), pp. 270–343; R. van Dülmen, *Die Utopie einer christlichen Gesellschaft. Johann Valentin Andreae (1586–1654)*, vol. 1 (Stuttgart: Frommann-Holzboog, 1978); R. Eidghoffer, 'Johann Valentin Andreae vom Rosenkreuz zur Panoptie', *Daphnis*, 10:2–3 (1981), 211–39; and idem, *Die Rosenkreuzer* (Munich: C. H. Beck, 1995).

30 Eidghoffer, 'Johann Valentin Andreae vom Rosenkreuz zur Panoptie', *Daphnis*, 10:2–3 (1981), 211–39; Marek Woszczek, 'Chemia, mistyka, rewolucja. Paracelsjańska religia przyrody jako destabilizująca trajektoria wczesnej nowożytności', *Klio. Czasopismo poświęcone dziejom Polski i powszechnym*, 46:3 (2018), 37–52.

31 For Hein, Dickson *Tessera of Antilia*, pp. 114–18 et passim.

his links with the Baltic area and briefly resided in Danzig. Most of the associates of Antilia also emanated from the broad Baltic region.

As Dickson has pointed out, the Antilians were a rare example of a utopian group aspiring to establish an actual physical settlement, in all likelihood distant from the places of residence of their inchoate fraternity. It was contemplated that whole families would relocate, with the result that it was necessary to take account of such practical problems as the education of children of the settlers, a sphere in which Andreae was also relevant.[32]

Hartlib agreed with this settler bias, among other things owing to his acquaintance with the ongoing flight of English Puritan congregations to the Netherlands or New England. In the event the Antilians completely failed to evolve a workable scheme. Each alternative was ruled out for convincing reasons. One of the most favoured ideas was migration to Virginia or New England, but this was unacceptable by reason of the strain of translocation to such distant places and the failure to locate a wealthy sponsor.[33] In spite of this dismal result, the Antilian myth resonated with Hartlib for the rest of his life. Dury also showed signs of some further interest. For instance, during his stay in Sweden in the 1630s, he collected information, including from Heinrich Hein, about the group's settlement plans in Russia and the Baltic. At this point Antilia was not specifically mentioned. Rather, the settlers took as their inspiration Andreae's little tract, the *Dextera porrecta*.[34]

Their failure to find a new homeland was symptomatic of a distinct infirmity of purpose among the Antilians on all fronts of their agenda. Although the membership included many worthy names, even their leaders tended to be overcommitted and inclined to lead a peripatetic existence. In the summer of 1628 Hartlib himself added to this problem by relocating to London. As the letters of Fridwald also confirm, the

---

32 In listing his pedagogical precursors, Comenius pointedly mentioned Andreae, whom he praised as the one 'who brilliantly discovered the diseases of the Churches and Politicians, as well as of the Schools, here and there in his golden writings'. For a full exposition of similarities in educational thinking of Andreae and Comenius, M. Mörhke, *Komenius und Andreā, ihre pedägogik und ihre Verhältnis zu einande* (Leipzig: Emil Glausck, 1904). Listed among the also-ran educators by Comenius is Phillip Glaum (1580–1650), who seems to have been the pedagogue most valued by the Antilian fraternity.

33 In the absence of personal sponsorship, Fridwald's later letters indicate that the Antilians fell into hands of a philosopher's stone fraudster.

34 G. Westin, *Durie in Sweden*, pp. 04–05, 15. As seen below, in 1646 Hartlib organised an English translation of this tract.

membership was constantly dwindling owing to deaths, perhaps reflecting the unfortunate coincidence that the fraternity was founded in the middle of a major plague epidemic. This wave of mortality eliminated Michael Zeller, who was another of the few Antilians directly linked to Andreae and his *Societas Christiana*.[35] Therefore, like the initial *Societas Christiana* of Andreae, the Antilians fell back on maintaining their fraternity through correspondence. Unfortunately, as Fridwald's letters demonstrate, key members such as Johann Abraham Poehmer and Hartlib himself were unreliable correspondents.

In his third letter to Hartlib, who was now in London, Fridwald promised to obtain copies of sets of rules, which he termed the '*Confessio*' and '*Legibus*', and to pass these on to Hartlib without delay. This message reveals that the Elbing fraternity had so far been operating in ignorance of such basic documents.[36] In letter four, Fridwald related that Johannes Koy (1583–1647), an important figure in the Antilian fraternity and later Burgomaster of Elbing, was entrusted with the *Leges societatis nostrae*.[37] The only other mention of the foundational documents occurs in letter six, which reveals that Fridwald was still not in possession of them, but he conveyed the surprising news that they or their summaries were in the possession of John Dury.[38] This remark raises the possibility that the

---

35   The major loss on this front was Michael Zeller, who seems to have been a patron and director of the whole scheme. Michael Zeller von Rastenburg is a link with Andreae's original *Societas Christiana*, perhaps from before 1620, and there is firm evidence from 1622 that he was trying to find a location in which to establish a residential base for this new society. He was a Viennese nobleman who was attacked as a Weigelian or Schwenckfeldian. For a full account of his career, U. Bubenheimer, 'Wilhelm Schickard im ontext einer religiösen Subkultur', in *Zum 400. Geburtstag von Wilhelm Schickard. 2. Tübinger Schickard-Symposion 25–27.6.1992*, ed. by F. Seck (Sigmaringen: Jan Thorbeck Verlag, 1995), pp. 67–69.

36   Fridwald to Hartlib, 18 July 1629, HP 27/34/3. The *Confessio* (1615) was the second of three initial Rosicrucian manifestoes. The '*Legibus*' might also be a Rosicrucian tract, but more likely is the '*Leges societatis christianae*' which survives in the Hartlib Papers, being first described by Turnbull *HDC*, pp. 74–75. It was first published in 2007 as an appendix to volume 6 of the collected works of Andreae. The *Leges* is generally regarded as the work of an associate of Andreae, but possibly it is by Andreae himself. The long list of rules in the Andreae *Leges* was subjected to detailed scrutiny by Dury. Turnbull dates this *Exercitatio* from between 1627–1630. The specific *Leges Antiliae*, also in circulation at this date, seems not to have survived. I suspect that these latter rules were the work of Poehmer.

37   Fridwald to Hartlib, 28 July 1629, HP 27/34/5.

38   Fridwald to Hartlib, 22 November 1630, HP 27/34/7.

three important manuscript writings of Andreae located in the Hartlib Papers, the *Leges societatis christianae*, the *Christiani amoris dextera porrecta*, and the *Christiani societas imago*, were disseminated by Dury rather than by Hartlib. In due course Dury cited the latter two tracts, and implied that he possessed knowledge of the *Leges* when, in one of his little-mentioned writings, he called for the better organisation of intellectual fraternities to work for the public good.[39] Although the Antilian group was destined for rapid extinction, the utopian initiatives of that period left a permanent impression on both Poehmer and Hartlib, as well as to a lesser extent on other of their associates such as Dury.

1.5 John Dury

The most important contact that Hartlib made in Elbing was with the 'English Preacher' in whom the Antilians had developed an obsessional interest.[40] It seems likely that the two met in late 1627. The first preserved letter from Dury to Hartlib dates from November 1628, when Hartlib had already been back in England for about a month. Therefore, they only overlapped in Elbing for about eight months, but this was clearly sufficient for them to develop a mutual understanding and the beginnings of a permanent friendship.

John Dury (c.1600–1680) belonged to the Durie family, the representatives of which had comprised a major force in Scottish Presbyterianism almost since its inception. Dury's birthdate is not certain, but c.1600 seems the most likely, which renders him a direct contemporary of Hartlib. Owing to the exile of his father, Dury's upbringing occurred in Leiden where his father was the minster to the Reformed congregation. He attended the Walloon College in Leiden from 1616 until 1621. Between 1624–1626 he experienced an unhappy period as a trainee pastor in Cologne, after which, in about mid-1627, he moved to Elbing, where until 1630 he ministered to English and Scottish Presbyterians connected with the Merchant Adventurers Company.

---

39 [Dury] *Meditatio de dissidio ecclesiastia*, HP 20/11/33A. Francis Bacon's *De augmentis scientiarum* was also cited in this context. Turnbull and Léchot are uncertain about Dury's authorship of this tract.

40 For the life of Dury from birth to 1630, P.O. Léchot, *Un christianisme 'sans partilitié'*, pp. 41–96.

In his first professional assignment in Cologne, Dury had formed friendships with fellow ministers Justinus van Assche (c.1600–1650), Johann Moriaen (c.1591–c.1668) and Petrus Serrarius (1600–1669) who, like Dury, experienced abuse at the hands of their intolerant congregations. During the next few years Dury introduced these prominent liberal thinkers to Hartlib. Except in the case where death intervened, this group remained in touch with both Dury and Hartlib for the whole period covered by this book.

From the outset, the relations between Dury and Hartlib were positive. They discovered a common interest in education. Dury revealed that he was engaged in educational writing, but in Elbing this work was interrupted owing to rival obligations. Then arose an even greater obstruction to his educational deliberations, when he discovered his calling for ecclesiastical peace among the Protestants. For Dury, this mission assumed the highest priority since it was a contribution towards redressing the chaos into which the Protestant cause was relapsing in many parts of Europe. In a mood of obvious excitement, Dury promised to submit to Hartlib his 'first thoughts on this business', an undertaking that, he conceded, was such an awesome test that few would even contemplate undertaking. For orientation Dury immediately resolved to take advice from William Ames, the veteran Puritan leader operating in exile in the Netherlands, a figure who was held in universal respect in nonconformist circles.[41]

Dury soon confided in Hartlib about the reasons for contemplating this transformation in his career. His grounds were specific, but they pointed in more than one direction. One account confines itself to purely personal reflections. At Elbing, in spare moments, the irenic issue occupied his 'ordinary meditations & laboured to ripen the matters belonging to this purpose for mine owne information in that which was to bee done'. Only when he was discharged from his post owing to the collapse of his congregation, 'because I had none other imployment, I knew noe better worke to bee taken in hand, & more essentiall to the Gospell then this of

---

41 Dury to Hartlib, 18 July 1629, BL Sloane MS 654, fols. 243r–244r. K.L. Sprunger, *The learned doctor William Ames: Dutch backgrounds of English and American Puritanism* (Urbana: University of Illinois Press, 1972).

publicke pacification'.⁴² Such factors resulted in the decision to commit himself to healing the rift between Lutherans and Calvinists.

In a more dramatic alternative account, Dury writes that he was summoned by a high-ranking Swedish official who had solicited his views on the 'pacification of the Churches,' without which the diplomat believed that the Protestant war effort would be fatally undermined. Hartlib may well have guessed that this invitation emanated from Dr. Jacob Godemann, who was at that time based in Elbing in his capacity as the Swedish diplomat charged, among other duties, with negotiations with the Elector of Brandenburg over various problems of mutual concern, especially issues relating to the ongoing international conflict.⁴³ Dury must have appreciated that an unimpeachable execution of this remit would launch him into the highest reaches of international Protestantism. He believed that by joining the ranks of the 'new Reformatours' he would participate in the transformation of 'the Churches of God which in these latter ages have beene called out of Babilon.'⁴⁴

Once introduced to Dury's new mission, without hesitation, Hartlib made this his own first priority, which, as observed below, cost him dearly. Dury often acknowledged this debt, never more graciously than in an important defence against his critics, where he conceded to Hartlib that 'there is no man in this Nation, to whom all my wayes and counsels have been so fully known as to yourself ever since the year 1627'.⁴⁵

---

42   Dury to Hartlib n.d., but Turnbull *HDC*, p. 128 suggests 1642, HP 6/10/2A.
43   For Godemann, D. Riches, *Protestant Cosmopolitanism and Diplomatic Culture: Brandenburg-Swedish Relations in the Seventeenth-Century* (Leiden: Brill, 2012), pp. 106, 116, 131–32.
44   Dury to Hartlib, 1 January 1629, BL Sloane MS 654, fols. 241r-242r. See Léchot *Dury*, pp. 87–88.
45   Dury, The Unchanged, constant, and single-hearted Peacemaker (1650), p. 1.

Fig. 2 Engraved title-page of Jan Amos Komenský (Comenius) *Opera didactica omnia. Variis hucusque occasionibus scripta, diversisque locis edita: nunc autem non tantùm in unum, ut simul sint, collecta, sed & ultimô conatu in systema unum mechanicè constructum, redacta* (Amsterdam: Laurens de Geer, printed by Christoffel Cunrad and Gabriel de Roy, with engraved title-page executed by Crisijn van der Passe the younger, assisted by David Loggan.

2. Communion of Saints

> As you know all who desire and wait for the inheritance of the Kingdom, and who desire to be considered true members of the mystical body, and to be companions of the communion of saints, let them run together with the same mind and the same opinion, united and compact, to the same goal, and contribute the second measure of the gift received, that which can be done for the building up of the body of Christ.
>
> John Dury, 'Restaurationis Universalis Cynosura & Amussis'.[1]

In the course of establishing their partnership during the few months in which he and Hartlib were together in Elbing, John Dury committed himself to a defined objective to which he adhered for the rest of his long life. Dury's strong sense of purpose was not evident in Samuel Hartlib, who was at that date well-educated and highly motivated, but was entirely unsure about the way forward. Elbing possessed none of the attractions it had offered for his recently deceased father. It was the subject of military occupation by an invading power. Among the many negative commercial effects was the flight of foreign traders, including those associated with the Merchant Adventurers, thereby eliminating the need for the services of John Dury.[2] The invention of Antilia was an imaginative device for seeking a better way of life for a segment of the regional elite, but no progress was made in locating a viable place of refuge.

Dury was not disconcerted by the transformation in his career. In many respects his situation in Elbing was irksome and he had discovered a preferable and possibly prestigious new vocation to which he sought an

---

[1] HP 17/19/2A-B. c.1652, addressed to Hartlib and Clodius. Léchot, *Dury*, p. 528, No. 153.

[2] Dury's polite but negative reply to the invitation to serve as chaplain to a prospective colony of settlers in New England, composed in late December 1628, describes himself as the preacher of the gospel to 'the remnant of the broken company of Merchants at Elbing'. HP 4/5/1A-B.

immediate transfer. Hartlib harboured no equivalent plan of action, but return to England possessed some obvious attractions, about which he had some understanding. Compared with much of the rest of Protestant Europe, Britain was a place of stability, prosperity and growth of empire. His mother's family had contributed to this outcome. These relatives, who were well-placed, might assist him. Furthermore, the variety of Protestantism that he had experienced while at Cambridge was exactly to his taste. That left the awkward problem of what occupational niche he should select. He had considered and rejected the clerical and legal routes. Reflecting the positivity of his extensive experience in the Academy system in Silesia, his conversations about education with Dury and the place of education in the planning of Antilia, he opted for becoming the proprietor of some kind of academy, an objective for which there was an obvious niche in the stultifying educational system of Britain.

On the evidence of his correspondence, Hartlib had arrived in London by the end of August 1628. Dury returned to England nearly two years later. In Hartlib's autobiographical summary he offered a vignette about his near relatives, which seems distinctly hyperbolic, but was in fact an understatement. His grandparents had three daughters, Elizabeth, Hartlib's mother, Margaretta, her younger sister, and a third, I assume the youngest, about whom little is known.[3] Elizabeth and at least three of her children remained in the Danzig area. Margaretta returned to England and in about 1604 married Robert Clarke, the son of an alderman and rich salter. Robert was himself a prosperous merchant from Bethnal Green. They had only one child who died young. Clarke died after only six years of marriage. Margaretta was the main beneficiary of his will. She went on to marry, as his third wife, Sir Richard Smythe, of whom the History of Parliament records 'his predilection for rich widows'. He also held a lucrative position at court. He died in 1628, thereby adding further to the wealth of Margaretta. She, known to Hartlib as Lady Smythe, as her third husband married Sir Edward Savage in 1629, one effect of which, again according to the History of

---

3   This daughter married one Mr Peake; there is a single reference to her in the Hartlib Papers, which is a letter from Herbert Palmer to Hartlib, dated 14 December 1644, where Palmer sends his regards to Mrs Peake and many others, HP 59/5/1A. There is a passing reference to this daughter and her marriage to 'a younger brother', one Mr Peake, in Hartlib's autobiographical notice. Turnbull *HDC*, p. 110.

2. Communion of Saints 31

Parliament, was that 'his position at Court was strengthened by his marriage to Lady Margaret Smythe, who was not only a rich widow but also a gentlewoman of Henrietta Maria's privy chamber'. Savage's strengthened position at court lined him up for further financial gains, an accumulative process that came to a sharp end with the civil war and was never retrieved. However he had the compensation of a substantial inheritance from Margaretta, who died in 1638.

With an understandable realism, Hartlib made no serious attempts to engage with Margaretta or her husbands. There were, however, some interesting coincidences. Sir Richard Smythe was the owner of Leeds Castle which, after his death, passed into the Culpeper family and soon to Sir Cheney Culpeper, one of Hartlib's closest friends. Smythe was a vestryman at St Stephen's, Coleman Street, during the period when John Davenport was its minister. It is an interesting coincidence that Hartlib joined this congregation just a couple of months after Smythe's death. Hartlib may well have witnessed the disbursements to the poor sanctioned in Smythe's will. Finally, Savage was an ally of Sir Richard Weston, whose essay on Brabant husbandry was retrieved and published by Hartlib (see chapter 4). That Hartlib had been noticed at St Stephen's is confirmed by an important letter from John Davenport, dated 27 October 1628, inviting Dury to become chaplain to a new community of colonists who were about to settle in Massachusetts. One main reason cited for the choice of Dury was a favourable opinion of him received from 'Mr Hartcliffe'.[4]

This piece of family history should have been a warning to Hartlib that the wealth of England was in the hands of a class that had no intention of redistributing it in the direction of him or his good causes. That lesson he painfully learned in the course of the 1630s, when he failed to raise anything like the level of funding required for maintaining himself and his family, or for hosting the visit of Comenius to England.

In 1628 and the following year, Hartlib had at least four different addresses, one of these being a lodging at Duke's Place, which soon

---

4   John Davenport and six senior figures from St Stephen's, Coleman Street to Dury, 27 October 1628, HP 4/5/1A-B. Hartlib's opinion was supported by Dr John Bastwick, who might have known Dury in Leiden in about 1620. Soon to become notorious, Bastwick is not usually mentioned in connection with St Stephen's. Turnbull *HDC*, pp. 128–29; F.J. Bremer, *Building a New Jerusalem*, p. 95.

became his main address for many years. Before this happened, on 20 January 1629, he married Mary Burningham from Reading. It seems that their first place of residence was the village of Dalston some four miles northeast of the City of London.

2.1 Academies and Educational Debate

The intention of Hartlib to establish an academy was rarely mentioned and known only to his closest friends. Among these was William Speede, a well-known figure in the Godly ministry, whose parish was in Chichester. In a flush of enthusiasm, he persuaded Hartlib to set up his teaching establishment in that minor cathedral city.[5] This was a location about which Hartlib knew nothing, and it had the effect of divorcing him from the friendship group that was developing in London. As later recalled, his aim at that moment was: 'erecting a little Academie for the Education of the Gentrye of this Nation, to advance Piety, Learning, Morality, & other Exercises of Industry not usual then in Common Schools'.[6] His commitment to this project was real and his initial reports were positive, but in practice, execution of his high ideals required systematic practical application and local knowledge, neither of which Hartlib possessed or seemed likely to acquire.[7] The resultant shambles prompted Speede's disappointment, while outsiders were left in puzzled ignorance. In his own letters Walter Welles addressed Hartlib as 'the schoolmaster in Chichester by the East Gate', but complained that Hartlib was revealing nothing about his professional activities in Chichester.[8] Such evasion could not be sustained. With Speede's help and encouragement, Hartlib returned to London. The one positive outcome of the Chichester academy project was Hartlib's employment of the young mathematician John Pell. This short experience soon matured

---

5   Turnbull *HDC*, pp. 16–19.
6   'Humble Petition to the House of Commons' [autumn 1660], White Kennett, *A Register and Chronicle* (London, 1728), p. 872. See also, Haffemeyer, *Les Lumières radicales*, pp. 74–75.
7   For his last positive report on the academy, Hartlib to Dury, 31 August 1630, HP 7/11/1A-3B.
8   Welles to Hartlib, 13 September 1630, HP 13/8/1A-2B.

into a close association on educational issues and then an enduring friendship.⁹

From the perspective of 1635, Dury looked upon Hartlib's Chichester experience more sympathetically. He stated that this undertaking aimed at

> a new and exact forme of schoolling, and more profitable way of education of children then ever was practised heretofore, wherein his zeale & forwardnes towards the publique good, & the inconstancy of those that were undertakers with him, to whome he did trust without diffidence, till all was past remedy made him quite a poore man for by his zeale towards the publicke good.¹⁰

Failing to learn from experience, Hartlib repeated the same objective when, upon his return to London, he made a further attempt to establish an academy, on this occasion in Hackney, in quarters made available to him by Robert Greville, the second Lord Brooke, who became one of Hartlib's most consistent benefactors.¹¹ This second attempt failed even more badly than the first.

The two academy fiascoes might convey the misleading impression of Hartlib's lack of serious regard for education. The evidence of his papers demonstrates beyond doubt that at this early stage in his professional career, education was his most absorbing interest. His notebooks are crammed with detailed information about every aspect of the educational discipline, including comprehensive information about bibliographical sources. He displayed sound knowledge of the bewildering range of German educational initiatives and their authors. He also preserved even minor summaries that Dury had supplied about his own draft educational writings.¹²

Most significant was the intense interest that Hartlib displayed concerning the latest educational thinking in England, the most striking feature of which was the debate that was taking place between Joseph

---

9   N. Malcolm and J. Stedall, *John Pell (1611–1685) and his Correspondence with Sir Charles Cavendish* (Oxford: Oxford University Press, 2005), pp. 26–34 for the academy episode and pp. 38–101 for the period of Comenius relevance.
10 Dury to 'Right worshipful', 2 November 1635, HP 3/4/10A.
11 Turnbull *HDC*, pp. 19–20. This episode figured briefly in the *Czech Didactica* of Comenius' DJAK 11, pp. 184 and 220. Alas, this source subscribes to the error that the patron of Hartlib's second academy was Bishop John Williams.
12 See for instance excerpts from Dury's letters concerning his educational views, HP 1/12/1A-B.

Webbe and William Brookes. Almost as soon as he had settled in London, Hartlib began corresponding with both of these combatants and he mediated their dialogue. The impressive bulk of their writings survives in the Sloane manuscripts, a small amount of which is replicated in the Hartlib Papers. At that stage Webbe had already a publication record, but nothing by Brookes was ever published, which is partly explained by his blindness. To remedy this impediment, Brookes took on Thomas Horne, who was a cousin of William Speede, Hartlib's host in Chichester. A further participant in this group was Hezekiah Woodward, a teacher and soon to become an outstanding writer on education and father-in-law of Horne.[13]

The true importance of the Brookes-Webbe exchanges was not appreciated until 1964, when Vivian Salmon published the first of her papers on this intriguing duo.[14] Salmon also rightly pays tribute to Hartlib for his perspicacity in recognizing that Webbe and Brookes were figures of major significance in the field of linguistics.

Hartlib's own notes make no claim to originality, but his commentary contains many points of interest, and sometimes evidence of his touching sensitivity, as for instance as displayed in the following excerpt:

> In teaching the Uses of the Creature, their senses must also bee exercised. eg. to carry the Child abroad to shew him the sune how it is in a continual imploiment never standing still so everyone must have a Calling and in it bee busy. So leading them into an Orchard to bid them to bow a yong Impe and then an old tree. So when wee are yong wee must bee taught. etc. The Parables in Scripture are of special Use in this particular.[15]

From this aside we can appreciate the glee with which Hartlib greeted the writings of Comenius, for which he still had a few years to await.

---

13   For Hezekiah Woodward, see *ODNB* Woodward (Mark Greengrass); Haffemeyer, *Les Lumières radicales*, pp. 308–09 et passim.

14   V. Salmon, 'Problems of Language Teaching: a Discussion among Hartlib's Friends', *The Modern Language Review*, 59:4 (1964), 13–24 and 'Joseph Webbe: Some Seventeenth-Century Views on Language Teaching', *Bibliothèque d'Humanisme et Renaissance*, 3:2 (1961), 324–40. See also Salmon, *The Study of Language in 17th-Century England* (Amsterdam: Benjamins, 1988), pp. 121–90. For the following sections, see Haffemeyer, *Les Lumières radicales*, pp. 121–90.

15   HP 22/1/10A.

2.2 Puritan Orientation

At this difficult moment Hartlib strengthened his ties with his friends, some of whom he known since his days in Cambridge. The effect was to bring him into closer touch with the increasingly embattled Puritan fraternity, one important element in which was the congregation at St Stephen's, Coleman Street, which he joined soon after his arrival in England. As noted above, in the month of his arrival he assisted them in their negotiations with John Dury concerning the possibility of his service to a fresh group of emigrants heading for New England under the auspices of the Massachusetts Bay Company. The usefulness of Hartlib's services to his friends is discernible from the letters that he received from William Speed and Walter Welles in the course of 1630 and 1631.[16] It is evident that they greatly valued his news about continental current affairs, especially relating to trends in the ongoing wars, and dealings among fellow Protestants, about which he supplied his friends with relevant documentation and literature from writers representing all points of view.

A document particularly relevant to Hartlib's early Puritan associations is a list of twenty-five donors dating from 1632 or 1633, which relates to a scheme for generating and distributing their approved brand of religious literature.[17] Peacey points out that this list closely relates to the membership of the Massachusetts Bay Company and the Providence Island Company. Collectively, the various sources demonstrate the impressive scale of the patronage network that Hartlib assembled during the 1630s.[18] Many of these donors, but not all, like his contacts in general, were prosperous and well-born lay people. Although Hartlib attracted

---

16 For both Speede and Welles, T. Webster, *Godly Clergy in Early Stuart England. The Caroline Puritan Movement, c.1620–1643* (Cambridge: Cambridge University Press, 1997), pp. 158, 256–57, 261 et passim. On Welles as an early influence on Oliver Cromwell, J. Morrill, 'The Making of Oliver Cromwell', in *Oliver Cromwell and the English Revolution*, ed. by J. Morrill (Longman: Harlow, 1990), pp. 36–42.

17 J.T. Peacey, 'Seasonable Treatises: A Godly Project of the 1630s', *English Historical Review*, 113: 452 (1998), 667–79.

18 A dozen of these names also crop up in a single short letter from Hartlib to Dury, 3 September 1630, HP 7/12/1A-4B. See also Dury, *The Effect of Master Dury's Negotiations for the Uniting of Protestants* ([London] 1657), p. 2 which reports his discussions with an impressive group, all of whom were also familiar to Hartlib: 'In *England* with the godly learned Non-conformist Ministers, such as were Mr. *Cotton*, Mr. *White*, Mr. *Davenport*, Mr. *Nye* and others; with the best of the Bishops,

most of his lay patrons on the basis of his sound reputation among the Puritan activists, he was also perceived as an unusual asset on account of his links with inventors and improvers throughout northern Europe. This wide range of dealings is well illustrated by Hartlib's friendly relationship with John Pym, which extended from about 1632 until his untimely death in 1643.[19]

An early example of Hartlib's activism outside his Puritan circle relates to John Richardson, the Bishop of Ardagh, for whom he supplied papers from Germany. At that date, 18 December 1631, Hartlib was still operating from 'Lord Brookes' house in Hackney'.[20] Their warm relationship continued. Soon Richardson thanked Hartlib for 'al your writings, papers, and newes' and sent him £5 for his troubles.[21] A short time later he confirmed that he had 'receaved many Intelligences from you, for Civil affayres, forrayne warrs, and Mr. Duries negotiation in Ecclesiastical pacification. I am much bounden to you for your love; & am much in your debt'.[22] Richardson then introduced Hartlib to William Bedell, the new Bishop of Kilmore and Ardagh, and also to James Ussher the Archbishop of Armagh, associations which made Hartlib extremely well-placed within the Irish clerical establishment.

2.3 Communications and Status

Hartlib's capacity to communicate effectively with the expanding community of his clerical associates and others required the efficient organisation of his growing archive of papers and letters, something that must have been achieved, given the relatively good order in which these were left after his death. A further asset to communication was his daybook, or Ephemerides. This began as it continued, with meticulously detailed records covering the years 1634 and 1635, which together amounted to more than two-hundred-and-fifty packed pages of notes. This record possessed a strong European flavour. Many strands of history are embraced by the Ephemerides, but at this date the dominant

---

      such as were Dr. *Davenant*, Dr. *Hall*, Dr. *Morton*, and others; with the best of the Prelaticall men, such as were Mr. *Mede*, Dr. *Featly*, and others'.
19 For Pym and Hartlib, Haffemeyer, *Les Lumières radicales*, pp. 180–86 et passim.
20 HP 5/46/1A.
21 Richardson to Hartlib, 5 May 1634, HP 5/16/1A.
22 Richardson to Hartlib, 30 December 1634, HP 5/11/ 3A.

element was his information regarding the energetic enterprises of the Puritan intelligentsia.

Hartlib's communications model was capable of being applied more generally. In the short term he was able to mount an international newsgathering service adjusted to the specialist interests of particular clients, and he was able to back this up with all kinds of additional intelligence according to the tastes of his patrons. Even at this early stage, he no doubt envisaged an even broader agenda that would lay the foundations for an Office of Address possessing a general kinship with Renaudot's *Bureau d'adresse et de rencontre* which, at that date, was in the process of being launched. This sequence of events will be further elucidated in chapter 5. Naturally, even in its basic form, this service was beyond the capacity of a single individual, but Hartlib quickly evolved the habit of employing a team of amanuenses, many of whom were emigrants from war-torn Europe. The second need was for an up-to-date news supply, which his existing European correspondents seemed happy to fulfil. The final requirement was for patrons to express their appreciation of Hartlib's services by covering both their costs and also the expenses incurred by his expanding inventory of schemes supportive of the public good.

Hartlib soon found that the costs of his services outpaced the income required to cover them and the maintenance of his family. As early as 1635, John Dury became aware of this desperate situation and wrote to a number of potential benefactors pleading for support for his embattled friend. By this stage, in the eyes of Dury, Hartlib had become: 'a Cursitor & an Agent for universall obiects in matters civill, ecclesiasticall, & scholasticall', and in a multitude of things 'profitable for the publicke good of every kind'. In sum Hartlib was:

> in a spirituall manner a Martyr... a true Minister of the publicke Communion of Saintes, for all his aymes & actions plainly intend & shew forth nothing els but the fruits of publicke edification, & holy communion in every kind... for Satan brought him to the greatest pinch of his poverty for his constant affection to religion, & his love to religious men, whome he did preferr before his kindred. And in that, when he was thus poore & persecuted withall, he yet in confidence to God, & love to publicke endeavours, made choice of the most painfull & laborious employment, that anie man almost can devise, he is to be thought.[23]

---

23 HP 3/4/11A-12B Communion of saints was much on Dury's mind at this date owing to his suspicion that his peace negotiators were not entirely sincere, hence

The above review demonstrates that Hartlib had served a hard apprenticeship since his arrival in England but, even as early as 1635, in the eyes of John Dury, his incontestable record of self-sacrifice had earned him the title of 'true Minister of the publicke Communion of Saintes'.[24] Such lavish expressions of regard seem out of order, but there is no doubt that by this date Hartlib had become known and valued among a wide circle of respected figures, and therefore he had already laid the foundations for the even higher regard that he was to attain in the following decade. As Hartlib's message to two of his aristocratic patrons indicates, he remained undaunted in his mission of service: 'If I know that my packets doe safely arrive, I will not faile God willing to discharge weekly my wonted duety and to represent a very spring of most delightfull objects. In the mean tyme beseeching God to be favourable unto Sion I take humbly my leave remaining alwayes....'. Coming on the eve of the civil war, such sentiments were guaranteed to serve Hartlib well in the eyes of these same patrons and their other well-placed associates, as they emerged as the ruling class of the new parliamentary regime.[25]

---

betraying the loyalty he owed to the communion of saints: Dury to Hartlib, 20 August 1635, HP 9/1/22B. In private messages, Dury even discussed ending his ecclesiastical negotiations and returning to Britain to work in a private capacity. Dury dispatched his call for support of Hartlib to at least six correspondents, none of whom were named in the drafts. The evidence suggests that the recipients may have included Charles Potts of the Middle Temple, Caspar Godemann, Isaac Pennington, John Pym and Lord Robartes. Other possible recipients were Sir Thomas Roe, Archbishop James Ussher, Lord Warwick and Sir William Waller.

24 For an even more extravagant assessment of Hartlib's devotion to 'the publicke good of the Sainsts and the communion thereof': Dury to an unnamed recipient, 21 January 1636, HP 6/4/7B-8A. On this basis, Dury proposed that Hartlib should be officially designated as the 'Agent for the Work of Peace Ecclesiasticall and other Profitable Ends', HP 9/1/109A-114B. In some letters in this sequence, the communion of saints was invoked as many as eight times. See, D. Willen, '"Communion of Saints": Spiritual Reciprocity and the Godly Community in Early Modern England', *Albion: a Quarterly Journal Concerned with British Studies*, 27:3 (1995) 19–41, which relates to many of Hartlib's friends, especially Lady Joan Barrington. For a characteristic source of authority: 'Saints by profession are bound to maintain an holy fellowship and communion in the worship of God, and in performing such other spiritual services as tend to their mutual edification; as also in relieving each other in outward things, according to their several abilities and necessities.' *Westminster Confession*, chapter 23/2, which ably reflects the perspective adopted by Lady Barrington, Dury, et al.

25 Hartlib to Edward Montagu, Lord Manchester and Lord John Robartes, 28 May 1640, HP 7/50/2A-B. For Robartes, Haffemeyer, *Les Lumières radicales*, pp. 185–86.

Indicative of the growing general regard for Hartlib was his nomination as the London agent for Karl Ludwig, the Elector Palatine, whose letters patent were issued on 23 April 1637. In all likelihood, this dignity was conferred owing to the intervention of the eminent Johann Joachim von Rusdorf (1589–1640), an important figure in the Palatine court. In recognition of this distinction, friends like Dury and Moriaen tended to address their letters to Hartlib as 'servant to the Prince Elector'. It is easy to overlook this aspect of the life of Hartlib, but in the 1640s, he became an active player in persuading parliament to confer generous financial settlements on both Karl Ludwig and his mother Elizabeth, Queen of Bohemia.[26]

2.4 Introducing Jan Amos Komenský

The Ephemerides for 1634 and 1635 and related evidence strikingly demonstrate that Hartlib added an important new strength to his programme through his discovery of the work of Jan Amos Komenský (Comenius, 1592–1670), who was not only the author of a burgeoning educational programme, but also an active writer touching on almost every sphere of human affairs. The sparkle of Comenius successfully reignited the heady ambitions of Hartlib's Antilian days and seemed to justify the assumption that everything was capable of betterment on an unimaginable scale.[27]

The exact chronology of Hartlib's acquaintance with the work of Comenius is difficult to establish. For instance, there is no evidence that either Dury or Hartlib were caught up in the flurry of excitement occasioned by the publication in 1631 of the first edition of the famous *Janua linguarum reserata*. From a couple of pieces of indirect evidence, it is assumed that Hartlib was indirectly in touch with Comenius from

---

26 For the letters patent, HP 7/14/1A-2B and Turnbull *HDC*, pp. 111–12. See also Rusdorf to Dury, 20 February 1636, for his lavish praise of Hartlib, HP 5/3/3A-B. For Rusdorf, Akkerman, *Elizabeth*, pp. 306–07 et passim.

27 Respecting relations between Hartlib and Comenius at this date, representative sources of reference include: Turnbull *HDC*; Blekastad, *Comenius*; Greengrass et al., *Samuel Hartlib and Universal Reformation*; Goris et al., *Gewalt sei ferne den Dingen*; Haffemeyer, *Les Lumières radicales*, pp. 98–100 et passim; and H. Hotson, *The Reformation of Common Learning*.

1632, which indeed may well be the case.[28] However, the first direct evidence of this association is a letter from the Scoto-Pole John Jonston to Hartlib, dated 1 March 1633, from which it is clear that Hartlib was already familiar with the work of Comenius. Jonston briefly and over-optimistically concluded that the *Didactica magna* was completed by this date, so allowing Comenius to press on with the pansophic philosophical project to which he attached great importance.[29] Even more important is the letter from Jonston to Hartlib dated August 1633. He noted that Hartlib's promise to supply some Verulamian manuscripts had greatly pleased Comenius, who recommended that Hartlib should entrust this delivery to reliable hands. The new *Seminarium* edition of the *Janua linguarum reserata* had recently been published in Danzig.[30] Jonston assumed that Hartlib had already seen this important source which, in light of the following paragraphs, seems likely. Comenius had also promised some further additions to this text under the title of *Vestibulum* (first published Leszno, 1633). Finally, Jonston recounted the rumour that one Anchoran was contemplating producing a version of Francis Bacon's *Sylva sylvarum*.[31]

Logically following on from this Jonston letter, on 9 January 1634, a date coinciding with the opening pages of the Ephemerides, Comenius addressed his first message to Hartlib.[32] This informative document, the very first and arguably the most important of all of his correspondence with Hartlib, merits detailed consideration. It is clear that Comenius had already developed firm impressions about Hartlib from 'your brother', that is Georg, Samuel's elder brother, who was

---

28   As for instance Turnbull *HDC*, p. 342.
29   Jonston to Hartlib, 1 March 1633, a reply to Hartlib's letter of 13 January that has not been traced. Since he was linked personally with Comenius and with Leszno, the headquarters of Comenius and the Bohemian Brethren, Jonston (1603–1675) was a sound witness, but he was very self-absorbed and from 1626 to 1636 was away from Leszno.
30   A German/Polish edition, with translations by Johann Mochinger and Andrzej Węgierski, Danzig 1633. Blekastad *Comenius*, p. 200; D. van Stekelenberg, *Michael Albinus 'Dantscanus'*, p. 240.
31   Jonston to Hartlib, August 1633, HP 44/1/2A.
32   Comenius *Korespondence* 26/1, pp. 154–62 and 163–66 (two distinct variants of this text). For an elucidation of these texts, see V. Urbánek, and M. Steiner, 'Otevřená brána Tvého přátelství: nová evidence o počátcích korespondence Jana Amose Komenského a Samuela Hartliba', in *Justus et Bonus: Ad honorem Jiří Beneš: křesťanská kultura a vzdělanost v českých zemích od středověku po Komenského*, ed. by O. Podavka (Prague: Filosofia, 2020), pp. 251–71.

clearly acting as an intermediary.[33] Georg's interest in fostering this relationship was no doubt increased by his own recent appointment as Rector of the Calvinist academy in Vilnius, a move that soon led him to disaster.[34] A further reason for gratitude to Samuel was the warm welcome that he had accorded to David Vechner and Jiří Laurin, the two emissaries dispatched by the Leszno Brethren to raise funds for their exiled communities experiencing distress in that region of Poland and neighbouring Silesia. London was a key player for various reasons, including the presence of the Dutch Church at Austin Friars, which was a consistently successful agency for fundraising on behalf of the embattled Czech Protestant community and the education of their young adults.[35] At some length, on the basis of Hartlib's proven record of support for the scattered remnant of his exiled community, Comenius assured him that he was already a firm friend. With respect to their common interest in education, he thanked Hartlib for sending relevant documents and publications, although these had not yet been received.

Regardless of the perilous condition of the Brethren and the many competing demands on his time, Comenius insisted on the primacy of education in his order of priorities since, after the war, on the Czechs' return to their native land, universal education lasting up to the age of above twenty would be fundamental to the task of social reconstruction. He explained that his *Janua linguarum reserata* was just a first stage in his schedule of educational writings. For further development he would

---

33 As pointed out above, Comenius and Georg Hartlib were contemporaries at the University of Heidelberg, which is the most likely location of their first meeting.

34 Georg became a victim of the mounting civil unrest of the Counter Reformation. In 1640 he was attacked and nearly killed by rioting students from the local Jesuit academy, after which he fled to Danzig and never returned. The substantial Calvinist minority in Vilnius was then subjected to vicious penalties from which it took half a century to recover. The plight of Georg was described in Eleazar Gilbert, *Newes from Poland wherein is declared the cruell practice of the popish clergie against the Protestants, and in particular against the ministers of the city of Vilna* (London: E.P. for Nathanael Butter, 1641), Wing G705. Perhaps for fear of stirring up further trouble, Samuel Hartlib was reluctant to comment on this tragedy.

35 Laurin was the brother-in-law of Comenius; David Vechner (1594–1669) was a valued lieutenant of Comenius, and the younger brother of Georg Vechner. The latter was also an important coworker of Comenius and a Socinian leader in his region. According to Comenius, this embassy to England was a complete failure, Comenius to Hartlib, 4 March 1641, HP 7/84/4A. See also O.P. Grell, *Dutch Calvinists in Early Stuart London: the Dutch Church in Austin Friars, 1603–1642* (Publications of the Sir Thomas Browne Institute, 11, Leiden: Brill, 1989), pp. 183–84, 203, 209.

require a team of helpers and relief from his administrative duties, tasks that Rafał Leszczyński (1597–1638), his rich and cultured patron, had agreed to support, but this good intention had suddenly collapsed, thereby completely undermining the reformer's future schedule of work.[36]

Notwithstanding such stressful circumstances, Comenius could nevertheless report significant progress, especially with respect to his spectacularly successful *Seminarium* or *Janua linguarum* (*reserata*) which, he explained, had been conceived as a breviary of the entire Latin language. He recognised that this was an audacious venture, but he wanted to test its reception. Hartlib, he exclaimed, knew all about this already, and he expressed relief that he counted among those who recognized the utility of this innovation. Also, he could disclose that he was near to completion of his *Didactica magna*, with the *Viridarium* and *Pansophia* next in line.[37] The core of the letter was an extended account of his thinking on the sequential order of learning, and the organisation of the Latin school system, which became respectively chapters twenty-two and thirty of the *Didactica magna*, the progress of which he also reported. A further important addition to Hartlib's knowledge was the gift of the recently published German edition of the *Informatorium maternum*, *Der Mutterschule*, whereby Hartlib would become the vehicle for introducing this important book into Britain.

Comenius envisaged that these ambitious plans would become the task of some forthcoming exile that he was envisaging ('*cupio admodum*

---

36 For the final illness and premature death of Leszczyńsky, Blekastad, *Comenius*, p. 120.

37 'Pansophia' is a term for the project as a whole. As seen below, Hartlib was instrumental in publishing the first of the more complete pansophic writings. As pointed out above, '*Viridarium*' is the title adopted for the third of six explanatory booklets planned for advising teachers in the vernacular school. Perhaps here, the reference is to the final stage in the teaching of languages, as for instance described in the draft *Methodus linguarum novum*, caps 11–12, HP 35/5/100A-B: 'By what appropriate synonyms shall we adopt for these distinctive grades in the study of languages: By virtue of the analogy between Languages and Horticulture, could we not without inelegance borrow names from the terminology of gardening? The grades are designated: I. PLANTARIUM: (the nursery where seedlings from the woodlands are placed in the sunny garden): II. SEMINARIUM: (where the saplings are planted, and prepared to spread themselves into a tree): III. VIRIDARIUM: (where everything is already green) and so in the end they would pleasurably learn to follow the creators of pleasant GARDENS.'

me in hoc exilio'). This was more than a hint that he had already abandoned the idea of making much further progress in Leszno. He therefore urgently needed to find a substitute for the support he had received from Rafał Leszczyński. Almost providentially, Hartlib seemed to offer himself as the next port of call. Hartlib himself seems to have inadvertently conveyed the impression to Laurin and Vechner that he could raise a whole-life pension of £100 a year for Comenius and whatever assistants he needed to employ.

Comenius was immediately inspired by the expectation that Hartlib was offering sanctuary to 'the whole body of youth in Christendom'. After all, England was, in the Czech's eyes, the most flourishing centre of rich and sympathetic patrons. At once Comenius volunteered Georg and David Vechner as eligible companions. Such a team might transform the whole programme of Comenius into a successful reality. Perhaps Comenius realised that he had carried hyperbole to an unreasonable extreme, but he had set a course that would in the not-too-distant future precipitate his relocation to London. Indicative of his confidence in England, Comenius ended his January 1634 letter with a reference to Petr Figulus, his fifteen-year-old pupil and future son-in-law, whom he had at that date entrusted to Cambridge for a key part of his education. As seen below, soon Figulus became the amanuensis to Dury and in due course he was one of Hartlib's most trusted correspondents.

The longer-known variant of the above letter pointedly alluded to the scandal of the Anchoran edition of the *Janua linguarum*, which weighed heavily on the mind of Comenius and must have been known to Hartlib. Strangely, Anchoran and his edition hardly feature in the Hartlib Papers, but this incident will be discussed further in chapter 4, in connection with Thomas Horne and his edition.

Much additional information about Comenius after the January 1634 letter is found in messages deriving from Caspar Streso.[38] In May 1635 Streso reported on a package of material that had been dispatched to Hartlib by Comenius in October 1634. This contained what he called

---

38 Caspar Streso (1603–1664): during this period an anchor of Hartlib's Dutch correspondence and an inexhaustible supplier of political news. Streso and Hartlib were in contact from about 1630.

the *pansophiæ suæ specimen*.³⁹ In addition, he implied that the Danzig agents of Comenius would be sending Hartlib further manuscripts and pamphlets that he had requested. Comenius himself could not supply the further material relating to the pansophic project on grounds of the complex nature of such an operation for Comenius himself. Finally, Comenius promised to report from time to time on progress with his pansophic work, but he required the winter to undertake more reading preparation and this might take up the summer as well.⁴⁰

In early December 1634, in an appendix to one of Streso's newsletters on continental political affairs, he inserted a brief note on Dury and another on Comenius. He regretted delaying attention to recent work by Comenius and expressed 'the wish I could see the sum of what Comenius sent you', confirming the above reports that, in the autumn of 1634, a substantial amount of material had been dispatched to Hartlib from Danzig and Leszno.⁴¹

A further letter from Streso to Hartlib, also written in December 1634, indicated Streso's growing interest in Comenius, and especially the recent acceleration of his pansophic programme. He seems to have received an assurance from Comenius that revision of his pansophic drafts, taking account of Streso's *technologia* and other reservations, would be completed in the following three months. Streso already feared that completion of the work on *pansophia* would require many hands. Accordingly, he pleaded with Hartlib to raise funds to support this project for its execution either in England, or elsewhere in Europe.⁴²

Most of the early references to Comenius in Hartlib's Ephemerides seem to derive from Conrad Bergius, who taught at Frankfurt an der Oder, before transferring to Bremen in 1629. The first of these notices seems to date from January 1634, the very first month of the Ephemerides. The early entries show particular regard for the character of Comenius. He was described as being Godly, enquiring and hard-working, but too

---

39 Perhaps *IN IANUAM RERUM sive TOTIUS PANSOPHIÆ SEMINARIUM*, an introduction to the pansophic project, composed at this date and surviving as a fragment in the Hartlib Papers, HP 35/1/1A-27B. A complete version of this and two related texts dating from about 1643 is located in St John's College, Cambridge Library, I.34. It is quite likely that these documents were in some way derived from Samuel Hartlib. For the standard edition, DJAK 14, pp. 13–48, 89–100.
40 Streso, summary of messages from Comenius to Hartlib, 24 May 35, HP 11/1/75A.
41 Streso, a note to Hartlib dated 4 December 1634, HP 11/1/20B.
42 Streso to Hartlib, 18 December 1634, HP 11/1/22A-B.

flexible, inconstant and credulous. Such alleged weaknesses of personality rendered him exploitable by advocates of dangerous ideas, including the most fearful of all, Socinianism, by which he had become 'intoxicated'. [43] As noted below, the openness of Comenius to dialogue and the prevalence of Socinianism in his environment inevitably opened him to the suspicion of Socinian leanings and indeed he never completely escaped from this accusation. But this allegation never affected Hartlib, for whom over the next few years Comenius became an ever-increasing priority.

This preoccupation was reflected in the contents of the Ephemerides, which contained a running report on the progress of every aspect of the work of Comenius. During 1634 Comenius found himself elevated to accompany both aspiring and established educational authorities of the day in Hartlib's updates of his schemes for educational improvement. For instance, with reference to the relatively neglected area of the upbringing of the youngest age groups, he itemised: ' *Infant education.* **1**. Comeni Informatorium **2**. An encyclopedia of particulars to be drawn up from Brukius, Pell, Evenius and Docemius **3**. 6 books of Comenius: and this up to the year 12'.[44]

By this date Hartlib was in possession of Comenius's gift of the *Informatorium*. He evidently appreciated its significance and commissioned an English translation, the draft of which in early 1635 passed to Pell for editing and improvement.[45] Perhaps on account of

---

43 Ephemerides, January 1634, HP 29/2/13A-B, and July 1634, HP 29/2/22A.
44 Ephemerides, c. November 1634, HP 29/2/57A, slightly edited for the sake of clarity. See also with a slight expansion: '**1**. *Informatorium Comenii his Muter-schule.* **2**. *Encyclopædia Brukiana Pelliana.* **3**. *Libelli 6. Comeni.* **4**. *Analysis Mundi Stresonis.* **5**. *Encyclopædia Popularis Vernacula. Mea, Eveni etc.* **6**. *Systema Historiæ universalis.* **7**. *Encyclopædia Eruditionis.*' HP 29/2/61A. Also relevant is HP 22/10/6A-B, which adds '*Janua Comeniana Vernacula*'. The first vernacular edition of the *Janua linguarum reserata* was the English/Latin, published in 1631 (under a different title and without acknowledging the authorship of Comenius), while the Czech language edition is dated 1633. As seen below, a more authoritative English edition dates from 1636 and emanated from Hartlib's friend Thomas Horne.
45 Malcolm/Stedall *Pell*, pp. 47–48. Pell warned Hartlib that this translation was likely to be obstructed by the Stationers' Company, something that Pell had recently experienced himself with regarding his *The English Schoole*. These authors (p. 48) also recall that the existence of an *Informatorium* English translation was mentioned by Comenius in October 1641.

Hartlib's inexperience as a publisher, this plan failed, but it was not, as seen below, entirely forgotten.[46]

The above idea of composing an encyclopaedia of basic data relevant to early education, drawing on material from diverse sources, was also in line with what Comenius himself advocated. Equally up-to-date was the allusion to the six reference booklets intended as a guide to the six stages of education in vernacular schools. These booklets were mentioned as a desideratum in chapter 29 of the draft *Didactica magna*, but they only slowly matured beyond the draft stage. In this context the six stages were engagingly designated as: *Violarum, Rosarum, Viridarum, Sapientiae Labyrinthus, Spirituale balsamentum* and *Paradisus animae*.[47] Completing these guides was, it seems, part of the work plan of Comenius for his visit to England. The seriousness of Hartlib's engagement with the Comenian scheme for early education is confirmed by variants and amplifications reported in the 1634 Ephemerides.[48]

The Jonston and Streso letters, like various other instances from the Ephemerides discussed above, demonstrate the emergence of intense curiosity on the part of Hartlib about the work of Comenius in the course of 1634. Signifying Hartlib's confidence in this new discovery, Comenius soon found a place in the shortlists of professors that Hartlib drew up for his putative model academy.[49] Quite rapidly in the course of 1634, Comenius became the dominating force in Hartlib's thinking about education and related matters. The Ephemerides quickly took on a new complexion, with *didactica* being adopted as a guiding

---

46 The first published version of the *Informatorium* was a German translation of a Czech original composed between 1629 and 1633. For a comprehensive study of the genesis and early history of this text, D. Čapková, *Předškolní výchova v díle J. A. Komenského, jeho předchůdců a pokračovatelů* (Prague: Státní pedagogické nakladatelství, 1968).

47 For Comenius's own account of this scheme, Blekastad, *Comenius*, p. 138.

48 HP 29/2/65B; 29/3/16A-B; 29/3/21B; 29/3/23A.

49 'Desid. Acad.: 1. Professor Theologiæ Practicæ desideratur. 2. Item. Professor Artis Vitæ. Duræanus, Pömerianus videtur 3. Professor Philosophiæ Experimentalis Verulamianus. In hunc finem scribendæ Paræneses et Consilia a Duræo. 2. Pömero. 3. Jungio. 4. Reinero. 5. Wats. 6. My Lord Herbert. 7. illo qui Wats perficit. 8. Comenio. 9. Gelebrand. 10. Twisso. etiam Verulamus in quodam loco de tali Collego.' Ephemerides 1634, Part 1, HP 29/2/19A-B. In other variants of this list Hartlib included the inner cohort of the Antilian fraternity, suggesting that there was smooth continuity between the Antilian and Comenian periods of Hartlib's academy and correspondency schemes.

principle for numerous of his many areas of interest.[50] As Comenius rose in importance, Brookes, Hartlib's hitherto predominant authority in educational matters, noticeably slipped into the background. Also eclipsed were the jungle of continental educational activists and contemporaneous German local didactic initiatives. Therefore, as Comenius blossomed, all of his competition withered on the vine.

The only other early surviving direct communication of Comenius to Hartlib is dated 17 October 1634.[51] Compared with the first one, this letter was routine and unimportant, albeit not without interest. The immediate occasion for this message was to thank Hartlib for his part in transmitting a gift in Reichthalers, worth about £7 sterling at that date. The rest of the letter relates to the role of Comenius in ongoing negotiations concerning church unity. This, he admitted, was a necessary exercise, but it was yet another factor obstructing further progress with his writing plans. He was caught up in yet another round of synods, this time trying to avert the rupture between the Polish and Lithuanian segments of the Bohemian Brethren. This was just one small element in the panoply of synods convened at this date to promote greater unity among the Protestant denominations in the face of the mounting Catholic ascendancy. Once better integration within the Brethren was achieved, the next step was a further round of synods aimed at an alliance between the Brethren and the Calvinist churches. This represented a further drain on the time of Comenius, but the exercise was unavoidable. Comenius insisted that he had not lost sight of his wider intellectual commitments, citing completion of pansophic writings as his main priority. Indeed, he told Hartlib to expect a sample of this work in the near future, a promise that was kept, but not until 1637.

The next preserved letter of Comenius to Hartlib was not until January 1638. The nearly four-year period following October 1634 is something of a paradox. Comenius's state of mind remained unchanged. He needed funds to obtain relief from his onerous duties and to support his escalating programme of writing. Although they formally remained

---

50 For instance, just for the period November 1635 to January 1636 (HP 29/3/50B-65B), the *didactica* heading was applied to thirty-five different subjects, many of which were mentioned more than once.
51 Comenius *Korespondence* 26/1, pp. 175–76; Hartlib Papers 7/103A-B; first published by D. Čapková and M. Kyralová, 'Unpublished Letters of J.A. Comenius', *Acta Comeniana*, 6 (1985), 165–68.

committed to Comenius, Hartlib and Dury became more engaged in their own projects, leaving Comenius to slip down their agenda. Dury persisted with his backbreaking timetable of ecclesiastical negotiations and quite often mentioned Comenius and the Brethren, but mostly in the context of interdenominational politics. When Hartlib plied Dury with documentation relating to Comenius, almost invariably he excused himself from offering a response. It is also clear that in the course of the 1630s, in consequence of other unavoidable demands on his time, Dury allowed his passion for education to fall into abeyance.

2.5 Evaluating Comenius

Hartlib kept alive his interest in Comenius, but at first only to a limited extent. All the relevant material in the Hartlib Papers from this date could be compressed into a negligible space. On the positive side, some of Hartlib's major allies offered expressions of good will. For instance, John Stoughton, who possessed a redoubtable record of fundraising for worthy causes, apologised that, because of persecution, the scattered forces of Puritanism, even in London, were unable to help. With evident regret, Stoughton concluded that Comenius would be prudent to make alternative arrangements for his future:

> By reason of the Hand of God among us we are all so scattered out of the City, and can commerce with so little Confidence in the City, that I know not what can be done. I was glad to heare that Mr Comenius inclined this way, in regard of the worke he is about, but considering the state of things among us I am absolutely of opinion that he resolved for the best.[52]

With respect to politicians, the increasingly powerful John Pym also advised procrastination:

> I shal bee exceeding gladd if I may bee an Instrument of any incoragement to that worthy man Comenius in those workes, & designes which he hath for the publick good. As soone as it shal please God to restore to us liberty of commerse & intercourse I shal be very desirous a consult with you how it may bee donn.[53]

---

52   John Stoughton to Hartlib, 7 September 1636, HP 46/11/3A.
53   John Pym to Hartlib, 26 November 1636, HP 31/3/1A.

There is also virtually nothing to report concerning rich benefactors. As an exception, Sir William Waller, who was in regular touch with both Dury and Hartlib from his home in Winchester Castle, responded courteously, but offered a blunt assessment:

> I thanke you very much for your constant weekly advertisements, accompanied with those many choice peeces of Mr Duræeus, Comenius, and others...Concerning both [Dury] and Mr Comenius, and those other noble spirits, I can say no more, but that I admire them, which is a kinde of saying nothing. [54]

Fundraising for Comenius and his team among the rich therefore fell upon death ears. Hartlib therefore largely relied on dribs and drabs from more humble sources, such as the two little donations recorded from the West Midlands:

> I receaved towards the promotion of Mr Comenius most hopefull worke, of the liberality & beneficiency of Mr Francis Billingsley of Astley [Abbotts, Shrophire] Esquire who contributed 20. shillings & of Mr Iohn Barton Master of Arts & high schoole-master then of Bridgenorth [Shropshire], but now of Birmingham; as also 20 shillings.[55]

Such well-intentioned, desultory acts of kindness were not uncommon, but they achieved nothing like the level of beneficence that Comenius had anticipated. Indeed, they exacerbated the mounting impoverishment that both Dury and Hartlib were experiencing. In 1637 Comenius was impressed by the alacrity with which Hartlib handled the publication and distribution of his *Conatuum Comeniorum Praeludia*, but he was unaware of the nightmare that Hartlib faced in covering his costs. Accordingly, by the time of the arrival of Comenius in England, his host was almost empty-handed.[56]

Reports from Poland, such as those from Johannes Arnold, testify to the worsening plight of the various Protestant sects, indeed in the very vicinity of Leszno, into which area Arnold himself had retreated by 1637. He commented that the financial aid received from Western Europe was

---

54 Waller to Hartlib, 25 September 1638, HP 32/2/7A.
55 Fragment of a receipt n.d., but about 1638, HP 23/2/21A.
56 For insight into Hartlib's financial affairs, M. Greengrass, 'The financing of a Seventeenth-Century Intellectual: Contributions for Comenius, 1637–1641', *Acta Comeniana*, 11 (1995), 71–87; 141–57.

insufficient to arrest the erosion of Protestantism in his region. He drew comfort from the example of English *'Puritanismus'*, the characteristics of which he believed should be imported to strengthen religious practice in his own communities. Arnold was obviously familiar with the affairs of Leszno. With respect to Comenius, he understood that he still had not completed his *Pansophia* and was working diligently on this project, but he had no intention of coming to England, and for many sound reasons that ruled out any such decampment. As a Senior of the Brethren there was no possibility of him abandoning all those churches that were always in need of his services.[57]

Arnold's testimony is helpful in clarifying the dilemmas facing Comenius. From his own perspective, Arnold feared that the reformer was not only hopeful of financial support from England for himself and his team, but also, he was considering settling there, at least for a fair length of time. Arnold also reminds us that a strong school of thought in Leszno would oppose any such exodus, or indeed any relief from his clerical and administrative duties. Arnold's report on this situation was helpful to Hartlib, but it must have alerted him to the risk of being burdened with responsibilities for which he was entirely unprepared.

In one important respect, in the late thirties Hartlib's anxiety about Comenius was slightly lessened owing to the growing strength of Hartlib's team. Of his seasoned associates in England, Theodore Haak and John Pell could be relied on to be supportive, although neither had played an active role in the dialogue with Comenius. More significant were the interventions of Johann Abraham Poehmer, Johann Moriaen and Joachim Hübner. Neither of the first two visited England, but at this date they corresponded with Hartlib about the affairs of Comenius. Poehmer had of course known Hartlib since the inception of the Antilian fraternity. They remained in intermittent but amicable contact. Poehmer's most active intervention on the Comenius front dates from 1638, and was made from Nuremberg, his family home. Poehmer was alarmed by the disputes that had broken out on the continent over the newly published *Conatuum Comeniorum Praeludia* (1637). This event was eagerly awaited on account of providing the first published insight into the pansophic ideas of Comenius. Poehmer, out of deference to Hartlib's commitment

---

57   Johannes Arnold to Hartlib, 6 March 1637, HP 45/8/1A.

to the *Praeludia*, was eager to lend support. However, concerning Comenius himself, Poehmer's loyalties were divided on account of his immersion at that point in the works of Tomasso Campanella which, as it happens, were also an important source of inspiration for both the metaphysics and the utopianism of Comenius.[58]

In his way, the polymath Johann Moriaen (1591–1668) was arguably the most ubiquitous of all Hartlib's foreign correspondents.[59] During the 1630s he became known to Hartlib and Dury, but his veritable bombardment of letters commenced only on 13 December 1638. These communications with Hartlib, mostly dispatched from Amsterdam, continued on an almost weekly basis for many years, including, of course, during the visit to England by Comenius, on whom he provided a running commentary.

Of this trio of foreigners, the most learned was Joachim Hübner (1611–1666), who settled in Oxford in the summer of 1636 and remained in England until 1642. Well-educated and outstandingly talented, this young intellectual lacked a settled vocation. He was exactly suited to assume command over Hartlib's Comenius assignments.[60] Hübner was not at this date entirely unknown to Hartlib, but it seems that he is mentioned only once in Hartlib's papers before 1636, in a passing remark dating from 1634, which itself hints that he was already known to Hartlib.[61] From November 1636 until the end of 1640 Hübner submitted almost weekly reports to Hartlib, mainly from Oxford. His direct correspondence with Comenius began on 7 October 1638 and eleven other letters followed, reaching an abrupt end on 7 December 1640. Most of these letters, like his correspondence in general, were lengthy

---

58 There is urgent need for a consolidated study of Poehmer. His presence in the Hartlib Papers is considerable, but under-estimated owing to misattributions. For his links with Comenius, Blekastad, *Comenius*, p. 151 et passim. See also much helpful material in Dickson *Tessera of Antilia*, pp. 110–35.

59 J.T. Young, *Faith, Medical Alchemy and Natural Philosophy: Johann Moriaen, Reformed Intelligencer and the Hartlib Circle* (Farnham, Surrey: Ashgate, 1998) for a fine review of major interests of Moriaen.

60 There is lamentable lack of modern commentary on the substantial body of Hübner's correspondence, but for an admirable summary of his biography and involvement in a liberal range of publishing projects, L.T.I. Penman, 'Areopagitica, freedom of the press, and heterodox religion in the Holy Roman Empire', *The Seventeenth Century*, 33:1 (2018), 45–61.

61 Streso to Hartlib, 20 July 1634, HP 11/1/142A. This note suggests that Hübner was already familiar with Dury.

and stylish. During this period, he mounted a virtuoso performance, demonstrating command of both classical and modern sources, and with respect to the latter, every species of activism, from Boehme and the Rosicrucians to the aspiring corpuscularians and mechanical philosophers. Unfortunately, his reputation was marred by habitual tactlessness, commonly expressing itself as condescension or indeed naked aggression. Some big targets were often chosen, for instance the eminent Johann Heinrich Bisterfeld, who in 1638 communicated to Hartlib his resentment at Hübner's monstrous misjudgment of his character and his capabilities as a philosopher.[62]

Comenius was at first fortunate. Hübner took a liking to his pansophic project and worked hard to edit and publish his *Conatuum*, the manuscript of which had reached Hartlib in the autumn of 1636. Hübner passed his first and most favourable comments on this text in December 1636.[63] The edition appeared in Oxford in the summer of 1637.[64] This was an auspicious moment since it marked the beginning of Hartlib's new career as a publisher. Alas, this well-meaning gesture occasioned the first perturbation in relations between Hartlib and Comenius. Unfortunately, publication had been undertaken without troubling to ask permission from the author. Secondly, this latest publication by Comenius was grist to the mill of the author's critics, who duly revived their accusations of heresy and Socinianism, suspicions that had also been raised in Oxford where they accounted for some delay in publication.[65]

For the moment harmony was restored and the way was prepared for a further amended edition of the now-retitled *Prodromus pansophiae*, which was issued in London.[66] After a further short delay, there was

---

62 [Bisterfeld to Hartlib], excerpt of letter, 17 September 1638, HP 27/7/1A.
63 Hübner to Hartlib, 25 November and 1 December 1636, *MGP*, pp. 68–72.
64 *CONATVVM COMENIANORVM PRAELVDIA EX BIBLIOTHECA S.H. OXONIÆ*, Excudebat GUILIELMUS TURNERUS Academiæ Typographus. ANNO MDC. XXXVII. STC 15077.
65 For a series of fifty adverse annotations on the *Conatuum* of Comenius by Hieronim Broniewski, a senior figure of the Brethren in Leszno, dated 5 January 1639, HP 7/64/1A-4B. The final note summarises the argument of Comenius and concludes: 'Hoc Socinianum est'.
66 Harmony was not quite achieved, as indicated by a letter from Hartlib to Tassius dated 21 April 1638, which complains that Comenius had not responded to his letters for the last six months, HP 28/1A-2B. In fact, on 26 January 1638 and again in September, Comenius had rehearsed to Hartlib his grievances about the *Conatuum* publication and related Leszno repercussions. On 8 March 1638

an English translation, which was not altogether appropriately titled *The Reformation of Schooles* (1642).[67] This title was no doubt calculated to appease British patrons, who were known to be enthusiastic about Comenius as an educational reformer, but were likely to be quite cool about the wider philosophical programme that had become the first priority of the Czech.

A false impression of Comenius's diminishing engagement with education was exacerbated by Hübner's behaviour over the *Didactica magna*, which was an ambitious synthesis, eagerly awaited and by the date of completion was destined for publication in England.[68]

Alarmed by the author's coupling of pansophic and didactic themes, Hübner set about the demolition of the *Didactica* in a tirade spread over four thousand words of a letter to Comenius, dated November 1639.[69] This began in an insulting and patronising manner by heaping praise on Marin Mersenne, whom Hübner portrayed as the kind of pansophic authority from whom Comenius would do well to learn before publishing anything more in this field. Then, with respect to the *Didactica magna*, he judged this sizeable text as quite unsuitable for publication. It failed to deliver what the title promised, and what it contained was inadequate, incoherent and unfounded. In view of its multiple failings Comenius was censured for daring to believe that this product as a suitable partner for the pansophic *Conatuum*. Hübner warned the author that he faced ridicule by the leading thinkers of the time unless the *Didactica* was sent back to the drawing board.

Moriaen's letter to Hartlib of 5 December 1639 illustrates the speed in which information was transmitted within the Hartlib community concerning Hübner's dramatic intervention. Moriaen was evidently shocked by the malign tone of Hübner's censure of Comenius's *Didactica magna*. He looked forward to hearing Comenius's response to this attack and was concerned by the damage the censure would inflict on the whole

---

Comenius submitted a short note concerning the plight of the Bohemian Brethren in Frankfurt an der Oder.

67 *A reformation of schooles designed in two excellent treatises, the first whereof summarily sheweth, the great necessity of a generall reformation of common learning* (London: Printed for Michael Sparke, 1642). Wing C5529.

68 The text of the *Didactica magna*, as delivered to Hartlib, is probably that preserved in HP 35/6/1A-145B, which is a variant of the first published version dating from 1657.

69 *KK*, vol. 1, 1898, No. 62, pp. 72–82. Repeated in *MGP*, pp. 141–57.

group of his associates. In the first place he demanded confidentiality in such exchanges, but this was not enough. He insisted that, before any further publications, there should be a meeting of those concerned, which would examine all ongoing work and reach a consensus before any further material was made public. He told Hartlib that he had written to Comenius with this proposition. This path of conciliation, although deeply subversive to the status of Comenius, seems to have been followed to some extent, allowing resumption of Hübner's communications with Comenius and talk of a close partnership, even the possibility of the transfer of Hübner to Leszno.[70]

Comenius was so shocked by the intervention of Hübner that at first he completely abandoned the idea of publication. The absence of an edition of the *Didactica magna* left Comenius without a fresh educational publication to his name at the date of his English visit. In normal times this would have embarrassed Hartlib and irritated English patrons, but, at the start of a civil war, all minds were otherwise engaged.

On reflection Comenius virtually ignored Hübner's strictures and published the *Didactica* quietly without any substantial alteration in his collected educational writings in 1657. It was never published separately during his lifetime, or for a very long period afterwards. It is only in modern times that it has come to be regarded as a major classic of modern education.

No doubt Hartlib took some comfort from the conclusion of the respected Professor J.A. Tassius, his Hamburg friend, who himself had reservations about *pansophia*, but concluded positively that 'Pansophics and better Didactics are now boiling over in all corners of Europe. So: even if Comenius has done nothing more, he has sown a veritable crop of stimuli in the hearts of all, and so must be thought to have achieved enough'.[71] Moriaen was even more enthusiastic about the *Didactica magna* than Tassius and announced that he was exploring the possibility

---

70 Moriaen to Hartlib, 5 December 1639, HP 37/49A.
71 Johann Adolf Tassius to Hartlib (n.d., but probably July 1638), *KK*, vol. 1, 1898, No. 53, p. 50. Hartlib echoed the verdict of Tassius, concluding that the *Praeludia*, although just a *seminarium*, might fare better than the projected finished product (*mehr gutes als das Werck selbt tun werde*). Hartlib to Tassius, 10 August 1638, Staats und Univ. bibliothek ep. 100, 60A.

of publication in the Netherlands, not only of the *Didactica magna*, but also other writings by Comenius.[72]

Regardless of the mishaps concerning the *Conatuum* and the *Didactica magna*, an all-round feeling took hold that England offered the best prospects for the future of Comenius and his collaborators. The above idolisation of Britain by Johannes Arnold was echoed by other correspondents of Hartlib throughout central Europe. The deteriorating situation of many Protestant minorities gave rise to largely unfounded conjectures about England being a haven of tranquility, enlightenment and magnanimity. Such bias generated some curious side-effects, as for instance with Johann Heinrich Bisterfeld, friend of both Hartlib and Comenius, who wrote of his yearning after '*Anglicam tranquillitatem*', a way of life thought characteristic of England, where scholars were free to study in peace, both day and night.[73] Poehmer held out Nuremberg and England as potential homes for Comenius and his team, but of these two places enjoying a golden peace, England was superior in its potential for patronage and benefaction.[74]

Given the plethora of favourable opinion concerning England among outsiders, Hartlib and Dury set about drafting petitions designed to enhance support for the relocation of Comenius and his team.

Various drafts of such documents are found in the Hartlib Papers, all of them anonymous. The most interesting is an elegant Latin entreaty, which describes the nation's plight in apocalyptic terms, and presents Comenius as a messianic figure, whose piety and erudition amounted to a kind of 'universal wisdom'. Proof of his transcendent importance was provided by his latest book, [the *Conatuum*] which was the 'key to the Book of Nature and the Scriptures, or an exact compendium of all the useful arts', otherwise known as *pansophia*. It was hoped that such a passionate appeal would unlock the purse strings of potential benefactors.[75]

If clarification about practicalities were required, this was amply covered in an anonymous petition headed 'Worthy Sir' which was undoubtedly drafted by Dury and might well have been circulated

---

72 Moriaen to Hartlib, 28 February 1639, HP 37/9A-B.
73 [Bisterfeld to Hartlib], excerpt of letter, 17 September 1638, HP 27/7/1A.
74 Poehmer to Hartlib, 1636, *MGP*, pp. 58–61.
75 Plea for the support of Comenius, n.d., [circa January 1639], HP 18/20/1A-2B.

under his signature. By contrast with the elegant Latin document, 'Worthy Sir' constituted a hasty, ill-thought-out and rambling recitation of possible personnel combinations and costs, but with no central thread of argument. The major defect was that the appeal for substantial resources was not matched by practicalities about such basic issues as to where the Comenius team would be located or what precisely they would undertake. It was therefore entirely obscure what benefit would accrue to the benefactors and the English nation.[76]

In his response to 'Worthy Sir' Moriaen noticed that there might be two or three collaborators in this package who, together with Comenius himself, would absorb at least £500 a year. Oblivious to the impracticality of raising such funds, he seemed untroubled by this estimate and assumed automatically that it would be spent in England, which he depicted as the most suitable location (*in Engelland am füglichsten*) for a project that would tap into the spirit of emulation for which the nation was noted.[77]

In his next letter, dated 19 April 1639, Moriaen signified his delight at the news from Hartlib that Comenius had now been invited to England. This perhaps suggests that Hartlib had by that point received some positive responses to the campaign for support of the Comenian team. Reflecting this mood of optimism, Moriaen suggested the addition of John Pell to this group in order to strengthen its mathematical expertise.[78]

On 12 August 1639 Moriaen thanked Hartlib for the transmission of yet a further work by Comenius, his *Pansophiae Christianae Lib III, De mediis homini ad fines suos concessis utendi modo*, for which Moriaen took the trouble to provide the full title. This is a further example of a manuscript which survives among Hartlib's papers.[79] Moriaen's letter also contains a bibliographical curiosity in the form of the title of a pamphlet, amply titled: *The Duties of such as wish for the advancement... of true Religion and An Exhortation for the worke of education intended by Mr Comenius*, which I suspect is either the 'Worthy Sir' document discussed above, or some

---

76 [John Dury], 'Worthy Sir...' etc., n.d., [circa January 1639], HP 26/23/1A-6B.
77 Moriaen to Hartlib, 7 March 1639, HP 37/11B-12A.
78 Moriaen to Hartlib, 19 April 1639, HP 37/21A-22B.
79 Moriaen to Hartlib, 12 August 1639, HP 37/36A. For *Pansophiae Christianae Lib III*, HP 35/2/1A-24B. See also G. H. Turnbull, *J. A. Komenského Dva spisy vševědné—Two Pansophical Works by John Amos Comenius* (Prague: Oaská akademie věd a umění ve Státním naki. učebia, 1951), pp. 7–18. DJAK 14, pp. 51–88, 101–07.

other pamphlet based on this source, which constitutes further evidence that Hartlib and Dury were seriously addressing their task of raising financial support for Comenius. Sadly, a letter from Dury to Hartlib, dated September 1639, admitted that their idea of some form of collegiate institution to support Comenius had made absolutely no progress.[80]

Notwithstanding a growing sense of forward motion, the Hartlib team remained inactive with respect to seeking support for Comenius in parliamentary quarters. An important set of communications sent by Hartlib to Sir Thomas Roe in August 1640 help to explain this lethargy. These exchanges focused almost entirely on the plight of Dury. Of Comenius, there was no mention at all.[81] If this documentation is representative, at this crucial time, it seems that Hartlib's allies were throwing all their eggs into a single basket, which was directed to the interests of Dury rather than Comenius.

2.6 Diversification

A further barrier to advancing the affairs of Comenius was Hartlib's habitual tendency towards diversification of his interests, in particular where this related to economic or scientific improvement. A particularly important case of Hartlib's scientific involvement related to his encouragement of the work of John Pell, who was one of his earliest associates, whose friendship persisted until Hartlib's death, after which he recorded accompanying Hartlib's body to its grave.[82] As evident throughout this study, Pell was relentlessly inquisitive, but the nucleus of his activities was mathematics, a discipline that he quietly advanced across a broad front and sometimes in concert with specialists who were

---

80   Dury to Hartlib, 13 Sept 1639, HP 9/1/94B. The occasion for this admission was the magnificent gesture of their friend Tassius, who 'was willing to leave all [of his library] to some Colledge of learned men that Studied to advance the public good of learning, by this meanes hee put mee to it to declare how farr our Collegiall Intentions were advanced, but I answered him in generalls not discovering our weakenes...'.
81   Hartlib to Roe, 10 August 1640, with supportive letters from Bishops Davenant and Hall, as well as reference to support from Archbishop Ussher and others. CPSD, vol. 463, 1–14 August 1640, pp. 569–70.
82   Malcolm/Stedall *Pell*, p. 185.

alien to the mentality of Samuel Hartlib.[83] Undoubtedly aware of the relevance of the plans of Comenius for the development of a pansophic programme, Pell stepped forward with his own brief and elegant scheme for the development of mathematics, which was eminently practicable and provided hints that Pell might superintend such a development. For reasons that are not clear, the decision was made to issue this plan as a kind of manifesto, known as *An Idea of Mathematics*, written in the form of a letter from Pell to Hartlib and first issued October 1638 as a folio broadsheet, without title, author's name, date or place of publication. This was produced in English and Latin versions, both of which were widely circulated by Hartlib. It should not be forgotten that the *Idea* counts as Hartlib's second publication venture.

The responses to this exploit were overwhelmingly positive, which was greatly to the advantage of Pell's reputation. As further noted in chapter 4, the *Idea* was reprinted in John Dury's *The Reformed Librarie-Keeper with a Supplement to the Reformed-School* in 1650, where it was entitled '*An Idea of Mathematics written by Mr Joh. Pell to Samuel Hartlib*'. All of this was then reprinted in 1651 to fill out the second edition of Dury's *The Reformed School*.[84]

Pell and Hartlib were in league again with respect to their promotion of Gabriel Plattes (c.1600–1644), who seems to have been in touch with them since late 1638. Plattes became integrated into Hartlib's orbit by the end 1639, in which context he particularly attracted the interests of John Pell and Theodore Haak.

Plattes' reputation was justifiably established by his agricultural tract, *A Discovery of Infinite Treasure*, and its mining counterpart, *A Discovery of Subterranean Treasure*, both of which were published early in 1639. Haak immediately briefed Marin Mersenne about these publications. The idea soon emerged that Plattes was the British equivalent of the illustrious Frenchman, Bernard Palissy (1510–1590).[85] Like Palissy, Plattes operated across the broadest of fields. The climax of his early

---

83 Malcolm/Stedall *Pell*, p. 96, with respect to Pell's mathematical exchanges with the patrician Royalist, Sir Charles Cavendish.
84 Malcolm/Stedall *Pell*, pp. 65–79.
85 Hartlib to Lords Robartes and Manchester, 28 May 1640: 'one Palissi to bee of the like disposicion & industry' to Plattes, HP 7/50/2A. For Plattes, see Koji Yamamoto, *Taming Capitalism before its Triumph* (Oxford: Oxford University Press, 2018), pp. 55–56, 112–13, 128–30, 181, 216.

publishing career was his *Description of the Famous Kingdome of Macaria*, issued in October 1641, a curious and fascinating little utopian pamphlet, no more than four-thousand words in length. Without any good reason *Macaria* has been widely attributed to Samuel Hartlib. Alas, there is no sound evidence that Hartlib was either the author or publisher.[86] It is even possible that Hartlib had no knowledge of Plattes' tract. It is nowhere mentioned in the Hartlib Papers, nor, it seems, in any other contemporary source. The discovery of the true interest of *Macaria* is a phenomenon of recent times, although, even now, the basic facts about this tract are often misrepresented.

2.7 Comenius in London

Hartlib may not have been directly involved with *Macaria*, but he was certainly not backward in alluding to the utopian literature, particularly the *New Atlantis* of Francis Bacon. In a lengthy letter of Comenius to Hartlib, dated 17 February 1641, he built on his panegyric to Francis Bacon, culminating with reference to Solomon's House, the ideal institution of learning advocated in *New Atlantis*.[87] In the fertile imagination of Comenius (seemingly inspired 'by the genius and eloquence' of Hübner) this idea was magnified into a Universal College of learned scholars devoted to the furtherance of all aspects of Universal Light. It is readily understandable how these ideas became assimilated into Comenius's own utopian work, *Via Lucis*, which was completed during his visit to England, but not published until 1668, when it was dedicated to the London-based Royal Society.[88] Just in case Hartlib was lacking in imagination, Comenius challenged him not to squander this opportunity for England to become host to such a universalist project. Specifically, he proposed a foundation in London comprising six to

---

86   For a full review of the *Macaria* issue, C. Webster, *Utopian Planning and the Puritan Revolution. Gabriel Plattes, Samuel Hartlib and Macaria* (Oxford: Wellcome Unit for the History of Medicine, 1979). Notably, the *Macaria* publisher, Francis Constable, never featured among Hartlib's chosen publishers. For Haak, Pell and Mersenne, Barnett *Haak*, pp. 39–42.

87   Comenius to Hartlib, 17 February 1641, HP 7/84/1B-4A; first published by D. Čapková, 'Unpublished Letters by Comenius', *Acta Comeniana*, 2 (1970), 286–87.

88   The most recent and exhaustive edition is U. Voigt, *Johann Amos Comenius Der Weg des Lichtes Via Lucis* (Hamburg: Felix Meiner Verlag, 1997).

seven scholars, who would then act as the hub of a communications network that would operate worldwide. By means of this foundation England would book its place in the forthcoming age of universal bliss, as was outlined by John Stoughton, their recently deceased friend.[89] On 7 March Comenius wrote yet again to Hartlib to remind him that the fate of the clergy belonging to the Brethren was much worse than on the previous occasion that he had raised this matter.[90]

In the spring of 1641 references to Comenius in Moriaen's letters to Hartlib became fewer and more marginal. On the other hand, a lengthy letter to him from Comenius, dated 7 March 1641, shows that Moriaen remained very much centre-stage. For his part, Comenius wanted to make personal acquaintance with Moriaen, Hartlib and Hübner. Also escape from Leszno seemed the only means to complete his pansophic studies, for which access to the library resources of the Netherlands or England was deemed to be essential.[91]

For Comenius, the fresh opportunity to visit England had arisen at an opportune moment, when he was no longer able to bear the weight of responsibilities demanded of him at his denomination's headquarters in Leszno, while also attempting to bring to a successful conclusion to the immense intellectual undertaking upon which he had embarked. He had therefore reached the situation of having few qualms about seeking shelter elsewhere in order to regain the momentum of the great tasks for which, he believed, he was divinely ordained. Unfortunately for him, divine ordination had not endowed the means or the political stability required to enable him to fulfil these ambitions.[92]

---

89 John Stoughton, *Felicitas ultimi sæculi: epistola in qua, inter alia, calamitosus ævi præsentis status seriò deploratur.... Nunc publici juris facta à S.H.* (London: R. Hodgkinson imp. D. Frere, 1640). No doubt, as its editor, Hartlib presented Comenius with a copy of this little book. The death in 1639 of the influential Stoughton was mourned by both Hartlib and Comenius as a major loss.

90 Comenius to Hartlib, 7 March 1641, HP 7/84/1A-B; Čapková, 'Unpublished Letters', 290–92.

91 Comenius to Moriaen, 7 March 1641, HP 7/84/1A-B; Čapková, 'Unpublished Letters', 293–94.

92 For its historiographical significance and general accessibility, special importance is attached to Hugh Trevor-Roper's scintillating essay, 'Three Foreigners and the Philosophy of the English Revolution', *Encounter*, February 1960, pp. 3–20. The other main sources: R.F. Young, *Comenius in England: the Visit of Jan Amos Komenský (Comenius)... to London in 1641–1642* (London: Oxford University Press, Humphrey Millward, 1932) ; Turnbull *HDC*, pp. 349–70; idem, 'The Visit of Comenius to England in 1641', *Notes and Queries*, 17 (1951), 37–42; idem, 'Plans of Comenius

The possibility of support for Comenius in England gained a higher public profile when his case was briefly mentioned in a sermon delivered by John Gauden to the Long Parliament in November 1640.[93] The relevance of this source to Hartlib was first revealed by Turnbull in 1927,[94] but it is only since about 1960 that it has attracted much attention, indeed more than is merited by the sermon itself. Gauden's somewhat adventitious remarks about Comenius, Dury and Hartlib occupy little more than a couple of paragraphs and a compressed footnote located on pages 42 and 43 of his 46-page sermon on Truth. When Gauden's text is examined closely, it is clear that his plea for financial support for Dury and Comenius is not associated with any expectation of their relocation to England. Hartlib is invoked as a possible intermediary between Parliament and the other two luminaries in the provision of more enhanced support. Gauden's sermon is therefore little more than a curiosity, but it does suggest that at the end of 1640 the point had not yet been reached when there was any general expectation of a visit to England from Comenius.

Regardless of qualms about the growing political turmoil in Britain in the early months of 1641, both Comenius and Hartlib developed a more positive attitude towards the Czech's exile in England. There were, however, differences of emphasis. Comenius envisaged that he and his team might play a constructive role in a college of the type envisaged by Francis Bacon, whereas Hartlib favoured the Czech visiting alone with the idea of inspiring greater support for his ideas concerning education and the advancement of learning.[95] Alas, for the period from May until September there is little evidence concerning the finalisation of Comenius's

---

for his Stay in England', *Acta Comeniana*, 17 (1958), 7–28; Blekastad *Comenius*, pp. 309–30; see also Haffemeyer, *Les Lumières radicales*, pp. 202–90.

93 *The love of truth and peace. A sermon preached before the Honourable House of Commons assembled in Parliament. Novemb. 29. 1640. By John Gauden, Bachelor in Divinity. Published by their command* (London: Printed by T.C. for Andrew Crooke in Pauls Church-yard at the Greene Dragon, 1641), 46 pages. Thomason E.204[10], Wing G362. John Gauden (1605–1662) was a long-standing, but not close, contact of Hartlib. This intervention by Gauden was no doubt prompted by one of his aristocratic patrons such as the Earl of Warwick. See Young, *Comenius in England*; Turnbull *HDC*, pp. 349–65; Young *Moriaen*, pp. 127–34.

94 G.H. Turnbull, 'The summoning of Comenius to England by Parliament', *The Central European Observer*, vol. 5, No. 2, April 1927.

95 Turnbull *HDC*, pp. 350–54 for a summary of the many relevant letters from the first months of 1641.

plans. His own testimonies about the circumstances of his visit to Britain are not entirely consistent. He cites pressure from Hartlib and his patrons, elsewhere the entreaties of bishops and leading churchmen and finally a summons from Parliament. The last of these explanations was in the past favoured in the literature, but it is entirely without foundation. Hartlib was not alone in engineering the choice of exile, but, reflecting the mounting political chaos in the British Isles, the strength of resolve among Hartlib's patrons and co-workers was noticeably subdued. In view of this confused situation and the tempting lures of Ludovicius de Geer for Comenius to settle in Sweden, it is doubtful whether Comenius ever believed that the English visit as more than an interlude. The duration of his stay was nine months, starting in September 1641, but, as Turnbull points out, 'the departure of Comenius from England must have been impending throughout the winter of 1641–2'.[96]

The great man's arrival in London was not heralded by fanfare. Even the date of this important occurrence is not entirely clear. Sir Cheney Culpeper, who soon assumed the task of trying to make a reality out of Comenius's dream of a Baconian college, first heard of the Czech's arrival in a letter from Hartlib dated 21 September 1641.[97] Shortly afterwards Nicholas Stoughton expressed his delight at this outcome and immediately donated £20 to help Hartlib with associated costs.[98] The Czech himself was under the illusion that his visit was sanctioned by parliament but, as noted below, this misapprehension was not shared by his hosts.[99]

---

96   Turnbull *HDC*, p. 364. A message to Hartlib perhaps from Moriaen, 17 October 1641, reports favourably on de Geer, and points to the advantages that Comenius would enjoy by taking the Swedish course of action. The informant estimated that de Geer was already supporting some 200 learned persons. HP 23/9A-B.
97   Culpeper to Hartlib, 29 September 1641, Culpeper *Letters*, p. 153. This letter is consistent with the remark of Comenius that he arrived on the day of the autumn equinox: *De novis studia Didactica continuandis occasionibus*, ODO ii introduction; Young *Comenius in England*, pp. 52–56. For Culpeper and Hartlib, see Haffemeyer, *Les Lumières radicales*, pp. 186–87 et passim.
98   Stoughton to Hartlib, 28 September 1641, HP 46/12/17A.
99   In the past much weight has been placed on the bold statement by Comenius: '*ibique demum me parliamenti jussu fuisse vocatum intellexi*', meaning that upon arrival he became aware that 'I had been summoned by order of the parliament'. *De novis studia didactica continuandis occasionibus*, ODO ii introduction; Young, *Comenius in England*, pp. 52–56.

The august visitor received a warm greeting, but little special attention. His residential arrangements amounted to lodging in Hartlib's humble home. The stream of curious visitors rapidly melted away, leaving Comenius for the most part in the company of Hartlib, Dury, Haak, Hübner and Pell. All of these were well-acquainted with the work of Comenius, but they were heavily committed with other obligations. With the exception of Sir Cheney Culpeper, who resided in Kent, none of the upper-class patrons of Hartlib were in a position to be of much assistance, largely because they were unavoidably preoccupied with the mounting political crisis. There was also a distinct lack of imagination on the part of Hartlib's patrons. As Dury reported to Hartlib: 'Sir William Boswell hee said that hee hadde all this while thought yow to haue beene a single man & of a good estate; but I informed him how yow stood, & what ingratitude was used towards yow by those whom yow furnished with intelligence, at which hee was silent'.[100] A further adverse factor to bear in mind is the precarious health of Hartlib himself, upon which Dury also commented and offered advice about amelioration.[101]

Although left almost destitute, without the anticipated support of coworkers, and with no promise of improvement, Comenius remained stoical and quietly attended to his work, with which he made remarkable progress. Already on 18 October 1641 he reported to friends in Leszno on his first impressions, which were accurate, realistic and not too pessimistic.[102]

In all likelihood, intended for the same group was a heavy work schedule, also dated 18 October.[103] From the outset Comenius appreciated that reforms on the scale he was envisaging required a group effort and an efficient division of this labour. Despite the harsh criticism emanating from Hübner, he was entirely unrepentant about his *Didactica magna*, which, he insisted, should be first published and then allowed to act as the linchpin for other educational projects. All sections of his *Informatorium der Mutterschul* also merited further

---

100 Dury to Hartlib, 30 May 1642, HP 2/9/1A.
101 Dury to Hartlib, 30 August 1642, HP 2/9/13A.
102 Comenius to friends in Leszno, 18 October 1641, Patera *Korrespondence*, 1892, Letter No. 32, pp. 113–16; Young *Comenius in England*, pp. 64–67.
103 *Ad excitanda publice VERITATIS & PACIS (hoc est communis salutis) ope DEI Studia Elaborandorum Operum Catalogus*, 8/18 October 1641, HP 7/90/1A-10B; Turnbull *HDC*, pp. 359–60 and p. 443, No. XVI.

editorial attention. He then proposed to expand advice concerning all grades within the Vernacular and Latin schools. The culmination of his effort was finalising guides to *panhistoria, pandognmatica* and *pansophia*. Finally, he turned to practical considerations, ending with specific ideas about division of writing labour between Comenius, Dury, Hübner and Pell, while Hartlib would occupy himself with the task of administration. This plan confirms that educational reform still occupied a high place in the order of priorities of Comenius.

With respect to patronage, the outlook was ominous, but some attempt was made to draw attention to the portentous opportunities offered by the presence of Comenius. The most conspicuous publicity concerning the visit was an anonymous pamphlet entitled *Englands Thankfulnesse*,[104] which was without doubt written by Dury and, as boldly stated on the title page, this petition was: 'Presented to the COMMITTEE for Religion in the High Court of Parliament'.[105] This tract, now a rarity, is important and impressive for various reasons, including demonstrating Dury's periodic ability to capture the mood of the moment. In this case he calculated precisely how to identify with the ideology of groups like the John Pym *junto* and their allies who were at that moment efficiently engineering the Parliamentarian ascendancy.

---

104 ENGLANDS THANKFVLNESSE, OR AN HVMBLE REMEMBRANCE Presented to the COMMITTEE for Religion in the High Court of Parliament, with Thanksgiving for that happy Pacification betweene the two *KINGDOMES*. *By a faithfull Well-wisher to this Church and Nation. Wherein are summarily discovered,* A maine and most subtile *Plot* of the *Pope* and his *Conclave* against *Protestancy*. Their true Method and Policy how to undermine the same. The best and principall meanes of re-establishing the *Palatin House*, and preserving all *Evangelicall Churches. As likewise, Three* speciall *Instruments* of the publike good in the wayes of *Religion, Learning,* and the preparatives for the *Conversion* of the *Jewes*. (LONDON, Printed for Michael Sparke Senior, dwelling in Green-Arbour, at the signe of the blew Bible. 1642). 16 pages. Wing E3057.

105 There is uncertainty about the identity of this Committee. It is usually thought to be the House of Commons committee of this name, but this huge committee was chaotic and ineffective. Perhaps more likely is the House of Lords committee for religion, established in March 1641, chaired by Bishop John Williams, who was supportive of Hartlib, and containing others who were also known to be sympathetic. This committee operated quite successfully and on a bipartisan basis. For an excellent summary, J. Van Duinen, '"Pym's Junto" in the Ante-Bellum Long Parliament: Radical or Not?' in M. Caricchio, G. Tarantino (eds.), *Cromohs Virtual Seminars. Recent Historiographical Trends of the British Studies (17th–18th Centuries)*, 2006–2007: pp. 1–5.

The pamphlet itself was published early in 1642, but it was likely to have been completed between the date of Comenius's arrival and 20 October, when the Long Parliament reassembled. This tract is particularly directed at interested Parliamentarians, among whom the text was distributed in advance of publication by Nicholas Stoughton (1592–1648), a Surrey dignitary who was already a confirmed admirer and editor of Comenius's work, and also a respected figure among influential Parliamentarians.

Those same Parliamentarians would have been particularly pleased that the title gave prominence to the 'happy Pacification betweene the two Kingdomes', an objective that had been formally declared on 10 August 1641. This represented a union that Dury had long advocated but had become reconciled to its impossibility. The Dury text opens by rejoicing at Britain's achievement of a special divine dispensation in being granted restoration of its spiritual and temporal life and liberty, thereby freeing the people from their 'wofull distresse and anxiety for the sense of evils present, and in dreadful expectation of worse things to come...when by your wisdom the abuse of our Christian Liberty in some matters of consequence shall be taken away, lest in many other things, by little and little it may turne into a licentious dissolution of all true Government' (p. 2). Such statements left no doubt about the author's anti-Laudian and reformist perspective. In fact, the tract as a whole was a sixteen-page political diatribe into which only a small section (pp. 9–11) on intellectual and social betterment constituted a minor incursion. This self-evident political bias was a stark contrast with the sermon of Gauden, who carefully abstained from any hint of anti-monarchical sentiment. Since the nation had qualified itself to be among God's people, Parliament was called upon 'to propagate unto all the world the glorious goodnesse of his Kingdome', an objective that would set the nation free to apply all the available talents to the reform of church and state.

Dury outlined three main priorities: firstly, the advancement of learning as outlined in Bacon's *De augmentis scientiarum*, an objective eminently suited to be entrusted to Comenius who, on the basis of already massive achievements, was expected to be granted the means to oversee a spectacular advance in both his educational and pansophical projects; secondly, the promotion of ecclesiastic peace, an objective clearly designed, for the very first time, to confer official sanction on the work of Dury; thirdly, a less familiar but at that date a rising priority: 'to make Christianity lesse offensive and more knowne unto the Jewes', a labyrinthine issue upon which the unplanned arrival of the capricious Johann Stephan Rittangel in England was viewed as a welcome, if unexpected, operation of divine providence.[106] The sudden and unpredicted availability of this exalted trio gave the nation the opportunity to facilitate their mutual cooperation in order that they might 'advance the publike good'.

Englands Thankfulnesse was a fitting celebration of the Comenius visit. It effectively conveyed the idea that Hartlib, Dury, Comenius and Rittangel were perfectly attuned to the prevailing mood of ideological transformation. However, in its eagerness to whip up support within Parliament, it conveyed a misleading impression of unanimity within the Parliamentary agency. Hence, a novice such as Comenius was tempted to believe that he was in receipt of Parliamentary sanction, which represented a misunderstanding that was difficult to correct. The involvement of Rittangel was little more than a myth. His arrival in England was precipitated by an unexpected incident at sea, well before the arrival of Comenius. Ever a reluctant visitor, he scurried away again in mid-November 1641.[107]

Dury, who had no misunderstanding about the limitations of Parliamentary unanimity, was reluctantly persuaded to compose a sequel to *Englands Thankfulnesse*, with the objective of providing more precise guidance about the intentions of the reformers. This challenge was met in *A Motion Tending to the Publick Good of this Age*, which must have appeared after *Englands Thankfulnesse*, with its preface being dated 31 December 1641, and the publication date being late March or early April 1642.[108] Although four times the length of *Englands Thankfulnesse*,

---

106 Laurence Sarson to Hartlib, 25 February 1644, HP 46/13/1A.
107 A letter of Moriaen to Hartlib, dated 18 November 1641 (HP 7/94A), reports that Rittangel had recently arrived back in Amsterdam and was already immersed in his rabbinic translations. This letter also confirms that Rittangel had stayed in Hartlib's house. There was therefore only a small overlap with Comenius. Also, in late September 1641, when Comenius arrived in England, Rittangel was in Cambridge.
108 [John Dury], *A motion tending to the publick good of this age and of posteritie, or, The coppies of certain letters written by Mr. John Dury to a worthy Knight at his earnest desire shewing briefly what a publik good is and how by the best means of reformation in*

this sequel must be judged an embarrassing failure, and therefore no help to the reputation of either Comenius or Dury. Indeed, in the first half of *A Motion Tending* it is difficult to locate any information relating to their reform objectives. This vacuous sermonising called upon each of their potential supporters to turn themselves into 'a spirituall house, and a holy Priesthood, to offer up spirituall Sacrifices acceptable to God, through Jesus' or to 'truly come unto him as lively stones, to be built up a spirituall house, and a holy Priesthood, to offer up spirituall Sacrifices acceptable to God, through Jesus'.[109]

After the reader had ploughed through some twenty pages of spiritual invocation, Dury at last revealed four practical propositions. The first related to education, but this was merely a call for schools to eliminate obstructions that 'breede evill habits, and make the Soules of men unfit for the apprehension of the mistery of Godlinesse in the profession of the Gospel'. The second proposal was the facilitation of ecclesiastical peace by means of 'correspondency and the Printing of treatises and letters; without which the negotiation of this matter towards Divines will bee wholly lame and imperfect'. The third was 'the erecting of a professorship of Practicall Divinity in every University; and one in *London* at *Sion* or *Gresham* Colledge'. Finally, Dury called for the establishment of a lectureship in London for 'teaching the common people' to make more effective use of the scriptures. Despite its narrow focus and eccentric choice of priorities, Dury urged that his threadbare prospectus would serve 'to the good of this age, and of Posterity for the propagating of heavenly knowledge in the Gospel'.[110]

Having run into the ground with his exposition, Dury suddenly changed tack and devoted the second half of *A Motion Tending* to three letters, of which only the first two, letters from himself to Culpeper and dating from January 1642, relate to serious issues of educational reform. Strikingly, the Culpeper letters make no reference to the four proposals listed above. Indeed, it would not be guessed that the first and second parts of the tract derive from the same hand. The first letter comprises a

---

learning and religion it may be advanced to some perfection, published by Samuel Hartlib (London: Printed by P.L. for Michael Sparke, Senior..., 1642) 40 pages. Wing D2874. N.B. Citations given below retain the erroneous pagination of the original.
109 *A motion tending to the publick good*, p. 17.
110 Ibid., pp. 21–22.

list of concise and practical recommendations for a series of guidebooks to assist the 'reformation of schools'.[111] The second letter amplifies the first, but is more specific about the issue of patronage. Since private patronage had failed 'in the midst of straights and infirmities', Dury called on Parliament to establish a permanent body, which would employ Agents to oversee the general reform of education.[112] Principal among these Agents should be Hugh Trevor-Roper's 'three strangers', who were bonded together by their: 'love to such objects through neglect of our selves we are put to a non-subsistence, I meane Master *Comenius*, Mr. *Hartlib*, and my selfe: For though our taskes be different, yet we are all three in a knot sharers of one anothers labours, and can hardly bee without one anothers helpe and assistance'.[113] These remarks clearly reflect the pact of mutual cooperation that was signed by Comenius, Dury and Hartlib on 13 March 1642.[114] Dury concluded that, under this new foundation, some important work 'might bee well done, and I will propose the matter to Master *Comenius* and Master *Hartlib*, to whom I have not as yet spoken of this particular'.[115]

The above sentiments confirm that Hartlib and his team believed that the time was ripe to embark on radical reform of education and that a new programme would be founded on Comenian principles. But the letters dispel any notion that Parliament had already made any commitment, or that Comenius possessed any special or official sanction. Also, since the letters admit that any hopes of private patronage had been dashed, the way forward was problematical. Finally, Hartlib's inner team, perhaps with the exception of Haak, were themselves on the verge of destitution. There was a real risk that by settling in London, Comenius would join the ranks of the destitute.

The specific challenge facing the reformers was to bring to fruition their plan for a collegiate community reflecting the aspirations of Bacon, Andreae or indeed the Antilians. This goal seemed at last realisable

---

111 Ibid., pp. 23–25.
112 Ibid., pp. 41–44.
113 Ibid., pp. 41–42.
114 '*Foederis fraterni...*' HP 7/109/1A-2B. This pact was retained in the minds of the signatories, among whom it was periodically invoked (Turnbull *HDC*, p. 363). The HP version of this document is clearly from a later date, for which purposes an additional name, William Hamilton, was added. Hamilton's acquaintance with Hartlib began only in 1648.
115 *A motion tending to the publick good*, p. 44.

on account of the annexation by Parliament of many ecclesiastical foundations, some of which were virtually redundant. Comenius, believing that he was under some kind of special dispensation from Parliament, expected that one of these institutions would be designated for his use.[116] The realities on the ground dictated that none of these objectives were practicable.[117] In principle Chelsea College was available for use, but in practice the Hartlib team proved incapable of making any progress on this front, or indeed with any alternative that might persuade Comenius to remain in England. On 10 February 1642 Dury wrote to Hartlib admitting that he had still not come round to drafting a plan for a 'College of Reformation'.[118] It seems that Dury was only undertaking this task to pacify Sir Cheney Culpeper, who retained an undiminished zeal for the Chelsea scheme. At this point Comenius was not mentioned by Dury. In his mind the primary beneficiary of Chelsea would be Dury himself. He pleaded for an annual remuneration of £150, on which basis he promised to rekindle his work for the public good. Dury's foot-dragging over the Chelsea scheme is easily explained. Since the beginning of 1642 he had experienced a complete change of mind concerning his future and had made a bid to become chaplain to the Princess Royal, Mary Stuart (1631–1660), the daughter of Charles I who, in May 1641, formally married Prince William of Orange, as a result of which she would be resettled in The Hague. At the date of their marriage Mary was nine and William fifteen.[119] Owing to the Civil War, this plan was revised and Mary left for The Hague at the beginning of May 1642. By this point Dury had accumulated sufficient support to gain the Princess Mary chaplaincy appointment and he duly repaired to The Hague at the end of May.[120] Culpeper heard this news with

---

116 For instance, S.G. Nordtröm and W. Sjöstrand (eds.), *Comenius' självbiografi* (Stockhom, 1975), pp. 154, 236, where Comenius reports that Culpeper was instructed by Parliament to tell Comenius and his associates to prepare for the successful conclusion of the whole matter.
117 Young *Comenius in England*, pp. 43–44, 53–55; Webster *Samuel Hartlib*, p. 36; Young *Moriaen*, p. 130; Blekastad *Comenius*, p. 315 states: 'The friends were admonished to have their plans ready, and after deliberations concerning housing a college of 12 scholars, they were offered Chelsea College and given an overview of its income'.
118 Dury to Hartlib, 10 February 1642, HP 2/7/1A.
119 Since the autumn of 1641 Dury had also negotiated becoming chaplain to the Earl of Leicester and his family, but this plan was quickly aborted. Turnbull *HDC*, pp. 223–24.
120 For a summary of these events, Turnbull *HDC*, pp. 224–26.

astonishment, particularly given that his hard efforts to secure a rich benefactor for the Chelsea scheme seemed finally to have succeeded.[121] Abandonment of the Chelsea project at that point was a further obvious impediment to securing the services of Comenius for Britain. Comenius was naturally aware of the chaos surrounding him. But he was also inured to instability and poverty, and such circumstances never impeded his intellectual productivity, gift of literary exposition, or indeed appetite for conducting a profuse international correspondence. By reason of these gifts, Comenius yet again demonstrated his capacity to turn defeat into victory. His record of productivity across a broad front was hardly affected by the straits to which he was subjected during his short sojourn in London.

The final letter by Comenius relevant to his stay in England is dated 10 June 1642.[122] This graceful expression of respects was addressed to all of his English friends, but his most cordial comments were reserved for Hartlib personally, whom he described 'as being born and sharpened to be the Instrument of God for arousing, sharpening and uniting men's inborn talents'.

Comenius finally acceded to the inducements offered by Ludovicus de Geer, and left England for the Netherlands, perhaps on 21 June, and thereafter made his way slowly to Sweden, where he arrived in August 1642. That was not the end of his travels, but he long remained in the iron grip of de Geer. This meant that he was in thrall to Sweden and Lutheranism, for which he and his fellow Bohemian Brethren in Poland paid a heavy price. After a dozen years away, he eventually returned to Leszno in 1654, only to be driven out again when, in 1656, the city was incinerated and the Brethren were once more driven into exile, as a result of which Comenius was propelled back to the Netherlands as an impoverished *exilant*.

Dury's flight from Britain also failed to bring about the security for which he yearned. He took up his court appointment immediately, but discovered he had been lured into a state of chaos. Yet again, just as on previous occasions, he found himself mired in intrigue, without adequate accommodation and unable to perform the services to which

---

121 Culpeper to Hartlib, 13 April 1642, Culpeper *Letters*, p. 167.
122 Comenius to Hartlib, 10 June 1642, HP 7/75A-B, which also exists as a printed broadsheet, headed *Exemplar Epistolae Comeni I.A.Comenii*, of the same date.

he aspired. He resigned in 1643 and secured a clerical appointment in Rotterdam, but again without satisfaction, after which he returned to England in 1645 and then, as described in the next chapter, he resumed his place of leadership within the Hartlib entourage, almost as if there had never been an intermission.

2.8 Israel's Call

When, in 1637, Dury characterised Samuel Hartlib's reformist mission, he emphasised its relevance to his own labours on ecclesiastical peace. He specially mentioned his friend's involvement in the Polish and German aspects of church unity, which had contributed to his 'knowne, trusted, & beloved' status throughout the Protestant world, as a result of which he had become one of the 'profitable members of the commonwealth of Israell'.[123] Again, in *Englands Thankfulnesse* (1642), Dury specifically appealed to Parliament to employ himself, Comenius and Rittangel, each of whom could 'be usefull unto the Common-wealth of *Israel* in a publike way'.[124] Dury was accorded an ideal platform to express his mature aspirations when he was selected by the House of Commons to deliver the Fast-Day sermon on 26 November 1645. The version published in the following year bore the title: *ISRAELS CALL TO MARCH OUT OF BABYLON UNTO JERUSALEM*. Like many of the previous Fast-Day sermons of the Civil War period, *Israels Call* was a virtuoso performance, deep in biblical learning, but also replete with challenging messages.

A sharp dichotomy was drawn between the party of Babylon and the architects of a revived Jerusalem. The former were destined to be destroyed, while the latter, if they acted with skill and fortitude, would be rewarded by being sanctioned to raise up the walls of the New Jerusalem.[125] This commitment was important because it would reinforce England's attainment of leadership in Protestant Europe, a status described as being 'Master of the family', 'the commonwealth of Israel' or 'children of Israel', upon whom God was keeping a 'speciall

---

123 Dury to Hartlib, c.1637, HP 26/23/75B.
124 Dury, *Englands Thankfulnesse*, p. 4; see also pp. 6 and 9.
125 *Israels Call*, sig. A2v.

eye'.[126] Such expectations of lavish reward seemed reasonable in light of Britain's achievement of spiritual superiority, above 'all other people of the world; for the Nations of great Britain have made a new thing in the world; a thing which hath not been done by any Nation in the world'.[127] Such a remarkable achievement was the counterpart of the call of the Israelites from Babylon to Jerusalem, which compared only with the state of the Jewish nation in the days of Nehemiah.[128] Having drawn this comparison, Dury habitually elided past with present and outlined the obligations of Parliament towards the 'citizens of Jerusalem' including the order to be observed in the newly erected 'Temple', so that the citizens of Jerusalem might enjoy full 'communion with God'. Thereby, all those who had groaned with pain under the bondage of corruption in Babylon would now 'come to the enjoyment of the glorious liberty of the Sonnes of God'.[129]

Thus far Dury (like Milton's *Areopagitica*, which also dated from 1645) echoed the revolutionary spirit of many other Fast-Day sermons delivered since November 1640.[130] His more specific contribution lay in the closing passages, where he warned that the new settlement of affairs entailed a radical overhaul of the whole educational sector, a task that merited high priority. His main targets were the universities, 'the Schools of the Prophets', which needed to be 'purged and reformed... with the soundness and purity of spiritual learning that they may speak the true language of *Canaan* and that the gibberishe of Scholastical Divinity... may be banished out of their society'.[131]

He also called for the monopoly of the current universities to be ended by the establishment of 'lesser' universities in 'every Province'.

---

126 Ibid., p. 22.
127 Ibid., p. 23.
128 *Israels Call*, pp. 24–25, 27, 29, 31, 34.
129 Ibid., pp. 34–43.
130 A. Guibbory, 'Revolution and Reformation. Parliament 'Fast Sermons,' the Elect Nation, and Biblical Israel', in his *Christian Identity: Jews and Israel in 17th Century England* (Oxford: Oxford University Press, 2010), pp. 89–120; C. Kennedy, 'Milton's Ethos, English Nationhood, and the Fast-Day Tradition in *Areopagitica*', *Studies in Philology*, 116:2 (2019), 375–400.
131 Of course, reminiscent of John Milton's *Of Education. To Master Samuel Hartlib* (1644), which complains that the universities had not recovered 'from the Scholastick grossnesse of barbarous ages', as a result of which students were 'deluded all this while with ragged notions and babblement' (p. 2), which itself echoed Milton's *Prolusions* II and VII from around 1630.

Consistent with these changes, Dury called for reform of 'all the inferior common Schools of all sorts of children and youths' with 'men of parts encouraged to have the inspection and oversight of them'. The current situation was untenable since these schools were 'useles, if not hurtfull to the common-wealth, by the matters of knowledge which are taught in them'. Finally, Dury also insisted that wholesale law reform was also necessary. Without all of these measures, the institutions of Babylon would not be rooted out and the new commonwealth would miss its chance to establish Zion on secure foundations.[132]

Embedded in Dury's conception of Britain's identity with Israel was the notion that both states were committed to an epic struggle to escape from Babylon and rebuild Jerusalem and its temple, ideas that were commonplaces of the Puritan mentality of that period. With respect to Dury and Hartlib, these notions can be traced went back to the beginning of their association. Hence, the third of John Dury's preserved letters, which was addressed to Samuel Hartlib, whom he described as a native of Elbing recently arrived in England with the objective to see attainment of the 'peace of Sion'. At that point Dury was uncertain about his own course of action, about which he intended to consult William Ames, the Puritan veteran, whom he called 'a true Israelite'.[133] In 1636, when efforts to gain financial support for his friend had virtually collapsed, in pleading Hartlib's case with potential patrons, Dury believed that 'God had given unto him to benefit the Commonwealth of Israel in matters of Religion and Learning'. At an earlier date, when prospects were more favourable, Hartlib reported his own notable success on behalf of Dury, in gaining the confidence of prominent Puritan divines, believing that the God of all mercies would now 'stir up the horse-men and charriots of this our Israel' to assist the further progress of their mission for ecclesiastical peace.[134]

Already, in 1634, Dury outlined the successes of Hartlib as:

> An Instrument of *God* appointed to tend upon this and all other public good enterprises... such Men should bee cherished and supported, for

---

132 *Israels Call*, pp. 47–49.
133 Dury to Hartlib, 18 July 1629, BL Sloane MS 645, 243r–244r.
134 Hartlib to Dury, 13 September 1630, HP 7/12/2A; Dury to St Amand, 11 November 1636, HP 6/4/15B.

they may bee made use of for extraordinary Workes; and in effect they are like the middle part of a wheele wherin all the beames or spackes [spokes] from the several parts of the circumference concurre to support the axel-tree of a Charet, so that in the Charet of Israel they are as it were the center wherupon the whole motion doth depend. If then hee can bee kept alive you shal finde that hee wil put life and quicken a hundert.[135]

The horsemen and chariots of Israel became a familiar and welcome image in the Puritan mind. For instance, in 1649 Cromwell warned Parliament not to forget its obligations to the people, who were, after all, 'the chariots and horsemen of Israel'.[136]

In many respects the peak of the aspirations of Hartlib and Dury was reached in 1653 with the imposition of the Nominated Assembly, which was a revised form of Major-General Thomas Harrison's millennially influenced idea of an assembly reflecting the spirit of the Old Testament *Sanhedrin* of seventy selected "Saints".[137] This biblically inspired innovation stirred Dury to compose some of his most impassioned policy statements. Concerning the general duties of the new assembly, in the manner of Harrison himself, he reminded them of the:

Duty incumbent upon me & you, as wee are inhabitants of Sion & members of the Commonwealth of Israel. And in this respect I conceive our duty is to looke stedfast... to that which is come to passe concerning the Kingdome of Israel, that Hee would exalt him that is low & abase him that is high, & would overturne that kingdome & that it should bee no more untill... the Messiah come whose right it is, to possess the nations & to receive the utmost endes of the earth for his inheritance; & if God hath thus determined his Counsell over his owne people, Israel, till Christ come: can wee expect it should bee otherwise among the Gentiles?[138]

As a consequence of the above appropriation of imagery about Israel and the course of Jewish civilisation, intellectuals such as Dury and some of his closest associates became preoccupied with Jews, their language and their culture. In 1641 the assimilation of the Hebraist

---

135 Dury to Charles Potts, 28 July [1634], HP 7/2/1A-B.
136 Letter from Cromwell to William Lenthall, Speaker of the House of Commons, 4 September 1651, *Letters and Speeches of Oliver Cromwell*, ed. by E. Murphy, M. Ó Siochrú and J. Peacey (Oxford: Oxford University Press, 2022), vol. 2, p. 225.
137 *The Memoirs of Edmund Ludlow*, ed. by C.H. Firth, 2 vols. (Oxford: Clarendon Press, 1894), vol. 1, pp. 346, 358.
138 Dury to 'worthy friend' [likely Hartlib], mid-1653, HP 1/1/1B.

Rittangel into their team was indicative of their growing obsession with all things Judaic. By that date Dury was also in touch with Menasseh ben Israel, whose initiatives in the course of time generated incremental relaxations that eventually removed obstacles to the further settlement of Jews in England.

The so-called philosemitism of this period has been the subject of some fine historical research, but it is necessary to remind ourselves that in those ecstatic days of revolution, the same philosemites were also likely to be absorbed in prophecy, messianism, apocalypticism and millenarianism, all of which inspired speculations about the imminence of some kind of transcendental crisis out of which an age of universal betterment would materialise. Such issues inevitably raised questions about the future of the Jews. The conclusion favoured by Protestant activists such as Comenius was neatly summed up by the Rosicrucian Michael Maier in 1618: those like himself who looked forward to a 'universal reformation in the world' envisaged in the not too distant future: 'One empire, one religion, one concord of the dissenters, of the Jews conversion... and to insist on similar things to these'.[139] The precise mode of assimilation of the Jews was a matter of intense discussion during the English Revolution, in which Hartlib and his associates played a conspicuous part.

As already noted, the final relish of the title page of their reform brochure, *Englands Thankfulnesse* (1642), declared that Dury, Comenius and Rittangel personally would serve as 'three speciall Instruments of the publike good in the wayes of Religion, Learning, and the preparatives for the Conversion of the Jewes'. Addressing Hartlib in 1645, Dury devoted an entire letter to the issue of conversion, concluding that 'I am still in the same mind I was in long a goe concerning the conversion of the Jewes, that God will certainly bring it to passe. Concerning the times and Seasons I dare say nothing; but I think they draw neere; because the fulnes of the Gentiles is comming in a pace'.[140] The mode of procedure envisaged by Dury and others was usually not intimidatory, but rather humane and constructive. Dury favoured educational schemes, broadly in line with the thinking of the 1647 proposal for the constituent colleges of a new University of London. In one of these,

---

139 Michael Maier, *Themis Aurea* (Frankfurt a.M: Nicholas Hoffman, 1618), p. 178.
140 Dury to Hartlib, 4 May 1645, HP 3/2/117A-B.

nothing might be spoken but... Hebrew, our Children would as easily learne by the eare, as the Hebrewes did and then all forraigne Protestants of worth in this westerne World would send their sonnes to the University of London, and our elder Brethren the Jewes, now, their conversion to the Christian Faith is at hand, some of you perhaps shall live to see many of them come out of the East and joyne with us their westerne English Brethren here in London.[141]

The issue of Jewish conversion sprang up throughout the reform literature of this period, even in an economic reform tract dated about 1649, where Benjamin Worsley claimed that one of the ancillary effects of his trade proposals would assist with 'endeavouring the Conversion of the Jewes, a worke as most Divines conceave shortly to be expected and without doubt at hand, and such as would not only bee a temporall, but a true and eternall Honour to them that sought or furthered it'.[142] At this very date, as outlined more fully in the next chapter, the collapse of Dury's plans for extending Hebraic studies was especially disappointing because it defeated 'all expectations which wee had to assist public designes and his workes of Iewish Conversion'.[143]

Within the Hartlib team there was serious interest in the ideas of the Collegiant, Adam Boreel (1602–1665), particularly during his visit to London between 1654 and 1659.[144] Boreel was a keen Hebraist, a personal friend of Menasseh ben Israel, and he was closely involved with the latter's embassy to London. When compared with his contemporaries, Boreel's estimation of the Jews was noticeably more positive. In his view, the desired final consummation of the church depended on the Jewish acceptance of Jesus of Nazareth as their messiah, but this objective would only be attained after Christians had radically reformed themselves.[145] Boreel featured prominently in the exchanges between Hartlib and Worthington in 1660. They were aware of differences of opinion about

---

141 Anon., *Motives Grounded for the Founding of a University in London* (1647), pp. 5–6. Consistent with this idea, Benjamin Worsley reported 'Our Layty having lately (especially about London) taken up the humor of learning and acquainting themselves with the Jewish Language, and beinge at the charge of establishing an Hebrew Lecture in the City in English'. [Worsley to Hartlib c.1648], HP 53/37/1A.
142 [Benjamin Worsley], Proffits humbly presented... [c.1645], HP 15/2/64A-B.
143 Dury, probably to Worsley, 29 January 1649, HP 1/7/1A-B.
144 F. Quatrini, *Adam Boreel (1602–1665), A Collegiant's Attempt to Reform Christianity* (Leiden: Brill, 2021), pp. 153–62.
145 Boreel to Dury, 22 November 1660, from F. Quatrini, *Adam Boreel*, p. 137.

Jewish conversion, but were inclined to side with Boreel, a conclusion that was enhanced by reference back to William Ames, the celebrated Puritan authority of earlier days who believed that 'The world may not expect any great happiness before the conversion of the Jews be first accomplished… the late learned Dr. Ames, who professed to his dying day the conversion of the Jews to be a most liquid scriptural truth, but could not approve of any of the Millennary tenets'.[146] Such a forecast represented a blissful outcome for the Christians but, however the pill was sugared, the prospect of the form of assimilation envisaged, even by the most liberal of the so-called philosemites, would have been utterly abhorrent to their Jewish targets.

As evident from the above exposition, a life of uphill struggle was the inevitable lot of the Communion of Saints in their striving to reach the New Jerusalem. In the view of Hartlib and Dury, such a life of hardship was a necessary experience. Hence there was no excuse for abandoning the cause. The final exchange regarding this theme we leave to John Davenport, who welcomed Hartlib into his congregation in 1628 and remained in touch with both him and Dury thereafter. Hartlib proclaimed to Davenport during the dark days of uncertainty occasioned by the civil war: 'If love in the Spirit inflamed with a Universally dilated Christian love did not find my heart, I should judge of myself as one utterly estranged from that Communion of Saints to which we labour to consecrate the utmost of all our studies and emploiments'.[147] Then, when the tide turned again for the worse at the Restoration, Davenport regretted the depletion in the ranks of those 'having & expressing a publick Spirit, in the Communion of Saints', fearing that they should not expect anything but 'the want of some publick Agents likeminded to yourselfe, that so wee may know how to Counterworke the Enemie, and to lift up prayers suitably to the Exigencies of the Churches'.[148] Such was the inevitable fate of those who had heeded the Call of Israel to affiliate themselves with the Communion of Saints.

---

146 Hartlib to John Worthington, 17 December 1660, Crossley vol. I, p. 245.
147 Hartlib to John Davenport, 30 January 1643, HP 7/35/1A.
148 Davenport to Dury, 25 June 1660, HP 6/5/1A.

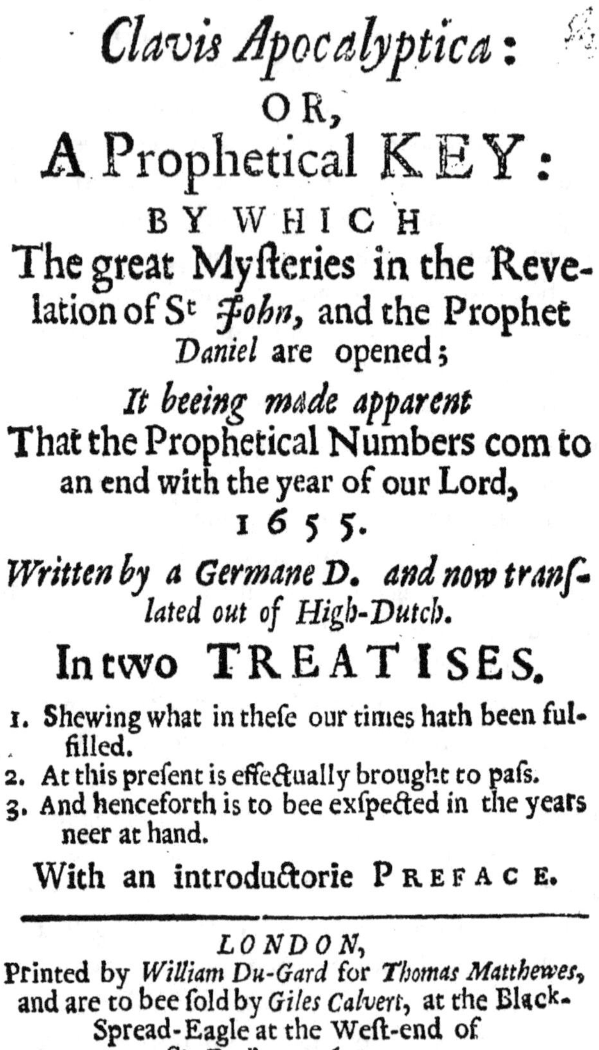

Clavis Apocalyptica:
OR,
A Prophetical KEY:
BY WHICH
The great Mysteries in the Revelation of S*t John*, and the Prophet
Daniel are opened;
It beeing made apparent
That the Prophetical Numbers com to
an end with the year of our Lord,
1 6 5 5.
Written by a Germane D. and now translated out of High-Dutch.

In two TREATISES.
1. Shewing what in these our times hath been fulfilled.
2. At this present is effectually brought to pass.
3. And henceforth is to bee exspected in the years neer at hand.

With an introductorie PREFACE.

LONDON,
Printed by *William Du-Gard* for *Thomas Matthewes*,
and are to bee sold by *Giles Calvert*, at the Black-
Spread-Eagle at the West-end of
S*t Paul's,* 1 6 5 1.

Fig. 3 Title-page of Samuel Hartlib, *Clavis apocalyptica, or, A prophetical key by which the great mysteries in the revelation of St. John and the prophet Daniel are opened; it beeing made apparent that the prophetical numbers com to an end with the year of our Lord, 1655: in two treatises: 1. Shewing what in these our times hath been fulfilled, 2. At this present is effectually brought to pass, 3. And henceforth is to bee expected in the year neer at hand* (London: Printed by William Du-Gard for Thomas Matthewes, and sold by Giles Calvert), Thomason 1260 [2], dated by Thomason Feb 27 1650; Wing H979.

3. The Hartlibian Resurgence

The arrival in England of Comenius in September 1641 coincided with the outbreak of hostilities in Ireland. Before the distinguished visitor had settled down, Parliament issued its Grand Remonstrance, a list of demands in which John Pym, one of Hartlib's most influential patrons, played a leading part. In the context of the ensuing political instability and loss of economic confidence, it is not surprising that there was a complete collapse in the expectations of the 'three foreigners' for a positive transformation of their fortunes.

Almost immediately after Comenius arrived, he reopened his discussions about transferring to Sweden. He departed from England on 21 June 1642. During his stay nothing happened to counteract his pessimistic estimate of the situation.

At exactly this date, after more than six years in Oxford and London, Joachim Hübner also left England for France and never returned. This was an immense loss to the Hartlib team, depriving them of their main player in the realm of international philosophical dialogue. Also, in June 1642 John Dury departed to take up his new role as chaplain and tutor to Princess Mary. These duties also brought Dury in contact with Elizabeth Stuart, the displaced Queen of Bohemia and Electress of the Palatine, who was the daughter of James I.[1] This appointment was relevant to Hartlib who, as noted above, served as the London agent for Elizabeth's son, Karl Ludwig, the Elector of the Palatine, a post that assumed

---

1   This was never a happy assignment, as for instance shown by a letter from Dury to Caspar Godemann, dated 27 June 1642, that is, very near the beginning of his new posting: 'the Princesse hath beene all this weeke at the Queenes Court Bathing with hir; tomorrow she is to returne againe hither: thinges are very unsettled amongst us; & I unprovided of a Lodging as yet, though I have urged it with importunity at all hands; I know not what the ende will bee, but the beginnings are slender & doubtfull', HP 2/9/6A-B. For the present chapter, see especially, Haffemeyer *Les Lumières radicales*, pp. 290–358.

importance in the mid-forties, when Parliament deliberated over the pensions awarded to Elizabeth and Karl Ludwig.[2] Sadly, none of Dury's postings in the Netherlands brought him satisfaction or security.

June 1642 therefore witnessed the departure of Hartlib's two most important associates.

Further serious losses among Hartlib's closest friends took place in the autumn of 1643 when John Pell secured a mathematics teaching post in Amsterdam, while the Palatinate refugee, Theodore Haak, was selected for a diplomatic mission to Denmark.[3]

One of the best-known examples of the irreversible loss of talent was the tragic death of Gabriel Plattes in December 1644. Prior to this Hartlib had conscientiously attempted to protect Plattes' interests, most notably when he addressed to Isaac Pennington, the Lord Mayor of London a long and detailed plea for support, calling Plattes 'a man of pretious use and many profitable abilities'.[4]

The nature of the Plattes tragedy was not known at this date, but this secret could not be concealed for very long: 'I can never forget... the world's base Ingratitude, that let such a man fall downe dead in the street for want of food, without a shirt to his back; none... being found to administer any reliefe to a man of so great merit'.[5]

This dark picture was amplified by Hartlib in 1660, on the verge of his own death: 'In his latter years I maintained him from week to week. But comming once from his lodging at Westminster to my house then in Dukes place being come to Charing Crosse he fell down and dyed suddenly, having not so much as a shirt about his body'.[6]

Replacement of lost talent was hampered by the continuing lack of suitable patronage. Hartlib welcomed the Bohemian refugee Georg Ritschel, who visited Oxford in 1641 and arrived back in London in 1645. In the following year he enrolled for a second time at the Bodleian Library. Owing to strained relations with Comenius, Ritschel was reticent to return to his service, but Hartlib was unable to find him a

---

2   N. Akkerman, *Elizabeth Stuart, Queen of Hearts* (Oxford: Oxford University Press, 2021), pp. 353–61 for Dorothy Moore and Hartlib.
3   Malcolm/Stedall *Pell*, pp. 102–21; Barnett *Haak*, pp. 51–70.
4   Hartlib to Pennington, 16 October 1643, HP 7/4/1A-8B.
5   Hartlib, *His Legacie*, 1651, p. 127 [by Dymock].
6   Hartlib to Winthrop, 16 March 1660, HP 7/7/2B. See Webster, *Plattes*, p. 34 for further contemporary accounts of Plattes' death.

substitute preferment. The abilities of Ritschel as a philosopher were confirmed by his *Contemplationes Metaphysicae* (Oxford, 1648) which, on Hartlib's recommendation, was dedicated to Sir Cheney Culpeper and Nicholas Stoughton, both of whom had evidently given Ritschel encouragement and financial support. In the absence of better prospects, Ritschel drifted into school-teaching in Newcastle and soon afterwards he took up a clerical post at Hexham.

Heinrich Appelius, who became brother-in-law to John Dury, experienced similar disappointment. In the light of Hartlib's favourable impression of this long-standing correspondent, Dury visited him in Amsterdam. The main interest of Appelius was medicine, but he was forced to fall back on school teaching at the nearby small town of Purmerend. Appelius was keen to settle in England and both Dury and Hartlib favoured this choice on account of making better use of his many talents.[7] Nothing came of this proposition but Appelius continued to be an invaluable source of intelligence, for instance, as indicated below, respecting the publishing schedules of Helmont and Glauber.

While Parliament incrementally strengthened its power, Hartlib suffered yet further setbacks. Especially damaging were the deaths of Robert Greville, the second baron Brooke in March 1643, John Pym in December 1643 and Sir Thomas Roe in November 1644, three mainstays among his patrons.[8] For a variety of reasons, other important contacts faded out of the picture: for example, Nicholas Stoughton, perhaps on account of disappointment owing to the collapse of the Comenius initiative, or John St Amand and others because of political alienation.

Such losses were additionally disadvantageous because they exacerbated Hartlib's poverty. The extent of this loss was vividly stated by friends who drew up a petition on his behalf: 'We therefore could not but become Petitioners in His behalf, that is heere a stranger, farr from his owne country; & not only deserted by his owne Naturall freinds & alies; but allso now deprived of those liberall supports which he was

---

7   Dury to Hartlib, 18 September 1642, HP 2/9/24B, hints that Appelius was already expected in England.
8   John Pym's association with Dury and Hartlib perhaps extended back to 1632. The Hartlib-Pym correspondence began in 1635 and continued until June 1643, just before the death of Pym. While the main content of these letters related to Pym's search for a solution to the problem of mine drainage, as noted in chapter 1, he also displayed lively interest in the work of Comenius.

wont to receive, from the most noble bounty of the late Lord Brooke, Sir Nathaniel Rich, Sir Thomas Barrington, Mr Knightly, Mr Pym and diverse others'.[9]

Reflecting the desperation of Hartlib's situation, a further petition was addressed on his behalf to the Lord Mayor and Common Council of the City of London, and signed by 'your Lordships friends and Servants', Lords Salisbury, Manchester and Pembroke, Sir John Clotworthy, Sir Gilbert Gerard and Oliver St John.[10] In response to his own sense of desperation, John Dury felt, not for the first time, that 'your Case doth lye heavie upon my spirit; because I see no trust to bee given to the hopes which are in men'.[11]

3.1 Stabilisation

Notwithstanding the depressing character of his situation, Hartlib remained remarkably resilient, even extending to preserving links that might easily have been severed. For instance, both he and Dury remained in touch with John Davenport, who had been known to Hartlib and Dury since their time in Elbing. As noted above, Hartlib joined Davenport's congregation upon his arrival in London in 1628. Davenport left England in 1633, but the two remained in touch. The warmth of their relationship is evident from a letter sent by Hartlib to Davenport in January 1642. Hartlib was heartened that Davenport sought to import into New England the educational ideas of Comenius. The depth of Hartlib's relationship with Davenport is evident from the labour he was willing to apply in the supply books and manuscripts that Davenport had requested. The Hartlib letter announced a first consignment of 'books and papers in the adjoined great Packet'. A further shipment 'of MS. and Bookes to your serious care and improvement' was promised at the next opportunity. The complicated transport plan to New Haven was then outlined at length.[12]

---

9   Draft petition to the Westminster Assembly, 1645, HP 7/30/1A-2B.
10   Dated 14 May 1645, HP 7/37/1A-2B.
11   Dury to Hartlib, 31 March 1646, HP 3/3/6A-B. At this moment Dury had just arrived in Winchester to take up his new clerical appointment.
12   Hartlib to Davenport, 30 January 1642, HP 7/35/1A-2B.

The extreme lengths of Hartlib's generosity have been outlined in previous chapters, and further cases will be cited throughout the rest of this study. This characteristic became widely known and was undoubtedly of critical importance in attracting fresh patrons and new talent into his orbit.

With respect to the recovery of Hartlib's momentum, his friendship with Sir Cheney Culpeper (1611–1663) was of pivotal importance. They met for the first time on 13 April 1641. Around this date Culpeper, who himself was not at all prosperous, signified his goodwill by making payments, presumably in support of the forthcoming visit of Comenius, an event that Culpeper had eagerly anticipated, and where he had made an important positive contribution. His correspondence with Hartlib began in the autumn of 1641 and extended until October 1657. Alas, as usual, only the Culpeper half of these exchanges has been preserved. The intensity of this relationship is evident from the fine edition of this correspondence edited by Michael Braddick and Mark Greengrass. The relationship between Culpeper and Hartlib certainly continued beyond their surviving correspondence, but seems not to have persisted into the Restoration. Hartlib and Culpeper were important to one another for many reasons, but on the patronage and political fronts Culpeper was fundamental in shifting Hartlib into the orbit of the Independent party, which was of course the rising power in the land.

To illustrate the weightiness of these associations, Culpeper and Hartlib were both much involved with John Sadler, the Town Clerk of London, who came to hold many other offices of state, as well as the headship of a Cambridge college. Sadler in turn was the son-in-law of John Trenchard MP, who was often in touch with both Culpeper and Hartlib. Sadler was also the cousin of Col William Sydenham, who was one of the many links that Culpeper and Hartlib enjoyed at the centre of the protectorate regime.[13]

Fundamental to the reorientation of Hartlib's perspectives was his friendship with the widow, Dorothy Moore (1612–1664), the daughter of Sir John King and Catherine Drury, and hence sister of Edward King, whose early death inspired Milton's 'Lycidas'. Particularly relevant

---

13   For Sydenham, Haffemeyer, *Les Lumières radicales*, pp. 403–04, 431–32. For Culpeper, A. Parr, 'The Laws of Nature and the Nature of Law: Insights from an English Rebel, 1641–57', *History of European Ideas*, 50:3 (2023), 370–91.

to Hartlib were Dorothy's family ties with Katherine Boyle (Lady Ranelagh), and her sister-in-law Margaret Jones, Lady Clotworthy.[14] All of these associations redirected Hartlib's energies towards Ireland and its established Protestant settlers. It may well have been his new relationship with Dorothy Moore that tempted Dury to contemplate becoming the household chaplain to Robert Sidney, the second Earl of Leicester who, in June 1641, was appointed Lord Deputy of Ireland by Charles I. Dury treated the possibility of this new assignment with seriousness, explaining himself in lengthy *apologiae* addressed to Hartlib and Sir John Temple.[15] Dury's appointment failed to materialise and Sidney never set foot in Ireland before he was dismissed by the king in November 1643.

The immediate occasion of Hartlib's contact with Dorothy was his sudden discovery that John Dury had formed an intimate relationship with this distinguished widow. How this partnership came about is not clear, but it was revealed to Hartlib in the summer of 1641, just after John Dury had repaired to the Netherlands and realised that he needed to employ Hartlib to facilitate his dealings with Dorothy who, with her two children, was domiciled in London, as the guests of the Dutch medical practitioner Dr Gerard Boate and his wife Katherine Manning in Aldermanbury. Hartlib was already familiar with Gerard and his younger brother Arnold, who was also a doctor. Arnold had already established a medical practice in Ireland; Gerard shifted his financial interests there and also began collecting geographical information about Ireland. Gerard was on the verge of transferring there when, in 1649, he died prematurely. As seen in chapter 4, both of the Boate brothers became important to Hartlib when he assumed an interest in and, soon, control over their *Ireland's Natural History* project.

Immediately upon his arrival in Rotterdam, John Dury pleaded with Dorothy to trust Hartlib 'as my friend, & freely make use of him to doe you service; for yow knowe hee will reioyce to gratifie yow for my sake in all things that shall lye in his power'.[16] There is every sign that Hartlib

---

14 For Dorothy Moore (Dury), L. Hunter, *The Letters of Dorothy Moore, 1612–64* (Aldershot: Ashgate, 2004). See also F.L. Maxwell, 'Calling for Collaboration: Women and Public Service in Dorothy Moore's Transnational Protestant Correspondence', *Literature Compass*, 14:4 (2017).

15 Turnbull *HDC*, p. 223 and Appendices II 4, 5(a) and (b), pp. 330–36.

16 Dury to Dorothy Moore, 6 July 1642, HP 2/5/1A-2A, Dorothy Moore *Letters*, pp. 03–05.

took this mission seriously. He even acted for her in instructing Gerard and his sister about the handling of Dorothy's investments in Ireland.[17]

From Hartlib's papers relating to the summer of 1642 it is evident that Hartlib had extended his Irish contacts to include Margaret Clotworthy and was engaged in transmitting confidential news between Margaret and various other Irish noblewomen concerning changes of personnel at the court of Elizabeth of Bohemia and the relevance of this to the future of Dorothy Moore.

Given that Margaret Clotworthy and her family lodged at the house of Katherine Boyle, Lady Ranelagh, in Great Queen Street, Covent Garden, it is quite possible that Hartlib may have met Katherine at that stage.[18] The first letter from Hartlib to Katherine is dated 17 October 1644. This confirms that she had supervised his dealings with the Committee of Both Kingdoms. Hartlib's letter makes it clear that the two of them had met on previous occasions and that she had already encouraged him to seek support from this particular committee.[19] These events mark the start of a close and harmonious association between Hartlib and Katherine Boyle that continued until the eve of Hartlib's death.[20] Their relationship underlines the strength of the bonds of friendship that developed among Hartlib's associates. This was illustrated on all kinds of occasions. A curious example was the case of the young visionary Sarah Wight, with which Hartlib's friends became engaged, I assume through the mediation of the prominent Baptist, Henry Jessey (1601–1663), who was a friend and correspondent of Hartlib. In the course of Jessey's record of conversations with Sarah, he transcribed her interviews

---

17 Dorothy Moore to Dury, pre-September 1642, HP 2/11/10A-D, *Dorothy Moore Letters*, p. 12.

18 Indicative of the close ties within the Ranelagh extended household, when Dorothy reported to Hartlib on her discussions with Sir Walter Strickland about Stuart court machinations, she specifically requested Hartlib to keep Ranelagh informed, and the letter was sent to her address, where it was to be available to Sir John Clotworthy. Dorothy Dury to Hartlib, 20 April 1645, HP 3/2/112A-113B, *Dorothy Moore Letters*, pp. 67–68.

19 Hartlib to Lady Ranelagh, 19 October 1644, HP 7/27/19A-B (draft); 7/27/18A-B (final). A letter of Dorothy to Hartlib of 29 September 1644 indicates that Hartlib and Katherine Boyle were in touch by that date.

20 For Ranelagh, the standard source is now M. DiMeo, *Lady Ranelagh: the Incomparable Life of Robert Boyle's Sister* (Chicago: University of Chicago Press, 2021). See also various studies in *Women's Life Writing & Early Modern Ireland*, eds. J.A. Eckerle and N. McAreavey (Lincoln, Nebraska: University of Nebraska Press, 2021).

with Katherine Ranelagh and Margaret Clotworthy, and also on the medical attendance of Gerard Boate and Benjamin Worsley, which was no doubt promoted by the two distinguished women visitors. All four of them had many things in common, including of course their mutual Irish connections.[21] This event was cited with approval a decade later in a letter from John Beale to Hartlib, where he made specific reference to *Exceeding Riches* and cited Katharine's involvement with Sarah as evidence that she wore a 'precious Jewel' of spirituality that constituted one of the greatest strengths of her personality.[22]

A further example of harmonised action related to the poverty into which Samuel Hartlib was sinking. As just noted, Katherine Ranelagh's first major act on his behalf was mobilising her allies on the newly established Committee of Both Kingdoms to redress Hartlib's financial insecurity. Although the secretary of this committee was Gualter Frost, a good friend of Hartlib, this manoeuvre was unsuccessful.

Separately, writing from Rotterdam, Dury disclosed that he and other friends there, no doubt including Dorothy, had confronted Hartlib's problem with the aim of securing for him 'some setled employment & office... that yow should not bee distracted for bodily wants, from the Comfort of serving the public in those aimes which are most eminently profitable for the advancement of Pietie & learning'. Evidently Dury was also thinking of his own security and expecting any office established for Hartlib in England would by necessity be associated with a 'correspondencie with foreign churches' for himself. He called upon Hartlib to take the initiative and use his own influence at the 'Assembly, Parliament and the Merchant Taylors' Company' to prepare the ground for action on behalf of the two partners.[23]

---

21 Henry Jessey, *The exceeding riches of grace advanced by the spirit of grace, in an empty nothing creature viz. Mris. Sarah Wight* (London: Printed by Matthew Simmons for Henry Overton, and Hannah Allen, 1647) [32], 159 pp. Wing J687. For Ranelagh and Clotworthy pp. 24–25, Boate and Worsley, pp. 26–27. Dury and Hartlib had various dealings with Jessey in the 1650s. An earlier contact is suggested by Heinrich Appelius's request for *Exceeding Riches*, soon after it was published, as well as a stray note in a letter from William Adderley to Hartlib in 1647. The Sarah Wight meetings would have exposed the two women not only to the iconoclastic Sarah, but also to Jessey and his radical allies John Saltmarsh and Thomas Palmer, and of course to lay people of similar persuasion. None of this would have worried Hartlib, but Dury would have disapproved, particularly because he was in the middle of a controversy with Saltmarsh at precisely that date.
22 Beale to Hartlib, 14 August [1657], HP 3/2/85A.
23 Dury to Hartlib, 28 July 1644, HP 3/2/45B.

3. The Hartlibian Resurgence

Having experienced unhappiness in her own situations in the Netherlands and witnessed similar distress on the part of her husband, Dorothy also subscribed to these aims and mobilised Walter Strickland (c.1598–1671), then the Parliamentary ambassador to the United Provinces, with whom she had established a good working relationship, to participate in negotiations about the welfare of both Hartlib and Dury. Strickland obligingly wrote to Herbert Palmer, his relative, who had just been appointed as the Master of Queens' College, Cambridge, and was also an influential figure both in the Westminster Assembly and at the Westminster Parliament.[24]

During the final months of 1644 Dury made further efforts to assist Hartlib, specifically by gaining the goodwill of three leading Independent members of the Westminster Assembly, and by furnishing Strickland with commendations from Dorothy and their Dutch friends. Strickland, who was unacquainted with Hartlib, was duly satisfied. It was also agreed to urge John Pell to press the Committee of Both Kingdoms to reconsider the matter of support for Hartlib.[25] Helpful to Strickland, on this occasion and generally supportive of Hartlib at this date was Oliver St John (c.1598–1673), who was well-connected, a powerful figure in Parliament and soon to hold senior judicial offices.[26]

In January 1645 Hartlib's team achieved an immediate, albeit token, success. The Committee for Both Kingdoms authorised a payment of £50, and prepared the ground for more regular support from Parliament.[27]

Notwithstanding active canvassing on Hartlib's behalf and vigorous efforts by Dury in the summer of 1646 to secure the office of Bodleian Library Keeper for him, nothing was achieved in Oxford.[28] At one point

---

24 For Strickland, Haffemeyer, *Les Lumières radicales*, pp. 310–15 et passim.

25 Dury to Hartlib, 9 January 1645, HP 3/2/85A. Culpeper regretted that Dury was 'buried in a Hampshire living' rather than in the 'brave and center and stage London', Culpeper to Hartlib, late autumn 1655, Culpeper *Letters* p. 240.

26 In 1651, Strickland, St John and John Thurloe, all associates of Hartlib, comprised a mission to negotiate with the Dutch in search of improved relations. S.C.A. Pincus, *Protestantism and Patriotism: Ideologies and the Making of English Foreign Policy, 1650–1668* (Cambridge: Cambridge University Press, 1996), chapter 4.

27 For Strickland's letter on Hartlib's behalf to the Committee of Both Kingdoms, 12/13 January 1645, HP 7/57A-B. For Hartlib to Stickland, 15 January 1645, expressing gratitude, HP 7/22/1A-2B (draft), HP 9/4/1A-2B (final).

28 C.J. Minter, 'John Dury's Reformed Librarie-Keeper: Information and its Intellectual Contexts in Seventeenth-Century England', *Library & Information History*, 31:1 (2015), 18–34.

an increase in the parliamentary pension to £300 was approved, but not activated. The pension awarded to Hartlib averaged out at about £100 a year, but it fell into abeyance after the death of Cromwell.[29]

Regardless of the futility of efforts to gain an adequate subsistence for Hartlib, these episodes indicated genuine sincerity on the part of his supporters. This is well illustrated by the short note received from the powerful Arthur Annesley who, as indicated in the final chapter, Hartlib again approached for assistance at the very end of his life: 'Yesterday after sermons Sir William Waller found a fitt opportunity to move your businesse in the house and was so well seconded by Mr Solicitor [Oliver St John] that three hundred pounds is ordered you and the care of settling you in a way of future subsistence is recommended to the Committee for the University of Oxford'.[30]

3.2 Active Reconstruction

Hartlib's many tasks of reconstruction were actively assisted by the return of John Dury to England in late July 1645. The latter's first priority was to establish himself in the Westminster Assembly. Dury was also awarded a clerical appointment at Winchester Cathedral, which he took up in March 1646, an assignment that lasted until December 1646, when he was called back to London to take charge of the three royal children, a role that he played until May 1649, after which there was a gap until October 1650 when he became the Assistant Library Keeper at St James's Palace, Westminster, which he vacated in March 1652. After that he led a peripatetic existence until the Restoration, without a settled income and facing similar problems to Hartlib with respect to insolvency.

In the summer of 1645 Dury plunged into his new duties in Winchester with his customary assiduity. Besides his direct contribution

---

29 For the details of these payments, Turnbull *Hartlib*, pp. 48–52; for the petitioning involved, Turnbull *HDC*, pp. 26–28. Henry Langley to Hartlib, 30 June 1651, HP 15/3/5A-6B confirms that at this date Hartlib's payments were in arrears. Langley was giving assistance in his capacity as Master of Pembroke College, Oxford.

30 Arthur Annesley to Hartlib, 1 April 1647, HP 66/3/1A. In 1660 Annesley was ennobled as the first Earl of Anglesey. Sir William Waller was a long-standing supporter of Hartlib, and a major figure in the Presbyterian party in Parliament. For Hartlib's heavily edited draft message of gratitude to Cromwell regarding the 1647 gratuity, see Appendix to this chapter.

to the Westminster Assembly and its manifold committees, he conducted pastoral work and, on behalf of the Assembly, set out on the onerous task of framing a new catechism. As if all of this was insufficient, he also pursued various controversies, the main one of these being against the radical preacher, John Saltmarsh.[31]

With the backing of Sir William Waller, his long-time patron, Dury soon fastened on the idea of redirecting major charities of Winchester, or indeed elsewhere in Hampshire. This opportunity inspired Hartlib to sketch out plans for all manner of educational and research organisations. The dating of these drafts is uncertain, but one is inscribed 'February 1646', which, because the items are interconnected, is a plausible date for the drafts as a whole.[32]

For boys and adolescents, he returned to the idea of an academy, and even drew up a list of about twenty potential students, many of whom were of aristocratic lineage. Most of the nominated parents were long-term patrons of Hartlib. The putative professors, Coxe, Dury, Pell and Worsley were also drawn from Hartlib's inner circle and they were duly reassigned to various of the other projects.[33] This Winchester Academy was soon lost among the plethora of other schemes that Hartlib devised for the better deployment of the skills of his growing band of collaborators. His aspiration was to achieve a practical expression of an underlying distinctly utopian notion.[34] Hence he adopted the term 'Verulamian' for the schemes as a whole.

The surviving drafts relating to this new project represent no more than first thoughts that were chaotic and fragmentary. There is no trace of later revisions. Hartlib envisaged a group of specialist units, some of

---

31 For Dury in Winchester, see M. Caricchio, 'John Dury, Reformer of Education Against the Radical Challenge', *Les Dossiers du GRIHL* (2009–2): *Dissidence et dissimulation*. Saltmarsh published more than ten pamphlets in 1646, some directed against the Westminster Assembly. He died in December 1647, so terminating his controversy with Dury.

32 The main examples are: HP 9/1A-6A, 33A-35B, 37A-B.

33 Dr Thomas Coxe was frequently mentioned in the Hartlib Papers. He was an associate of John Sadler, and treated Sadler's relative Col William Sydenham, through whom he met his later famous young brother Thomas Sydenham, whom Coxe is reported to have introduced to medicine.

34 For the live interest in the older utopian writers see Ephemerides 1649, where Wiliam Petty discussed the rival merits of Thomas More and Francis Bacon, concluding that 'Mores Utopia a true patterne of a rightly constituted Commonwealth and which might easily be put in practise'. HP 28/1/20A.

them exercising teaching functions, but the emphasis was firmly on the advancement of learning. The main interest of these drafts is the identity of Hartlib's prospective recruits, which reveal his thoughts concerning the disposition of expertise at the date of composition.[35]

Because these speculative schemes perished *in embryo*, one might conclude that they are hardly worth mentioning. But they are valuable in casting an insight into the mentality of Hartlib who, sensing the steady expansion of his band of associates, recognised the need for a more structured basis for their field of operation. Therefore, in order to achieve the most effective deployment of expertise, he planned a structured division of labour among his specialists. He was, of course, operating in the spirit of the Verulamian Solomon's House, and other utopian fictions, but with a much better sense of the practicalities on the ground. On the basis of this and other related initiatives, Hartlib deserves some modest recognition in future histories of workforce planning.

The names included in Hartlib's lists reflect the content of the correspondence of Dury and Hartlib at that date. For instance, Dury specifies Culpeper, Godemann and especially Theodore Haak, in connection with a scheme for Oxford that was designed for both 'Pietie & Learning', with the aim of making the university 'more glorious than any other in the world'—a quotation that reveals the grandiose expectations of Dury and Hartlib concerning the significance of their designs.[36]

The proposal for the Oxford institute, which was at his elitist end of the spectrum, envisaged that John Sadler would become the rector, while the specialist chairs were to be divided between Adam Boreel, Robert Boyle, Dr Thomas Coxe, Sir Cheney Culpeper, John Dury, Caspar Godemann, Thomas Harrison, John Pell and Benjamin Worsley. The supplementary specialist associates included Dr Justinus van Assche, Dr Gerard Boate, Hugh L'Amy, Peter le Pruvost, J. S. Rittangel and Levinus Warner.[37] The nominations for the most senior posts of such

---

35 Already, in 1634 Hartlib sketched plans for an academy containing four, revised to ten professors, together with names and their specialisms. As at Winchester, this was a cosmopolitan conception. Ephemerides 1634, 29/2/19B and 23B. See chapter 2, n.36.
36 Dury to Hartlib, 25 August 1646, HP 3/3/30A-B.
37 HP 47/9/37A-B, untitled, undated, but perhaps early 1646, that is a few months before Oxford came under Parliamentarian control.

figures as John Sadler, Oliver St John and Francis Rous, reflect Hartlib's confidence about being able to draw upon the services of rising talents among the political elite of the day. By including so many names from outside Britain, it also clear that Hartlib's units would rely on foreign correspondents, an arrangement that was analogous to Dury's stress on correspondence ['correspondency', 'correspondencies'] as a vehicle for facilitating progress in his own field of ecclesiastical negotiation.

In Hartlib's schemes, the sciences and their practical applications were the predominant focus of attention, but there were some other unusual strengths. For example, van Assche, Boreel, Rittangel and Warner were orientalists. Rittangel made much of his personal acquaintance with Karaite Judaism in Lithuania, while Warner was a major collector of oriental manuscripts, among which an important component related to Karaism.[38] As noted in chapter 5, Warner also played a key role in organising a major project for translation of the Bible into Turkish.

For Dury and most of the other orientalists, as noted in chapter 2, their work was not just an antiquarian exercise. They were drawn to Hebraic studies on account of their messianic convictions. Hence Dury, while sending his regards to fellow oriental enthusiasts (Moriaen, the latter's rich relative Pergens, Boreel and van Assche), regretted that, because of the failure to obtain state support for his collegiate plans, there would be a major setback in the quest for conversion of the Jews.[39]

Failure to establish any one of the projected academies or research groups, while something of a setback, was no impediment to the revival of Hartlib's team of eager participants, many of whom led a peripatetic existence, as for instance Rittangel who, after London and Amsterdam, gravitated to Königsberg, or Levinus Warner, who became a diplomat in Constantinople. Hartlib's enhanced team therefore operated from a variety of locations, but still retained a sense of integrity on account

---

38 This collection was deposited in the University of Leiden Library and remains there as one of its famous possessions. The Karaites rejected the authority of Oral Law, insisting on the direct, independent, and critical study of the Bible. Karaites were ardent exponents of the Mikra (Tanakh, Hebrew Bible) as the exclusive source of religious law. For Rittangel's short stay in England, see chapter 2.

39 Dury, probably to Worsley, 29 January 1649, HP 1/7/1A-2B. This letter is a defence of his proposals for 'the knowledge of Orientall tongues and Jewish mysteries' made in his *Seasonable Discourse* published in April 1649. The relevant parallel to Hartlib's schemes of 1646 is the impressive petition, *Motives for the present founding of an University in the Metropolis London*, 1647, pp. 05–06 for a college of Hebrew studies.

of their elaborate correspondence network, the maintenance of which was not without its problems. The Hartlib Papers record numerous examples where exiles turned to Hartlib for assistance in maintaining links with their places of origin. Hartlib himself seemed indifferent to this wide dispersal of talent. Indeed, this diversification seemed to offer positive advantages. Hence locations such as Amsterdam acted as new centres of gravity, rendering this city in the eyes of Hartlib in some respects in advance of London in its importance. Hence, it is noticeable that this study draws frequently on correspondence from Amsterdam-based figures such as Appelius, Boreel, Moriaen, Rulice and Serrarius, or for more limited durations, Rand and Worsley, and also the refugees Comenius and Figulus from 1658 onwards, all of which demonstrates the positive value that Hartlib derived from his friends in Amsterdam and other Dutch locations, including for a time Dury himself, Dorothy Moore and John Pell. It should also not be forgotten that this diversification also extended to the location of fresh patrons, among whom Laurentius de Geer was a supreme example. Intercommunication was therefore so well established in the Hartlib fraternity that plans for the concentration of talent in a single base, especially in an isolated location like Winchester, might, as Culpeper reminded Hartlib, even have been counterproductive.

The stillbirth of the above plans is of less importance than their value as indicators of the substantial body of talent upon which Hartlib could draw, which was a considerable achievement, especially considering the bleak period that he had just endured. Also evident was the existence of strong bonds of association within this core grouping. The buoyant morale within this critical mass also inspired a thirst for the recruitment of yet further participants.

3.3 Benjamin Worsley, Robert Boyle and William Petty

A key figure in the above lists was Benjamin Worsley (1618–1677), long underrated but now subject to an explosion of interest and the subject of a fine biography.[40] Little is known about the early life of Worsley, but in 1639 he was admitted to the Barber-Surgeons Company. He went on to

---

40 T. Leng, *Benjamin Worsley (1618–1673): Trade, Interest and the Spirit in Revolutionary England* (Woodbridge: Royal Historical Society/Boydell & Brewer, 2008).

practise medicine, including in Ireland where he was appointed Surgeon General to the army. In 1644 he returned to London where he continued his medical work. The year 1644 was the first recorded date that Worsley treated Samuel Hartlib. Hartlib had been tormented by ill-health, particularly kidney stones, since at least 1642. Among the treatments he listed in 1644 was the one delivered by Worsley. This event in itself was trivial, but it necessitates a radical revision of the date of their first contact, which is usually given as the summer of 1645.[41] The latter date is still relevant because it was not until then that we possess any evidence concerning the wider activities of Worsley. Once again Culpeper was the chronicler of Worsley's emergence into the limelight. By the end of 1645 Worsley was not only engaged in a wide range of specific projects but had outpaced L'Amy and Pruvost with respect to more ambitious and integrated planning for economic reform. The most ambitious synthesis of his ideas was his 'Proffits humbly presented to this Kingdom', which is now recognized as a major contribution to the economic thinking of that period and an important element in the background to the Navigation Acts. 'Proffits' was actively edited by Hartlib and first circulated by him in the autumn of 1645.[42] Hartlib's annotation *'opera parliament'* shows that he was fully aware of the importance of this document.

While Hartlib was absorbing the impact of Benjamin Worsley, he was also contemplating ever more ways of mobilising his forces. In the autumn of 1645 Culpeper was much attracted by Hartlib's latest idea of some kind of Verulamian college for the advancement of learning, which Culpeper insisted should be located in London. The first of Culpeper's relevant letters expressed extraordinary optimism about the prospects for this college, declaring that it could fulfil the greatest of Bacon's expectations and 'prove a straitininge to those motions, discoveries & improvements, as are potentially in all well principled indeavors and are (by God's blessing) like to emerge from ours'.[43] It is tempting to

---

[41] Hartlib medical notes, 1644, HP 60/4/6A.
[42] Culpeper to Hartlib, autumn 1645, Culpeper *Letters*, pp. 248–49. For an edition of this text, Webster *Instauration*, Appendix V, which is derived from HP 15/2/61A-64B, in the hand of Worsley. Two other versions of 'Proffits humbly presented' exist at HP25/3/7A-10B and 54/32/1A-7B. For Proffits, see also S.C.A. Pincus, *Protestantism and Patriotism: Ideologies and the Making of English Foreign Policy, 1650–1668* (Cambridge: Cambridge University Press, 1996), pp. 47–51.
[43] Two undated letters from Culpeper to Hartlib, probably autumn 1645, Culpeper *Letters*, pp. 238 and 242.

link these remarks with a small fragment which is located adjacent to Hartlib's initial sketches discussed above. This is a virtually blank sheet containing draft headings. It boldly announces '*Opera Parliamenta et* of the Whole Kingdom' by which was meant a '*Collegium Verulamianum Experimentorum*'. Apart from that, the only other words are '*Reditus* Mr Worsley of saltpetre when it comes to the city', which is enigmatic, but clearly indicates that Hartlib was already sensitive to the intriguing character of Worsley and the intrinsic profitability of his saltpetre project, the high status of which was also signified by the prominent position that this was accorded in his 'Proffits humbly presented'.[44] Following his auspicious launch, Worsley was thenceforth rarely absent from the centre of the stage.

In 1646 the short-lived Verulamian college scheme rapidly faded from view, partly on account of being superseded by plans for an Office of Address, an ambitious design, which is fully discussed in chapter 5. As was often the case, Culpeper was the weathervane in the early history of the Office of Address project. In February 1646, when first alerted, he was sceptical, but in March he announced his conversion and set about proselytising on behalf of the Office of Address among his allies within the Independent group in Parliament.

Notwithstanding such major distractions, Hartlib continued to play a major role in the leadership of the intellectual community, retaining his old associations and steadily expanding his field of able recruits, many of the most outstanding of whom were strikingly young, as for instance Robert Boyle (1627–1691), John Hall (1627–1656) and William Petty (1621–1689).

Generally, Hartlib's first contact with Boyle is given as 1647, but a much earlier date is likely. As noted above, Boyle was known to Hartlib by February 1646, when his name was included in various of the draft schemes for education and research. This suggests that in all probability Boyle first came to Hartlib's attention at an earlier date, perhaps during 1645. Lady Ranelagh, Boyle's older sister, was likely to have been Hartlib's informant, and later might well have been the stimulus for the Boyle-Hartlib correspondence, which began in March 1647. Boyle's link with Worsley began a somewhat earlier. In the autumn of 1647 Boyle,

---

44 HP 47/9/27A. For Worsley's saltpetre project, Leng *Worsley*, pp. 22–25.

Culpeper, Hartlib and Ranelagh became engaged in friendly exchanges about the funding of the Office of Address.[45]

The high spirit of excitement exhibited by the young Robert Boyle when making his first foray into the scientific community has naturally become indelibly linked with Hartlib's name. Boyle's stray use of the term Invisible College to characterise the group with which he was attached has provoked a disproportionate amount of attention. Reflecting on the Invisible College as it affected Hartlib, at this date he was so besieged by rival engagements that I now regretfully conclude that the Invisible College never amounted to more than an incidental element in his packed agenda.[46]

It was not until late 1647 that the many-sided talents of William Petty became evident to Hartlib.[47] As indicated in the next chapter, Petty's first publication, *Advice of W.P. to Samuel Hartlib* (1648) outlined more efficiently than any other source an educational programme towards which Hartlib and his agents were stumbling. This tract established Petty as an indispensable asset to Hartlib. Strangely, in the short-term Petty's *Advice* failed to attract the notice it deserved. As Culpeper's letters confirm, much more interest was attracted by Petty's many engagements as an inventor. As the following chapter intimates, invention was the main goal to which Petty himself at first aspired. Hartlib and Petty remained in touch until the eve of Hartlib's death, an outcome that was

---

45 Culpeper to Hartlib, 10 November 1647, Culpeper *Letters*, pp. 312–13; Hartlib to Boyle, 16 November 1647, M. Hunter, A. Clericzio and L.M. Principe (eds.), *The Correspondence of Robert Boyle*, vol. I (London: Pickering & Chatto, 2001), pp. 63–64. For examples from the extensive recent literature on Boyle: M. Hunter, *Robert Boyle, 1627–91: Scrupulosity and Science* (Woodbridge: The Boydell Press, 2000); idem, *Boyle: Between God and Science* (London/New Haven: Yale University Press, 2009); L. Principe, *The Aspiring Adept: Robert Boyle and His Alchemical Quest* (Princeton: Princeton University Press, 1998).
46 I agree with Lauren Kassell, who concludes that 'Marcombes, Tallents, and Hartlib were not participants and that the invisible college's prime mover may have been Benjamin Worsley, a former physician turned projector in Ireland, who was closely associated with Hartlib and who also corresponded with Boyle between November 1646 and February 1647'. *Oxford DNB* entry: 'Invisible College'.
47 Important is Hartlib's initial characterisation of Petty: 'The author of them (History of Trades) is one Petty, of twenty-four years of age, a good linguist in other vulgar languages besides Latin and Greek, a most rare and exact anatomist, and excelling in all mathematical and mechanical learning, of a sweet natural disposition and moral comportment'. Hartlib to Boyle, 16 November 1647, Boyle *Correspondence* I, pp. 63–64 (lightly edited).

not easily sustained on account of the enmity that developed between Petty and Worsley.

Worsley, Boyle and Petty all feature prominently in the remaining sections of this study, but such major names represent only one facet of Hartlib's recruitment drive. Until recently, much less interest has been taken in the minor figures who attached themselves to his team. In practice, these lesser-known newcomers added an important new dimension to the Hartlib fraternity and undertook duties on behalf of Hartlib that represented his urgent desiderata. Indicative of the interest and importance of these newcomers are John Hall and William Rand. These two were contemporaries, both from Durham, and they became discontented undergraduates when at Cambridge, an experience that emboldened them to confront convention and commit themselves to a more active and original contribution to intellectual affairs. Each, separately, found his way to Samuel Hartlib in order to pursue more effectively the reformist objectives to which they both aspired. Each made an impressive literary contribution. In character, Hall was the hare, and Rand the tortoise. Both of them died young, thereby cutting short their impressive record of literary and social activism.

3.4 John Hall

John Hall (1627–1656) was from Consett in Durham. He entered St John's College, Cambridge, in May 1646. This he found a tiresome experience, but he rapidly proved his ability as a creative writer. His first book, composed when he was only nineteen, was *Horæ Vacivæ, or Essays. Some occasional Considerations* (1646).[48] At the age of twenty he entered Gray's Inn, where he found his first congenial intellectual home in the Black Ribband group led by Thomas Stanley. From there he graduated to Samuel Hartlib, under whom he climbed the intellectual ladder and wrestled with what were seen as leading intellectual issues of the day. Up to the point of his untimely death before the age of twenty-nine, Hall proved to be a prolific and resourceful writer, who graduated from being a minor literary celebrity to become a major social and political

---

48 This was also the occasion for his first portrait, a frontispiece engraving by William Marshall, the superscript of which announced that Hall was then nineteen.

3. The Hartlibian Resurgence

activist and skilful controversialist, qualities that facilitated his ascent into the realms of the governing elite of the day.[49]

Of major importance in this upward mobility was his association with Samuel Hartlib. Although Hartlib was an experienced engineer of intellectual dialogue, he was hardly prepared for the whirlwind that John Hall represented. Between December 1646 and about May 1647, from his stations in Cambridge and London, he fired off some twenty-five often frenetic letters to Hartlib and undertook missions on behalf of his host at lightning speed.[50]

On Hartlib's side, his expectations for Hall were limited. He was short of reliable translators, especially for the stock of manuscript writings that he had accumulated over many years. Hall's first assignment, very modest in scale, was the translation of two short tracts on Christian brotherhoods drafted by Johann Valentin Andreae some thirty years earlier, which had been guiding lights to Hartlib and his allies during their Antilian phase.

Not content with these morsels, Hall agitated to translate *Christianopolis*, Andreae's important utopian tract. Moreover, he claimed to be near to completing a translation of another major utopian work, Campanella's *Civitas Solis*.[51] Hall's short flirtation with the utopian idea was nevertheless the most concentrated attention on this theme in the whole of the Hartlib Papers. These imaginative initiatives were ignored by the likes of Culpeper, but they struck other of Hartlib's associates favourably, as shown by Robert Boyle's praise for Hall's

---

[49] The following account of Hall in 1646 and 1647 connects with N. McDowell, *Poetry and Allegiance in the English Civil Wars: Marvell and the Cause of Wit* (Oxford: Oxford University Press, 2009).

[50] For a preliminary description of these letters, G.H. Turnbull, 'John Hall's Letters to Samuel Hartlib', *Review of English Studies*, 4:15 (1953), 221–33, and also McDowell's contextualised interpretation.

[51] John Hall, *A Modell of a Christian Society... The Right hand of Christian Love Offered* (Cambridge: Roger Daniel, 1647) Wing H352, dedicated to Hartlib. It seems that only about one hundred copies of this two-part publication were produced, of which only one survives (Oxford Bodleian Library, 8 W.84.Th.) For the English and Latin texts, G.H. Turnbull, 'Johann Valentin Andreae's Societas Christiana', *Zeitschrift* für Deutsche *Philologie*, 73:4 (1954), 407–32 and 74:2 (1955), 151–85. It seems that these two Hall translations were reprinted as appendices to Hall's posthumous, but now lost, *Of the advantageous reading of History* (1657), the title page of which is preserved in HP 14/1/11A-B. Hartlib apparently took little interest in Hall's proposal to translate *Christianopolis*, or when the idea was repeated by John Graunt in 1653, Ephemerides 1653, HP 28/2/57A.

utopian projects as a whole.[52] Recognising Hartlib's thirst for ideas about furthering intellectual organisation, Hall transmitted to him the details of his own 'Designe' for a 'utopian Academy', a plan which had originated within the Stanley group and at that stage was designed for a narrowly defined social and intellectual elite. Hall hinted that he himself envisaged a cooperative venture of the kind favoured by Hartlib.[53] In the utopian academy context, Hall requested details of Sir Francis Kynaston's *Constitutions of the Musaeum Minervae* (1636), which Hartlib speculated was a precursor to the Stanley academy scheme.[54] Hall's subsequent letters betrayed his support for Hartlib's idea of a 'universal correspondency', which was something of a utopian venture in itself and represented just one arm of the sprawling plans for an Office of Address, which also attracted Hall's curiosity.

It is evident that Hall saw Hartlib as his means of gaining access to intellectuals who were congenial to the Parliamentarian ascendancy. John Milton, Benjamin Worsley and Robert Boyle were his chosen targets. Milton ignored Hall's overture. In his exchanges with Hartlib, Boyle spoke well of Hall, but he was evasive about being in direct contact. Only Worsley unhesitatingly responded to Hall's request, on this occasion for an opinion on the intricate metaphysical issue of the science-religion relationship.[55] One positive benefit received by Hartlib from his work with Hall was contact with a further translator, in this case Jeremy Collier, also of St John's College, Cambridge, who, as outlined in the following chapter, produced a translation of a metaphysical text by Comenius. As in the case of Hall's Andreae translations, Collier's book

---

52   Boyle to Hartlib, 8 April 1647, Boyle *Correspondence* I, pp. 54–55. It is perhaps with Hall in mind that Boyle wrote of Hartlib that his recent communications had predominantly assumed 'the nature of Utopian'. Boyle to Hartlib, 8 May 1647, Boyle *Correspondence* I, p. 58.
53   For *Christianopolis*, Hall to Hartlib, 13 April 1647, HP 60/14/30A-31B. For *Civitas solis*, Hall to Hartlib, [1 March 1647] HP 60/14/39A-40B, and 11 March 1647, HP 60/14/37A-38B, indicating the speed of Hall's work, from conception to near completion in about ten days.
54   Hall to Hartlib, 20 April 1647, HP 60/14/32A-33B, and [26 April 1647], HP 60/14/35A-36B. See also G.H. Turnbull, 'Samuel Hartlib's Connection with Sir Francis Kynaston's "Musaeum Minervae"', *Notes and Queries*, 197 (1952), 33–37.
55   Leng *Worsley*, pp. 30–31. A few further letters from Worsley to Boyle exist, mainly from the late 1650s. The most 'remarkable' (Leng, p. 114) among these is one deriving from late 1658 or 1659 (Boyle *Correspondence* I, pp. 301–18), which is a wide-ranging discussion of the philosophy of medicine. In my view this letter is not by Worsley but by John Beale.

was also dedicated to Hartlib. Unlike Hall, Collier remained in active touch with Hartlib and was in due course nominated for an important post of responsibility in one of the reformer's ambitious plans for a national educational administration.

After a hectic few months, the association between Hall and the whole of the Hartlib group fell away as rapidly as it had begun. One of the few indications of Hall's later activities is a single sheet in the Hartlib Papers containing a transcription of a title page dated 1657, therefore shortly after Hall's death. This is a particularly precious document, since it provides the only evidence that Hall's translations of Andreae were ever reprinted. Even more important, this title page is the only indication that what is now generally called Hall's 'A Method of History' dating from 1645 was ever published at all.[56] Hesitancy about publication, unusual for Hall, was perhaps prompted by his heavy indebtedness to a published version of a lecture delivered by Degory Wheare, the Camden Professor of Ancient History, in Oxford in 1623. Wheare himself was contributing to a debate that had long been raging among humanist scholars.[57]

Humble Motion

Once Hall had drifted out of Hartlib's orbit, as noted at the outset of the next chapter, his work took on a more overtly political role. The prime product of this new phase in his work was the pamphlet *An Humble Motion to the Parliament of England concerning the Advancement of Learning and Reformation of the Universities* (1649; Wing H350). More than half of this 45-page octavo tract (pp. 01–25) was absorbed with florid preliminaries extolling Parliamentarian military achievements and challenging the Rump Parliament to complete its civilising mission by undertaking major tasks of reconstruction, with emphasis on a

---

56 J. Raymond, 'John Hall's "A Method of History"': A Book Lost and Found', *English Literary Renaissance*, 28:2 (1998), 267–98. See also HP 14/1/11A, where the title is '*Of the advantageous reading of history*'. Raymond located a manuscript copy of this text in the Bodleian Library.

57 Degory Wheare, *De ratione et methodo legendi historias dissertatio* (London: John Haviland, 1623) and later editions of 1625 and 1637. Wheare himself was indebted to previous authors such as Bartholomaeus Keckermann. For general context, *Historia: Empiricism and Erudition in Early Modern Europe*, ed. by G. Pomata and N.G. Siraisi (Cambridge, Massachusetts: MIT Press, 2005).

radical reform of the universities. Running through the entire text were asides which added up to a demand for transferring the balance of power within the Commonwealth to a forward-looking intellectual elite, a class that could be trusted to manage the affairs of state in a scientific and enlightened manner, a conclusion that coincided with the aspirations of Hartlib's group at that very date. Hall was also developing a more directly political programme, in his case involving a decisive shift towards overt republicanism. In general Hall was in line with educational policies advocated by Hartlib's team at this date, but he was much in advance of them in the extent of his confrontational rhetoric. However, with respect to the specificity of his reform proposals, he was much in arrears of William Petty's *Advice on the Advancement of Learning*, a source that he might not even have consulted.

Hall's brief survey of the reform of the 'idle Pedantick Brotherhoods' of the universities, which occupies the second half of the *Humble Motion* (pp. 26–45), was built on the style and ethos of Milton's pamphlets, especially his *Of education* (June 1644, dedicated to Hartlib and considered in the next chapter), and his *Areopagitica* (November 1644). With respect to the weaknesses of pre-university education he was entirely in step with Hartlib and Dury, to whom he obliquely paid tribute in his remarks about their 'wonderfull deale of courage, attempting the discovery of a new world of knowledge'.[58]

After the completion of his *Humble Motion*, Hall was preoccupied by his service to the state. Among these duties was accompanying Oliver Cromwell and the New Model Army on their expedition against the Scottish army, which culminated in a decisive victory at the battle of Dunbar, which occurred on 3 September 1650. The following day Cromwell revealed this signal event to the Speaker of the House of Commons. Naturally the letter was mainly an account of the battle itself. One paragraph struck an entirely different note. It warned that in their preoccupation with military affairs, Parliament should not forget its obligations concerning its people, who were, after all, 'the

---

58 For assessments of the *Humble Motion*, R.L. Greaves, *The Puritan Revolution and Educational Thought* (New Brunswick, New Jersey: Rutgers University Press, 1969), pp. 59–61 et passim; A. McGruer, *Educating the 'Unconstant Rabble': Arguments for Educational Advancement and Reform during the English Civil War and Interregnum* (Newcastle upon Tyne: Cambridge Scholars Publishing, 2010), pp. 125–32.

chariots and horsemen of Israel'. Once the 'proud and insolent' section of the population was under control, Parliament should attend to 'the oppressed, hear the groans of the poor prisoners in England, be pleased to reform the abuses of all professions… and if there be any one that makes many poor to make a few rich, that suits not the Commonwealth'. Such polices, the paragraph concluded, would bring the 'true glory of your Commonwealth'.[59] The proximity of these proposals to the known outlook of Hall naturally raises the question: was Hall himself responsible for this reformist element in the content, or even perhaps the letter as a whole?

Mataeotechnia Medicinae Praxews

The *Humble Motion* is conventionally considered Hall's sole contribution to the social reform debate, but he made yet a further, more extensive statement of his views in a tract nominally ascribed to one Noah Biggs, entitled *Mataeotechnia Medicinae Praxews* (1652), henceforth *MMP*. Like Hall's *Humble Motion*, *MMP* was addressed 'To The PARLIAMENT' and both called for determined Parliamentary action. The evangelical zeal that pervades *MMP* inspired the conclusion that there was a 'devastatingly close link between the religious and political outlook of the new Cromwellian regime and medical reformism of Biggs'.[60] This is a perfect representation of the situation, except that the authorship of *MMP* needs to be reassigned to John Hall.[61] The evidence adduced in favour of John Hall's authorship of *MMP* amounts to an unquestionable case. This conclusion ought to raise the profile of *MMP*, introduce a further dimension to our understanding of John Hall and also add fresh insight into the character of political radicalism during the Commonwealth and Protectorate.

---

59 Letter from Cromwell to William Lenthall, 4 September 1651, in *Letters and Speeches of Oliver Cromwell*, vol. 2, ed. by E. Murphy, M.Ó Siochrú, and J. Peacey (Oxford: Oxford University Press, 2022), p. 225.

60 P. Elmer and O.P. Grell, *Health, Disease and Society in Europe, 1500–1800* (Manchester: Manchester University Press, 2003), p. 129.

61 Chymiatrophilos, *Mataeotechnia Medicinae Praxews. The Vanity of the Craft of Physick. Or, a New Dispensatory* (London, for Giles Calvert, 1651/ London, for Edward Blackmore/ and London, no stated printer or bookseller), 264 pp., quarto, Wing B2888. For the reassignment of the authorship, C. Webster, *In Times of Strife* (Oxford: Taylor Institution Library, 2023), pp. 99–106.

No other author of the period, young or old, could excel Hall as a stylist, scholar or deft political apologist. In this case his failing was his poor grasp of technical aspects of medicine and only limited acquaintance with the writings of Helmont, the medial reformer selected as his hero.[62] Nevertheless, Hall knew enough about the current political climate to appreciate that Helmontianism offered him a stick ideally suited for beating the back of the medical establishment. In this endeavour, Cromwell's letter to Speaker Lenthall might also be interpreted as a licence to embark on this course of action.[63]

The twelve-page preface to *MMP* constitutes a literary and intellectual *tour de force*, in its style well up to the standard of John Milton. This effective and excoriating attack on the academic and medical establishment and advocacy of reform was similar in its rhetoric to the work of other medical reformists of this period, but it reached a literary plane that none of his rivals could match, and indeed was superior to what he himself had achieved in the *Humble Motion*. Hall made authors like John Dury, whatever their pious intentions, seem pedestrian and unappealing, a factor which must have handicapped their impact.

The preface was specifically declared as a response to Cromwell's instruction to reform the abuses in all professions and to take into account the public good in all policy decisions. Such a context demanded 'the reformation of the stupendous body of Universal Learning, Languages, Arts and Sciences', of which medicine was one element. In assuming such a mission, Britain should remember that it was the first nation to sound the 'Trumpet of Reformation to all Europe'. To be consistent with this precedent: 'Let not England forget her precedence of teaching other Nations how to live'. Another line of attack, no doubt intended as praise for the Rump Parliament, underlined the analogy with the ongoing missions against priests and presbyters. It was therefore consistent to apply the reformation to all things 'Moral, Oeconomical, and Political'.[64] Britain should therefore aspire to become the 'Cathedral to other Nations'

---

62 For recent relevant work on Helmont, G.D. Hedesan, *An Alchemical Quest for Universal Knowledge: The Christian Philosophy of Jan Baptist Van Helmont (1579–1644)* (London: Routledge, 2016); idem, 'Alchemy, Potency, Imagination: Paracelsus's Theories of Poison', in *Poisons in European History*, ed. by A. Cunningham and O.P. Grell (London: Routledge, 2016), pp. 01–17.

63 *MMP*, Preface p. [1].

64 Ibid., Preface p. [4].

and 'give out Reformation to the world, both in religion and Arts'. This may seem like an insurmountable ambition, but Hall reminded readers of the 'lofty Genius of this Nation', a factor that had yielded outstanding success in its promotion of the Arts which 'daily have sensible increases, and receive new additions, new light, and further perfections'.[65]

Hall went on to rehearse his critique of the universities in much the same terms as in the *Humble Motion*, calling on their faculties to abandon their cold and lazy habits in order to take advantage of the exciting advances and new discoveries that were evident in all fields of the sciences, especially chemistry.[66] Even when they were more industrious, the efforts of the faculties were dissipated owing to their preoccupation with classical authorities such as Aristotle and Galen. These were no more than 'painted Butter-flyes' never penetrating beyond the 'Bark and superficial outside'. Consequently, scholars remained remote and alien from the 'Centre and true Marrow' of the sciences, or the secrets of physics.[67]

Decadence was not confined to the universities. At considerable length he lambasted technicians in general for being 'illiterate, rude, and the dregs of men', therefore incapable of rectifying the errors of their reason or taking advantage of knowledge in their fields. To add to this neglectful situation, the minority of technicians with real ability, his 'sad friends of Learning', had the misfortune to receive absolutely 'no publike encouragement'.[68]

The Preface of *MMP* ended with some recommendations for further action by Parliament. These were not particularly specific or indeed easy to translate into workable legislation, but they nevertheless constituted an appropriate climax to this essay. Hall proposed the establishment of an 'Academy of Philosophical Freedom' designed to encourage dialogue between intellectuals from many different backgrounds with the goal of reducing erroneous beliefs over the whole field of the 'Literary Republike of Universal Learning, Languages, Arts and Sciences'.[69] As is evident from the following section, Hall's Academy of Philosophical

---

65 Ibid., Preface p. [5].
66 Ibid., Preface p. [6].
67 Ibid., Preface p. [9].
68 Ibid., Preface p. [7].
69 Ibid., Preface p. [10].

Freedom was remarkably similar in its aspirations to the 'Society of Graduate Physicians' proposed by William Rand in 1656.

In contrast to its strikingly effective preface, the inflated body of *MMP* descended into a disorganised and self-indulgent gabble. Therefore it was completely lacking in the kind of elegance that Hall displayed in the analytical section of *The Grounds and Reasons of Monarchy*, characteristics that guaranteed this essay a permanent place in literature of political theory. *MMP* was the longest piece of prose writing ever produced by John Hall. The preface was well up to the level of his best, but the book as a whole must count as a disappointing lapse in Hall's sparkling career as a reformer and controversialist.

3.5 William Rand

Like John Hall, William Rand (1617–1663) came from Durham. The two shared many things in common. Both were dissatisfied with Cambridge, but they were able classical scholars, whose skills as translators were eagerly employed by Samuel Hartlib to strengthen this aspect of his publishing crusade. Rand declared that his 'greatest ambition is that I may, if possibly, injoy my privacy to translate & and write such things as I have propounded unto my selfe, and doe other things aimeing at the publick good'.[70] Rand was more reticent than Hall, but both were thoughtful and radical, qualities that facilitated their assimilation into Hartlib's inner team, from which Hall migrated, but Rand remained. His striking intellectual qualities and literary productivity drew him to the attention of Lady Ranelagh. With good reason, Rand is now beginning to attract attention in many spheres of interregnum scholarship.

William's father was James Rand (c.1585–1642), who became a successful London apothecary and married Elizabeth Joyce (d.1658) from Enderby, Leicestershire. William was the eldest surviving child of the apothecary's small family. He followed other members of his family into medicine, but he was more inclined to general intellectual affairs, leaving his younger brother James Jr. (1618–1686) to continue his father's practice and business, something that he achieved with

---

70 Rand to Hartlib, 10 January 1653, HP 62/17/3B.

outstanding success.⁷¹ Both William and James Jr. became associates of Samuel Hartlib.

William Rand attended St Catharine's College, Cambridge, where he matriculated in 1633, and obtained his B.A. in 1637 and M.A. in 1640. Little is known about his life in Cambridge, but he made no secret of his distaste for the 'vain ostentations' of the current academic system.⁷² His letters to Hartlib contain long digressions on husbandry and natural history designed to underline the extent of his emancipation from the scholastic academic system and his sympathy with Hartlibian aspirations for rural improvement. It was therefore natural that, when the time arrived, as noted in chapter 4, he contributed thoughtful essays on the theory of vegetation to the third and final edition of Hartlib's successful *Legacy*.

Rand's friendship with Samuel Hartlib, Benjamin Worsley and others in this group dates from about 1646. It seems that Worsley introduced Rand to Pierre Gassendi's biography of the famous French polymath, Nicolas-Claude Fabri de Peiresc (1580–1637), after which Hartlib suggested that the young scholar might undertake a translation of this book. Hartlib's faith in the importance of this project was accentuated when Joachim Hübner reminded him that Peiresc's correspondence had done more to advance knowledge than the entirety of the rest of the academic establishment. Hübner speculated that Hartlib's planned Office of Address might achieve a similar objective.⁷³ Understandably, in view of the scale and difficulty of this undertaking, the young Rand found the task too daunting to attempt.⁷⁴ Hartlib then tried out the Peiresc proposal on Thomas Smith of Christ's College, Cambridge, but he also was defeated by the task.

In late 1648, perhaps with the aim of completing his medical studies, Rand commenced a lengthy visit to the Netherlands, where he travelled widely, spending most of his time in Amsterdam, where he experienced a cultural scene that greatly impacted on his outlook. He registered at

---

71 James Rand became a prominent and rich figure in the Society of Apothecaries. As noted in the final chapter, James was one of the two signatories of the important petition recommending public support for Hartlib's Agency for Learning.
72 Rand to Hartlib, 18 July 1651, HP 62/30/1A.
73 Hübner to Hartlib, 15 April 1647, HP 59/9/9B.
74 Pierre Gassendi, *De Nicolai Claudii Fabrici de Peiresc, Senatoris Aquisextiensis, Vita* (Paris, 1641).

the universities of Utrecht in 1649 and Leyden in 1652. He also visited and was impressed by Louvain University. It is not clear where his MD was granted, but perhaps he followed the pattern of his relatives, Samuel and Ralph Rand, by obtaining a Groningen MD, although this is not recorded.[75] After spending nearly five years in the Netherlands, Rand returned to London in May 1653.

Rand's first surviving letter to Hartlib dates from 1651, but the *Ephemerides* contains half a dozen relevant references to Rand from the year 1648, raising a variety of points of common interest, and indicating that Rand already had a diversity of social contacts.[76] At this stage he was not formally a medical practitioner, but his reading extended into this area. He was particularly impressed by the medical writings on fevers by Gómez Pereira (1500–1567), most likely his *Novae veraque medicinae* (1558), which used an attack on Galen's theory of fevers to mount a bold innovatory approach to natural philosophy and medicine. Rand was impressed by this platform for the 'Restauration of Medicine'.[77]

Rand's letters from this period show that he was independent-minded and not afraid of controversy. For instance, he broke ranks with many of his friends by agreeing with the verdict of Sir Thomas Browne's *Pseudodoxia epidemica*, that J. B. van Helmont, the renowned medical reformer, was a plagiarist who 'had much of the mountebank in him'.[78] Perhaps even less welcome to Hartlib was Rand's adverse response to John Dury's *Reformed School* (1650), where the declared non-sectarian Rand was alarmed by Dury's overtly sacerdotal and formulaic approach to education.[79]

---

75 R. W. Innes Smith, *English Speaking Students of Medicine at the University of Leyden* (Edinburgh: Oliver and Boyd, 1932). For summaries of Rand's peregrinations, see his preface to his *Mirrour of True Nobility and Gentility*, and to his translation of Francken in Hartlib's *Chymical Addresses*.

76 These included Hartlib's associate Benjamin Worsley and perhaps the young William Petty, John Sadler and Francis Rous, both politicians, John Sweeting the Stationer, one Moore of Stratford, an inventor, John Tradescant Jr. the collector, William Hamilton the Scottish gentleman scholar, and the intending teachers, William Aldrich and Joshua Rawlin.

77 Ephemerides, early July 1648, HP 31/22/13A. The same point was elaborated in Rand to Hartlib, 1 September 1651, HP 62/27/1B-3A.

78 Rand to Hartlib, 1 September 1651, HP 62/27/1A-B.

79 Rand to Hartlib, 18 July 1651, HP 62/30/1B-3B. For Rand on Hobbes, J.R. Collins, *The Allegiance of Thomas Hobbes* (Oxford: Oxford University Press, 2005), pp. 99–101, 112, 128, 130. Collins calls Rand 'an obscure English physician' (p. 191): now, no longer!

Rand was also one of the earliest known commentators on the *Leviathan* of Thomas Hobbes, who was repeatedly mentioned in his letters to Hartlib and Worsley in the summer and autumn of 1651. He voiced some of the usual reservations, but was generally favourable, praising Hobbes's work as 'a world of fine cleare notions'.[80] Recent commentators on Hobbes have been intrigued by Rand's artful adaptation of Hobbes to his own republicanism, anticlericalism and liberalism in matters of faith.[81]

Satanae Stratagemata

Independently, perhaps on account of his Socinian leanings and belief in religious toleration and liberty of conscience, Rand developed an interest in the writings of Iacopo Aconcio (Jacobus Acontius, c.1492–c.1567), a leading figure of the second generation of the Radical Reformation. Rand discovered that Aconcio's works, especially his *Satanae Stratagemata* (1565), were also being championed by Dury and Hartlib.[82]

Hartlib was reminded of the suspicions attached to Socinianism when his plan for publishing a translation of the *Conatuum* of Comenius in Oxford was held up owing to the accusation that this text was tainted by Socinianism.[83] The first translation of a Socinian work to be published in England was *A vindication of liberty of religion* (1646), a short but effective defence of liberty of conscience written by Johannes Crell (1590–1633), one of the leading Socinians of his generation and Rector of the Raków Academy, who was a figure well-known to Hartlib. This tract was recently described as a 'truly remarkable work'. [84] On

---

80 HP 62/30/3B. For Rand and Helmont, A. Clericuzio, 'From Helmont to Boyle', *British Journal for the History of Science*, 26:3 (1993), 303–34. Oblivious of the acute observations by Rand, in recent times Lonie has drawn attention to the importance of Pereira on fevers, while Pagel has stressed the role of both Pereira and Campanella as precursors of Helmont on fevers: I.M Lonie, 'Fever Pathology in the Sixteenth Century: Tradition and Innovation', *Medical History*, Supplement No. 1 (1981), 19–44; W. Pagel, *Joan Baptista Van Helmont* (Cambridge: Cambridge University Press, 1985), pp. 158–61.

81 J. R. Collins, *The Allegiance of Thomas Hobbes*, pp. 191–92; J. Parkin, *Taming the Leviathan* (Cambridge: Cambridge University Press, 2007), pp. 99–101.

82 Rand to Hartlib, 1 September 1651, HP 62/27/4A.

83 Hübner to Hartlib, 12 June 1637, *MGP* 26, No. 66, pp. 91–92.

84 Johannes Crell, *A learned vindication of liberty of religion* ([London, s.n.] 1646), Wing C6897, which is a translation of Crell's *Vindiciae pro religionis libertate*, written in 1632 and first published in Amsterdam in 1637. The 1646 English edition, attributed to 'N.Y.', was the first vernacular translation. This was followed by a Dutch translation in 1649, French in 1689, and Polish only in 1957.

account of envisaging a firm separation between civil authorities and communities of believers, Crell went well beyond Aconcio in allocating unlimited independence of action to believers who, under the stern gaze of entrenched regulatory bodies, commonly faced terrible retribution, even for minor infringements.

The *A vindication of liberty in religion* translation is often ascribed to John Dury, an assumption that materially adds to his reputation as an advocate of liberty of conscience, which in turn makes him an obvious candidate for collaborating in the *Satanae Stratagemata* translation project. Crell's tract was indeed a helpful precursor to the Aconcio translation, but there is no convincing evidence to support Dury being identified as 'N.Y.', the declared translator of the 1646 edition of the *Vindication*. Also, any reading of the translator's preface suggests a level of radicalism that was deeply objectionable to the risk-averse Dury. For instance, the translator insisted that magistrates should grant the widest toleration of religion to their subjects, to the extent of allowing 'the common people to search the Scripture, and to try the spirits by them as the only Judge'. Without such latitude, these authorities would 'destroy the ground of their Reformation'.[85]

Such radical thoughts, like many other sentiments expressed in the preface, were entirely alien to Dury. On the other hand, the translator might have been drawn from the Hartlib entourage, where for instance, Henry Robinson was a firm advocate of freedom of conscience, but his publications indicate no interest in Socinianism. Perhaps a more likely candidate is Benjamin Worsley, who has the advantage of being as much a 'N.Y.' as Dury. That ought to be a hypothesis worthy of serious consideration. Worsley was known for his Socinian sympathies, as expressed for instance in a letter to Hartlib in which he specifically drew attention to a recently published ethical work by Crell, which he believed constituted an impressive exercise in demonstrating the compatibility between Aristotle's *Ethics* and New Testament moral teaching. Also, no fewer than eight books by Crell feature in Worsley's library catalogue.[86]

---

85 Crell, *A learned vindication of liberty of religion*, 'To the Reader'.
86 Lengthy extract of a letter from Worsley to Hartlib, 28 May 1649, Royal Society, Boyle *Letters*, 7.1, fol. 1B; also, the Worsley library sale catalogue, dating from 1678. If Worsley was indeed the translator of Crell's *Vindication*, this project may have been undertaken when he was already in contact with Hartlib. The text by Crell under consideration in Worsley's letter to Hartlib of 1649 was the *Ethica christiana*,

As noted above, Worsley's association with William Rand took place in London in 1646. Since in 1651 Rand indicated that his own interest in Socinian writings was long standing, this factor may have helped in 1646 to cement his friendship with Worsley. When Rand and Worsley renewed their acquaintance, this time in Amsterdam between 1648 and 1649, both of them further advanced their knowledge of Socinianism and both sought to propagate interest in these ideas among their English friends.[87]

In England Aconcio's moment came in 1648 with the publication of a translation of the first half of *Satanae Stratagemata*. Excitement about Aconcio increased during the 1640s, especially with the Independents, among whom *Satanae Stratagemata* took on the status of a manifesto. It was helpful to their campaign that, according to Thomason, on 24 February 1648, the first four chapters of Aconcio's work were issued in translation under the title *Satans Stratagems*.[88] The book was dedicated to Generals Fairfax and Cromwell, and also to the Lord Mayor of London. It was accompanied by an Epistle to the Reader by John Goodwin, and also a letter dated 9 February 1648 from John Dury to Samuel Hartlib. Dury praised Aconcio without reservation, including for 'the depth and solidity of his Judgment in everything'. He also thanked Hartlib for arranging the translation and he expressed warm gratitude to Hartlib's friend, the anonymous translator. The identity of this translator has been subject to much speculation, but until now no convincing solution has been forthcoming. Among the favoured possible candidates, John Goodwin of St Stephen's, Coleman Street, commands the most support, but others, including John Milton, have also been canvassed as possibilities. [89]

---

written c.1623, but usually said to be first published in 1650. Worsley's letter suggests that the book was available in Amsterdam in early 1649. This letter from Worsley also probably connects with a letter from Dury to Hartlib dating from 1649, where Dury urgently requests to purchase any of the writings of Socinus or Crell, HP 4/1/31A. For Crell's *Ethica christiana*, M. Schmeisser, 'Johannes Crells aristotelische Ethi... in den ersten Jahrzehnten des 17. Jahrhunderts', in *Religiöser Nonkonformismus und frühneuzeitliche Gelehrtenkultur*, ed. by F. Vollhardt (Berlin: Akademie Verlag, 2014), pp. 101–20.

87 Leng *Worsley*, pp. 46–47.
88 *Satans Stratagems* was printed by John Macock and sold by both Giles Calvert (Wing A443A) and by John Hancock (Wing A443). The Hancock printing was marked by Thomason 'Feb.24'.
89 Most recent writers follow the editor of the Scholar's Reprint edition of *Satans Stratagems* by settling on John Goodwin as the translator: R. E. Field ed., *Satans Stratagems* (Delmar New York: Scholars' Facsimiles and Reprints, 1978). This view

The whole choreography of this publication suggests an event of significance. As one recent commentator concludes, the project 'bore witness to the coalition of intellectuals, printers, booksellers, military commanders and sympathetic politicians ranged against the imposition of religious uniformity'.[90] Naturally, because they were perceived as favouring granting licence to every kind of separatist and heretical voice, all concerned with *Satans Stratagems* were subject to immediate and fierce abuse from the Presbyterian party, among whom Francis Cheynell was one of the most seasoned and bellicose campaigner.

Among the alleged culprits of the *Satans Stratagems* episode, Cheynell was angry about Dury's participation, but he was inclined to treat this fellow member of the Westminster Assembly with leniency. The greatest blame was aimed at the anonymous translator, whom Cheynell tried unsuccessfully to identify. The translator's expressed intention to publish a full translation incensed Cheynell, who was determined to halt the delivery of a further dose of the 'quintessence of those poysonous dregs which are in his third Book'.[91]

In view of Hartlib's known sympathy for the doctrinal positions of Aconcio, it is not surprising that his experience and services were solicited in the search for a translator. The fact that this project was cut back to only the first four out of Aconcio's eight chapters, albeit still amounting to nearly 60,000 words, rendered the task more manageable. Hartlib, with ineffable judgement, turned to Rand for this important assignment. This translation was undertaken on the eve of his departure to the Netherlands, which occurred later in 1648. He was therefore well out of the way, and protected by anonymity, by the date of Cheynell's search for the culprit. Without further evidence, the idea of Rand's involvement in the 1648 Aconcio edition might have remained in doubt. But further light on this problem is shed by the documentation concerning the reissue of *Satans Stratagems*, which occurred in July 1651, when the title was changed to *Darkness Discovered, or the Devils Secret Stratagems*, still with no indication of the identity of the translator.

---

is also taken by J. Marshall, *John Locke and Toleration* (2006), who also wrongly adds that the book was dedicated by Dury to Hartlib.

90   J. Coffey, *John Goodwin and the Puritan Revolution* (Woodbridge: Boydell Press, 2006), p. 160.
91   Francis Cheynell, *The Divine Trinity* (1650), p. 444. For Cheynell's attempt to identify the translator and his fury over the latter's further publishing plans, pp. 443–44.

However, Rand's correspondence from Amsterdam respecting the 1651 reissue and his plan to complete the translation leaves no doubt about his identity as the translator of *Satans Stratagems*.[92]

Rand remained committed to his eight-chapter Aconcio edition, but in 1654 it became clear that Hartlib was no longer particularly interested in this project, a lapse no doubt dictated by Dury, who invoked the 'unseasonableness of the time' argument, probably reflecting his own sensitivities about his current ecumenical negotiations.[93] It seems that, as the climate worsened, seasonableness drifted into the indefinite future and propitious conditions never again returned. But Rand's translation was not entirely forgotten. In 1664 John Worthington recalled the Latin editions of Aconcio, noting that Dury was attacked for his part in the 1648 edition, and he claimed that 'the rest was also finished, and I think Mr Hartlib had it'.[94] Perhaps on account of the delicacy of the situation, there is no trace of the text of Rand's eight-chapter edition in the Hartlib Papers.

The Mirrour of True Nobility

With the encouragement of Hartlib and James Rand, who himself by this stage was also actively working with Hartlib, William Rand returned to London, probably in the late spring of 1653. He married Ellen, perhaps in 1657, but his wife soon died and was interred at the Bethlem burial ground on 7 May 1658.

Not deterred by the failure to publish his full Aconcio edition, Rand retained his curiosity about the business of translation. He called on Parliament to adopt a more proactive approach to the book trade. He advocated official sponsorship of books that merited translation or promotion for the 'publick advantage', instancing Livy's *Histories* which, in translation, he believed, would serve as 'a great rub in the way of the advancement of the Interest of his [Hobbes'] Leviathan like Monarchs'.[95] A further improvement, in this case designed to weaken the exploitation of authors by the Stationers' Company, was his proposal

---

92 For further information, see my *In Times of Strife*, pp. 120–22.
93 Dury to Hartlib, 16 September 1654, HP 4/3/32 A.
94 John Worthington to George Evans, 18 November 1664, Crossley II,Part 1, pp. 143–44.
95 Rand to Worsley, 11 August 1651, HP 62/21/2A.

for a 'Collegiate association' of authors to secure their complete control over their intended publications.[96]

Rand had not forgotten Hartlib's delayed Peiresc project. He undertook to translate the third edition of this biography, published in The Hague by Adrian Valcq in 1655. Faithful to the massive detail of Gassendi's text, Rand communicated to his English audience a remarkable insight into the rich cultural legacy of French antiquarians and naturalists in the age of Peiresc. As Rand explained to his readers: from an early age, Peiresc showed inexhaustible curiosity about every kind of natural knowledge. In the course of his enormous travel schedule, he gained the confidence of leading innovators of the day, including Galileo. His contemporaries quickly appreciated that Pereskius had 'taken in hand the helm of learning and began to guide the Common-wealth of letters'.[97] Hence, Peiresc in his generation was without an equal in the whole of Europe.

In view of these momentous conclusions, Peiresc admirers would have recognised that Rand's demanding task was well worth the extended effort that it had required. With remarkable speed, Rand not only produced an accomplished translation of Gassendi's work, but also included supplementary material by other authors, which rendered his work even more useful. This was dispatched by the translator to John Evelyn on 12 February 1657, an event that was duly recorded in Evelyn's diary on 5 March. Displaying remarkable prescience on the part of Rand, the dedication to the young John Evelyn designated him as the epitome of Peirescian virtue.[98] Rand's translation was the only complete vernacular edition of the Peiresc biography until 1770, when a French translation made its appearance.

The Society of Graduate Physicians and Miscellaneous Literary Projects

Rand was bent on a literary career, but discovered that his financial means were insufficient to continue with the congenial lifestyle that he

---

96 Rand to Hartlib, 14 February 1652, HP 62/17/1B-2A.
97 *The mirrour of true nobility and gentility*, pp. 44–46.
98 *The mirrour of true nobility and gentility being the life of the renowned Nicolaus Claudius Fabricius, Lord of Peiresc* (John Streater for Humphrey Moseley, London 1657), Wing G295. The preface is signed: 'William Rand. From my house, near Cripplegate in London, January the 30th 1656[/7]'.

had adopted in Amsterdam. He therefore somewhat reluctantly decided to return to London and embark on a medical career.

The most significant initiative of Rand's later years was his audacious reform proposal, dating from 1656, advocating a 'Society of Graduate Physicians', an institution that was designed to break the monopoly of the London College of Physicians.[99] In this he was following in the footsteps of John Hall. He disagreed with Hall about the merits of Helmont, but he shared a similar negative view of the London College. For the sake of all academically qualified doctors like himself who were disinclined to affiliate with the existing College, he proposed an alternative voluntary option, which would grant an opportunity for practising medicine in London without fear of harassment by the entrenched College. Rand believed that a formally constituted body endowed with full legal protection was the only means by which free practitioners could withstand the depredations of the College Fellows. He argued that the new society would attract the 'more studious, modest, reserved, publick & humble spirited' practitioners, leaving the rump of the 'ambitious, covetous, domineering & selfish sort' to gravitate to the existing College. As well as associating together for reasons of legal defence, Rand outlined obvious advantages relating to the improvement of professional standards. In consequence of the broader culture of the members, they would make a decisive contribution to the advancement of 'all naturall Discoveries'. In other words, they would establish themselves as the natural basis for a London-based permanent scientific society. Furthermore the Society might become an 'induction to the establishment of a third Universitie'. Finally, Rand urged that, compared with the intrinsically unsound monopolistic London College, his Society would fit better with the pluralistic pattern of existing city institutions.

Because of the tendentious nature of the above proposal Rand warned Hartlib to limit circulation to 'such as you know are averse to the colledge'. Otherwise, the scheme would surely be 'countermined'. He was confident that Hartlib would immediately recognise the merits of this scheme, since it would provide him with a body of experts available

---

99 HP 42/10/1A-4A, which comprises a letter from Rand to Hartlib dated 15 August 1656, and an undated memorandum headed 'Propositions relateing to those Graduate Physitians of any Universitie, that have bin there licentiated, & are now resident in London & not incorporated nor desirous to incorporate with the present College'. See C. Webster, 'English Medical Reformers: background to the Society of Chymical Physitians', *Ambix* 14:1 (1967), 16–41.

for consultation on the many proposals upon which he required professional advice.

Additional information about this scheme is entirely lacking. The fact that it was revealed to Hartlib at the home of Katherine, Lady Ranelagh, perhaps suggests that she might have been one of the discussants. In that case she might also have mentioned the idea to her brother Robert Boyle and perhaps to some others in her impressive entourage. Rand was likely to have found a viable constituency of support for his new institution, but opted not to spearhead a collision with the College and its allies, a decision that would have disappointed a whole fraternity of doctors and others with medical interests who elected to distance themselves from the established College. The late John Hall would have been mortified by Rand's reticence. The Society of Graduate Physicians therefore joined the ranks of social reform measures from this period that were condemned to perdition by their unseasonableness. Nevertheless, Rand bequeathed a set of ideas relating to his profession that contains many points of relevance to issues that surfaced at much later dates and still remain unresolved.

In his last years, Rand produced a few further minor publications, and considered undertaking a translation of Edward, Lord Herbert's great *De Veritate*, by any standards a daunting task, but also faced practical difficulties that proved impossible to surmount.

John Evelyn perceptively noted an element of tension in the activities of Rand. On the one hand he was a gifted translator, but he was also an able natural philosopher. Evelyn pleaded with Rand to devote himself more to the advancement of the sciences: 'for the future be engaged in communicating to the world something of use, light and encouragement to practical Philosophy, as it concerns nature, and the Restauration of Sciences, as you have already fairly begun'.[100] Rand lost none of his appetite for cosmological speculation or theological debate. He remained sympathetic to Socinianism and actively promoted the Mortalist heresy, but his literary urge had lost its momentum. Also, he relapsed into poor health and experienced periodic episodes of depression. With the collapse of the Republic, he sank into obscurity. Following the traditions

---

100 Evelyn to Rand, 9 April 1657, Evelyn *Letterbooks*, vol. 2, p. 202.

of his immediate family, on 22 January 1663 this worthy reformer was buried at St Pancras, Soper Lane.

3.6 Apocalypticism

It is easy to forget that one of Hartlib's most successful publications was his edited text *Clavis apocalyptica*, published in February 1651, therefore when Britain had reached a notable high point of millennial, messianic and apocalyptic speculation. Apocalypticism was not new to Hartlib. It was, for instance, an important part of the context for the Antilian experiment, which was itself merely one manifestation of a trans-European Rosicrucian furore.[101]

At the roots of Rosicrucianism were apocalyptic motivations, the characteristics of which were apparent in the very first published announcement of the Brotherhood, the precious little pamphlet, *Antwort An die lobwürdige Brüderschafft der Theosophen vom RosenCreutz* (1612), by Adam Haslmayr (1562–1630). Haslmayr notably intimated that the Rosicrucian programme was firmly anchored in the work of Theophrastus von Hohenheim (Paracelsus) who, besides promulgating his revolutionary scientific programme, was also a committed apocalyptically inclined prophet.[102]

Joseph Mede

The next serious engagement of Hartlib with apocalyptic and millennial issues came about through his association with Joseph Mede of Christ's College, Cambridge, whom he may have met during his student days in Cambridge, but certainly they maintained an amicable and active correspondence from 1634 until 1638, a few months before Mede's

---

101 Dickson *Tessera of Antilia*, pp. 101–44; V. Urbánek, *Eschatologie, Vědění a Politika. Příspěvek k dějinám myšlení pobělohorského exilu* (České Budějovice: Jihočeská Univerzita, 2008).

102 L. de Vries, 'Rosicrucianism promised' in *Reformation, Revolution, Renovation. The Roots and Reception of the Rosicrucian Call for General Reform* (Leiden: Brill, 2021), pp. 215–91; C. Gilly, Adam Haslmyr, *Der erste Verkünder der Manifeste der Rosenkreuzer* (Amsterdam: In de Pelikan, 1994); C. Webster, *Paracelsus: Medicine, Magic and Mission at the End of Time* (New Haven and London: Yale University Press, 2008), pp. 210–43.

death.[103] Naturally, at the centre of their exchanges was Mede's *Clavis apocalyptica*, which he had first published in 1627. Hartlib assisted Mede by distributing this book among his contacts in the Netherlands. Mede's interpretation was in direct competition with that of Thomas Brightman dating from 1609. The method of approach of the two writers was entirely different, but their interpretations were broadly similar, except for the crucial twentieth chapter of Revelation. Brightman accepted the traditional Augustinian approach by locating the beginning of the first millennium of Revelation 20:2 in the fourth century. In this scheme the conversion of the Jews would not take place until the year 2300. Mede took both millennia literally. One focus of his interpretation was Revelation 16, which recounted the pouring out of the seven vials. According to his system of synchronisms he worked out mathematically that from the fourteenth century onward, each outpouring represented a shorter time-frame than its predecessor. The fourth vial reached the Thirty Years War and the triumphs of Gustavus Adolphus; the fifth, yet to come, would mark the destruction of Rome; the sixth, the conversion of the Jews and the Collapse of Turkish power; after which the seventh vial, coinciding with the seventh and last trumpet, would usher in the Second Coming of Jesus Christ, who would initiate the millennium and its age of glory. Mede therefore opened up the promise of imminent apocalyptic transformations, the exact chronology of which became the subject of heated debate.

Felicitas Ultimi Sæculi

The slide into civil war, and all the associated contingencies, elevated issues connected with the apocalypse into a universal preoccupation. John Coffey characterised this situation with respect to the core activists

---

103 J. Jue, *Heaven Upon Earth. Joseph Mede (1586–1638) and the Legacy of Millenarianism* (Dordrecht: Springer, 2006); S. Hutton, 'The Appropriation of Joseph Mede: Millenarianism in the 1640s' in *Millenarianism and Messianism in Early Modern European Culture: The Millenarian Turn*, ed. by J. E. Force and R. H. Popkin (Dordrecht: Kluwer Academic Publishers, 2001), pp. 03–14. For the wider Puritan background, see W.M. Lamont, *Godly Rule: Politics and Religion, 1603–60* (London: Macmillan, 1969); P. Toon (ed.), *Puritans, the Millennium and the Future of Israel: Puritan Eschatology 1600–1660* (Cambridge and London: James Clarke Co., Ltd., 1970); C. Gribben, 'The Eschatology of the Puritan Confessions', *Scottish Bulletin of Evangelical Theology*, 20:1 (2002), 51–78.

of the Parliamentarian party, who were 'fired by a sense that they were participating in the great end-times war with evil. From leaders like Pym, Vane and Cromwell, to humble foot-soldiers like Nehemiah Wallington', they were inspired 'with apocalyptic fears and hopes. Without the book of Revelation, indeed, there may have been no English civil war'.[104] With respect to the leading voices of the Puritan movement, Tai Liu concludes that their 'vision of a glorious millennium of Christ's kingdom here on earth' was no longer the preserve of a feckless minority, but became 'a central theme in Puritanism during the whole course of the Puritan Revolution'.[105]

Respecting the sermons delivered before Parliament, Coffey concludes that England, as the New Jerusalem, became a leading theme and also 'The Israel paradigm and Revelation, the language of the godly nation and of the global apocalypse were fused together in Puritan rhetoric with explosive effect'.[106]

The conclusions summarised in the previous paragraph will be familiar to the reader from the contents of chapter 2, especially the concluding section of 'Israel's Call'. Also relevant is Hartlib's third publication, *Felicitas Ultimi Sæculi* (1640), which he edited as a sign of respect for his recently deceased friend, John Stoughton, a leading figure and famous activist among the Godly preachers of the 1630s. Stoughton's display of florid classical elegance and Hartlib's accompanying editorial remarks in a similar vein form a notable contrast with his new-found preoccupation with technicians like Gabriel Plattes. Beneath the patina of classical elegance in *Felicitas Ultimi Sæculi* nestled evidence of apocalyptic leanings. Striking is Stoughton's use of this presentation as a vehicle for promulgating the programme of Francis Bacon, as heralding a new age of enlightenment, in fulfilment of Daniel 12:03–04, ordaining that 'many shall run to and fro, and knowledge shall be increased'.[107] In addition, the specification of Dury, Comenius, Alsted, Bisterfeld and

---

104 J. Coffey, 'The Impact of Apocalypticism during the Puritan Revolutions', *Perichoresis*, 4:2 (2006), 117–48 (pp. 125–26); Haffemeyer, *Les Lumières radicales*, pp. 77–84.

105 T. Liu, *Discord in Zion: The Puritan Divines and the Puritan Revolution 1640–1660* (The Hague: Martinus Nijhoff, 1973), p. 3.

106 Coffey, 'The Impact of Apocalypticism', p. 124. See also, C. Hill, *Antichrist in Seventeenth-Century England* (London: Oxford University Press, 1971), pp. 69–98.

107 Webster, *Instauration*, pp. 03–20.

Johannes Piscator as additional heralds of the new age, was meant to draw attention to Stoughton's special interest in apocalypticism and his solidarity with leading lights among intellectuals in Eastern and Central Europe.[108] Especially interesting is Stoughton's dedication to Tolnai Dali János, which would have been applauded by his embattled Puritan associates. Tolnai had studied in the Netherlands before spending the period 1633 to 1638 in England, during which he was especially influenced by William Ames. On 9 February 1638, he and his fellow Hungarian students formed the "London League", with the aim of spreading Puritanism in Hungary by renewal of the Reformed Church. In the autumn of 1638 he was appointed director of the Reformed College of Sárospatak by Prince György Rákóczi I, which proved to be unsustainable on account of his Puritan reputation, a factor that was integral to his promotion of Francis Bacon and Comenius.[109] In view of these associations, it is not surprising that Hartlib reinforced this message by including in the *Felicitas Ultimi Sæculi* his own dedication to Prince György Rákóczi. Beneath its classical façade, *Felicitas Ultimi Sæculi* was therefore in major respects a device for smuggling past the censors a piece of propaganda on behalf of militant, international Puritanism. The presence of the Hungarian Puritan visitors to London was not entirely forgotten, as is evident from a surprising remark made by Milton in his *Areopagitica*: 'Not for nothing that grave and frugal Transylvanian sends out yearly... not their youth but their staid men, to learn our language and our theologic arts', which suggests that the Hungarians impressed him, just as was the case with Stoughton and Hartlib.[110]

Great End-Times

Once the air cleared, and the freedom of expression was partly unleashed, apocalypticism enjoyed a long spell of assertiveness. The palatability of this was vividly displayed in the sermons delivered to

---

108 Especially influential in England in the apocalyptic context was Johan Henrich Alsted's *Diatribe de mille annis Apocalypticis* (1627; English trans. 1643), the genesis of which was influenced by Piscator. H. Hotson, *Paradise Postponed: Johan Heinrich Alsted and the Birth of Calvinist Millenarianism* (Dordrecht: Kluwer Academic, 2001).
109 M. Bucsay, *Geschichte des Protestantismus in Ungarn* (Stuttgart: Evangelisches Verlagswerk, 1959), pp. 107–15.
110 Milton, *Areopagitica* (1645), CPW, II, p. 264.

3. The Hartlibian Resurgence

Parliament, where, in 1645, Dury played his part with his *Israels Call*. The same ethos was evident at this date in the writings of Milton and the Cambridge Platonists.[111]

Of the successive dramatic shifts that were experienced during the 1640's, the most seismic occurred in December 1648, with the military occupation of Parliament and expulsion of some 270 M.P.s, leaving some 200 to sit as the Rump Parliament. These events paved the way for the rapid trial and execution of Charles I on 30 January 1649.

These momentous changes inevitably provoked extravagant responses. For instance, the execution of Charles I was interpreted as a justified act of tyrannicide, necessary for preparing the ground for the eventual rule of Jesus Christ. The millenarian issue reached such a peak that it spawned the Fifth Monarchist movement, which with remarkable speed gained and preserved its traction across all social classes.[112]

The Rump Parliament was at first viewed as being ideally suited to carry out the management of all civil affairs. The nation seemed for the first time fully equipped to dominate its colonies and assume leadership among its Protestant counterparts. When it came to a situation of disagreement with its allies, as in the case of the Netherlands, it was assumed that Britain was righteous and therefore justified in the use of force to bring miscreants into line. Benjamin Worsley, aided by Dury and Hartlib, in 1649 and 1650 actively advised the government on foreign and colonial policy, and even made recommendations for the reform of Parliament in order that such radical objectives could be more readily achieved.

Also high on the agenda as an end of times objective was 'conversion' of the Jews. As shown in chapter 2, this was an issue upon which there was a diversity of opinion, but there was general support for greater attention to Judaic studies and language. Indicative of some expressions of more positive attitudes towards the Jews was the publication in 1650 of Moses Wall's translation of Menasseh ben Israel's *The Hope of Israel*. This initiative prepared the ground for Menasseh ben Israel's visit to

---

111 B.K. Lewalski, 'Milton and the Millennium', in *Milton and the Ends of Time*, ed. by J. Cummins (Cambridge: Cambridge University Press, 2003), pp. 13–28; S. Hutton, 'Mede, Milton and More: Christ's College Millenarians', in *Milton and the Ends of Time*, pp. 29–41; C. Hill, *Antichrist in Seventeenth-Century England*, chapter 3.

112 B. Capp, *The Fifth Monarchy Men. A Study in Seventeenth Century English Millenarianism* (London: Faber & Faber, 1972); C. Hill, *Antichrist in Seventeenth-Century England*, pp. 131–40.

England, which began in September in 1655 and ended in October 1657. He aimed and failed to secure a more definite readmission of Jews, a goal upon there was no consensus. It is possible that agreement to hold the 1655 Whitehall Conference on this subject was partly inspired by expectations of their imminent conversion. The conference itself merely served to underline splits of opinion on all the main issues of contention. For whatever reasons, in ensuing decades the obstacles to Jewish residence in England continued in their glacial drift towards relaxation.[113]

Clavis Apocalyptica

Hartlib made his most dramatic intervention in the apocalyptic debate with *Clavis apocalyptica*, which was published in February 1651. The adoption of Mede's title was no accident. The expectation was aroused by the ample title page that this book was bringing Mede's work to its natural conclusion, by revealing precisely what was to be expected in the year 'that is near at hand'.[114]

Hartlib dedicated this book to Oliver St John, his friend and patron, also a leading figure in the Rump Parliament, Lord Chief Justice of the Common Pleas, and, according to Capp, a known sympathiser of the Fifth Monarchists.[115] *Clavis apocalyptica* certainly caught the mood of the moment and was a commercial success. In 1651, the first edition went through about half-a-dozen variant reprints and there were fresh editions thereafter.

As with many of the books published by Hartlib, *Clavis apocalyptica* was a compilation, in which most interest was attracted by its third and longest component, the anonymous *Apocalypsis Reserata. or the Revelation*

---

[113] Representative of the more recent literature: B. Coulton, 'Cromwell and the Readmission of the Jews to England', *Cromwelliana* (2001), pp. 21–38; E. Glaser, *Judaism without Jews* (London: Palgrave Macmillan, 2007); and H.D. Lee,'The Readmission of the Jews and the Power of the Civil Magistrate: Thomas Barlow on the Jews and Natural Law', *The Seventeenth Century*, 38:4 (2023), 575–96.

[114] *Clavis Apocalyptica or A Prophetical Key by which the great mysteries in the revelation of St. John, and the Prophet Daniel are opened; It beeing made apparent that the Prophetical Numbers com to an end with the year of our Lord, 1655.... Shewing what in these our times hath been fulfilled. 2. At this present is effectually brought to pass. 3. And henceforth is to bee exspected in the years neer at hand* (London: printed by William Du-Gard for Thomas Matthewes and are to bee sold by Giles Calvert, 1651). Wing H979.

[115] Capp, *The Fifth Monarchy Men*, p. 40.

of St. John (pp. 40–163). This is preceded by an insignificant ancillary apocalyptic exposition, and before that an exhaustive seventy-nine-page 'Epistolic Discourse from Mr. John Durie to Mr. Sam: Hartlib', dated 28 November 1650.

Most of the modern academic attention has revolved around the identity of the author of the *Apocalypsis Reserata*. Until quite recently the favoured choice was the celebrated Abraham von Franckenberg, which was not wide off the mark, but Martin Mulsow convincingly demonstrated that the author was an associate of Franckenberg, Michael Gühler, a tax official and eventually a secretary in the court of Duke Johann Christian of Brieg. Both Franckenberg and Gühler belonged to the Silesian intellectual community that had emerged during Hartlib's later teenage years, which is well-characterised by Mulsow, and is also outlined in the first chapter of this study. Hartlib remained in touch with Franckenberg until his death in 1652.[116]

The Gühler commentary is both narrow and broad. As he revealed to a Privy Counsellor in Brandenburg, his exposition focused upon chapters 11 and 16 of Revelation. His next aim, which was not realised, was a separate study of Revelation 20, with the purpose of further consolidating his earlier conclusion that 'the thousand years of the peaceable and quiet Kingdome of Christ are at hand'.[117] In practice the 1651 commentary drew on all corners of Revelation, and indeed, on the whole Biblical prophetic canon. Gühler frankly admitted that Mede provided the guidelines for his own work and the stimulus for his main and reiterated conclusion, that the millennium would commence at an imminent date. Announcing that he was in line with Mede and four other authorities whom he cited, Gühler concluded with certainty that the year 1656 would be marked by 'great revolution and changes'.[118] Mede himself thought that the biblical Apocalypse would occur prior to 1716, and he hinted that the years between 1654 to 1657 would be especially significant. Consequently, Gühler was not out of line with this and other respected opinions when he adopted 1656 as the most

---

116 M. Mulsow, 'Who Was the Author of the *Clavis Apocalyptica* of 1651? Millenarianism and Prophecy between Silesian Mysticism and the Hartlib Circle', in *Millenarianism and Messianism in Early Modern European Culture Volume IV*, ed. by J.C. Laursen and R.H. Popkin (Dordrecht: Kluwer Academic, 2001), pp. 57–75.

117 Excerpt of a translation of a Gühler letter from Brieg, 7 April 1653, HP 43/43B.

118 *Clavis apocalyptica*, p. 25.

significant year in his calculations. A similar point of view was adopted in tracts by the Fifth Monarchist, John Tillinghast, which may well have been influenced by Gühler's exposition.[119]

For the *Clavis* reader, a noteworthy feature of this presentation was its Silesian Protestant terms of reference. The nearest Gühler came to spelling out immediate prospects was his prediction that in 1655 the exiled and oppressed Evangelical Professors 'would receive unexpected help from God, revive them again, return to their homeland and establish them more powerfully than ever before'.[120] As for the promised 'thousand years of the peaceable and quiet Kingdome of Christ' for the population as a whole, in this exposition, this was demoted to the sidelines.

The pride of place in *Clavis apocalyptica* was accorded to the long introductory Epistolical Discourse written by John Dury, who gave prominence to the letter of Comenius to Hartlib, by which Gühler's tract was delivered to England, which then became the basis for the publication undertaken by Hartlib. Dury explained that his review of the apocalyptic theme in general was an act of solidarity with the exiled Bohemians and others in their situation. He welcomed Gühler's exercise as a gift from God to the distressed churches in the interim before God would 'make an end of his work among them', something that was 'now shortly to be accomplished'.[121] Dury then expanded at length on 'the expectation of the fulfilling of the apocalyptical promises', something that he assured foreign visitors was much on the mind of their allies in England, but also even among the Jews 'who were also made sensible of the approaching change of their condition'. The Jewish issue was additionally important because it indicated the emergence of a 'universal concurrence' that the Lord was 'hastening to finish his work in righteousness'.[122] Dury identified Gühler's work as an abridgement of Mede's interpretation of Revelation, utilising the same method of

---

119 John Tillinghast, Generation-worke (London, 1653–1654), Knowledge of the Times (London, 1654); for discussion, Capp, *The Fifth Monarchy Men*, pp. 192–93. For an estimate of Tillinghast, John Beale to Hartlib, 26 March 1659, HP 51/106A-B. For the rash of predictions relating to 1656 and related years, C. Hill, *Antichrist in Seventeenth-Century England*, pp. 112–13.
120 *Clavis apocalyptica*, pp. 87–89, 132–34; for the preceding suffering of the Silesian Protestants, pp. 79–86.
121 Ibid., Preface, p. 05.
122 Ibid., Preface, pp. 06–07.

3. The Hartlibian Resurgence

synchronisms, but applying this to experience of the author's own part of Europe at this later date, and reaching the conclusion, consistent with Mede, that the apocalyptical climax was imminent.

On the above basis, the reader might have expected Dury to sympathetically prepare the ground for Gühler's exposition, but that was not the case. I suspect that Dury, on account of his disapproval of Gühler's basic methodology, largely ignored his exegesis, to which he made hardly any specific reference, even ignoring Gühler's lengthy 'Objection No. 2', which refuted the 'mystical' interpretation that was the main objective of the Dury exercise.

Dury underlined the fallibility of all attempts at exact chronological prognostication, insisting that a large element of mystery was endemic to all apocalyptical visions. Such a conclusion was rendered inevitable on account of the philosophy of scriptural interpretation that he had been developing for nearly twenty years. Consequently, discovering the 'keys' to unlock biblical prophecies was a sophisticated operation, the difficulty of which should not be underestimated.[123] Dury went on to define 'the universal Rules of Prophetical Interpretation' before applying these in a chapter-by-chapter review of the Book of Revelation, which took no account of the fact that Gühler drew on many Biblical prophetic sources, and on Revelation only to limited extent. Again, contradicting Gühler, the concluding remarks of Dury's 'Epistolical Discourse' were entirely lacking optimism, instead warning the Protestants of the dangers of false prophets, quarrels, bestial animosities and civil war. He warned that Protestants were still playing into the hands of the Beast. He frankly admitted that he saw no evidence that 'the Bride is come out of the Wilderness, or that we have gotten the conquest of the Beast, and over the false Prophet'.[124] Dury conceded that there would be an end to these desecrations, but he offered no prospect of the day when Satan 'bee bound up from seducing the Nations of the Earth'.[125] These dark and pessimistic conclusions were, of course, a world away from Dury's stated belief that the 'Lord is hastening to finish his work in righteousness', and other similar remarks which featured in the opening pages of his Preface and indeed in his later correspondence. Dury's confusion and

---

123 Ibid., Preface, pp. 19–21.
124 Ibid., pp. 75–06.
125 Ibid., p. 79.

revisionism must have shocked both Gühler and Comenius, who had not trusted their mission to Dury with the expectation of anything like this conclusion.

Regardless of incompatibility of its various elements, *Clavis apocalyptica* was a success and was remembered on account of Gühler rather than Dury. Hartlib's own leanings and associations were also firmly towards Comenius, Figulus and Gühler, rather than with Dury. For the next decade Figulus continued to ply Hartlib with intelligence respecting the desperate situation of distressed Protestant communities in their homelands and with accounts of incidents suggesting hints of impending restitution. Figulus had been involved in the Gühler project since the outset, and had recounted the state of affairs in Silesia with equal alarm, including noting that the Jesuits had discovered the identity of the author of the *Clavis*, after which the Habsburg Emperor had placed a hefty reward upon his head. Figulus assured Hartlib that Gühler 'remained confident that there would be an execution of 'those things which are expressed in the 18 Chapter of Revelation and England to bee the chief Actor in it'.[126]

Readers of the *Clavis* would also have observed that Hartlib's opening statements possessed obvious resonance with the apocalyptic vogue of that date. Indeed, this was so obvious that it provoked a passionate message of blessing to Hartlib from Morgan Llwyd, the notable Welsh saint. Llwyd designated Hartlib as 'a teller of such great things as all the Prophets and Apostles and saincts in all ages waited for'.[127] This letter was communicated to Hartlib by his friend Henry Jessey, who was by this point also a committed Fifth Monarchist. From much earlier, Hartlib was familiar with Vavasor Powell, a close companion of Llwyd, by this date also an ardent Fifth Monarchist. Hartlib, Llwyd and Powell were also linked by their enjoyment of the friendship of the influential and radically inclined Sir Richard Saltonstall, and through their common interest in Jacob Boehme.[128] The widespread belief in an apocalyptical future was

---

126 Figulus to Hartlib, 3 July 1654, HP 43/46A-B.
127 Morgan Llwyd to Hartlib, 30 October 1652, HP 65/8/1A.
128 B. Capp, *Fifth Monarchy Men*, especially chapter 5; G.R. Nuttall, *The Welsh Saints 1640–1660* (Cardiff: University of Wales Press, 1957), pp. 33–54. In 1659 Jessey, Powell and Saltonstall were among the signatories of the petition in support of the Good Old Cause, *Essay toward settlement on a secure foundation*, September 1659, Wing 3295A.

noted by Christer Bonde, the Swedish diplomat, who disclosed to King Charles X the popular belief in London that jointly, Sweden and England were destined imminently to overthrow the papacy.[129]

The last reference that I have located concerning the influence of Hartlib's *Clavis apocalyptica* relates to Thomas Venner's *A Door of Hope*, dating from January 1661, which is a famous Fifth Monarchist manifesto, associated with the tragic death of its author.[130] The *Clavis apocalyptica* episode was in various respects a significant intervention in various respects and it very much reflected the mood of the times. In view of his long and varied association with these ideas, Hartlib was ideally placed to publicise prophecies reflecting an Eastern European perspective. As the situation of Protestants in his homeland further deteriorated, he became ever more involved in their affairs, especially with respect to facilitating negotiations concerning greater cooperation among the Protestant powers and providing relief for the growing tide of distressed exiles.

Lux in tenebris and the Aftermath

Hartlib was soon drawn again into the middle of apocalyptic affairs, this time with respect to Comenius and his large collection of prophecies generated by three of his most valued protégés, in its published form, entitled *Lux in tenebris* (1657).[131] Owing to the significance of its political relevance, Comenius was immensely attached to this project. In the first place, he hoped that these prophecies would galvanise Protestant states to unite on their Eastern flank against the Habsburgs. In the second

---

129 Christer Bonde to Charles X, 23 August 1655, in *Swedish Diplomats at Cromwell's Court, 1655–1656*, trans. and ed. by M. Roberts (London: Royal Historical Society, 1988), Camden Fourth Series 36, pp. 142–43.
130 B. Capp, '*A Door of Hope* Re-opened: The Fifth Monarchy, King Charles and King Jesus', *Journal of Religious History*, 32:1 (2008), 16–30. See also S. Hutton, 'Henry More and the Apocalypse', *Studies in Church History. Subsidia*, 10 (1994), 131–40, for More's debt in the 1660s to Dury's Preface to the *Clavis Apocalyptica*.
131 *Lux in tenebris: hoc est Prophetiae donum, quo Deus ecclesiam Evangelicam (in regno Bohemiae et incorporatis provinciis) sub tempus horrendae eius pro evangelio persequutionis, extremaeque dissipationis ornare, ac paterne solari dignatus est ; Submissis de statu ecclesiae in terris, praesenti et mox futuro, per Christophorum Cotterum Silesium, Christianam Poniatoviam Bohemam, revelationbus vere divinis, ab anno 1616 usque ad annum 1656 continuatis* ([Amsterdam] 1657).

place he wanted Cromwell to prepare Britain to participate in a fresh wave of military interventions. He believed that Hartlib could play a decisive role in the achievement of this latter objective.

From 1654 onwards, Comenius kept Hartlib informed about every step in his thinking on apocalyptic affairs. Then he reported on progress towards publication of *Lux in tenebris*, and finally on arrangements for printing and distribution. Already, at the beginning of March 1654, Hartlib, in the course of their exchanges about various apocalyptic issues, informed Moses Wall about *Lux in tenebris* and offered to supply him with a manuscript copy of this work.[132]

Before that, Comenius dispatched three copies of the manuscript in a special vellum binding for the use of the Lord Protector. These, he insisted, should be handed to Cromwell personally by Hartlib. A further seven sets of the manuscript were also supplied for those in high office in England.[133] A more liberal distribution was permitted when the handsome published version arrived in England in January 1658. Hartlib promptly dispatched *Lux in tenebris* to his friends, among whom it was received with favour. John Beale was the most active discussant and he even communicated his response direct to Comenius. Beale's attitude was ambivalent, but Hartlib assured Pell that, concerning the controversial Drabik, Beale had concluded that 'I cannot at all doubt but, in the main, God is in it'.[134]

Worsley also considered the book in some detail, which led him to discuss the question of prophecy in general. He rejoiced that he and Hartlib were alert to the realisation that 'this is a Time wherein the Lord calls for watching & waking and hearkening more then ordinary'. This sentiment connects with an even more passionate pronouncement made by Worsley to Lady Ranelagh, where he predicted that all the prevailing evils connected with darkness 'shall all of them have an end; shall all of them have an end together; And that the end of them all is really et truly

---

132 Moses Wall to Hartlib, 19 March 1654, HP 34/4/9A, perhaps the first reference to *Lux in tenebris* in the Hartlib Papers.
133 Comenius to Hartlib, 18 July 1657, HP 7/111/21A-22B. Comenius insisted that he was not issuing abstract prophecies, but 'commands to the Leading Statesmen of the world, which they must not ignore, they whom the Lamb has called to be his allies in the war against the Beast. Among them will come those of your Nation'. (21B).
134 Hartlib to Pell, 18 March 1658, Vaughan *Protectorate*, II, p. 450.

already at hand'.¹³⁵ Also relevant to the persistence of the apocalyptic obsession among Hartlib and his friends is an anonymous note attached to a diplomatic letter dated 27 December 1659, which concludes: 'From this letter I see that Mr. Schlezer is a 'Schwarmer' [separatist]; for Hartlieb (who is an Elbinger, also a man of learning) is the patron and advocate of all new prophets. Figulus is a preacher, is married to Comenius' daughter, pretends visions, which he also had printed, and prophesies great things for Sweden'.¹³⁶

The dream of Comenius and Figulus concerning a united Protestant mission against their Counter-Reformation enemies promptly fell to pieces. In the first place Hartlib was taken aback by some of the predictions, including some unflattering references to Cromwell in the prophecies of Drabik. Secondly, the initial favourable military adventure in Central Europe was soon replaced by irredeemable disaster. Comenius clung on to his prophetic hopes, but his reputation was not assisted by realities on the ground.¹³⁷ This was not quite the end of the *Lux in Tenebris* story in England: an English translation by Robert Codrington was published in 1664, and this went into a second edition in the same year.¹³⁸ This seems to have made only a negligible impact. By this point the Fifth Monarchists as a coherent movement were finished. But the academic interest in the apocalypse was by no means exhausted, as for instance was witnessed by the Platonists and Isaac Newton in Cambridge.¹³⁹

Whether for reasons of hope, despair or curiosity, as shown in the following chapters, Hartlib also remained preoccupied with apocalypticism and millennialism for the rest of his life. Indeed, within his last few exchanges with John Worthington were expressions of regret concerning Ezerel Tong's failure to publish his much-vaunted

---

135 Worsley to Hartlib, 20 January 1659, HP 33/2/11A-12B; Worsley to Lady Ranelagh, 20 April 1659, HP 33/2/13A.

136 D. Riches, *Three Marriage Alliances: Diplomatic Culture in Action* (Leiden: Brill, 2013), p. 177. Lady Ranelagh's letter to Hartlib dated 31 December 1656, indicates that she also was on friendly terms with Schlezer, HP 39/2/50B. For Schlezer, Haffemeyer, *Les Lumières radicales*, pp. 434–42.

137 For Comenius and the foreign policy of György Rákóczi, G. Kármán, *Confessions and Politics in the Principality of Transylvania 1644–1657* (Göttingen: Vandenhoeck & Ruprecht, 2020), chapter 10.

138 *The Prophecies of Christopher Kotterus, Christiana Poniatovia, Nicholas Drabicius* (London: R. Pawlet, 1664).

139 S. Hutton, 'Henry More and the Book of Revelation', *Studies in Church History*, 10 (1994), 131–40.

apocalyptic study, and also a desperate plea from Comenius with respect to the plight of the Protestants in Hungary and Poland, all of whom were facing imminent slaughter (*'ad mactandum destinatos eripe'*). Finally, Hartlib's very last letter to Worthington included a summary of a letter that he had just received from Serrarius, announcing the certainty of the imminent redemption of their 'Israel'.[140]

---

140 Crossley I, Part 2, pp. 69 and 71 (Tong), p. 166 (Comenius), pp. 108–09 (Serrarius); S. Hutton, 'Henry More and the Book of Revelation', *Studies in Church History*, 10 (1994), 131–40; idem, 'Mede, Milton, and More: Christ's College Millenarians', in *Milton and the Ends of Time*, ed. by J. Cummins (Cambridge: Cambridge University Press, 2003), pp. 29–41.

Fig. 4 Title-page of Iacopo Aconcio, *Darkness discovered. Or the Devils secret statagems laid open...* [translated by William Rand] (London: printed by John Macock for William Ley, 1651), Thomason E634 [2], dated by Thomason 7 July; Wing A442.

4. Man of the Moment

That this turne of time may not be capable of a noble alteration... I not onely deny, but even evince the contrary. For what more seasonable opportunity can we have, then that we see the highest spirits, pregnant with great matters, and in despite of these Tumult and Troubles which inviron them of every side, labouring with somewhat; the greatnesse of which they themselves cannot tell, and with a wonderfull deale of courage, attempting the discovery of a new world of knowledge?[1]

4.1 Changing Times

As the revival of his fortunes progressed, Hartlib increasingly identified himself with the ascending Parliamentary regime. His partisanship became ever more explicit. Reflecting the almost invulnerable position of the Parliamentarians, in 1647 he wrote of his honour in serving the 'Commonwealth of Israel' in which 'this Parliament, and such as joyne with it in this Publike Cause, are more solemnly and strongly engaged to advance the Glory of God by the Reformation of this Church and State, then any other Protestants are'.[2] Soon, his publications were as a matter of course dedicated to Parliament and to the Parliamentarian political and military leadership.

The same path was followed by John Hall, whose strong Parliamentarian leanings were evident from his first contacts with Hartlib. Soon Hall plunged into direct political activity with his revival of Marchamont Nedham's newsbook, *Mercurius Britannicus*, which operated under Hall's authorship weekly from May to August 1648. In 1650 he became one of the main authors of *Mercurius Politicus*.

---

1 John Hall, *An humble motion concerning the Advancement of Learning* (1649), p. 21.
2 *Considerations tending to the happy accomplishment of Englands Reformation* (1647), Preface and p. 2.

In a distinct acceleration of Hartlib's drive for reform in the field of higher education, as noted in the previous chapter, Hall issued an audacious pamphlet, *An Humble Motion to the Parliament of England concerning the Advancement of Learning and Reformation of the Universities* (1649). Taking up the call of Hartlib's *Considerations tending*, Hall proclaimed that, 'You have done great things for us, and equal to what hath been done in any Nation', which led to the above corollary, calling for Parliament to take advantage of the ongoing revolution by seizing the opportunity to exploit 'the new world of knowledge' that lay before them. The remainder of his *Humble Motion* was devoted to this theme.³

Hall was duly rewarded. The Council of State granted him a pension of £100 per annum, with the expectation that he would continue to serve the interests of the Commonwealth, an arrangement that worked satisfactorily until shortly before Hall's final sickness and death. As also noted in the previous chapter, one of Hall's early acts in his new capacity was to write his devastating attack on Galenic medicine and the College of Physicians of London, in defence of Helmontian medicine and the freedom of medical practice.⁴ Hall typified the youthful spirit of excitement and hopefulness that found wide expression in the wake of the Parliamentarian ascendancy.

The extent to which Hartlib was enmeshed with Independent political leadership is evident from a letter of John Dury to Francis Rous, where he extolled the joint commitment of himself, Rous and Hartlib to virtue, learning and the public good 'against the common enemies thereof', who represented malignity, error, violence and deceit. In this, Rous, as the stepbrother of the late John Pym, in the view of Dury, carried a special responsibility for upholding Pym's commitments. Prominent among these was the furtherance of the work of Hartlib, who was 'Mr Pyms intimate and familiar acquaintance', whom Pym had throughout supported on account of his commitment to the 'good of many'. On this account, Dury called upon Rous to join with his ally Oliver St John and others in securing continuing governmental support for Hartlib and his 'service for the publicke'.⁵

---

3   Hall, *Humble Motion*, p. 13.
4   Webster, *In Times of Strife*, pp. 99–106.
5   Dury to Rous, 7 February 1646, HP 7/32/1A-2B.

In 1649 Dury continued along the same path directly with Oliver St John, by then the Lord Chief Justice of the Common Pleas. Dury told St John that John Trenchard M.P. and John Sadler (Town Clerk of London) had asked him to brief Lieutenant General Cromwell and Commissary Gualter Frost, 'all Mr Hartlib's friends in the House and Councell of State', concerning Hartlib and his proposed Office of Address, in order that they could correct 'the Committee of Oxford's neglect of the orders of the House' and also investigate additional sources of support for him.[6] St John was indeed Hartlib's most august politician supporter. The warmth of Hartlib's admiration for him was made evident in the Dedication to St John of the *Clavis apocalyptica* (1651). Sadler was one of Hartlib's most avid and consistent correspondents. Gualter Frost Sen. was a personal friend of both Hartlib and Dury, and was a particularly valuable asset owing to his senior positions in the administration, ending up as Secretary to the Council of State. After Frost's death in 1652, his post went to John Thurloe, with whom both Hartlib and Dury were also in regular contact, but without much evidence of personal interaction.[7]

Hartlib's continuing linkage with the political elite is well-illustrated by the Committee for the Advancement of Learning established by the Nominated Assembly. This committee operated between July and December 1653. Half of the fourteen initial members of the committee were well-known to Hartlib (Col. Thomas Blount, Jonathan Goddard, Sir Robert King, Henry Lawrence, John Sadler, Walter Strickland and Col. William Sydenham), while Francis Rous, another friend, was the Speaker of that Parliament. Sir Robert King, the brother of Dorothy Dury, had in 1649, received from Myles Symner an enthusiastic endorsement of William Petty's *Advice* and Hall's *Humble Motion*, an incident that was indicative of a wider consensus among Hartlib's friends concerning

---

6   Dury to Oliver St John, 26 February 1649, HP 4/1/23A. Thomas Westrow M.P., an ally of Trenchard, to Culpeper, 20 February 1647, recalled Cromwell's active interest in the Office of Address, Culpeper *Letters*, p. 290. See also *ODNB* John Sadler (R.L. Greaves). For St John, whose wife was a cousin of Cromwell, see *ODNB* Oliver St John (William Palmer), Worden *Rump*, pp. 178–84 et passim. For Sadler, St John and Hartlib, Haffemeyer, *Les Lumières radicales*, pp. 309–16 et passim. For Cromwell and Hartlib, Haffemeyer, *Les Lumières radicales*, pp. 406–58 et passim.

7   For Thurloe, P. Aubrey, *Mr Secretary Thurloe. Cromwell's Secretary of State 1652–1660* (London: Athlone Press, 1990); Haffemeyer, *Les Lumières radicales*, pp. 419–28 et passim.

the need for university reform.⁸ Hence, in turn, King was supportive of Symner's plan to establish an innovative new academy in Ireland.⁹

Hartlib's political usefulness mainly related to domestic affairs, but he was also valued for his international associations. A moment of special importance arose in 1655, when the issue of Britain's participation in an international Protestant alliance re-emerged on the agenda. London became a gathering place for diplomats from most of the leading Protestant powers. Important among these representatives was Johann Friedrich Schlezer, the representative of the Elector of Brandenburg and a long-time associate of Hartlib, who stayed at his house for the whole duration of his lengthy visit. Comenius asked Hartlib to instruct Constantin Schaum, the agent of Transylvania, and ordered Hartlib to arrange for Schaum a confidential meeting with the Lord Protector.¹⁰ According to Hartlib's records, Schaum spent much time at Hartlib's house from April to August 1655 and left behind a veritable feast of idle gossip.

From his station in Switzerland John Dury fixed on this moment to attempt a decisive intervention in these negotiations. His profile was elevated by his apparent success in unifying the Protestant Cantons, and even more by his value as a source of intelligence concerning the Waldensian crisis, which was alarming to the whole of Protestant Europe. Even before the Waldensian massacre on 24 April 1655, Dury called for more action from England to alleviate the distress of this persecuted minority.¹¹ At this date Hartlib was also aware of the increasing plight of the Bohemian Protestants in Poland. In April 1655 Figulus forwarded to him a letter from Comenius expressing a sense of desperation about the prospects for his community in Leszno, and accepting the inevitability of their renewed exile. In the following December Comenius concluded that there was no way of escape for him and his people, a prediction that was gruesomely fulfilled with the conflagration of Leszno on 26 April 1656.¹²

---

8   Myles Symner to King [1649], HP 47/6/1A-B.
9   BL Sloane MS 427, f.85.
10 Comenius to Hartlib, 23 January 1655, HP 7/72/5A.
11 Dury to Hartlib, 1 April 1655, HP 4/3/89B.
12 Letter from Comenius to Figulus, early April 1655, quoted in Figulus to Hartlib, 16 April 1655, BL Add MS 4364, ff. 49B-50A; letter of Comenius to Figulus, early December 1655, quoted in Figulus to Hartlib, 15 December 1655, BL Add MS 4365, ff.49B-50A. For the Leszno disaster, see [Comenius], *Lesnae excidium anno 1656 in Aprili factum fide historica narratum* [Amsterdam, 1656], DJAK, 9/11, pp. 345–53.

Dury dwelled on the crisis facing Protestant minorities in his calls for a renewed effort to generate a more aggressive alliance of leading Protestant powers. Key to his argument was an eight-point plan for achieving agreement between Calvinists and Lutherans, which had been drafted by the Theological Faculty at Upsala University in 1637 and in a revised form handed to Dury shortly afterwards at the end of his pre-Civil War Swedish negotiations. Dury viewed this paper as an ideal vehicle for cementing relations between Britain and Sweden, and also as a platform for building a wider Protestant alliance. Hartlib was entrusted by Dury with the elaborate process of distributing letters and documents that poured from his pen during late 1654 and the early months of 1655.[13] There is firm evidence that this documentation reached its targets, but no indication of any abiding influence.[14]

4.2 The Hartlib Partnership Continued

The previous chapter outlined the robust recovery of Hartlib's assembly of active associates after the disappointments of the early years of the Civil War. A key indicator of this revival was the further proliferation of his correspondence, the full fruits of which became evident during the period covered by the present chapter. This decade undoubtedly witnessed the high-water mark of Hartlib's career. He sponsored a torrent of publications, expanded the range of his associations and activities, and was recognised as a major public figure, key to the process of universal betterment that the new rulers wished to inspire. He could even be said to have been almost assimilated into the body of the civil service of the new administration.

---

13 See particularly, Dury to Henry Lawrence, Lord President of the Council of State, 14 November 1654, HP 4/3/58B-59B, which transmits his eight-point plan for religious unification.

14 One example of a positive response: Peter Julius Coyet, the Swedish representative, reported to Charles X that he had received 'a very remarkable letter' from Dury, which he was passing on for the King's consideration. Coyet to Charles X, 24 August 1655, in *Swedish Diplomats at Cromwell's Court, 1655–1656*, trans. and ed. by M. Roberts (London: Royal Historical Society, 1988), Camden Fourth Series 36, pp. 144–45. Roberts concludes that Hartlib and Dury were in close touch with Cromwell, but he doubts that they exercised much influence on him (p. 143). See also, Roberts, 'Cromwell and the Baltic', in his *Essays in Swedish History* (London: Weidenfeld and Nicolson, 1967) chapter 6.

Signifying the buoyancy of Hartlib's labours, the text of his Ephemerides for the 1648–1658 period was ample and continuous. It was not quite as voluminous as for the opening years, 1634 and 1635, and there was also a striking change in the subject matter. As already discussed, the centre of gravity of the early years was the minutiae of the proceedings of the Godly brotherhood. This later period was dominated by the collation of data concerning innovation in every sphere of the economy. Accordingly, it is only a minor exaggeration to describe the Ephemerides for this period as an economic data bank. It was organised in such a manner that Hartlib could readily extract the latest news on everything from pharmacy to the cultivation of woad.

Much of Hartlib's later correspondence reflected this shift in the bias of interest. But there continued a lively concern about the prevailing issues of theological and cultural debate. This broader cultural frame of reference is for instance reflected in Hartlib's correspondence with John Worthington (1618–1671), which is one of those rare cases where both sides of the correspondence are preserved. The first extant letter, which is from Hartlib to Worthington, is dated 20 November 1655. Incidental evidence suggests that they had been in sporadic contact at least since 1651. In the James Crossley three-volume edition of Worthington's *Diary and Correspondence*, which itself is a masterpiece of Victorian scholarship, the letters exchanged between Hartlib and Worthington occupy about 300 pages. This edition is of course a bedrock for all later serious work on Hartlib. John Worthington was Master of Jesus College, Cambridge, and for a year Vice-Chancellor of the University. Within that university he was widely known and in touch with important groups such as the Cambridge Platonists, among whom was Ralph Whichcote, to whom Worthington was related through marriage.

The first substantial reference to Worthington occurred when, on behalf of Hartlib, he urged Henry More to write further on the operation of spirits in the human mind.[15] The first mention of Worthington in the Ephemerides occurred in the autumn of the same year, which is also the first evidence relating to Worthington's lengthy and important mission to retrieve the scientific manuscripts of his fellow Lancastrian,

---

15 More to Hartlib, 2 February 1652, HP18/1/9A.

Jeremiah Horrocks, who had tragically died in January 1642 at the age of twenty-two.

As the case of Robert Boyle indicates, the major exchanges of letters were not always an unmitigated success. As noted in the previous chapter, Boyle first came to Hartlib's attention in the autumn of 1645, but their correspondence commenced only in 1647. More than fifty letters were exchanged between them over the next twelve years. At first the young Boyle expressed his gratitude that the eminent Hartlib was willing to participate in such a dialogue. The first preserved letters were all on Boyle's side. Thereafter the tide shifted, until in the final years almost all the preserved letters emanated from Hartlib. Letters from these years followed Hartlib's customary practice of adapting the content to the presumed needs of the relevant discussant, while also appending notes on such topics of the day as personal affairs, health issues or political news. At first Boyle relished the mishmash served up by his respected elder, but, as his curiosity about specialised scientific issues intensified, he must have found Hartlib's letters increasingly irrelevant and even tiresome. Reflecting this growing gulf of expertise, Hartlib increasingly complained about Boyle's lack of response to his letters, until, at the end of November 1659, their correspondence ground to a halt.

4.3 Education and Training

Of all the diverse activities of Samuel Hartlib, education is the most widely remembered. As described above, this commitment was built upon his own early educational experience. It was then part of his planning of Antilia during his final days in Elbing. There also, at his first acquaintance with John Dury, they discovered that their main common interest was education. Education then became the vocational priority of Hartlib upon his arrival in England. This same commitment was next the inspiration for his famous partnership with Comenius. In view of such factors, it comes as no surprise that Hartlib is most remembered as a principal agent for the betterment of schooling, with irons in the fire in almost every other sphere of education and training.[16] The

---

16 In chronological order: Margaret James, *Social Policy and Problems during the Puritan Revolution, 1640–1660* (London: Routledge, 1930); W.A.L. Vincent, *The State and School Education 1640–1660 in England and Wales* (London: S.P.C.K, 1950); R.L.

influential Foster Watson concluded that under Hartlib's leadership, as 'the most enterprising man of his age', England reached 'the verge of an organisation of elementary, if not secondary, education'.[17] Here, Hartlib was mobilised to drive forward the system of universal education to which Foster Watson and his allies aspired. The more recent literature is diverse in its outlook, but it is united in recognising that state implementation of reforms in education was vastly in arrears of the changes envisaged by campaigners. Whatever the limitations of their influence on public policy, it must be accepted that the period from 1640 to 1660 witnessed a massive level of activity in the field of education on the part of a substantial number of advocates, among whom were many of outstanding ability, whose interventions are undoubtedly of significant historical interest.

Shortly after his return to England in the summer of 1645, Dury outlined three major priorities for this new phase of his work, of which the third was 'to assist Some others in the Counsels of reforming Schooles, & of educating youth in Languages in vertues & in humane Sciences. which are the main fundamentalls of a Solid Reformation, and without which none of all our other endevoures, will reach effectually unto the good of posterity'.[18] This proved to be a more arduous commitment than he had anticipated. Reporting to Hartlib about progress with his drafting of *The Reformed School*, Dury lamented the lethargy in the pace of advances in education, which he ascribed to 'these distracted times'. Nevertheless he concluded: 'it may be a satisfaction to our minds, that we have not been wanting to our generation, so farre as God hath enabled us to trace the wayes of doing service to the publick; and that we have not buried our talents in the ground when opportunities have

---

Greaves, *The Puritan Revolution and Educational Thought. Background for Reform* (New Brunswick, New Jersey: Rutgers University Press, 1969), C. Webster, *Samuel Hartlib and the Advancement of Learning* (Cambridge: Cambridge University Press, 1970); R. O'Day, *Education and Society 1500–1800* (Harlow: Longman, 1982); A. McGuer, *Educating the 'Unconstant Rabble'. Arguments for Educational Advancement and Reform during the English Civil War and Interregnum* (Newcastle upon Tyne: Cambridge Scholars Publishing, 2010); A. Beeton, 'Not infected with the venom of the times: the Rump Parliament and Places of Learning, 1649–53', University of Oxford D.Phil. dissertation, 2022, which contains a helpful review of the recent literature, including other sources than those listed above.

17   F. Watson, 'The State and Education during the Commonwealth', *English Historical Review*, 15:47 (1900), p. 61.
18   Dury to 'My Lord', c.August 1645, HP1/8/2A.

been offered to us to employ them.'[19] The following sections attempt a balanced assessment of the diverse range of campaigns for educational betterment that involved Hartlib and those most associated with him, duly taking account of the insurmountable odds to which Dury alluded.

4.3.1 British Comenians

In a response to John Davenport's request for Hartlib's assistance in the development of education in New Haven, Hartlib replied that he had kept the New England leaders fully informed about 'Mr Comenius and his endeavours which I have laboured also to keepe alive these many years'. This, he explained, was an important aspect of his wider programme to promote 'true Reformed Learning and some other profitable means for the good of those most Christian and Heroick Plantations where the Lord hath so graciously pitched your tent.'[20] At Hartlib's request, John Dury amplified this message by outlining where Comenius stood in the development of his programme of educational writings and explaining in detailed terms how the Comenian principles could be applied in New England.[21] The assistance offered to Davenport was of immediate relevance. He was at this date involved in establishing a secondary school in New Haven, and in the supervision of the newly established Harvard College.[22] As a leading architect of the thriving new communities of Massachusetts, education was never far from his thoughts.

As is evident from the previous chapter, Hartlib became the main advocate of Comenius in England, and this was fully appreciated by Comenius who, after his departure from London, remained in touch with Hartlib, supplied him with specimens of his latest writings, and in general kept him well-briefed about progress with his own elaborate writing plans.

In practice Comenius was little mentioned in the work that Hartlib published in the 1640s. A notable exception was a passing reference made in Dury's first outline of the proposed Office of Address for

---

19 Undated letter, Dury to Hartlib, likely the autumn of 1648, published as an appendix to the first edition of *The Reformed School*, but deleted thereafter.
20 Hartlib to John Davenport (NOT John Winthrop), 30 January 1643, HP 7/35/1A-B. See also, Haffemeyer, *Les Lumières radicales*, pp. 97–105.
21 Dury to Davenport, 7 August 1642, HP 6/149A-B.
22 Bremer, *Building a New Jerusalem*, pp. 202–03, 292–93.

Communications, suggesting that the new Agency would: 'help to perfit M. *Comenius* Undertakings, chiefly in the Method of Teaching Languages, Sciences, and of Ordering Schooles for all Ages and Qualities of Scholars'.[23]

Hartlib published only one other work by Comenius, which was an English translation of *Pansophiae diatyposis*. This was a development of the *Pansophiae prodromus*, and written at about the date of the latter's English translation. In some respects the *Diatyposis* is a more lucid statement of the metaphysics of Comenius than the more encyclopaedic *Pansophiae prodromus*. Regardless of its intrinsic merits, *A Patterne of Universal Knowledge* (1651) would have reached only a limited audience and is now a very rare book. The translator was Jeremy Collier, a youngish intruded Fellow of St John's College, Cambridge. His friend, John Hall of the same college, who was already an active translator for Hartlib, seems to have volunteered Collier for this project.[24] Hartlib liked the outcome, among other things because the preface by Collier, and the text itself (p. 172), included flattering praise of Hartlib. Here, Collier also made the first published claim that Comenius was invited to London by the English Parliament.[25]

Hartlib remained in touch with Collier, who went on to teach at the Aldenham Free School, a post that he occupied from 1649 to 1653, when he was dismissed.[26] He obtained other teaching posts, the last being in Ipswich, from which he was dismissed in 1664. Hartlib maintained a good opinion of him, as indicated when he nominated Collier to be the secretary of the putative national Council for Schooling, for which see below.

Concerning the direct reception of Comenius in England during the Commonwealth and Protectorate, Hartlib played little part. In the spring of 1647, two years ahead of its publication, Comenius furnished Hartlib with a manuscript of the *Methodus linguarum novissima* (in

---

23 *Considerations tending to the Happy Accomplishment of Englands Reformation* (1647), p. 47.
24 For Collier, T. Boster, 'Jeremy Collier the Younger, 1650–1726', University of Pittsburgh, Ph.D. dissertation, 2008. For Jeremy Collier the elder (1630–1669), pp. 08–36.
25 *A Patterne of Universal Knowledge* (London: T.H. for Thomas Collins, Northampton, 1651), Thomason E.1304[1], Wing C5527.
26 The Aldenham School, Hertfordshire, was established in 1597 and still exists, now as a prep. school.

Czech, *Didaktika analytická*), which resides in the Hartlib Papers. Hartlib and his friends displayed little interest in this important work. It seems that Hartlib made no effort to publish a translation of this development of the *Didactica magna*, nor the *Didactica magna* itself, the existence of which he had known about since the early 1630s. The author supplied him with the complete text in 1638, which is presumably the copy that is located in the Hartlib Papers.

As a mitigating factor in the Comenius story, it must be mentioned that Hartlib was a serious patron of Cyprian Kinner (c.1600–1649), who had briefly worked for Comenius, in whose educational writings he continued to be critically engaged. Kinner and Hartlib had been friends since their schooldays. They conducted an intense and revealing correspondence from June 1646 until Kinner's death, which occurred during his short and tragic visit to London. He seems to have arrived in January, and was dead by the end of April 1649. We possess little information about this visit, but Dury wrote a note of introduction for him in late February 1649: 'The Bearer heerof Cyprian Kinner, Dr. of the Civill law & of Phisick beeing a man of very eminent parts for Godlines & Uniuersall Learning, & now called upon to improove his extraordinary Talent & Abilities for the Reformation of Schooles & Education of Children'.[27]

Ahead of Kinner's visit, Hartlib arranged for a translation of his *Diatyposis*, which was a self-conscious attempt to adjust the educational programme of Comenius.[28] After Kinner's death, Hartlib prepared for further publications built on Kinner's unpublished work, but nothing of this materialised. As indicated by a petulant letter from Dury to Hartlib, published as an appendix to the first edition of his *Reformed School*, Kinner was not entirely forgotten. Since Dury was wounded by rumours that his own book plagiarised Kinner, he felt the need to point out that good ideas often occur simultaneously to more than one person.

A further missed opportunity with respect to Comenius related to his famous *Orbis sensualism pictus*, the early development of which

---

27 Dury to Oliver St John, 26 February 1649, HP 4/1/23B, as edited by Hartlib.
28 *A continuation of Mr. John-Amos-Comenius school-endeavours, or, A summary delineation of Dr. Cyprian Kinner Silesian, his thoughts concerning education... translated out of the original Latine, transmitted to Sam. Hartlib, and by him published* (London: for R.L., 1648).

was known to Hartlib. Constituting an item of special history of the book importance, Hartlib's papers contain a sixteen-page proof copy of an excerpt of this text, as it was printed in Sárospatak in 1653, which contains a title page, preface, associated text and a set of associated woodcut illustrations.[29]

Further helpful evidence is a list of schoolbooks sent by Comenius to Hartlib informing him of titles that would be reissued in Nuremberg. The final part of this list, dating from February 1656, that is, shortly before the destruction of Leszno and exile of Comenius, included only three items, one of which was the 'Lucidarium. sive Orbis Sensualium pictus cum Figuris 4o. [pp.]160'.[30] The first complete edition of *Orbis pictus* was the German/Latin version published in Nuremberg in 1658. The second edition seems to be Charles Hoole's English/Latin version, which appeared in 1659. This was a remarkable scoop for Hoole, with which Hartlib was not involved.

Unsurprisingly, Hoole was known to Hartlib, who noted in 1656: 'The 20 of May one Paul or Hoole [Charles Hoole] that hase lived some years in Mr Bals [Thomas Ball] of Northampton house came the first time to mee being most zealous for Reformation of Schooles or a Schoole of Teachers counting it one of the greatest works to bee intended in a National Reformation'.[31]

Charles Hoole (1610–1667) was one of the most successful teachers and educationalists of this period. After a varied career in the North, he returned to London in about 1646, after which he built up a career as a private school teacher. At the date of his meeting with Hartlib, he ran a school at Token House Green, Lothbury. His principal educational writing was *A New Discovery of the Old Art of Teaching School* (1660), which is one of the most important British educational writings of the century. The *New Discovery* was overlooked by Hartlib, as was Hoole's English translation of Comenius's *Orbis sensualium pictus* (1659).[32]

---

29 HP 7/106/1A-8B. At this stage the title was *Vestibuli et Januae Linguarum Lucidarium*. For a thorough assessment of this proof, G.H. Turnbull, 'An Incomplete Orbis Pictus of Comenius printed in 1653', *Acta Comeniana*, 1:2 (1957), 35–52.
30 HP 7/65/2A.
31 Ephemerides 1656, HP 29/5/7/2B.
32 J. Gianoutsos, 'A New Discovery of Charles Hoole: Method and Practice in Seventeenth-Century English Education', *History of Education*, 48:1 (2019), 01–18.

Of similar importance to Hoole, is Hezekiah Woodward (1591/2–1675), author of the seminal *A Childes Patrimony* (1640) and *A Light to Grammar* (1641). As Mark Greengrass points out, it remains the case that Woodward's significance as an educationalist remains insufficiently recognised.[33] Part of the blame for this neglect of Woodward lies with Hartlib, which it is difficult to comprehend. He knew Woodward extremely well. Their links extended back to Hartlib's early days in London. It is likely that Woodward was on the sidelines of the debates between Webbe and Brookes. Hartlib and Woodward corresponded over a long period, yet Woodward's writings on education never featured in their letters or elsewhere in the Hartlib Papers. Yet Hartlib followed Woodward's career closely. He must have known that Woodward had taught at the Free School, Southwark, and then privately, also in London for several years, before serving as the vicar of Bray, Berks., from 1649 until 1660, the date of his ejection. The closeness of their relations and the generosity of Woodward were both evident when he sought Hartlib's assistance over the promotion of his former usher:

> Mr Archer, I think, you know, for to be my usher; he is now preferred to the free schoole in Northampton; Truely I persuade myself, hee will be a blessing to the town and place both. My desire is that you would write to Mr Ball minister of chief note there, that he might have what encouragement Mr Ball could be a meanes to gaine him for the town. Surely, Sir, you may adde this one Word more, That you have some reason to think that his way of teaching etc. etc. Mr Archer understands, that Mr Ball has a high esteeme of you, which moved me to entreat a word to him on his behalf.[34]

Ball was indeed a close friend of Hartlib and this plan evidently worked. Ferdinand Archer, formerly usher at the Free School, Southwark, is noted by Venn as being appointed the headmaster of Northampton School in 1647.[35]

---

33 *ODNB* Hezekiah Woodward (Mark Greengrass); M. Smoluk, 'Hezekiah Woodward', in *1st International Interdisciplinary Conference, 2013, Proceedings,* pp. 584–88.

34 Hezekiah Woodward to Hartlib, 1 March 1647, HP 34/1/5A.

35 The Northampton Free School was founded in 1541. It is now the Northampton School for Boys.

At this point it is also necessary to draw attention to Hartlib's neglect of Thomas Horne, Woodward's son-in-law and a further underestimated educationalist who captured Hartlib's interest between 1630 and 1635, but thereafter was lost from view. Hartlib therefore failed to observe that Horne translated Bathe's *Janua* in 1634 and the *Janua linguarum reserata* of Comenius in 1636, or indeed Horne's later educational activities and publications, which amounted to a considerable achievement before his premature death in 1654.[36]

Horne's attention to Comenius was prompted by the action of Jean Anchoran, a minister of Huguenot origin who toured widely in northern Europe in the early thirties. It seems that Anchoran spent much time in Danzig between 1630 and 1633. Evidently, he learned of the existence of the *Janua linguarum reserata*, and persuaded Comenius to give him access to the text, perhaps even before it was published. This enabled Anchoran to prepare a parallel Latin/English/French edition, which was published in London only three months after the first edition, which Comenius published in Leszno in 1631. Anchoran's was therefore the second edition of the *Janua* and the first vernacular translation. This was a major commercial success, which called for a series of further reissues over the next few decades. To the anguish of Comenius, absolutely nothing of the promised profit was paid to him. The injury was worsened by Anchoran's adoption of a different title and by his artful failure to disclose that Comenius was the author.

For good reason, seemingly unknown to Hartlib, Thomas Horne was dissatisfied with Anchoran's effort and decided to produce a rival version which was published in 1636.[37] Although attracting much less attention than Anchoran, Horne's edition was original, more comprehensive and superior to Anchoran's in every respect. The *Janua linguarum reserata* market was therefore a very packed field in which no fewer than fourteen editions were issued between 1631 and 1662.[38]

---

36 G.M. Boswell, 'Thomas Horne (1608–1654)', in *British Rhetoricians and Logicians, 1500–1660: Second Series*, ed. by E.A. Malone, vol. 281 (Detroit, Michigan: Gale, 2003), pp. 145–53.

37 *Janua linguarum reserata, or a seed-plot of languages and sciences* (London: printed by Robert Young, sold by Thomas Slater, 1636), STC 15077.3.

38 For a comprehensive review, D.F. Cram and J. Maat, 'Comenius, Dalgarno and the English Translations of the *Janua linguarum*', *Studia Comeniana et Historica*, 26 (1996), 148–60.

Neither the Anchoran nor the Horne editions of the *Janua* seem to have attracted much attention from Hartlib.

Also overlooked by Hartlib as an educational writer was Henry Robinson (1604–1673?), who was first noticed by Hartlib in 1641. In 1642 Robinson told Hartlib about a Kentish doctor who was an admirer of Comenius and wanted to be in touch with him.[39] Robinson and Hartlib were in active contact at least until 1653. Their main common interest was the Office of Address and the Land Bank. As Calafat has recently noted, 'Henry Robinson's writings and pamphlets offer a rare mix of works by a London merchant interested in tolerance, trade, economy, social reforms, law, education and politics.'[40] Perhaps inspired by the deficiencies of Dury's *Reformed School*, Robinson called for a system of free schools throughout England, where all children, both boys and girls, would be taught up to the age of university entry by properly remunerated teachers and writing masters. He was insistent that each student should receive at least one hour a day of individual tuition. Robinson further insisted that schools should be within easy walking distance from the children's homes. His most original idea was that all children should be taught to swim.[41]

4.3.2 The Hartlibian Educational Cohort

John Milton

In view of the shortcomings discussed above, the question naturally arises, which of the education writings of this period were associated in some way with Samuel Hartlib? Of the many candidates, John Milton's *Of Education* (June 1644) is by far the most noted. This guaranteed a permanent presence for Hartlib in the history of English literature. Hartlib himself seemed to be oblivious of his good fortune. The eight-page letter addressed to Hartlib by Milton was a primitive little

---

39 Ephemerides 1642, HP 30/34B-35A.
40 G. Calafat, 'For a "Livorno-on-Thames": the Tuscan Model in the Writings of Henry Robinson (1604–1673?)', *The Seventeenth Century*, 37:4 (2022), 01–30, p. 01.
41 Henry Robinson, *Certain proposalls in order to the peoples freedom and accommodation* (London: M. Simmons, 1652), pp. 24–26, Wing R1670.

pamphlet, issued without the name of a publisher or a date.[42] With good reason it is assumed that Hartlib was the publisher, while the pamphlet was most likely produced by Thomas Underhill, a stationer who had been employed by Hartlib a few months earlier to generate an edition of a letter of similar proportions by John Dury.[43]

Milton's tract has rightly been endowed with literary importance, and the case has been made for its influence on associates of Hartlib. However, at the date of its publication, the letter seems to have generated little interest among Hartlib's correspondents. *Of Education* was sent by Hartlib to Dury and Culpeper. Each acknowledged it in a few words and without enthusiasm. On the positive side, John Hall was a Milton enthusiast and certainly had Milton very much in mind when he composed his *Humble Motion* in 1649.[44] Dury's *Reformed School* of 1650 was also clearly influenced by Milton's *Letter*. It is likely that the liberally minded Hartlib would also have welcomed Milton's study and he would not have been disconcerted by the refusal of Milton to follow the austere path of the German didactics. On the basis of his curiosity about Sir Francis Kynaston's academy and other academies reflecting the French model, Hartlib welcomed other propositions of the same kind. But it is likely that the models uppermost in Hartlib's mind were the academies that he had personally experienced in Silesia, which proved beyond doubt that a rewarding humanistic education could be imparted without recourse to any of the stifling conventions applying in universities.[45] It is therefore reasonable to suspect that Hartlib's own failed academy in Chichester or the one that he evolved in early 1646

---

42 John Milton, *Of Education. To Master Samuel Hartlib* [1644], Thomason E.50 [12], Wing M2132. p. 1 is inscribed by Thomason, 'By Mr John Milton 5 June 1644'. *Of Education* comprises eight densely printed pages, amounting to about 8,000 words.

43 Dury, *Letter to Lord Forbes on the Necessity of a Common Confession of Faith*, dated by Thomason 15 November 1643.

44 For recent studies relevant to Hartlib, T. Raylor, 'Milton, the Hartlib Circle, and the Education of the Aristocracy', in *The Oxford Handbook of Milton*, ed. by N. McDowell and N. Smith (Oxford: Oxford University Press, 2011), pp. 382–406; A. Bromley 'The Impact of Milton's *Of Education* on the Hartlib Circle's Understanding of Public and Private', *The Seventeenth Century*, 39:2 (2024), 241–60. See also Haffemeyer, *Les Lumières radicales*, pp. 105–09, for the academy of Balthazar Gerbier.

45 As indicated by Hartlib's reference to the objectives of his 'Illustre Collegium', he modelled himself on Melchior Lauban, the Rector of the Brieg academy, whom he admired for his general public spiritedness and commitment to good relations between the various religious denominations. Hartlib also remembered sending

would not have been much different from Milton's own private academy or its ideal representation outlined in *Of Education*.⁴⁶

John Dury

Milton was not mentioned in the reading list drawn up by Jeremy Collier, John Hall's particular friend. This list emanated from the energetic and successful schoolmaster from Hitchin, Hertfordshire named Joseph Kempe, who deserves to be better-known.

Hartlib recounted that Kempe, who was 'Mr [Jeremy] Colliers acquaintance, the 14. of April began to impart to him [Dury's] *Reformed Schoole, Library keeper, Discourse of Agency of Learning* and W. Petty's *Advice*. Hee hath a very great schoole and 30. or 40. borders, is very ingenuous but cannot have much time to helpe the advancement of Learning'.⁴⁷

Joseph Kempe was clearly absorbed in recent writings by John Dury, particularly *The Reformed School* in its 1651 second edition, which also contained *The Reformed Librarie Keeper* and Pell's *An Idea of Mathematicks*. The *Discourse of Agency of Learning* was likely to have been the second part of Dury's *Seasonable Discourse* of 1649, the first part of which was in some respects a preamble to the much awaited *The Reformed School*.

Hartlib had been calling on Dury to publish his essays on education since about 1630. Dury made many positive gestures, but education was repeatedly sacrificed owing to inclement circumstances or other priorities. A more realistic occasion only arrived after Dury's return to England in 1645, when, with some prompting from Hartlib, the opportunity for educational writing returned to the agenda. In April and May 1646, Dury displayed enthusiasm for writing on education for the nobility and elaborating his views on academies. A practical

---

Lauban the texts of four unpublished writings by John Dury. Letter of Hartlib to unnamed recipient, 22 October 1632, *MGP* 26, pp. 24–28.

46 Especially relevant at this point are two sketches for academies by Hartlib dating from about 1646, one headed 'Opera Parliamenta Academy' (HP 47/9/1A-6B) and the other 'Mr. Milton Academie' (crossed out), and substituted 'Mr. Lawrence Academie' (HP 47/9/34A-36A).

47 Ephemerides 1651, HP 28/2/14B. Kempe was a Cambridge graduate who, in about 1635, established a boarding school at 'The Biggin,' a manor house in Queen Street, Hitchin, Herts, formerly a house of the Gilbertine order. Many Cambridge students studied under Kempe, who died prematurely in 1654.

demonstration of his thinking in this sphere was provided by his 'advices' prepared as guidance for a young student about to enter Oxford with the goal of entering the ministry.[48]

There were plenty of other diversions for Hartlib and Dury, including a sudden impulse to reform the Bodleian Library and install Hartlib, perhaps in conjunction with Dury, as the new Library Keeper.[49] The Hartlib Papers give little insight into the progress of Dury's educational writings. The letters comprising *The Reformed Librarie-Keeper* date from 1646.[50] Perhaps originating from the spring of 1649, in the course of his ruminations about a Kinner festschrift, Hartlib drew up two relevant lists relating to education: the first was a list of Dury's early writings in Latin, the second outlined various recent items in English, which included 'The directory of Boyes et Girles; The directory of Logick to his Children. Ioh. Pelli Idea. Math.'. This latter list describes the content of Dury's *The Reformed School*, except that the directory for girls was absent, which is a glaring omission.[51] This evidence confirms that, as is self-evident, *The Reformed School* is an artificial compilation of essays that are not organically related. It must also have been apparent to the informed reader that *The Reformed School*, as it was published in mid-1650, offered little that was not already contained in the ample literature on the education of the nobility, of course including Milton's *Of Education*.[52]

We possess no insights into Kempe's response to Dury's writings but, from the little available evidence, it is difficult to dissent from Dury's editor's conclusion that 'Dury's work does not appear to have exerted a

---

48 HP 68/4/2A-4A. The recipient was Smart, perhaps the John Smart, who matriculated in 1648 and remained in Oxford until his death in 1666.
49 C.J. Minter, 'John Dury's Reformed Librarie-Keeper: Information and its Intellectual Contexts in Seventeenth-Century England', *Library & Information History*, 31:1 (2015), 18–34.
50 Dury, *The reformed Librarie-keeper* (London: 1650), Wing D2882.
51 This omission must relate to 'Of the Education of Girls' by Dorothy Dury, BL Sloane MS 649, fols. 203–05, first published in Turnbull *HDC*, pp. 120–21. For a fairly positive account of *The Reformed School* and Dury's approach to the education of girls, McGuer, *Educating the 'Unconstant Rabble'*, pp. 134–37. On Dury, also positive, is S. Sohma,'A Consideration of the School Class Arrangement Devised by John Dury', *Studies in the Humanities and Sciences*, 39:1 (1998), 117–37; W.A.L. Vincent, *The State and School Education*, p. 80, devotes only a few sentences to *The Reformed School*.
52 John Dury, *The Reformed School* (London: Printed by R.D. for Richard Wodnothe, n.d.) Wing D2883. Opinion is divided on the publication date, but 1650 seems the more likely.

marked influence, even in its day'.[53] I have located only two responses to Dury's book in the Hartlib Papers. The first is a letter written by Heinrich Appelius, Dury's brother-in-law, who makes only the briefest observations, but he was emphatic that 'I see not yet what to adde to my brother Duries reformed schoole: onely this is for the learned, but what course is to bee taken with all the schooles in everie cittie & village?' He adds with respect to teachers in local schools, the only relevant 'Receipt' was 'Give wages, we get workers'. As a consequence of such observed shortcomings, it is no surprise that Dury desisted from further publication in the field of education. The second response emanated from William Rand who, at length, expressed disagreement with Dury's catechetical bias, which Rand believed represented an unacceptably sacerdotalist approach towards education. [54]

Hartlib was presented with a promising opportunity for action to advance education by the convening of the Committee for the Advancement of Learning by the Nominated Assembly. This committee was in existence between July and December 1653.[55] As noted above, the committee was strongly biased in Hartlib's favour, while his friend Francis Rous was Speaker of that Parliament.[56] It is clear that the lengthy draft 'Some Proposalls towards the Advancement of Learning' was specifically designed for this occasion. The author was certainly Dury, who no doubt believed that he was acting as the spokesperson for the Hartlib group as a whole. His twenty-two-page memorandum was in reality a repackaging of *The Reformed School*, lacking in all the basic presentational characteristics of a properly constituted parliamentary paper.[57] It was not therefore the basis for any practical outcome. Unsurprisingly, 'Some Proposalls' vanished from sight, leaving almost no mark in the Hartlib Papers,

---

53   *The Reformed School by John Dury*, ed. by H.M. Knox (Liverpool: Liverpool University Press, 1958), p. 10.
54   The first recipient was Heinrich Appelius: Appelius to Hartlib, 23 August 1650, HP 45/1/43A; the second was William Rand: Rand to Hartlib, 18 July 1651, HP 62/30/1B-3B. The third was William Hamilton, who acknowledged, but offered no comment, Hamilton to Hartlib, 22 July 1650, HP 9/11/21A.
55   *Journal of the House of Commons*: vol. 7, 1651–1660 (London, 1802), 20/21 July 1653, p. 287, for the establishment of this committee and the nomination of its 14 members.
56   In 1654 Hartlib dedicated to Rous his *The True and Readie Way to Learn the Latin Tongue*.
57   For the text of 'Some Proposalls', Webster, *Samuel Hartlib*, pp. 165–92; McGuer, *Educating the 'Unconstant Rabble'*, pp. 150–55 for a more positive assessment.

which is a pity considering that the timing was opportune. Everything seemed in order to achieve at least a modicum of advance in the field of educational reform. However, the relevant committee left no trace of its existence and no such occasion presented itself again during the tenure of the Parliamentary regime.

William Petty

Compared with Dury's dry and pedantic exercises, Joseph Kempe would have judged William Petty's *Advice* to be a positive inspiration.[58] This, his first proper publication marked the young Petty as the man of the future. Samuel Hartlib, as the dedicatee, thereby added a little more to his own place in history. Petty graciously acknowledged the help of Hartlib by devoting the opening pages to publicising the Office of Address.

As was recounted by Petty himself, his purpose was:

> To provide for Poore, advance trade and make all manufactures flourish, England should bee endeavoured to bee made the shop of Europe and it with other Countries the Markets. To doe this All Trades and Workmen should bee encouraged and all manner of compendious ways invented wherby they may come to undersel the Manufactores and commodities of all other Countrys. This would bee better then to strengthen their monopolizing Corporations in ignorance and idlness.[59]

This programme placed Petty's advice in perfect alignment with Worsley's economic development schemes, as already outlined in 'Proffits humbly presented to this Kingdome', or thereafter, as demonstrated in the following section of this study dealing with 'The Thirst for Betterment'. Petty's originality lay in his delineation of a comprehensive educational programme designed to support these economic objectives.

---

58   THE ADVICE OF W.P TO Mr. SAMUEL HARTLIB. For the Advancement of some particular Parts of LEARNING (LONDON: 1648)—with a preprint dated 1647. Wing P1914A, preface signed 8 January 1648. Webster *Instauration*, pp. 70, 81–85 et passim; McCormick *Petty*, pp. 66–74, 85–86, 109. *ODNB* Petty makes no reference to the *Advice*. See also Haffemeyer, *Les Lumières radicales*, pp. 92–96.

59   Ephemerides, c.April 1649, HP 28/1/14B.

In line with the radical tone of his advisory platform, Petty could not resist characterising the targets that his *Advice* would extinguish: 'There would not then be so many Fustian and Unworthy Preachers in Divinity, so many pettifoggers in the Law, so many Quack-salvers in Physick, so many Grammaticasters in Country-schooles, and so many Lazy-serving men in Gentlemens houses, when every man might learne to live otherwise in more plenty and honour'.[60]

At the date of its publication Petty's *Advice* was virtually unnoticed among Hartlib's correspondents, who tended to be focused on Petty as an inventor. However, there were notable exceptions, as for instance Myles Symner, who expressed himself most vigorously in support of Petty in a letter to Sir Robert King, the brother of Dorothy Dury. In Petty's plans he detected an ideal model for deflecting youth away from the universities, which he denounced at length for the sterility of their culture.[61] Much the same attitude was expressed somewhat later by Robert Wood, who was Symner's close friend. He rejected the obsession with the teaching of languages as an 'unpracticable chimæra', but the idea of 'Colleges of Artificers I thinke might be of excellent use & might perhaps be a meanes & make way for the History of Trades... after the way of natural Historie, which would in my opinion prove the most desirable worke I can thinke upon for schooles'. Wood wanted such objectives to be supported by legislation, with parliamentary Commissioners charged with enforcement. He added 'that many Grammar schooles... do more hurt then good to the Commonwealth, as well as to many of those scholars that are brought up in them'.[62] As indicated below, Petty's ideas were also very much in Hartlib's mind when he formulated his plan for a Council for Schooling. As witnessed by their intimate correspondence, in the course of which Hartlib was assisting Petty to secure a post in Oxford, Petty's warm relations with Hartlib continued after the publication of the *Advice*.[63]

---

60 Petty, *Advice*, p. 13.
61 Myles Symner to Sir Robert King [1648], HP 47/6/1A-B.
62 Wood to Hartlib, 14 October 1657, HP 33/1/7A.
63 See especially a testimonial from Dury and Hartlib to the Committee of Parliament for the regulation of the Universities, 16 August 1650, Osborn Collection, Yale, Document 8.

Samuel Harmar

Another innovative figure in Hartlib's orbit was Samuel Harmar. Hartlib brought him to the attention of Lady Ranelagh, who was immediately impressed. Thereafter she carefully followed the progress of his work. When mentioned at all, Harmar tends to be known on account of his pamphlet, *Vox Populi, or, Glostershere's Desire* (1642), which establishes him as a pioneer of tax-funded education for the poorer classes, albeit just for Gloucestershire, but it is assumed that he aspired to more extensive employment of his proposals. Until now this has been entirely a matter of conjecture.[64]

Lady Ranelagh and Hartlib help us to settle this issue. Her letters to Hartlib make it clear that Harmar was working for the realisation of his scheme in London, but also, she hoped that this would set a precedent for more universal application. Hartlib's replies to the Ranelagh letters are not available, but at precisely this date he noted that Harmar had observed that: 'My Lord Mayor hath a desire that every ward (25. there bee) of London may erect and maintaine a Charity schoole and Good Men and women to bee Instructors of the said Poore Children of both sexes. We crave your prayers for the prosperity of it, that Christ's kingdom in little ones may more and more bee advanced'.[65]

Various other relevant references to Harmar occur in Hartlib's papers, in all about twenty covering the period 1645–1658. Many of these relate to poor relief and therefore often also to education. Both Harmar and Hartlib cherished high hopes for the London Corporation for the Poor established in 1649, which both of them canvassed as a vehicle for the education of the poor.[66] They harboured positive expectations about the wealthy William Pennoyer (1603–1670), who was an Assistant in the Corporation for the Poor. Hartlib's assessment of Pennoyer was fully justified, as confirmed by his will, which in 1670 disbursed considerable sums on the welfare of the poor, especially with respect to education, as

---

64 F. Watson, 'The State and Education', *English Historical Review*, 15:57 (1900), pp. 63–64; M. James, *Social Policy*, pp. 315, 318–20; Vincent, *The State and School Education*, pp. 19–20, 31–34, 36, 84, 91; *ODNB* Samuel Harmar (R.L. Greaves), Webster, *Instauration*, pp. 208–10. Harmar is overlooked by Turnbull *HDC*.

65 Lady Ranelagh to Hartlib, 3 November and 31 December 1656, HP 35/2/56B and 57A. Ephemerides 1657, 29/6/20B.

66 It is noticeable that in Hartlib's well-known pamphlets on Poor Law reform, although education features in his titles, the texts contain little on this subject.

is still conspicuously memorialised by the Pennoyer Centre at Pulham St Mary in Norfolk. Besides the Pulham school, Pennoyer endowed schools in Whitechapel and Hay-on-Wye, Herefordshire where he was born, as well as scholarships at Harvard College.[67]

Hartlib's observations on individual schools and teachers litter the pages of the Ephemerides. Some of these instances, like Martin Holbeach (Holbeck) of Felsted are well remembered.[68] With respect to others, such as Joseph Kempe of Hitchin, Hartlib's single entry in the Ephemerides seems to comprise the main source of information about their activities.

4.3.3 Higher Education and Training

Although actively concerned with reforming the two English universities and favourable to university expansion, Hartlib was even more engrossed in collecting information about projects for specialised institutions designed for the training of teachers, facilitating the collective working of skilled artisans, or the training of their apprentices. Hardly anything was achieved, yet he never tired of recording the work of the colourful innovators who evolved these novel schemes.

A Ministry of Education

As noted above, as early as 1642, Samuel Harmar advocated systematic expansion of education on the basis of administrative counties. Hartlib, and later Lady Ranelagh, became Harmar's allies when he shifted his campaign to London. In 1646, Joshua Rawlin, in connection with his supportive remarks about the educational work of Hartlib and Comenius, noted that there was in circulation the idea of an 'Association of Ministers and others' in every county, which should assume a variety of functions, including the examination and regulation of all teachers in grammar schools.[69] No doubt this idea was again in mind when, in

---

67 H. Clutten, *School's out a History of Pennoyers School and its benefactor, William Pennoyer* (self-published,1994).
68 It was noted that Hartlib's friend, Moses Wall, was allied with Holbeck by marriage, Ephemerides, c.May 1649, HP 28/1/15B.
69 Joshua Rawlin to Hartlib, 9 February 1646, HP 10/10/1A.

1648, a group of leading local Puritans met in Maidstone to discuss the granting of state support for Hartlib and his public service projects.[70]

On 3 April 1649 Hartlib noted that Dr [John] Bathurst had outlined a plan for a state-controlled and tax-funded body responsible for the training and regulation of all teachers.[71] Bathurst was a figure of status at this date, and he was also a physician to Cromwell. He endowed two schools in his home county of Yorkshire, the statutes of which specifically mentioned the importance of practical mathematics.[72] A similar idea emanated from George Snel, also in 1649, and at a nearby date of 30 June.[73] Given that Snel provided greater detail, it is quite likely that Bathurst and Snel were talking about the same proposition and that this originated with Snel rather than Bathurst. Snel more ambitiously envisaged a kind of Ministry of Education 'that should superintend the Schooles and Education throughout the whole kingdom'. This would not only regulate teachers, but also establish a system of 'rural colledges in every county towne or city' which would 'teach or learne nothing but that which is useful', specifically 'all Arts, Sciences and faculties in the mother tongue etc. with the Art of Husbandry, Health etc. etc.'. Snel's utilitarian scheme of education had much in common with Petty's *Advice*, but Snel was a much older man and seems to have devised his plans quite separately. His views were publicised in a short, rather eccentric tract, which was no match for Petty's rival presentation.[74]

It is quite likely that Hartlib's meetings with Bathurst and Snel, as well as his association with Rawlin and Petty, helped to ignite Hartlib's plan for a Council for Schooling. One puzzle about this little-noticed idea is its dating, which is not indicated in the document. For various reasons I favour the latter part of 1649. It is striking that both Bathurst and Snel figure prominently in the document. Both are named at the head of the document where, emphatically, Hartlib instructs that 'Dr.

---

70 Joshua Rawlin to Hartlib, 15 May 1648, HP 10/10/7A.
71 Ephemerides 1649, 28/1/14A.
72 Webster *Instauration*, pp. 211, 216–17, 296, 318.
73 Ephemerides 1649, HP 28/1/23B-24B. George Snel (c.1581–1656) from Fremington, Devon, attended St John's College, Cambridge, where he became a fellow. Then a D.D. from St Andrews, followed by a clerical career in Chester, but in 1645 he was deprived of his living, after which he became a private tutor in London. His brother was a London goldsmith.
74 George Snel, *The Right Teaching of Useful Knowledge* (London: William Dugard, 1649), 22 pages. Thomason E.1377[3], Wing S4393A.

Snel to bee one of the Council', and reports that Dr Bathurst's unnamed benefactor would endow this Council with £1000, in return for which the Council would be expected to subsidise Cressy Dymock's work on the betterment of husbandry (by which was probably meant the training of husbandry workers).

The presiding eight-member Schooling Council included Dury, Nedham and Pell, and these reappeared among the Commissioners. Petty figured among the Councillors, but was not a Commissioner.[75] The eight names listed as 'Commissioners for the Act of the Council for Schooling' were, in order: John Dury, John Pell, William Rand, Georg Horn, Christian Rave, Marchamont Nedham, John Milton and Jeremy Collier (secretary).[76] All of the names on this list were directly associated with Hartlib, and each possessed a proven record of involvement in education. The least known in this context was William Rand, but his suitability would not have been questioned. His first letters to Hartlib notably expressed dissatisfaction with the education on offer at Cambridge. His views on reform were similar to those expressed by John Hall in 1649. As a friend of Joshua Rawlin, Rand would also have been familiar with the ideas in circulation about the formation of a better administrative system for all segments of the school system.

Inclusion in this list of Rand, the historian Georg Horn and the orientalist Christian Rave, all of whom were resident abroad at this date, suggests that the Council for Schooling would operate in tandem with the projected Agency for the Advancement of Universal Learning, which was explicitly mentioned at the head of the Council of Schooling document. As described in the next chapter, the development of schooling was at first accepted as a function associated with the proposed Agency for Learning, but this idea was gradually abandoned.

In the course of the 1650s, none of the various plans for a radical extension of opportunities for children's education came to fruition.

---

[75] A surprise name among the Councillors is Sir Francis Nethersole (1587–1650), which is the only reference to him in the Hartlib Papers. In 1638 Nethersole founded a school at Polesworth, Warwickshire, for poor children of both sexes, which was endowed in 1655. Hartlib may well have known Nethersole on account of his relations with Elizabeth of Bohemia. For Nethersole, see Akkerman, *Elizabeth Stuart*, pp. 127, 143 et passim.

[76] In case of doubt concerning Nedham, McGuer, *Educating the 'Unconstant Rabble'*, pp. 186–90 et passim. For Nedham, also Haffemeyer, *Les Lumières radicales*, pp. 300–04 et passim.

However, idealists such as Lady Ranelagh never lost heart. Even in the troubled atmosphere of January 1659 she noted:

> I do indeed expect a meeting here this afternoon of the two good men you mention, (she means Mr. Wood & Mr. Potter) and my brother Boyle, & another ingenious person [Worsley or Petty?], in order to the carrying on of that work (education of children) which tho' it may seem small & contemptible to those who judge according to appearance, cannot but be esteemed truly great by those who are assisted to judge righteous judgment. [77]

Training Colleges

As just indicated, Cressy Dymock was much in Hartlib's mind when framing his Council for Schooling. Dymock was not only a husbandry improver; he also proposed to establish a training college specifically for husbandry, a scheme that would have met with the approval of George Snel. Hartlib viewed this idea as sufficiently weighty to merit a separate publication containing a preface by Hartlib himself.[78]

Many of the plans that evolved were realisable as technical workshops, but as educational institutions such ideas tended to be vague and impracticable, as for instance in 1654 when Hartlib told Boyle that John Trenchard M.P., a friend of Hartlib, was transferring his Vauxhall property to Edward Somerset, the second Marquess of Worcester (1601–1667), to house Caspar Kalthoff (1606–1664) and his son, expecting that this would also pave the way for a college of artisans. Hartlib hoped that this project might also involve Cressy Dymock, 'though I had rather he should superintend a college of husbandmen whensoever it can be founded'. [79]

On a completely different front, John Dury solicited further information about a 'Reformed Colledge in which Mr Rushworth [presumably the influential lawyer and politician, John Rushworth] hath a hand'.[80] This prompted Dury to contemplate the future career

---

77 Letter of Lady Ranelagh quoted in Hartlib to Worthington, 30 January 1659, Crossley I, p. 166.
78 Cressy Dymock, *An essay for the advancement of husbandry learning, or propositions for erecting [a] Colledge of Husbandry*, 1651, Wing H985A/D2970A.
79 Hartlib to Boyle, 8 May 1654, Boyle *Correspondence* I, pp. 178–79. At this date John Pell was serving as a diplomat in Zurich.
80 For John Rushworth, Haffemeyer, *Les Lumières radicales*, pp. 144, 229 et passim.

of John Pell, listed above as a member of the projected Council for Schooling, who already had spent nearly a decade as a successful lecturer in mathematics in Amsterdam and Breda: 'I wish Mr. Pell were the head of a Colledge. I believe hee would doe well therin, although I think hee would doe as well in a New plantation with his Mathematicall & naturall & Politicall abilities, for hee hath a complication of all these together in a setled iudgment & well-ordered affections towards God'.[81] The conviction that the best prospects for the furtherance of education lay, not in England, but in New England, is consistent with advice given by Hartlib and Dury to John Davenport of New Haven, as cited at the head of this chapter.

The New College at Durham[82]

The significance of this initiative has long been recognised and the course of its history is by no means obscure, as for instance witnessed by C.E. Whiting's history of the University of Durham published in 1932. Yet, even recent standard sources of reference continue to ignore the existence of this institution, as for instance when it was concluded that 'The history of the college is obscure, and the patent may never have been put into effect'.[83] In practice, as indicated below, the Durham scheme was well thought out, implemented on a realistic basis and it included some capable staff, who advanced the scheme stepwise until it suddenly ground to a halt in the chaos surrounding the collapse of the Republic.

Sustained local pressure for such an establishment began in 1650. Cromwell's instinct to break the Oxford and Cambridge monopoly and favour an innovative and practical alternative might well have been accelerated by his association with John Hall, Hartlib's young associate, who was at this date a member of Cromwell's staff. Hence, Cromwell

---

81   Dury to Hartlib, 6 November 1655, HP 4/3/128A. Malcolm/ Stedall, *John Pell*, chapter 4.

82   Webster *Instauration*, pp. 233–38; for the earlier literature p. 233, note 446, the most relevant to Hartlib and his papers being G.H. Turnbull, 'Oliver Cromwell's College at Durham', *Durham Research Review*, 3 (1952), 01–07. See also A. Green, 'The First Durham University', *Symeon*, Issue 8 (2018), pp. 06–09 for a helpfully illustrated account.

83   M. Burden, *A Biographical Dictionary of Tutors at the Dissenters' Private Academies, 1660–1729* (London: Dr. Williams's Centre for Dissenting Studies, 2013), p. 196; similarly, Aylmer, *The State's Servants*, p. 317.

might well have been alert at this date to Hall's *Humble Motion* of 1649, and perhaps even the draft of his follow-up attack on the College of Physicians of London, which was published in 1652.[84] Hall might also have played some part in the composition of two relevant letters from Cromwell to Speaker Lenthall. The first was written immediately after the Battle of Dunbar, calling on Parliament to embark on the path of improvement, with the priority of correcting 'the abuses of all professions'. The second, written in Edinburgh a few months later, instructed the executive to set in motion a plan for converting the Deans and Chapter estates in Durham into a 'College or School for all the Sciences and Literature'.[85] During the pitifully slow process of implementing Cromwell's orders concerning Durham, he and his agents would also have become familiar with the veritable flood of further manifestoes demanding the reform of Oxford and Cambridge, perhaps the most notorious of which was John Webster's *Academiarum Examen* (1654).[86]

Possibly in response to this pressure for change, Ezerel Tong called on Samuel Hartlib:

> The 2. of January came the first time to my house the Minister in Kent [Ezerel Tong] and one that should bee Master of a College. Hee desired the foundation of a Mechanical schoole and acquainted mee with the whole designe of founding a College of Sciences with several schooles and a library a[nd] worke-house in Durham.[87]

Hartlib went on to describe Tong as:

> a right Agitator for Learning and Mechanicks to employ the Printesses when they are in their shops, to better purposes then to stand idle. The fore-said College is related to the Northern Counties, the schooles being to supply that College. There is a thousand Acres belonging to it which may bee mightily improved. That college is one of the Ancientest, of 8

---

84 Webster, *In Times of Strife*, pp. 91–106.
85 Cromwell to Lenthall, 4 September 1650 and 11 March 1651, in *The Letters, Writings and Speeches of Oliver Cromwell*, volume 2, ed. by E. Murphy, M. Ó Siochrú and J. Peachy (Oxford: Oxford University Press, 2022), pp. 335, 427–28.
86 John Webster's tract, and a closely related sermon by William Dell, *The Tryall of Spirits* (1653), were included in a list of nine books selected for dispatch to Morgan Llwyd, a correspondent of Hartlib. John Webster wrote the biography of William Erbery, the author of two further of these nine tracts: G.F. Nuttall, 'A Parcel of Books for Morgan Llwyd', *Journal of the Friends Historical Society*, 53:3 (1992), 180–88.
87 Ephemerides 1655, HP 29/5/2B.

hundred years... most of which is under ground. The buildings are very much decayed and yet were by Mr. Tong's industry very much advanced. Lord Lambert is his great friend besides the Gentlemen of the Northerne County, Sir William Strickland, my Lord Ayres [George Eure, 6th Baron Eure], Colonel [Robert] Lilburne etc. etc.[88]

Other supportive information from the Ephemerides indicates that Tong was in 1655 already scouting for scholars who might be recruited to Durham. In January 1656 he noted that the Durham College already possessed an income of £400 and expected a similar amount upon reversion. All of the above evidence demonstrates that Durham College was in an advanced state of preparation before the Privy Council committee first took up the issue at the end of January 1656. Perhaps in recognition of the facts on the ground, Hartlib and Tong were added to this committee in August 1656. The financial settlement relating to the college was not formally disclosed until the Letters Patent were issued on 15 May 1657. In general, this document was consistent with the scheme that Tong had outlined more than two years previously. However, there was one major departure from what Hartlib and Tong had anticipated: rather than being the provost, Tong was just one of the dozen fellows specified in the Letters Patent. The provost of the new institution was the more senior Philip Hunton (1602–1683), author of the important *Treatise on Monarchy* (1645), a tract that was destined to attract the attention of generations of political theorists. As indicated by Tong's vignette of the founding fellowship and his subsequent notices to Hartlib, he found entirely acceptable the selection of Hunton as Provost:

> One Sprig [William Sprigg] is a fellow of Durham College excellent for Drawing and painting and very Optical also.
> Mr Vaughan [Thomas Vaughan] another Fellow undertaking in two years to fit scholars for University for Latin and Hebrew.
> Hinton the Mr [Master] of it an indisputable schollar.
> Also [Joseph Hill] a Fellow of Magdalene College a Universal schollar—one of the Professors or Fellows.[89]

Although Tong was never the provost of the Durham College, no doubt with the encouragement of his powerful backers, he dominated

---

88 Ephemerides, January 1655, HP 29/5/2B, 3B-4A. Eure had been an M.P. in the Nominated Parliament.
89 Ephemerides, c.July 1657, HP 29/6/17A.

the institution for the whole of its short life. Also, Hartlib's interest in Durham never wavered.

The Durham scheme came into being without incident. The new institution seemed very open to innovation and the seventeen initial appointees contained many open to the latest developments in the sciences and with a keen interest in economic progress. Among these were included such figures as Johann Sibertus Kuffeler, Georg Ritschel, William Sprigg, Ezerel Tong and Robert Wood, all of whom were in touch with Hartlib. Tong in particular kept Hartlib well-informed about the progress of the new institution.[90] The very first of the potential recruits for Durham mentioned by Tong to Hartlib was the colourful Thomas Vaughan, whom he described in January 1655 as 'a very learned Man a Minister, who is haunted with a Platonical genius who talkes to him at nights. Hee is very didactical and hath many several Tables to teach more readily the Grammar of the Latin Tongue and hath given *specimina* in teaching of Languages'.[91]

Of the staff possessing outstanding tutorial abilities, Richard Frankland stands out. His next career step led him to become an outstanding pioneer of dissenting academies. There is no evidence that Frankland owed this appointment to Tong, but he was well-connected among the leading patrons of the new institution. The eminent Edmund Calamy later recalled that 'Mr. Frankland was pitch'd upon as a very fit Man to be a Tutour there'.[92]

In 1659, there was a plan to expand activities at Durham, which would have taken spending to above £3000 p.a., enough to allow funding for an associated grammar school and the admission of forty poor scholars each year. Given his long-term commitment to the education of the poor, Hartlib would have been particularly supportive of this comprehensive plan of the operation of the Durham educational charity.[93]

One of the most far-sighted of the initial appointments at the Durham College was Robert Wood, who was nominated as the Professor of Mathematics. Wood was an inspired choice for Durham, but the

---

90 Webster *Instauration*, pp. 234–38.
91 Ephemerides 1655, HP 29/5/5A.
92 Calamy, *An Account of the Ministers...Ejected or Silenced after the Restoration in 1660* (London, 1713), p. 285.
93 Hartlib to Worthington, 20 April 1659, Crossley I, p. 127. For the seventeen appointees in Durham and their work, Webster *Instauration*, pp. 234–38.

evidence concerning his association with Durham warns us against premature judgements about the operation of this institution. The first hint of Wood's selection for Durham dates from June 1656, when he frankly admitted his surprise about this unexpected preferment. Wood recognised that he owed this honour to the intervention of Lady Ranelagh, who had freely satisfied his 'desires about the preferment', for which he expressed his gratitude. The fact that Wood's letter went on to thank Hartlib for supplying basic information about the Durham scheme suggests that he also was involved in this appointment. Since Hartlib had taken a serious interest in his welfare, Wood asked him to supply further information about Durham as it became available. Wood expressed his surprise that this news had already operated to his advantage in Ireland, where there was an 'unwillingnesse to part with me then otherwise I could have expected'.[94]

Therein lay the seeds of doubt about the move to Durham. In March 1657 Wood again mentioned circulation of a rumour that he would take up the mathematics post in Durham, but thereafter there was an ominous silence until January 1659, when he cited a report, likely from his friend William Sprigg, again describing the satisfactory state of affairs at Durham.[95]

It was not until August 1659 that Wood unselfconsciously admitted that 'I will not mention my being chosen at Durham, because being otherwise engaged I never went there'.[96] This warns us that, for all that Durham was a veritable hive of activity owing to the resourcefulness of Ezerel Tong and his friends, the majority of the seventeen appointees were likely to have been absentees. Supportive of this conclusion, the biographies of most of those for whom such records exist, including the *ODNB* entry on Wood, tend to make no mention of any link with the Durham College. Neither Sprigg nor Wood resigned their fellowships at Lincoln College, Oxford, despite the first being located in Durham and the other in Ireland during the late '50s. In the case of Kuffeler, whose appointment was certainly engineered by Tong, there is no evidence that he ever absented himself from his workshop in London.

---

94 Wood to Hartlib, 24 June 1656, HP 33/1/5A-B.
95 Wood to Hartlib, 4 January 1659, HP 33/1/39A-B. For Sprigg's account, Webster *Instauration*, p. 235.
96 Wood to Hartlib, 31 August 1659, HP 37/1/64A.

The New College in Dublin

The young Robert Wood, an intruded Fellow of Lincoln College, Oxford, introduced himself to Hartlib in March 1656. Their active communication continued until the beginning of 1662, therefore just before his patron's death. Shortly after his first meeting with Wood, Hartlib introduced the young man to Lady Ranelagh. This contact worked to the benefit of both of them and soon developed into a relationship of some intimacy. As just mentioned, Hartlib and Lady Ranelagh obtained for their young protégé the appointment as Professor of Mathematics at the new University of Durham. Wood failed to pursue this overture, but it undoubtedly assisted his reputation in Ireland, and soon helped to secure his appointment as an assistant secretary to Lord Deputy Henry Cromwell.

By the date that Lady Ranelagh first heard of the plan to establish a new college in Dublin, preparations had been dragging on for some time.[97] No doubt, while she was in London, Hartlib said nothing about this scheme because there was little tangible to report. Hartlib relied on Robert Wood for further news. In May 1656 Wood confessed his embarrassment that 'I cannot yet send you any good newes... yet I do not despaire but that in time I may, at least when our Governors have leisure to go about settlinge the Colledge'.[98] A month later, there was still little tangible to recount, but Wood retained confidence that the scheme would take effect. There was one highly important positive development: James Ussher's famous library had been secured for the new college: 'the Bishop of Armagh Bookes for the new Librarie, being bought & now paid for, will shortly be brought over'.[99] Shortly afterwards, Wood confirmed that 'My Lord Henry Cromwell, the Chancellor of the University, is about a very noble Designe, of making another Colledge in this City, & putting things unto a better way for the Advancement of ingenuous Learning, of which I may shortly perhaps give you a fuller account'.[100]

---

97   For a general review, Barnard, *Cromwellian Ireland*, pp. 206–12. The Act of Parliament sanctioning this project is dated 8 March 1652. The responsible committee included a few contacts of Hartlib, most notably Ralph Cudworth.
98   Wood to Hartlib, 13 May 1656, HP 33/1/1B.
99   Wood to Hartlib, 24 June 1656, HP 33/1/5B.
100 Wood to Hartlib, 23 November 1656, HP 33/1/8A.

This portentous announcement proved to be something of a false start. During the next few years, the new college was mentioned rarely in Wood's letters, but in early 1659, he was able to announce substantial progress:

> The Commitee appointed for the New College & Universitie have mett often, but have yet made no great progress in the Business, nor have they fully pitch't upon the place for the New College, though it has been much debated. But one thing I can acquaint you with since I wrot last, My Lord Lieutenant has very nobly bestowed Corke house (which was his owne, & worth £3,000) with the Garden &c. upon the University, to make publick Schooles of, & to be a receptacle for the new Library, which himselfe & the Army upon his recommendation purchased not long since at £2,500 besides incident charges. I shall not undertake to commend him for it the worke it selfe speakes sufficiently.[101]

Citing another recent letter from Wood, Hartlib repeated this information but with the important added detail of itemised spending. Wood's latest and final report is important because it confirms that the idea of the new college was still in play. However, a substantial part of the stated budget was directed to the existing university college, or into related educational charities.[102] As Barnard correctly concludes, there is virtually no evidence that this scheme, even if it had been realised, would have embodied any of the innovatory features that existed at the Durham College, or indeed the equivalent 'better way for the Advancement of ingenuous Learning' that had initially been promised for Dublin.

Universities: The Future

During the interregnum there was a widespread feeling that the Oxford and Cambridge monopoly on university education should be terminated. In Dury's *Israels Call* sermon in 1645, he pleaded with parliament to establish universities in every province.

As noted in chapter 3, Hartlib's team prepared an elaborate plan for a University of London comprising a large assembly of specialised constituent colleges. At the same date, a convincing petition supported

---

101 Wood to Hartlib, 4 January 1659, HP 33/1/39A.
102 Hartlib to Worthington, 20 April 1659, Crossley I, p. 127.

the same objective.[103] Also relevant, in 1656 William Rand's proposals for a Society of Graduate Physicians envisaged that this would be a constituent college of a new university of London.

John Beale's fertile imagination generated parallel and interactive schemes for colleges linked with Offices of Address that were initially planned for London, but were intended very soon to extend to all major places of trade. These colleges were expected to work in close collaboration. Beale was insistent on a non-doctrinaire approach to education, and on a high degree of reference to modern subjects such as the sciences, both pure and applied.[104]

Moses Wall agreed with Hartlib that London, 'which is no formall University, & hath no stipends for students, [is] worth both our Universities ten times over, for the benefitting of mankind by an industrious searching out of truths in all kinds, and by printing many profitable books'. In general, he concluded: 'I wholly dislike the way of our Universityes; instead of 2, I would have 5, or 6 in the Nation'.[105] As noted in the next chapter, in 1659 and 1660 Ezerel Tong, on the basis of his Durham experience, evolved a scheme that would draw upon tithes and other ecclesiastical resources to establish universities in many of the cathedral cities, or equivalent institutions in every major county and in groups of smaller counties. He was insistent that such institutions should make tertiary education accessible to young people from poorer backgrounds.

Such demand for new universities rapidly drained away during the Restoration and formally speaking it was not revived until the nineteenth century. But there was a distinct continuity, particularly with the spawning of dissenting academies. For instance, in Yorkshire, the Rathmell Academy quickly materialised as the initiative of Richard Frankland after his ejection and the termination of his post at the Durham College. Many others among the throngs of the ejected ministers hosted private tutorial groups, some of which developed into fully fledged academies.[106]

---

103 *Motives for the present founding an University in the Metropolis* [London, 1647].
104 Beale, 'For a Colledge', undated but perhaps 1657, HP 31/1/77A-80B, and 'Office of Address', 10 January 1657, HP 31/9A-12B.
105 Wall to Hartlib, 22 January 1659, HP 54/4/21B.
106 J. W. Ashley Smith, *The Birth of Modern Education: The Contribution of the Dissenting Academies, 1660–1800* (London: Independent Press, 1954); D.J. Appleby; *Black*

4.4 The Thirst for Betterment

In what was a generally agrarian economy, it is not surprising that husbandry was at the centre of Hartlib's campaign for economic renewal. His wider enthusiasm for innovation and inventions, for instance relating to drainage, accordingly also often bore links with husbandry. As early as 1643, building on his partnership with Gabriel Plattes, Hartlib urged the Mayor of London to take the initiative and champion:

> The founding of a Speciall House or Colledge for the tryall & approued communicacion of all manner of solid & desirable Invencions & Experiments. I am confident that the embraceing & hearty promocion of these Mocions as it will discouer the excellency of that manifold trust reposed in that Honourable Assembly by the whole Kingdome; so it will bring a certaine & most inestimable benefit to all men of what degree soever.[107]

Hartlib's many technically minded associates as a matter of course appreciated that they were contributing to his general repertoire of 'Designes for all Experimental as well as Mechanical Learning', the ambitious horizons of which Worsley invoked, when he outlined a programme of innovative schemes upon which he and his partners were working, with the expectation that by such means the 'Commonwealth of England might in few years bee made the richest (if that bee the happiest) and the most flourishing Country in the world'.[108]

It is therefore not surprising that Iliffe's survey of technical innovation in mid-century London concludes that Hartlib's Ephemerides

---

Bartholomew's Day: Preaching, Polemic and Restoration Nonconformity (Manchester: Manchester University Press, 2007); Mark Burden, *A Biographical Dictionary of Tutors at the Dissenters' Private Academies, 1660–1729* (London: Dr. Williams's Centre for Dissenting Studies, 2013).

107 Hartlib to Isaac Pennington, 16 October 1643, HP 7/4/3A.
108 Worsley to [Hartlib], 11 June 1649, Royal Society, Boyle Letters 7.2, 1A. These sentiments were consistent with the call for recruitment of foreign artisans, as outlined in a manifesto, 'Proffits humbly presented to this Kingdom' c.1645 (text in Webster *Instauration*, pp. 539–46). For the general assessment of this subject-area: P. Slack, *The Invention of Improvement. Information and Material Progress in Seventeenth-Century England* (Oxford: Oxford University Press, 2015); K. Yamamoto, 'Reformation and Distrust of the Projector in the Hartlib Circle', *The Historical Journal*, 55:2 (2012), 375–97; idem, *Taming Capitalism before its Triumph* (Oxford: Oxford University Press, 2018), pp. 117–30 et passim.

comprises 'an astonishingly rich description of inventive activity in the capital', carried out variously by budding entrepreneurs, scientists, technicians, or humble artisans.[109] It is a matter of importance that these innovators included a group of founders of the Royal Society, many of them being at this point at a formative stage in their scientific apprenticeship. Historians of science of the past have tended to dismiss such technical activities and forays among the lower social orders by young scientists as juvenile foibles, rapidly regretted and discarded upon their scientific maturation. Upon closer examination, it is evident that collaboration with technicians such as lens makers was essential to the evolving astronomical work of a whole fraternity of Royal Society founders. Equally, any botanist pioneer like John Ray was dependent on the investigative work and *hortus siccus* of Edward Morgan, the Welsh explorer and London gardener. Likewise, any serious entomologist would have been foolish to ignore the insect collections and fine artwork of Alexander Marshal.

4.4.1 Technical Innovation

Hartlib's relationship with Johann Sibertus Kuffeler (1595–1667), the son-in-law of the famous Cornelius Drebbel, constituted the most extensive of his contacts with the technical innovators of his generation. His first recorded mention dates from 1635, when Kuffeler's inventions relating to stoves of all sizes were noted.[110] Hartlib took soundings on innovations connected with bread making, to which Johann Moriaen returned a bleak response, suggesting that in this field and more generally, the inventive capacity of Kuffeler had ground to a halt and warning that the true seriousness of this setback would become obvious in the course of time.[111] Hartlib remained undeterred. From 1635

---

109 R. Iliffe, 'Hartlib's World', in *London and Beyond: Essays in Honour of Derek Keene*, ed. by M. Davies and J.A. Galloway (London: London University Press/Institute of Historical Research, 2012), pp. 103–22 (p. 105); idem, 'Capitalizing Expertise: Philosophical and Artisanal Expertise in Early Modern London', in *Fields of Expertise: A Comparative History of Expert Procedures in Paris and London, 1600 to Present*, ed. by C. Rabier (Newcastle upon Tyne: Cambridge Scholars Publishing, 2021), pp. 55–84. For Hartlib and betterment, see also Haffemeyer, *Les Lumières radicales*, pp. 470–502.

110 Ephemerides 1635, HP 29/3/44A.

111 Moriaen to Hartlib, 30 June 1639, HP 37/3/1A.

until 1660 Hartlib listed more than a hundred cases of improvements championed by Kuffeler and his associates. An indicator of the special relationships that developed between technician and patron is provided by the agreement between Kuffeler, Hartlib and Ezerel Tong, allowing for a loan of £100 to the inventor, in return for a promise to direct his labour to the welfare of the Commonwealth, in the course of which the loan would be repaid from the profits that his inventions were calculated to generate.[112]

A good example of potential synergy between the inventor and the rising scientist is provided by the Kalthoff-Petty interaction, in which Petty was seventeen years the younger. Caspar Kalthoff, already mentioned above, was no mean figure. He came from a successful cosmopolitan family, whose high reputation derived from their work as gunsmiths. Kalthoff settled in England to work with the royal court. He seems to have attracted the attention of Hartlib in 1639. His reputation was sufficiently sound for Hartlib to instigate a pact between Kalthoff and Sir Christof de Berg, in which they agreed to pool their wisdom.[113] After this, Kalthoff was absent from Hartlib's papers until 1649, after which for about five years there were many references to him. On the Kalthoff-Petty relationship Benjamin Worsley was Hartlib's main informant. After many months during which Worsley acted as the intermediary between the two innovators, he concluded that 'If Kalthof and Petty might bee joined together they might doe wonders, as well for their owne benefits privately as otherwise... For Kalthof hath great relations and advantages, not only from his parts, but from his friends and interest in the Court and in many eminent Persons in this Land'.[114]

Petty was pursuing so many different avenues of adventure that his partnership with Kalthoff fell into abeyance. Nevertheless, this conjunction was significant because both investigators came to realise the potential of steam power. Kalthoff was the more experienced and he was better equipped to carry forward such investigations. All the evidence points to his success, in partnership with Edward Somerset, in devising a

---

112 For the text of this agreement, HP 26/49/1A-2B. For Kuffeler, Haffemeyer, *Les Lumières radicalse*, pp. 424–27 et passim.
113 Kalthoff-Berg Contract (in German) signed at Duke's Place, January 1640, witnessed by Hartlib, Haak and Hübner, HP 48/4/1A-2B. See Haffemeyer, *Les Lumières radicales*, pp. 424–27 et passim.
114 Worsley to Hartlib, 28 May 1649, Royal Society, Boyle *Letters*, 7.1 f.1A.

working steam power device, often called a 'water-commanding engine', which was described in Worcester's *Century of Inventions* written in 1655 and was certainly demonstrated in public at least by 1656.[115] Hartlib's commentary offers insight into the huge horizons opened up by William Potter's marketing scheme for Kalthoff's new drainage engine:

> 1. for clearing of Mines from Water (the profits of which Kalthof counted to bee equal if not exceeding the Revenues of any king). 2. for Watering of Town's or bringing of water into Townes. Cities etc. 3. for taking of all Mills upon rivers to make them Navigable etc. 4. for flooding or watering of Lands. which also Sir Cheney Culpeper suggested. 5. for imploying of many thousands if not hundred thousands of Poore People that may bee set to digging of Mines. The Earl of Worcester motions that all the mines might bee farmed by the Protector which by the improvement of the fore-said addition would come to a Million of yearly Revenue by which meanes all Taxes might bee taken off.[116]

Among Hartlib's correspondents there was distinct naivety concerning the social impact of economic innovations of this kind. However, some of the leading innovators were sensitive to social realities and also to the likelihood of resistance that their schemes were likely to inspire. To the objectors, Cressy Dymock replied: 'And therfore this will bee a maine objection against this Remedy or Invention because it will deprive poore People of emploiments. But the common Receipt may serve turne which is that those heads which invent such devices can invent also many others how to set poore People a worke.'[117] Elsewhere, Dymock ingeniously cited John Wilkins' *Mathematical Magic* in his favour respecting the need to overcome the intrinsic opposition of human nature to any kind of change.[118]

As evident from the above account of Kalthoff's drainage device, the prevalent yearning for success within the innovation lobby inevitably generated a propensity to unrealistic expectations. One sign of this weakness was the tendency to view any experiment with mechanical contraptions as some kind of approach to solving the problem of

---

115 For a short review, Stephen Hughes, 'Early steam engines', *TICCIH Bulletin*, Number 74 (2016), p. 06.
116 Ephemerides, c.January 1654, HP 29/4/2A-B; letter from Potter to Hartlib and Kalthoff, 18 January 1655, HP 30/3/3A-4B.
117 Ephemerides 1648, HP 31/22/ 7B. Ephemerides, c.January 1654, HP 29/4/2A-B; letter from Potter to Hartlib and Kalthoff, 18 January 1655, HP 30/3/3A-4B.
118 Dymock to Hartlib, 29 September 1649, HP 62/50/5A.

perpetual motion. Even a modest realignment of a plough was likely to be invested with an almost magical aura. In order to attract sponsors, artisans naturally fell into the habit of encouraging exaggerated expectations. Into this trap fell many of the sponsors whose experience is recorded in the Hartlib Papers, including both Comenius and Samuel Hartlib himself. The latter's naivety was fully exposed when in 1658, Hartlib, having again reached the verge of destitution, admitted that he had invested £100 per annum for several years in the perfection of Cressy Dymock's 'engine of motion' and was earnestly searching for others who would join him in this partnership. There were of course no takers for this desperate mission. Then, in the very next letter, he expressed high confidence in the economist and inventor, William Potter, who had constructed a perpetual motion machine. Not to be deterred, Hartlib reviewed the whole question of perpetual motion for the benefit of John Winthrop, regretting the failure of Comenius to arrive at a successful outcome, notwithstanding fifteen years of effort, yet expressing confidence that both Potter and Nicholaus Mercator were on the verge of triumph.[119]

4.4.2 Chemistry and Alchemy

In the technical field an obvious parallel to the temptation of perpetual motion was the tendency of the striking and productive vogue of interest in applied chemistry to drift into a preoccupation with alchemical transmutation. As some important research has demonstrated these two facets were inextricably linked.[120]

Hartlib was attracted to chemistry, iatrochemistry and alchemy for many reasons, including his especially close ties with Robert Child and

---

119 Hartlib to Winthrop, 16 March 1660, HP 7/7/1B-2A. Hartlib had followed the progress of Potter's work on perpetual motion since 1650. For an agreement of Richard Eccleston, a London merchant, to invest in the Dymock-Hartlib 'engine' scheme, 6 November 1650, HP 58/10A-11B.

120 Young, *Moriaen*; W. Newman, *Gehennical Fire: The Lives of George Starkey, An American Alchemist in the Scientific Revolution* (Cambridge, Massachusetts: Harvard University Press, 1994); B. Moran, *Distilling Knowledge: Alchemy, Chemistry, and the Scientific Revolution* (Cambridge, Massachusetts: Harvard University Press, 2005). W. Woodward, *Prospero's America: John Winthrop, Jr., Alchemy and the Creation of New England Culture, 1606–1676* (Chapel Hill: University of North Carolina Press, 2010).

George Starkey, as well as his personal acquaintance with many other of the leading players among the British chemist-alchemist activists of the day, and inevitably on account of Friedrick Clodius being his son-in-law.[121]

A glimpse into the alchemical fraternity was provided by Robert Child, writing to Hartlib in 1652, when he confirmed being as much preoccupied with chemistry and alchemy as with husbandry. The main feature of this letter was his expression of concern about the ebullient George Starkey.[122] Child also briefed Hartlib about the inner circle of Thomas Henshaw's 'college', which included: 'Dr Currar, Mr Ashmole, & if Mr Henshaw [who] doth sometimes visit you,... I would faine know, if Mr Walker etc. do go on in their Colledge'.[123] This so-called college was a descendant of the 'chymical club' dating from 1650, where the prime movers were Child, Thomas Vaughan, Thomas Henshaw and Francis Webbe. According to Hartlib, the aims of this group were: '1. to collect all English Philosophical Books or other Chymists. 2. all MS. 3. to translate and publish them in one Volume. 4. to make all Philosophers acquainted one with another and to oblige them to mutual communications.'[124] With the exception of Currar, all these college and club associates were already known to Hartlib. Henshaw was indeed a visitor to Hartlib's house. Hartlib even made notes on the activities of Henshaw's father and mother.[125]

Among the points of interest in the above list is the dominance of names who were well outside the Puritan and Parliamentarian ambit, indicating that, when circumstances dictated, both Child (a staunch Presbyterian) and Hartlib fraternised without anxiety with those of alien persuasions. This inclusivity also applied to those outside the list, including such notable names as Sir Kenelm Digby and John Evelyn. From this point of view, perhaps the most striking name in Child's list was Obadiah Walker, whom Ezerel Tong suspected of Catholic leanings, which indeed was the case, as proven after 1660 by Walker's record

---

121 V. Keller and L.T.I. Penman, 'From the Archives of Scientific Diplomacy: Science and the Shared Interests of Samuel Hartlib's London and Friedrick Clodius's Gottdorf', *Isis*, 106:1 (2015), 17–42.
122 For this phase in the young Starkey's career, Newman, *Gehennical Fire*, pp. 54–89.
123 Child to Hartlib, 5 October 1652, HP 15/5/19A.
124 Ephemerides 1650, HP 28/1/61B.
125 For Hartlib's characterisation of Walker, Ephemerides, c.August 1650, HP 28/1/66B.

as Master of University College, Oxford, where he became a notable promoter of James II. Henshaw, who was formerly Walker's student, also came into his own only with the Restoration.

The many who trespassed into the occult were of course aware that their findings were not universally accepted within the scientific community. It is therefore not surprising that Benjamin Worsley, an ardent seeker in these fields, insisted that one of his essays should be 'wholly suppressed unless it be', referred by Hartlib to liberal minds like John Sadler, Thomas Streete, John Beale, John Sparrow or Elias Ashmole, 'but no more to Oxford: for they doe not understand it'.[126]

The objectives of the Chymical Club remind us that the interregnum period witnessed a vogue in the ancestral knowledge of chemistry, alchemy and iatrochemistry. Hartlib's papers record many examples of such interests, for instance, when Lady Joan Barrington, well-known to him already as a Puritan celebrity, supplied him with an alchemical manuscript containing the work of two recent seekers, John Dee and Edward Kelley, but also much earlier writings by George Ripley and Thomas Norton, and even one attributed to St John of Bridlington.[127] The sense of the inextricable bond between past and present is well-reflected in the statement, possibly by Robert Child, concerning the explanation of organic fertility, where he insisted on the relevance of a 'multiplicity of Opinions of learned Philosophers (as Aristotle, Rupesc. Sendivog. Norton, Helmont, Des Cartes, Digby, White, Plat. Glaubre) concerning this Subject [which] sheweth the great difficulty of this Question'. A powerful testimony to the depth with which this course was prosecuted is provided by the impressive *Theatrum Chemicum Britannicum*, published by Elias Ashmole in 1652.[128]

---

126 Worsley to Hartlib, 14 October 1657, HP 42/1/10B. For the warmth of relationship between Sparrow, Worsley and Hartlib, see Worsley to Hartlib, 20 January 1659, HP 33/2/11B.

127 Ephemerides 1640, HP 30/4/67A. For Hartlib's relations with Lady Joan Barrington's son Sir Thomas Barrington, Haffemeyer, *Les Lumières radicales*, pp. 134–35, 162, 187–88 et passim.

128 *Theatrum Chemicum Britannicum. Containing Severall Poetical Pieces of our Famous English Philosophers* (London: Printed by J. Grismond for Nath: Brooke, 1652). For further detail on Ashmole's alchemical enterprises at this date, volume one of *Elias Ashmole: His Autobiographical and Historical Notes, his Correspondence, and Other Contemporary Sources Relating to his Life and Work*, 5 vols., ed. by C.H. Josten (Oxford: Oxford University Press, 1967).

Paracelsus

A more tangible objective of high priority during the 1650s was arranging for the English-reading public to have better access to the writings of Theophrastus von Hohenheim (Paracelsus), an author whom the Germans had long enjoyed reading. To Hartlib, Paracelsus was a familiar figure from his youth, partly because Silesia was a hotbed of Paracelsian activity, including being the base for Johannes Huser (1545–1601), editor of the impressive collected editions of the *Bücher und Schrifften*, 10 volumes, 1589–1591, and *Chirurgische Bücher und Shrifften*, 1605 and 1616. For a long period Huser was a physician in Glogau/Głogów, Lower Silesia. One of the main sources for the work of Huser was the extensive Paracelsus manuscript collection of Johannes Montanus (1531–1604) of Striegau /Strzegom in Lower Silesia. Striegau and Glogau were less than 100km apart.

In England, the medical establishment was generally hostile to radical reformers, of whom Paracelsus was arguably the leading figure. But there was a growing feeling that Paracelsus should be taken more seriously, which was precisely the viewpoint of Benjamin Worsley, who confirmed this in no uncertain terms to Hartlib: 'There is another a Countryman of your owne: next & before all others, I commend Paracelsus, who was a cleare & Rationall man, though intoxicated now & then partly with the sight of his owne knowledge, & partly through the extraordinary opposition & reproach he mett with'.[129] Among those less satisfied with Paracelsus was Clodius, who complained that 'Paracelsus writes often sophistically but not so Helmont, who is said also to have made Notes upon *Chirurgia Universalis Paracelsi*'.[130]

By 1650 there had been a vigorous Paracelsian movement in Britain for the best part of a century, but there were no translations acceptable as genuine or cognate with the authentic writings. At this point the situation changed abruptly. Between 1650 and 1660 no fewer than nine substantial volumes of translations were published, giving the English readers for the first time access to some of the most important expositions of the ideas of the reformer. Among the translators some were notably Puritan in their outlook, of whom two, John Harding and Henry Pinnel, were rival

---

129 Worsley to Hartlib, 14 February 1656, HP 42/1/6B.
130 Ephemerides 1651, HP 28/2/24A.

clerics working from the same village: Brinkworth, in north Wiltshire. Of these translators only one, John French, the author of the first of these translations to be published, seems to have been known to Hartlib.[131]

Helmont

A major priority at this date for Hartlib and his friends was keeping abreast with the work of Jan Baptist van Helmont (1579–1644) and Johann Rudolph Glauber (1604–1670), both of whom were active in the Low Countries, where they exercised a profound influence. The Hartlib Papers record profuse references relating to these two, now famous, scientific figures. This evidence signifies the manner in which Hartlib's team employed its own well-developed network in that region to garner the latest news on these two and many lesser innovators in the fields of chemistry and iatrochemistry.

After the death of Helmont in December 1644, attention focused on preparations for publication of the massive collected edition of his work, the *Opus medicinae*, which was published by Elzevir in Amsterdam in 1648. The very first mention of Helmont received by Hartlib derives from a letter sent by Heinrich Appelius to Hartlib from Amsterdam, dated 13 August 1644. On the basis of the recently published *Opuscula medica inaudita*, he described Helmont as representative of a 'new way to worke in philosophy et in Physick differing from Roman churches & Aristotle & Chemists, will not disappoint the expectations of the diligent labourer'. He concluded that the paradoxical style of Helmont's writings placed him on a level with Bacon, Comenius and Kozak. In June 1646 Appelius revealed that the text of Helmont's drafts had still not been delivered, but already the publishing arrangements had been agreed. This massive undertaking was to be handled by a cooperative comprising the Elzevir Press and the workshop of Johann Fabel. The latter was renowned as a publisher of books by authors representing diverse and often marginal viewpoints. It was therefore singular good fortune that Fabel was also a willing source of intelligence. Appelius estimated the expected size of *Ortus medicinae*, the upper limit of which turned out to be correct. According to his next letter, dated 2 May 1647, Appelius had managed

---

131 For further information respecting the Paracelsus translations, Webster *Instauration*, pp. 275–303.

to obtain from Fabel a few copies of one of Helmont's works (perhaps *Opuscula medica inaudita*), two of which Appelius was sending to Hartlib. At this stage the definitive printing process had just begun. To his great satisfaction, on 26 August 1647, Appelius announced that the printing of *Ortus medicinae* was half complete. Hartlib was assured that Fabel would supply him with a copy of the *Ortus medicinae* as soon as printing was completed.

The next problem for the enthusiast was the sheer inaccessibility of Helmont's writings. In that context Hartlib was cheered to hear that one 'Mr Mosle the Physitian doth practise the Art of collecting upon Helmont making an Index or Concordance upon him.'[132] Clodius reminded Hartlib that indexing the 800 pages of the Helmont edition was a minefield: 'Those that make Indices in Helmont especially parallelisms may be grossly mistaken if they understand not the difference between the preparation of the Alcahest and the Lapis. For commonly they are confounded and a World of Chymists have split themselves upon this rock'.[133] No doubt assisted by his status as Hartlib's son-in-law, Clodius had no shortage of patients and elevated himself into becoming one of the most vociferous Helmontians of this period. With prescient judgement he fixed upon the important Helmont principle that 'All things can bee resolved into their water, out of that several other Experiments can be made [respecting water]'. Not only was Helmont's theory that water was the basic source of living matter backed by what seemed like a crucial experiment, but also through this conclusion he was challenging not only the theories of matter of the ancients, but also the rival ones favoured by the Paracelsians. Among those enthralled by Helmont's idea was Robert Boyle, whose famous *Sceptical Chymist* (1661) constituted a compelling reassessment of Helmont and rival theories of matter.

In the course of the two decades after 1650, Helmontianism became the main badge of modernism in the field of British medicine. Hence, it was with obvious pride that in 1660 Hartlib declared that 'I believe my son in law a great Helmontian (Frederick Clodius by name) hath as

---

132 Ephemerides 1652, HP 28/1/43B. This information was supplied to Hartlib by Thomas Harrison, the expert on the organisation of knowledge, indexing etc.
133 Ephemerides 1652, HP 28/2/3A.

good if not better chyrurgicall medecins. He cures perfectly the cancer and Kings evill'.[134]

The Helmontian tide even made its incursion into the medical elite, where Walter Charleton, the rising star in the College of Physicians, for a short period in the early 1650s enthused about Helmont and published translations of his work. As noted in the previous chapter, among Hartlib's associates, there was generally a favourable attitude to Helmont, which John Hall took to extreme lengths, while others, notably William Rand, remained entirely unconvinced.

Glauber

Helmont's *Ortus medicinae* paved the way for the writings of his younger contemporary, Johann Rudolph Glauber, whose first important work, the *Furni novi philosophici*, was published by Hans Fabel in five stages between 1647 and 1649. This was arguably his most successful and important work, certainly the one that established his fame.

As in the case of Helmont, Hartlib monitored the progress of the original edition, then the English translation and finally he was much engaged with the wider transmission of information about Glauber's innovations. As a source of information, once again Appelius was important.[135] The first recorded mentions of Glauber in Hartlib's papers emanate from three letters that he received from Appelius dated 7 and 12 June, and 5 September 1644.[136] From these letters, it is obvious that Hartlib had been enquiring about Glauber at an earlier date. This assumption seems to be supported by the existence of two versions in Hartlib's papers of a sales leaflet advertising Glauber's furnaces, which are firmly dated 1643.[137] These are headed *Furni Novi Philosophici Utilitates*, a title soon to be repeated in the publication for which Glauber became famous. These informative documents were designed to stimulate sales of his patent furnaces, of which various models existed.

---

134 Hartlib to Winthrop, 16 March 1660, HP 7/7/4B.
135 For relations between the Hartlib group and Glauber, Young, *Moriaen*, pp. 198–207 et passim.
136 HP 48/1/62A, 45/8A and 13A.
137 HP 16/8/1A-4B (Latin); HP 63/14/48A-49B (German).

Appelius revealed that his own patron, as well as Moriaen and other medical enthusiasts, was well satisfied with Glauber's products.

Over the next couple of years Hartlib recorded little about Glauber, but in 1647 his campaign resumed. Particularly interesting is the letter of 26 August, in which Appelius patiently and at length replied to a list of fifteen, often pedantic, queries from Hartlib, specifically about Glauber. That Appelius was able to field such a tedious interrogation, demonstrated that he was on intimate terms with Glauber, and was therefore able to communicate information that would, in normal circumstances, be difficult to obtain. Through Appelius, Hartlib discovered that Glauber was in a restless state. Although not his first choice, he opted to settle in Arnhem, partly because this was the seat of the Kuffeler family's cloth dyeing business. With this move Glauber decided to terminate the direct supply of his famous furnaces. The main reason for this reorientation was to broadcast 'to the whole world' his proposals for improving the design of furnaces. He already envisaged that his work would be widely available in translation. This change of approach, he calculated, would also provide him with greater opportunity for writing, in which sphere he harboured ambitious aims, which were indeed amply fulfilled. In 1646 he published Part I of his *Furni novi philosophici*. Hans Fabel then issued Part II in 1647, Parts III and IV in 1648 and the final Part V in 1649.

On 16 October 1646 Appelius dispatched to Hartlib Part I of the *Furni novi philosophici*, an event that probably established Hartlib as the first person in Britain to handle a publication by Glauber. The same conclusion might well have applied in 1648 when a special effort was made to supply him with the *Ortus medicinae* of Helmont.

Throughout the prolonged *Furni novi* printing process, for publicity purposes and to raise funds, the author distributed advance samples, a few sheets at a time. By 1660 Glauber had published no fewer than twenty separate titles, many of these being substantial and innovatory in character.[138] In 1651 an English translation of the *Furni novi* was executed under the direction of John French, an influential figure, who was actively in touch with Hartlib.

---

138 J.R. Partington, *History of Chemistry*, vol. 2, pp. 341–61.

In October 1647 Hartlib resumed his interrogation of Appelius, this time making it clearer than in his previous questionnaire that he was acting on behalf of an unnamed 'Gentleman' who was contemplating becoming a paid visitor to Glauber's workshop, but this person would only defray the costs if Glauber could guarantee generous profits in return. It is tempting to speculate that Hartlib was acting on behalf of Sir Cheney Culpeper, for whom Glauber, at this date, was an obsession.[139] It is much more likely Hartlib was representing the more entrepreneurially minded Benjamin Worsley, whom Culpeper described as devoting himself to 'the trade of ingenuity and knowledge'. On that basis Culpeper hoped that Worsley would agree to acting as the 'Factor' to a Glauber mission business partnership headed by Culpeper himself.[140] The appeal of Glauber to eager innovators like Culpeper and Worsley had many dimensions, but high in their expectations was the likelihood that more powerful furnaces would smooth the path to generating the transmutation of metals, and thereby opening a great door to science and a gateway to riches.

This elevated mission was no doubt in mind when Worsley arrived in the Netherlands in January 1648, where he remained for almost two years. For Worsley, this period was packed with action on many fronts, but the strand specifically relating to Glauber and his furnace innovations cannot be overlooked.[141] Worsley lost no time in making contact with Glauber, and this was further facilitated by the chemist's return to Amsterdam in the summer of 1648. In his report to Hartlib dated 11 June 1649, Worsley assured his financial backers that they were in line for a return of 30 or even 40 per cent on their investments, even though the furnace upon which all of this depended was not yet in operation.[142] A letter from Moriaen to Hartlib of the same date confirmed this disappointing news, in addition to which Moriaen had been badly injured at the trial of his own version of the new furnace.[143] Moriaen

---

139 S. Clucas, 'The Correspondence of a Seventeenth-Century 'Chymicall Gentleman', *Ambix*, 40:3 (1993), 147–70.
140 Culpeper to Hartlib, 20 October 1647, Culpeper *Letters*, p. 308. For Culpeper and innovation generally, see K. Yamamoto, 'Reformation and Distrust of the Projector in the Hartlib Circle', and idem, *Taming Capitalism before its Triumph*, pp. 109–30.
141 Leng *Worsley*, chapter 2, for Glauber, pp. 38–40; Young *Moriaen*, pp. 219–26 for 'Worsley's Alchemical Mission to the Netherlands'.
142 Worsley to [Hartlib], 11 June 1649, Royal Society, Boyle Letters 7.2. 1A-2B.
143 HP 37/137A-B.

was fearful that both Worsley and Glauber would be dismayed by the risk of failure of his much-anticipated new laboratory and furnace. On the positive side, Worsley, for the benefit of Hartlib's data bank of Mechanical Learning, outlined in some detail five distinct improvements in distillation apparatus and furnace design upon which he was working. Particularly impressive in retrospect is the evidence that he was making rapid strides towards replacing metalwork with glass in his distillation apparatus. In this Worsley was not so much a follower of Glauber as an investigator of similar standing. Such positive gains represented important steps in the modernisation of the distillation process, which, in the mind of Worsley, might have compensated for the catastrophic commercial failure of the main object of the original Glauber mission. A memorandum specifically concerned with distillation, and likely dating also from June 1649, confirms that Worsley's attention was gradually shifting away from furnaces and the transmutation of metals to the refinement of distillation techniques as these applied mainly to highly refined beverages and medicaments, innovations that he canvassed as being equally necessary and lucrative.[144] The 1650s saw a rash of laboratory developments in England. The participants ranged from Robert Boyle to Friedrick Clodius. Hartlib revealed to Boyle that Clodius headed a consortium which was establishing a 'chemical college or laboratory' that was already stocked with three furnaces, and a further five were planned, which would permit the 'command of any kind of operation whatsoever'.[145]

Hartlib's attitude to operators in the field of transmutation was vague and inconsistent, as was also the case with John Dury. On the whole Dury was cautious, but he reacted positively about a group engaged in the 'great work' of *lapis philosophorum* proceeding in Hamburg under the supervision of Johannes Tanckmarus.[146] This high opinion of Tanckmarus was shared by Hartlib's European friends, and this, despite

---

144 [Worsley], 'Of the distillation or Drawing of spirits some Animadversions', HP 26/33/9A-B; W. Loibl, 'Johann Rudolph Glauber and the "Glassy" Consequences', *Journal of Glass Studies*, 49 (2007), 81–101, for Glauber and his immediate followers in Germany.
145 Hartlib to Boyle, 14 September 1658, Boyle *Correspondence* I, p. 294.
146 Ephemerides 1653, 26/2/45B. Tanckmarus of Hamburg was described by Hartlib as 'a great Chymist and Mr Dury's special acquaintance'. Ephemerides 1651, HP 20/2/22A.

the evidence that he and two other clients of Hartlib had been driven out of Lübeck for their involvement in the spread of fanatical literature.

4.5 Husbandry Revolution

Hartlib's papers, especially those relating to the later years, contained discussions of every variety of technical innovation, but the greatest weight of evidence relates to husbandry. Among Hartlib's associates the term 'husbandry' was preferred over its synonym 'agriculture', which was also commonly used but to a much lesser extent. Hence, it is not surprising that Samuel Hartlib's husbandry endeavours, especially his well-known associated publications, figure prominently in modern assessments of writings in this sphere. Indeed, it is entirely understandable that Fussell should label the period from 1640–1660, 'The Age of Hartlib'.[147]

As noted in chapters 2 and 3, Hartlib's serious engagement with major husbandry improvers began with his acquaintance with Gabriel Plattes. After the latter's premature death, high expectations arose concerning the possibility of some weighty posthumous publication, which Hartlib was slow to dispel. Clarification was delayed until 1660, when he explained: 'I have a Mss of his about experiments of husbandry, which though it be near of 40 sheets or more,... yett there is little of new solid knowledge, yett such as it is I have profered to divers stationers, yett all of them have counted the manuscripts not worth printing'.[148] Such an outcome would have been a profound disappointment, but, as

---

[147] Generally, see: M. James, *Social Problems and Policy*, pp. 109, 112, 115–17; G.E. Fussell, *The Old English Farming Books, from Fitzherbert to Tull 1523–1730* (London: Crosby Lockwood, 1947), pp. 36–55; E. Kerridge, *The Agricultural Revolution* (London: Allen and Unwin, 1967), pp. 181–325; Webster *Instauration*, pp. 465–83; J. Thirsk, 'Plough and Pen: Agricultural Writers in the Seventeenth Century' in *Social Relations and Ideas: Essays in Honour of R.H. Hilton*, ed. by T. H. Aston et al. (Cambridge: Cambridge University Press, 1983), pp. 295–318; T. McComick, 'Food, Population, and Empire in the Hartlib Circle, 1639–1660', *Osiris*, 35 (2020), 60–83; Oana Matei, 'Husbandry Tradition and the Emergence of Vegetable Philosophy in the Hartlib Circle', *Philosophia*, 16:1 (2015), 35–52, and related publications by her cited in the Bibliography below.

[148] Hartlib to Winthrop, 16 March 1660, HP 7/7/2B.

seen below, the Plattes archive was still sufficiently viable to yield one of the major items included in the third and last edition of the *Legacy*.[149]

Cressy Dymock

Hartlib did not allow this tragic loss of Plattes to inhibit his thirst for further enlightenment relating to all the spheres of innovation pursued by his deceased protégé. Fortuitously, in the spring of 1648 there emerged Cressy Dymock (c.1605–1660), a candidate who bore some striking resemblance to Plattes, including, somewhat ominously, being perpetually destined to live in insecurity and hardship.[150] Dymock's great year was 1649, after which his poverty worsened and the high hopes among his patrons gradually tailed off. Nevertheless, Hartlib remained supportive and he even published Dymock's work in a handful of short tracts and also by essays included in editions of the *Legacie*. These and his unpublished correspondence show beyond doubt that Dymock was a fluent writer and effective publicist for his wide-ranging reform package. Most of what he proposed was already familiar ground to his potential benefactors, but Dymock was adept at synthesising many different elements into a convincing blueprint. Central to his plans was the imposition of some kind of enclosure system, which was of course controversial, but increasingly attractive among Hartlib's panel of experts. Typically, Robert Child condemned the system of commons, which was thought to operate for 'the good of the Poore but makes them live basely poorly and idly... But if the Land were put all into gardening and enclosures it would maintaine twice as many People as now it doth'.[151] In similar terms Captain Floyd expressed his specific support for Dymock's enclosure plan.[152]

Dymock acknowledged the objections, but he convincingly argued that all classes would benefit from his plan. His case was supported by an

---

149 The first (1651) and second (1652) editions are *Legacie*, the third and final edition (1655) is *Legacy*.
150 *ODNB* Cressy Dymock (Mark Greengrass). For Dymock, Haffemeyer, *Les Lumières radicales*, pp. 480–81 et passim.
151 Ephemerides 1650, HP 28/1/66B.
152 Ephemerides 1653, HP 28/2/46B. Floyd was a nautical captain, with plantations in the Caribbean. He was actively engaged with Hartlib during 1652 and 1653.

impressive cost-benefit analysis. He was then able to demonstrate his system on his cousin's farm at Wadworth, now a suburb of Doncaster. Central to the success of his scheme was his newly invented 'Engine', a kind of seed drill, of which he was inordinately proud. He noted his cousin's astonishment at the successful operation of this instrument.[153] Shortly afterwards, the discerning William Brereton was also impressed by Dymock's 'Instrument': 'Dymock's Way of Husbandry or Instrument of Setting of Corne needs not the manure of any Ground for the Seed is manured before it bee put into the ground. And besides it ploughs, harrows and sows at once'.[154] Since there is no good reason to question the reliability of this evidence, the advanced seed drill was in successful operation long before this features in the standard histories of seed drilling.

As illustrated by the plea from Robert Boyle and his associates Sadler, Hartlib, Dury, Worsley and Robinson, Dymock was earnestly entreated 'to goe on in making Experiments of those particulars which wee desire and expect from you, both in your Manure and Engines of Motion', while remaining faithful to this group rather than being distracted by others.[155]

After 1653 Dymock rapidly faded from view. The above account by Brereton from 1655 was the last significant mention of Dymock in the Ephemerides. Dymock's last letter to Hartlib was dated December 1656. In this, a desperate plea for help, Dymock apologised for his failure to keep in touch. Notwithstanding this decline, a stray letter from William Petty to Dymock, seeking advice on the management of his estates, demonstrates that Dymock was still at that date respected as a reliable expert on agricultural practices.[156]

Walter Blith

In addressing his problems of estate management, Petty relied also on Walter Blith's *The English Improver*, the first edition of which was published in 1649, and which during the 1650s became firmly established as the standard single-authored agricultural work. Blith set the standard for the

---

153 Dymock to Hartlib, 15 April 1653, HP 55/2/6A.
154 Ephemerides 1655, HP 29/5/32A.
155 Boyle to Dymock, 15 March 1650, Boyle *Correspondence* I, p. 88. HP 62/2A.
156 Petty to Dymock, 16 July 1658, HP 66/23/1A-2B. For Dymock, see K. Yamamoto, *Taming Capitalism before its Triumph*, pp. 117–30.

new round of literature in his area of interest, central to which was 'the Advance and Betterment of their land'. This book by a practising farmer and captain in the Parliamentarian army met the mood of the moment and merited a second edition in 1652, which was much expanded and more lavishly designed, including with good illustrations, such as a fine engraved title page carrying the headline 'Vive la Republick'. To leave no doubt about the author's loyalties, this edition was dedicated to Lord President Cromwell, the Council of State, and Parliament more generally. None of this glamour detracted from the intrinsic worth of the contents, which are of outstanding quality.

There is little direct evidence about Hartlib's connection with Blith, but in 1652 he distributed the second edition to such experts as Robert Child and Ralph Austen, both of whom gave a favourable response. Furthermore, it is evident that Hartlib was at that date personally in touch with Blith, who even offered to assist Austen with the publication of his own first book. This proves that Blith was very much alive in July 1653, but Hartlib's letter to Austen of 21 October announced Blith's death which, in November of that year, Austen sincerely lamented.[157]

Ralph Austen

Austen was by no means a negligible figure. He engaged in a productive correspondence with Hartlib that probably began in 1651 and extended to May 1661. Austen generated more than seventy letters to Hartlib. Austen's proposal for a monograph on fruit trees met with Hartlib's approval and it was duly published in 1653. As an advertisement for this book, Hartlib published a short but worthy tract by a deceased anonymous author which constituted further publicity for fruit trees and contained much useful information on this subject.[158]

In the late 1650s John Beale struck up a friendly rivalry with Austen concerning their joint passion for fruit trees and cider. Austen served

---

157 Austen to Hartlib, 26 July and 1 November 1652, HP 41/1/10A and 12A. This evidence disposes of the *ODNB*/Wikipedia error, which gives Blith's death as 1654. Austen's *Treatise of Fruit Trees* was published in Oxford in 1653 and dedicated to Hartlib. For Blith, see K. Yamamoto, *Taming Capitalism Before its Triumph*, pp. 126–30 et passim; and for Austen, pp. 191–94 et passim.

158 *A Designe for Plentie, By Universall Planting of Fruit Trees* (London: printed for Richard Wodenothe [1652]).

in the humble capacity as Registrar to the Parliamentary Visitors to the University of Oxford and regarded himself as a dedicated servant of the Commonwealth.[159] In this capacity he assumed importance to Hartlib and indeed acted as his main agent in Oxford.

Sir Richard Weston

An opportunity for Hartlib to make a direct incursion into the field of husbandry publication arose in 1649, when William Spenser drew his attention to an unpublished essay emanating from the Catholic and Royalist Sir Richard Weston (1591–1652), of Sutton Place near Guildford, Surrey.[160] This tract was composed during Weston's exile in the Low Countries during the Civil War. The sound quality of his analysis proved that Weston was an experienced husbandman. He was also an inveterate inventor, whose main project was a huge scheme for a canal in the south-east of England. His Brabant and Flanders manuscript lay neglected until a copy was obtained by Edward Basnett, who passed this to William Spenser, a good friend of Hartlib. Quite separately, Robert Boyle also secured this manuscript.[161] It seems that in the process of transmission the authorship became obscured.

Once this document was obtained by Hartlib, he precipitously grasped the opportunity for publication. His edition of this modest twenty-six-page pamphlet appeared, according to Thomason, on 29 November 1650.[162]

---

159 For Austen, *ODNB* Ralph Austen (James Turner), and also his 'Ralph Austen, an Oxford Horticulturist of the Seventeenth Century', *Garden History*, 6:2 (1978), 39–45; D.C.R. Austen, 'Puritanism and Natural Philosophy Revisited: the Case of Ralph Austen (c.1612–1676)', *The Seventeenth Century*, 39:3 (2024), 359–99.

160 For Weston, *ODNB* Sir Richard Weston (Ernest Clarke/Mark Overton); Haffemeyer, *Les Lumières radicales*, pp. 443–44, 478–81 et passim.

161 'A poore Cavallier that hath compounded at 2. high rates, is the observer or now the true Experimenter in the West of the Brabant Husbandry, whereby hee hath regained those fines. With him Mr Boyl is very well acquainted and promised to give a full account of it'. Ephemerides, November 1650, HP 28/1/83A.

162 *A discours of husbandrie used in Brabant and Flanders; shewing the wonderfull improvement of land there; and serving as a pattern for our practice in this commonwealth* (London: William Dugard, 1650), Thomason E.613[12], Wing W1482. The first issue was erroneously dated 1605, which was corrected to 1650 in a reissue. Dugard was a friend of Hartlib. He was a successful schoolteacher as well as publisher. For Dugard and Hartlib, Haffemeyer, *Les Lumières radicales*, pp. 200–01 et passim.

Perhaps in imitation of Blith, Hartlib dedicated his Weston text to the Council of State and followed this with a politically orientated Address, emphasising that this modest introduction to the 'advancement of agriculture' related to the part of the economy that was 'the wellspring of wealth in all well-ordered societies'. Hartlib frankly admitted that his own experience in husbandry was negligible, but he believed that Providence had led him to associate with real experts, for whom he was destined 'to become conduit pipe thereof towards the Publick'.

Up to this point Hartlib seems to have taken little interest in the authorship of the *Discours*. Perhaps he already knew that this document was of Catholic and Royalist origin. In any case, around this date he informed William Spenser that the author was Weston, and Spenser confirmed that this was also his understanding.[163] The pamphlet was evidently a success, prompting Hartlib to issue a second and corrected edition, this time declaring that it was the work of 'Sir Richard Weston late of Sutton... his Legacie to his Sons... 1645'. This second edition was issued by Dugard in 1652 and a third in 1654. Hartlib attempted to make contact with Weston in May and December 1651, but to no avail. Weston died in May 1652.

It seems that Hartlib had no memory of a much earlier account that he had received about Weston from his friend John Pell, from whom he heard that 'One of the greatest Experimenters and triers of all manner of Projectes is one called Sir Richard Weston... In Sussex hee hase bought abundance of barren ground, which hee hase enclosed, and tryed all manner of experiments upon it'.[164] Also of interest is the evidence that at least three of Hartlib's informants were in direct contact with Weston during 1651. Edward Basnett noted that Weston had experimented with 'the Clover-grasse and sowing of Turneps with great successe'.[165] Around the same date Petty said that Weston told him that he relied on his own clover seeds, which he found superior to any imported from abroad.[166] Finally, around 1657 Robert Wood told Hartlib that his own

---

163 William Spenser to Hartlib, 9 December 1650, HP 46/7/9A.
164 Ephemerides 1639, HP 30/4/26A.
165 Ephemerides 1651, HP 20/2/7B.
166 Ephemerides 1651, HP 20/2/10A.

opinions on clover husbandry had been directly received from Weston, which must have been before 1652.[167]

Hartlib His Legacie, First and Second Editions

In view of this initial success, Hartlib was emboldened to capitalise on the Weston *Discours* experience. The main product of this next stage in his husbandry publication programme was his *Hartlib His Legacie*, which is arguably the best-known and most successful production of his publishing career. This was also an uncharacteristically shrewd piece of publicity near the start of his direct entry into publishing in this subject area. This initiative was also a boost to his already productive partnership with the publisher, Richard Wodenothe, who must have been responsible for the fine title page, at the very head of which in bold capitals was announced 'SAMUEL HARTLIB'. The book is dated 1651; the preface is signed 24 February, while Thomason inscribed '10 May' on his copy.[168] The *Legacie* title page was of course an appropriation of the title page of the Weston edition, but with Hartlib's surname inserted in place of Weston's. Also emphasising this connection, the book was called an 'enlargement' of the 'Discourse of Husbandry used in Brabant and Flanders.' The first section was simply a reprint of the Weston *Discours* edition of 1650, which Hartlib was also on the point of reissuing separately.

The saving grace of the volume was the anonymous 'Large letter concerning the Defects and Remedies of English Husbandry', the author of which was Robert Child (1613–1654).[169] Child's essay occupied 108 pages of the total page-length of about 140. Child's contribution was an excellent complement to the work of Walter Blith, a source which

---

167 Two undated notices from Wood to Hartlib, HP 26/67/1A-2B and 26/87/1B.
168 *Samuel Hartlib his legacie: or An enlargement of the Discourse of husbandry used in Brabant and Flaunders; wherein are bequeathed to the Common-wealth of England more outlandish and domestick experiments and secrets in reference to universall husbandry* (London: Printed by H. Hills, for Richard Wodenothe at the Star under St. Peters Church in Cornhill, 1651). Thomason E.628[11], Wing H989.
169 For Child, *ODNB* Robert Child (Stephen Clucas); G. H. Turnbull, 'Robert Child', *Publications of the Colonial Society of Massachusetts*, 38 (1947), 21–53; Webster *Instauration*, pp. 431–33 et passim; W. R. Newman, *Gehennical Fire: the Lives of George Starkey*; M.E. Newell, 'Robert Child and the Entrepreneurial Vision: Economy and Ideology in Early New England', *The New England Quarterly*, 68:2 (1995), 223–56.

seems to have been unknown to him at that date. With this act Child proved himself to be the backbone of Hartlib's activities in the fields of husbandry and natural history, besides retaining his long-standing involvements in chemistry, alchemy and technology.

Since the Weston tract was already in existence and continued to be issued separately, without Child's decisive intervention, the *Legacie* would not have been worth publishing. Hartlib's preface was perfunctory and dismal in quality. Even his most uplifting sentiment was not particularly edifying: 'we may hope through Gods blessing to see better dayes, and to be able to beare *necessary* and *Publique burdens* with more ease to ourselves, and benefit to *Humane Society* then hitherto we could attaine unto'. Hardly any of the fragments, of which comprise the last twenty pages of the book, were worthy of publication.

Notwithstanding such drawbacks, the book was a success. A second edition appeared in the early summer of 1652, 'augmented', but only by eight pages. Some extra content was introduced by compression of the typesetting, hence impairing the legibility of the whole book.[170] The added material constituted a series of ten letters extending from July 1651 to January 1652, which were anonymous, but obviously emanated from Arnold Boate. A further addition was a twenty-five-page alphabetical list of Boate's 'interrogatories' relating to *Irelands Naturall History*, which constituted the most interesting feature of the new edition.[171] From their content it is evident that the Boate letters were to some extent inspired by Hartlib, who seemed to have been oblivious of Boate's intention to contradict the Large Letter by Robert Child that constituted the bedrock of the same book.

Regardless of such shortcomings, the first two editions of the *Legacie* cemented Hartlib's reputation as a leading player in the field of husbandry, as for instance shown by communications from the string of enthusiasts recorded in his Ephemerides. For instance, in 1653 he noted:

---

170 *Samuel Hartlib his legacie: or An enlargement of the Discourse of husbandry used in Brabant & Flaunders: wherein are bequeathed to the common-wealth of England, more outlandish and domestick experiments and secrets, in reference to universall husbandry. The second edition* (London: Printed by R. & W. Leybourn, for Richard Wodenothe, in Leaden-Hall Market, next door to the Golden Hart 1652). Wing H990.

171 For the Interrogatories project, Webster *Instauration*, pp. 428–34.

The 29. May on Saturday one came to mee the first time who gave mee his name as followeth under his owne hand. John Nevil of Thorney in the County of Nottingham six miles from Lincolne. Hee came mainly to be acquainted with me about my published Books of Husbandry himself being a great Experimenter of Husbandry.[172]

Irelands Naturall History

Irelands Naturall History... now published by Samuel Hartlib Esq. (Wing B3372) was a further opportunistic exploit of Hartlib, which was probably published in the early summer of 1652, and therefore almost simultaneously with the *Legacie*. The *Naturall History* derived from a manuscript produced by Gerard Boate in about 1645, which was recovered by Hartlib after Gerard's death in 1650. Since, as noted in chapter 2, the Boate family was well-known to Hartlib, it is likely that he was given free access to Gerard's work. The book was published over-hastily, leading to imperfections and limitations that were frankly admitted by all concerned. Hartlib freely conceded that he had issued an 'imperfect work'.[173] He therefore set about locating a specialist capable of achieving a superior standard in an anticipated second edition. Fortuitously Robert Child had moved to Ireland in May 1651 and immediately began a systematic survey of the husbandry and natural history of this country, the progress of which was recorded in a dozen, mostly lengthy, letters to Hartlib dating from August 1651 to 8 October 1653. He was therefore the ideal person to take over responsibility for a major revision of *Irelands Naturall History*, a project upon which he worked conscientiously until his own premature death sometime between February and April 1654. For this purpose, the interrogatories were a key asset. Hartlib distributed these widely, including five copies sent to Robert Boyle. Hartlib was heartened by the early arrival of responses to the interrogatories, perhaps the first of these being from Thomas Field, a humble carpenter and expert on soap production, whose home was in Dublin. Field was modest about his abilities, but his text was well up to the required standard.[174]

---

172 Ephemerides 1653, HP 28/2/62B.
173 Hartlib to Boyle, 28 February 1654, Boyle *Correspondence* I, pp. 154–63.
174 Field to Hartlib, 27 March 1654, HP 31/14/1A-4B. Field visited Hartlib on 12 July 1654, Ephemerides 1654, HP 29/4/24B.

Following the pattern that was becoming established in Hartlib's publications, the *Naturall History* was dedicated to Oliver Cromwell and also Charles Fleetwood, the Lord Deputy of Ireland. The dedicatory Epistle was signed by Hartlib. It is clear from his exchanges with Dury in Switzerland that, once again, this component was drawn up by Dury rather than Hartlib. It is also clear that Dury had never seen the book, nor was he familiar with its list of contents.[175] Accordingly, the pious sentiments of the Epistle show no engagement with the book. The single point of interest in Dury's input is his suggestion that the current 'replanting' of Ireland provided an opportunity to recruit exiled Bohemians, other Protestants in similar distress, and also some 'well affected' specialists from the Low Countries. The importance he attached to this controversial idea explains why he gave precise instructions about the distribution of the draft epistle to the reader. In particular he was insistent that it should be seen by Richard Bradshaw, the British Agent and Deputy of the Merchant Adventurers in Hamburg. Perhaps Dury believed that Bradshaw might exercise influence on members of the Council of State to support this idea. Comenius, speaking on behalf of the exiled Bohemian community, reiterated their determination to return to their homeland and therefore he conclusively rejected the Irish notion.[176]

An insight into the materials that Child would have incorporated into his interrogatories is provided by extracts communicated by Hartlib to Boyle.[177] Over the next few years, other of Hartlib's associates in Ireland, especially Myles Symner and Robert Wood, took up the challenge and intermittently worked through the interrogatories and prepared informative revisions of the *Naturall History*, but completion of the planned definitive edition was undermined by disorganisation and lack of leadership on the part of Hartlib. Finally, the project was completely disrupted by the chaos in Ireland during the collapse of the Republic.[178]

---

175 Dury to Hartlib, 2 and 24 April 1652, HP 4/2/15A-B and HP 4/2/29A-B.
176 Comenius to Hartlib, 9 February 1658, HP 7/11/9A.
177 Child to Hartlib, 2 February 1652, HP 15/5/18A; Hartlib to Boyle, 8 May 1654, Boyle *Correspondence* I, pp. 169–70.
178 Myles Symner seems to have been the leading investigator, and likely main author of a set of relevant notes, HP 62/45/1A-7B. Symner (Milo Sumner) is an interesting figure, deserving of more attention than he has received. For basics, Barnard, *Cromwellian Ireland*, pp. 210–28 et passim.

Hartlib His Legacy: The Third Edition

The third edition of *Hartlib His Legacy* appeared in the spring of 1655. Already, as indicated in Hartlib's letter to Robert Boyle of May 1654, work on this radically revised and extended version was already well-advanced. Hartlib declared to Boyle that this new version would include a substantial additional essay by 'the late Dr. Child', the aim of which was a decisive refutation of the late Arnold Boate's polemical letters from Paris included in the second edition. Hartlib promised that this new essay would include 'diverse excellent observations and experiments, which, are like to enrich these nations, if their industry be not wanting'. Furthermore, he predicted that Child's work in Ireland would constitute a 'good foundation of life for that honest country'.[179]

On this occasion Hartlib's ambitions were largely fulfilled. Here Wodenothe reverted to the excellent design standards adopted for the first edition. One of the few negative features was the direct input of Hartlib himself. Once again, he failed to generate an introduction proportionate to the scale of the challenge. Instead of an uplifting preface from himself as the editor, he substituted a short excerpt from page 223 of John Norden's *The Surveyor's Dialogue* dating from 1607.

The third edition of the *Legacy* was almost twice the length of the second.[180] As previously, much of the content comprised short items that ranged from a single paragraph to a few pages. In this version the reader would have been relieved to find a detailed introductory eleven-page synopsis.

This edition reproduced virtually the whole of the second edition, with the notable exception of the Ireland interrogatories, which were circulated separately. This arrangement left Child's 'Large Letter' in pride of place, occupying the first ninety-eight pages. The next section was of similar length and comprised mostly short extracts, the notable exception being the fourteen-page critique by Arnold Boate of the 'Large

---

179 Hartlib to Boyle, 8 May 1654, Boyle *Correspondence* I, p. 171, quotation slightly abbreviated.

180 *Samuel Hartlib, his legacy of husbandry wherein are bequeathed to the common-wealth of England, not onely Braband and Flanders, but also many more outlandish and domestick experiments and secrets (of Gabriel Plats and others) never heretofore divulged in reference to universal husbandry: with a table shewing the general contents or sections of the several augmentations and enriching enlargements in this third edition* (London: Printed by J.M. [John Macock] for Richard Wodenothe, 1655), Wing H991.

Letter' by Child, which is immediately followed by a forty-page defence by Child. Fortunately for the reader, both the Boate and the Child contributions contain a good deal of interesting observation respecting husbandry and the natural sciences. The reader would also have been grateful to Hartlib for devoting the following section of more than fifty pages derived from a hitherto unpublished work from the archive of Gabriel Plattes. The later sections of this third edition contained some contributions of a more theoretical character, introducing the reader to the latest thinking on the principles of botany. These logically followed on from the 'Question concerning Fruitfulness' which had appeared in Dymock's *Division for Setting out of Land* in 1653. In the first part of the *Division*, Hartlib had squeezed in a series of short pieces, which might have been surplus material left over from the second edition of the *Legacie*. The most important of these items is the anonymous 'A great Question concerning Fruitfulness, offered to all ingenious Searchers of Nature' (p. 16), which influenced Worsley's thinking in the run up to his Phytological Letter. Touching the authorship of the 'great Question' there are various credible candidates, but currently I favour Robert Child, partly because this piece seems to relate to his never completed *De Fertilitate*, which was composed at precisely this date.

The first and most important element in this later section of the *Legacy* comprised 'A Philosophical Letter Concerning Vegetation', which was followed by three short extracts relating to the same subject. Each of these derived from letters to Hartlib contained in the Hartlib Papers. The first emanated from Benjamin Worsley, dated 16 May 1654, the second from Johann Moriaen, dated 19 December 1654, and the third from William Rand dated 18 July 1651.[181]

The Vegetation letter is of special interest on account of being an early expression of a scheme that soon found expression in Worsley's 'Phytological Letter', which in a lucid style delineated a comprehensive botanical research programme. This now celebrated essay appears as an anonymous document in the Hartlib Papers, about which various erroneous conclusions about the authorship arose before it became accepted that it was the work of Worsley.[182]

---

181 The sources for these letters (located in the *Legacie*, pp. 217–21) are (in order): HP 66/15/1A-4B; 55/14/18A; 62/30/1A-4B.

182 'A Copy of a Phytologicall Letter written to Mr. Hartlib', HP 8/22/1A-4B. Originally published in 1692, with the assumption that it was written by Robert

William Potter and the Land Bank

Perhaps offered as a bonus to readers, the penultimate pages (290–99) of the third edition were dedicated to promoting the concept of the Land Bank. This idea was directly relevant to ongoing concerns about unemployment, poverty and the stagnation of trade, including husbandry, but it also possessed a more general economic significance.[183] The Land Bank system was designed to circumvent the many hazards associated with current banking practices. These stemmed from many sources, but prominent among them were such issues as counterfeiting, or dependence on the supply of precious metals. The method proposed to solve this problem was introduction of a universal credit based on factors possessing a stable value such as land. It was argued that the raising of bank credit only by or upon land would 'multiply money' to a maximum determined by the value of land in the nation as whole, thereby potentially operating as a major boost to commerce and to the general wealth of the nation. The main initiative for the circulation of the Land Bank idea was William Potter's *The Key to Wealth: Or a New Way for Improving Trade* (1650), but it was also known through the writings of Henry Robinson, an established contact of Hartlib, whose views on this idea were recorded in the Ephemerides, about July 1649.[184] This entry confirms that Potter and Robinson were in direct contact with one another and also that they were keen to keep Hartlib in their ambit: 'One Potter is the Author to the designe and Book *Of the Key to Wealth* a very ingenious Gentleman of Mr H. Robinsons acquaintance. The scope of it is How to drive a Trade without Monies'.[185]

Boyle. For an apparently compelling argument for William Petty's authorship, Tony Aspromourgos, 'The Invention of the Concept of Social Surplus: Petty and the Hartlib Circle', *European Journal of Economic Thought*, 12:1 (2005), 01–24. For attribution to Worsley, Leng *Worsley*, pp. 104–05, and 202 where it is dated April 1657.

183 C. Wennerlind, 'Money: Hartlibian Political Economy and the New Culture of Credit,' in *Mercantilism Reimagined: Political Economy in Early Modern Britain and its Empire*, ed. by P.J. Stern and C. Wennerlind (Oxford: Oxford University Press, 2014), pp. 74–94; K.A. Moore, 'The Blood that Nourishes the Body Politic', *Early American Studies*, 1 (2019), 01–36.

184 Ephemerides 1649, HP 28/1/26B and 29B. Regarding this project Dury proclaimed 'what more could be desired for encrease of publick or privat riches'.

185 Ephemerides 1650, HP 28/1/68A.

Regardless of the preparatory work of Robinson and Potter, the Land Bank would have been unfamiliar to most of the *Legacie* readership. For Hartlib a popular presentation of this subject was a shrewd piece of marketing. The advertisement for this item in the synopsis was entirely favourable to the promoter of this scheme, one 'Mr William Potter (a Gentleman of great deserts and of a most publique spirit)'. The essay was certainly not produced by Potter, but by a writer having a firm command of the general problem area, and without any partisan leanings. The presentation was crisp and highly accessible. The author evidently possessed an instinct for lucid analytical exposition. This exposition deserves much more notice than it has received. Hartlib gives no clue about the identity of the author, but few of his associates would have been capable of such a demanding task.

Light may be shed on the authorship by the exposition of the Land Bank issue that had been published by Hartlib in 1653. This constituted a twelve-page essay, stemming from another anonymous author, who also clearly possessed a sound command of the subject. This essay was granted a separate title page, but it was relegated to the status of an appendix to Cressy Dymock's thirty-three-page pamphlet *A Discoverie for Division or Setting out of Land...imparted in a letter to Samuel Hartlib esquire*.[186] With respect to the authorship of this compelling 1653 Land Bank exposition, detective work by the editors of the Culpeper Correspondence has established that this was the work of Sir Cheney Culpeper. This seems to be this activist's only known publication, unless, of course, he was also the author of the anonymous Land Bank exposition in the 1655 edition of the *Legacy*.[187] At the moment there seems to be no other likely alternative author.[188]

---

186 *A DISCOVERIE For Division or Setting out of Land, as to the best Form. Published by Samuel Hartlib Esquire, for Direction and more Advantage and Profit of the Adventurers and Planters in the FENS and other Waste and undisposed Places in England and IRELAND. Whereunto are added some other Choice Secrets or Experiments of Husbandry. With a Philosophical Quere concerning* the *Cause of Fruitfulness. AND An Essay* to shew *How all Lands may be improved in a New Way to become the ground of the increase of Trading and Revenue to this Common-wealth* (London: Printed for Richard Wodenothe in Leaden-hall-street, 1653), Wing H990.

187 Culpeper *Letters*, pp. 293–94. Yet a further essay on this subject, anonymous and undated, opening with a discussion of the Amsterdam Bank, is at HP 17/14/1A-2B.

188 Other possible authors known to Hartlib were Benjamin Worsley and Robert Wood, but there are arguments against both. Certainly, the 1655 author was familiar with Worsley's *Proffits humbly presented*.

It should be added that discussion of the Land Bank proposition did not end at this point. It was widely canvassed that the Land Bank as more suitable for the New World than the Old. The strangest version of this alternative in the Hartlib Papers is the suggestion that the Land Bank was best applied in the West Indies. Martin Noell, one of the richest of all the British *nouveau riche*, was nominated for this undertaking. Nothing came of this and it is unlikely that Noell would have warmed to participating with the Hartlib team. Further exchanges about the Land Bank and related economic issues, even touching upon the efficient minting of farthings, sprang up on the eve of the Restoration, on this occasion instigated by Robert Wood in Dublin, who aspired to generate economic reform schemes that might be applied in Ireland. Once again Hartlib was the mediator of these exchanges.

As with other embryonic reform projects, this one was also overtaken by events. However, in this case there were two positive outcomes. First, Wood was invited to serve on the Restoration Irish Council of Trade, and for this purpose he produced a document headed '*The Advancement of Trade*', which was to be circulated to this committee with the aim of establishing the principle that 'Land, which is the only reall security. To be [rendered a] reall & true security'.[189] Secondly, as noted in the next chapter, the Land Bank issue arose at Rota club discussions in the late spring of 1660. These were the last trace of the Land Bank in the experience of Hartlib and his friends, but the idea remained in play, particularly in New England, where it is established that the first advocates of this idea were directly influenced by Potter personally and by the Culpeper essay contained in Hartlib's *Discoverie for the Division of Land*, which is a fitting tribute to William Potter, Cheney Culpeper and Hartlib for their tenacity in pursuing the diffusion of this important proposition.[190]

---

189 Wood to Hartlib, 23 March 1661, HP 33/1/73A-74B.
190 J.K. Horsefeld, 'The Origins of Blackwell's Model of a Bank', *The William and Mary Quarterly*, 23:1 (1966), 121–35 (pp. 124–26).

Fig. 5 Engraved title-page of *Biblia święta: to jest, ksiegi pisma swietego starego y nowego przymierza* (Amsterdam: Christophel Cunrad, 1660).

5. *Phosphore Redde Diem!*

WILL'T ne'er be morning? Will that promis'd light Ne'er break, and clear those clouds of night? Sweet Phosphor, bring the day.

Francis Quarles, *Phosphore redde diem*[1]

5.1 Family Affairs

Little space in this study has so far been devoted to the practicalities of Hartlib's life in London. This short resumé aims to repair this omission. It is certain that, on his arrival in London, Hartlib briefly occupied one of Lord Brooke's spacious houses, specifically that located in Hackney, which, as noted above, became home to one of Hartlib's ephemeral academy projects. By February 1631, he had switched to Coleman Street. This also was a temporary arrangement. By the summer of 1631 he had relocated a short distance away to a house near the Vine in Duke's Place in the parish of St Katherine 'Cree Church', which was near to Aldgate.[2] There he remained until about April 1650, when his family transferred to a house in Angel Court near to the Charing Cross. His final move, as a widower, which was probably made in November 1659, was to Axe Yard, King's Street, Westminster. At Axe Yard he shared the house with Samuel Jr. and his family.[3] It seems that the Clodius family moved

---

1 Quarles' poem was derived from Martial, *Epigrams*, Bk. VIII:21, the Latin first lines of which were quoted by Hartlib to Boyle, 15 November 1659, Boyle *Correspondence* I, p. 385. For helpful illustrations, drawing upon the Agas maps of London, relating to Hartlib's main places of residence, see Haffemeyer, *Les Lumières radicales*, Figures 1 and 2, pp. 19 and 21.

2 Willam Hamilton to Hartlib, 17 December 1649, HP 9/11/28B gives Hartlib's address as Duke's Place 'against the trees in the open cowrte'.

3 Wood to Hartlib, 8 December 1658, HP 33/1/36A, mentioned that Hartlib had 'removed to his sons'.

at about the same date to another house in Axe Yard. This relocation made Hartlib Sr., Hartlib Jr., Clodius and their respective families near neighbours of the young Samuel Pepys.

Concerning Hartlib's family life, little is known. His mother and two sisters, and Georg, his elder brother and his family, almost never feature in the Hartlib Papers. Concerning Hartlib's mother, who lived on in Danzig, Petr Figulus reminded Hartlib that 'shee is much greeved at her sonne's negligence in writing to her. For hee hath not written to her but once, soone after his arrival at London... His Mother's heart cannot chuse but bee sorely troubled about it'.[4] If this is representative, it is not surprising that his family members appear only perfunctorily in his papers.

Hartlib's marriage to Mary Burningham of Reading took place on 20 January 1629. Relations with the Burningham family seem to have been limited, but cordial. Many of Hartlib's correspondents ritually sent their regards to Mary and her family, but almost always without naming any of them. There occur just a handful of specific references to Mary, most of them relating to ill-health, as for instance in 1654, when Hartlib recounted to Boyle that his 'poor wife hath been sick unto death', but, with the aid of laudanum, this emergency was brought to a rapid end.[5] Among Hartlib's correspondents, the most consistent interest in Mary was shown by Petr Figulus who, on 22 November 1658, communicated a lengthy and heartfelt expression of grief upon hearing of her death. Here he called her 'your truest & faithfullest Companion & fellow bearer of all your distresses & burdens.'[6] From the evidence preserved in Hartlib's papers it is easy to imagine the scale of the burden carried by Mary. Always handicapped by meagre resources, she hosted an unending stream of Protestant exiles who were referred to Hartlib's care. She housed and supervised Hartlib's team of amanuenses, most of whom were also exiles. Mary then needed to care for more important guests, some of whom stayed with Hartlib for months, and finally she had to

---

4   Figulus to Hartlib, 16 March 1658, HP 9/17/3A.
5   Hartlib to Boyle, 28 February 1654, Boyle *Correspondence* I, p. 162. Mary's medical care may well have come from her cousin Anthony Metcalfe, a practising doctor, who was their neighbour at New Court.
6   Figulus to Hartlib, 22 November 1658, HP 9/17/49A.

make provision for the endless stream of casual daily callers, many of whom were recorded in the Ephemerides.

It is easy to see why, in such challenging circumstances, the Hartlib parents lost sight of their obligations to their three children. None of their births were mentioned in Hartlib papers and little is known about their existence. There is every sign that their care and education fell into abeyance. Considering Hartlib's famed dedication to education, and his respect for educated women, his apparent indifference to education within his own family constitutes something of a shock. It is evident that his preoccupation with the affairs of the world was so intense that it excluded care of himself or any of his closest family members.

The eldest was Samuel Jr. who, it seems, was born in 1631. Mary, their eldest daughter, was perhaps born in 1633, and Anne (known as Nan) the younger daughter around 1639. Obviously concerned about the Hartlib children, John and Dorothy Dury, during their brief spell in Rotterdam in 1645, made preparations to assume care of Samuel Jr. and Mary, but these arrangements collapsed, partly on account of Mary's ill-health.[7] The opportunity for the Durys to intervene reoccurred in 1647, when Dury was in charge of the royal children at St James's. Samuel stayed with the Dury family for some months. This expression of generosity perhaps helps to explain Dury's overt disappointment about Hartlib's failure to visit his wife Dorothy and her sick child in 1654 when they were alone owing to Dury being detained abroad.[8]

During his teens Samuel Jr. made an almost universally unfavourable impression. During 1652 he was billeted at the home of Giles Andrew at Epping, an episode which seems to have been uneventful. Shortly afterwards he entered the government clerical service, where he occupied a variety of minor posts, before reaching a more senior position in the late 1650s which even allowed him to have a working relationship with John Thurloe, Secretary of the Council of State. In this context he played an active role in the attempt to gain public support for the Dury/Hartlib benighted Agency for Learning. Also on the positive side, Samuel Jr. seems to have been helpful to many of Hartlib's friends. John Beale even

---

7   Dorothy Dury to Hartlib, 20 April 1645, HP 3/2/112A. For Dury's expression of concern over the 'sadde case' of Samuel Jr., Dury to Hartlib, 27 October 1647, HP 3/3/45A.

8   Dury to Hartlib, 1 July 1654, HP 4/3/13A.

euphemistically posited: 'Can your Worthy son Hartlib... thinke fit to bring in a newe modell of a house of Peeres by Privy counsellours, field-officers, & their adherents'.[9] By 1658 Samuel Jr. was already married and resident at Axe Yard, Westminster, where he was a neighbour of Pepys, who was also his colleague in the civil service. His profile was then further enhanced when his widowed father joined him at his Axe Yard address. In September 1661, he and his wife were invited to attend the funeral of John Pell's wife. His government service continued into the Restoration, but his reputation became increasingly clouded. Friends of Hartlib Sr. in the Netherlands evolved a plan whereby Samuel would assist in engineering a potentially lucrative business scheme evolved by Laurentius de Geer, but, notwithstanding many reminders from John Dury, Samuel failed to respond. He drifted into increasing trouble until, around 1670, he fled to the Netherlands and never returned.[10]

Each of the two daughters of Hartlib found apparently suitable marriage partners, both of continental origin, but from very different social classes. In late 1653 Mary married Friedrick Clodius.[11] From early 1654 Hartlib's correspondents respectfully called him 'son Clodius'. He seems to have been known to Hartlib since the second half of 1651, when he sprang into life in the Ephemerides, which for that period contained an impressive range of references deriving from him. Clodius was never slow to advertise and exaggerate his credentials. For instance, with respect to the rich and influential Wendelius Sybilista, Clodius promised information about a powerful cure, Sybilista 'being his special friend to the Duke at Wolfenbüttel and learned in *omni scribili*. Being very rich and having but one daughter whom he offered for marriage to Mr Clodius. The same that hath written a Preface to [the famous traveller Adam] Olearius' booke'.[12] As noted in the previous chapter, Hartlib and Dury were so much overcome by the new arrival that, in 1652, they entered into a formal pact with him, promising exalted achievements from their joint operations. Strangely, Clodius was then virtually unmentioned in

---

9   Beale to Hartlib, 22 March 1659, HP 51/101A-B.
10   Turnbull *Hartlib*, pp. 42–47.
11   Keller and Penman, 'Science and the Shared Interests of Samuel Hartlib's London and Friedrick Clodius's Gottdorf'.
12   Ephemerides, early 1652, HP 28/2/28B. The book mentioned here is Olearius's famous *Beschreibung der muscowitischen und persischen Reise* (Schleswig, 1647).

the Ephemerides until immediately after his marriage, when the parade of his intelligence resumed in earnest.

One extremely sad experience recorded by Hartlib was his daughter Mary's miscarriage, after which Hartlib noted on the following day that she was left 'very weak'.[13] Clodius was of course a controversial figure, but this may not have impinged on his marital relationship. On the other hand, his erratic behaviour was, in the end, deeply wounding for Hartlib. Dury lamented that Hartlib's health problems were compounded by 'your Son Clodius misdemeanours' and 'the wrong he doth to you', which Dury believed would also alienate Hartlib's friends.[14]

With respect to his younger daughter Anne/Nan, Hartlib opined: 'let them [competing suitors] know that my daughter hath had many suitors, some Landed-men to which I would not give my consent. I liking well the wealth but not the persons as I ever did my son in Law's manners and comportments to this day'.[15] The fortunate suitor in this contest was Johannes Rothe (knighted by Charles II: Sir John Rode), who combined wealth, aristocratic status and an enquiring intelligence.[16] Their wedding, on 10 July 1660, was held at Goring House. Pepys, who attended the event, described the occasion as one of 'very great state, cost, and noble company'. Also worth quoting is the coarse remark of Pepys on 1 July 1660: 'I saw Mynheer Roder, that is to marry Sam[Jr.] Hartlib's sister, a great fortune for her to light on, she being worth nothing in the world'. Between April and June 1661, the smooth progress of her pregnancy and the birth of her first child, a boy, were faithfully recorded in the weekly letters from Dury to Hartlib.

5.2 Oppressive Pain

Respecting Hartlib's own personal affairs there was no issue more pressing than his indifferent health. This issue became desperate in the late 1650s, but the roots of this problem can be traced back much earlier. Hartlib kept a rough record of his kidney stone and related ailments

---

13 Hartlib to Boyle, 14 September 1658, Boyle *Correspondence* I, p. 291.
14 Dury to Hartlib, 12 August 1661, HP 4/4/3A.
15 Hartlib to Worthington, 3 August 1660, HP 20/1/2B.
16 F. Sierhuis, 'Transnational Networks and Radical Religion: Johannes Rothe and the Construction of Prophetic Charisma', *Renaissance Studies*, 36:1 (2021), 142–62.

from 1642 until 1645.[17] Already in the autumn of 1642 Dury noted that he had in The Hague spoken to 'Dr Havernfeld concerning yowr pissing of blood; hee saith that that may come rather from another cause then from the stone of the kidneyes chiefly seeing yow have no constant paine; but if it were found certainly to bee the stone, hee would send yow a little glasse with water which would cure it'.[18] This proved to be the first of a multiplicity of interventions by European medical specialists on Hartlib's behalf. In 1644, Hartlib's first known contact with Benjamin Worsley also related to a treatment for stone.[19]

By 1656 Hartlib's distress concerning his ill-health was more prevalent and disturbing. In August 1656 this factor prompted his resignation from the Privy Council Committee on the new Durham College. In graphic terms, his draft letter of resignation lamented that for 'many months I have groaned under a compilation of most paineful diseases of the stone, strangury and the piles. And though I have used many medicines yet to this hour my paines continue upon mee. So that I cannot stir abroad or doe almost anything else'.[20] The spectrum of interrelated pathological conditions described at this point, all beyond the capacities of medicine as it existed at that date to relieve, represented a dire warning that Hartlib's life was already endangered.

During 1657 almost every month featured letters from Hartlib's friends communicating sympathy about his illnesses and offering a profuse range of potential cures, or the identity of promising-looking practitioners. During this period his sickness was so debilitating that his letters were habitually written by his amanuenses.[21]

The year 1658 saw no evidence of relief. Hartlib wrote to Pell about his kidney and bladder stones, 'both of which still do put me to impossible torments. I void still every day five, six, or seven stones, pretty big ones...'[22] Once again, many of Hartlib's letters were written by intermediaries. By this point advice and medicaments were flooding

17 HP 60/4/6A-11B.
18 Dury to Hartlib, 9 October 1642, HP 2/9/37A.
19 HP 60/4/6A.
20 Hartlib, draft letter to Sir Walter Strickland, August 1656, HP 30/5/10B.
21 See for instance, the very first letters from John Beale to Hartlib, where sickness impeded his attention to the drafts of Beale's *Herefordshire Orchards*, HP 31/1/6A-18B.
22 Hartlib to Pell, 2 February 1658, Vaughan *Protectorate*, II, pp. 446–47.

in from many parts of Europe. The following years witnessed basically no amelioration in his condition. He continued to report stone in his kidney and bladder, also ulcers in the bladder, piles, the voiding of blood, strangury etc. Friends began to express their anxiety about the irreplaceable loss to public service that Hartlib's death would represent. As Figulus baldly stated: 'the Publique & the cause of many good and very usefull Endeavours to the Common Good are sorely endangered'.[23] Similarly, a week later, Figulus exclaimed more fully: 'For if nowe you should bee taken awaye, a great losse it should bee in England for the whole Protestancy everywhere. An Instrument of such universall qualitie, so much exercised & able to doe & to promote good on all sides to all men, in all occasions is rare nowe adayes'.[24]

In the final stages of Hartlib's life, we have access to an unusual bulk of first-hand witness statements, which is something of a rarity and, in our case, of particular interest. I am therefore taking the liberty at this point of quoting these testimonies more fully than is the usual practice.

To his new friend, John Winthrop of Connecticut, Hartlib admitted that in recent years he had been 'in the middst of very many trialls and horrid pains arising from the stone in the bladder, wherewith I have been afflicted near these 4 years, most of which time I have been confined to my house'.[25]

Disregarding his own pitiful condition, Hartlib still found time to plead for aid to other friends in need. In one case, he recounted having written to John Evelyn and Colonel Edward Harley in support John Beale's long-standing claim to the mastership of St Katherine's Hospital in Ledbury, Herefordshire. The letter ended abruptly after a single paragraph with the writer's lament that: 'No more at present my tormenting fits comming too fast upon mee but that I am now and ever...'[26]

By the beginning of 1661 Hartlib's fears had worsened: 'I have a dangerous disease besides the tormenting, hanging about me. If it

---

23 Figulus to Hartlib, 19 July 1658, HP 9/17/11A.
24 Figulus to Hartlib, 26 July 58, HP 15/9/5A.
25 Hartlib to Winthrop, 16 March 1660, HP 7/7/1A.
26 Hartlib to 'Right Noble Sir', likely Arthur Annesley, recently ennobled as the Earl of Anglesey, BL Add.MS 15948f, fols 100A-B. Likely May 1660, on account of close similarity with Beale to Hartlib, 19 May 1660, HP 31/1/70A-B.

should encrease, I hope God will shorten my days... It's called in English the dead palsey, which is a more dispatching disease, then the other grievous disease'.[27] Hartlib was right to fear dead palsy, by which he meant paralysis on one side of the body, now known as stroke.

At the end of that year, he remained pessimistic: 'My health is still very hazardous, and more tormenting than before; ...The stone is like a bull enraged, that will not fall with one blow'.[28]

During the last few months of his life, friends persisted in offering helpful hints about assistance, most often about stone-cutting experts and their methods. Hartlib graciously thanked his well-wishers and declared an interest in their panaceas, while being resigned to their ineffectiveness.

Most of Hartlib's last letters to Worthington include some remark about his desperate condition. On 16 December 1661 he complained that 'I labour under the pain and tormenting effects of it [the stone], that I have reason to despair of my life'.[29]

On 14 February Hartlib confessed that in view of being 'tormented in body' this was likely to be his last letter to Worthington, which, alas, was exactly the case.[30]

While appreciating the desperation of the situation, Worthington expressed the hope that 'your pain of the stone, though grievous to endure, is not so near the putting a period to your days of service here; but that as heretofore you have been preserved when it was thus with you, it may be so still, and that you may live to enjoy that contentment which you promise yourself'.[31] Worthington's supportive remarks unwittingly turned out to be an adjuration that perfectly fitted the solemn circumstances in which it was delivered. It is quite likely that, as Hartlib feared, he was on the morning of 10 March subject to yet another stroke, which on this occasion proved to be fatal. He was buried at St Martin-in-the-Fields on Wednesday 12 March 1662.[32]

---

27 Hartlib to Worthington, 1 January 1661, Crossley I, p. 257.
28 Hartlib to Worthington, 2 November 1661, Crossley II, Part 1, p. 68.
29 Hartlib to Worthington, 16 December 1661, Crossley II, Part 1, p. 93.
30 Hartlib to Worthington, 14 February 1662, Crossley II, Part 1, p. 107.
31 Worthington to Hartlib, 24 February 1662, Crossley II, Part 1, p. 111.
32 For sources, see Turnbull *Hartlib*, p. 72.

5.3 Hard Times

During the last year of the Protectorate, especially after the death of Oliver Cromwell in September 1658, Hartlib and his friends were apprehensive about the future. As Martin Grundmann wrote, 'we doe not know how soon the night may overtake us'.[33]

Following Cromwell's death, Hartlib suddenly discovered that it was impossible to retrieve his guaranteed state allowance. As he exclaimed to Robert Boyle: 'my pensions of two hundred pounds a year being founded upon his highness's and council's orders, and privy seals, now utterly made null. Last our lady-day I should have received seventy-five pounds out of the exchequer; but it being delayed till this change of government, there is no hope to get one penny of it'.[34]

This disjunction was a serious issue, prejudicing any chance of him ever again executing the range of services that he had customarily provided, including of course the supply of intelligence to the various agencies of central government.

He fell back to an even greater extent on the support of patrons and groups of friends. Especially important in this respect was Laurentius de Geer who, with prompting from his secretary, Petr Figulus, was in the habit of generously rewarding Hartlib for his services. As de Geer achieved familiarity with Hartlib's programmes, he was even prompted to reconsider his own plans for the future. As Figulus observed: 'Your many hearty Expressions to this purpose [the public good], you make in your Letters, & especially tending to stirre up the spirit of Monsieur de Geer to resolve so generously as hee seemes to begine to use his temporall Estate to further such laudable & Godly endes'.[35]

The possibility of Hartlib playing a more active role in the philanthropic efforts of de Geer rapidly evaporated. In 1656, with the exile of Comenius to Amsterdam, the Czech naturally became the priority for de Geer. At this sensitive moment Hartlib unwisely pressed de Geer to support Moriaen, which evoked the caustic response from de Geer that Moriaen would not have faced financial ruin if he had resisted the temptations of alchemy. Comenius wisely reminded Hartlib

---

33 Grundmann to Hartlib, 15 March 1659, HP 10/5/9A-10B.
34 Hartlib to Boyle, 17 March 1659, Boyle *Correspondence* I, p. 354.
35 Figulus to Hartlib, 11 October 1658, HP 9/17/34A.

that de Geer would not react kindly to those who exerted unreasonable pressure on him.³⁶ Figulus also admonished Hartlib that in light of his experience with Moriaen, de Geer had become suspicious 'about yours & Mr Morians &c publicke Concernements' and more broadly that he harboured 'some secret feare & doubtings of all the like Inventions & Endeavours'. Fortunately for Hartlib, his assistance was essential for facilitating the heavy publishing commitments of Comenius, at this date specifically with respect to the *Lux in Tenebris* as discussed above in chapter 3, and also with the distribution of the massive *Didactica Magna*, which had just been published in Amsterdam, of course at the expense of de Geer. This was an event of such importance that de Geer at one point instructed Figulus to join Hartlib in London to help with the distribution.³⁷

In the main Hartlib was thrown back on minor donations from private sources. For instance, in 1659 Worthington collected £10 from colleagues in Cambridge. Most of these were long-standing associates of Hartlib and Worthington, such as the three Platonists, Ralph Cudworth, Henry More and Benjamin Whichcote. There were also three less expected names, but all known to Hartlib at this date: Samuel Craddock (until 1656 a Fellow of Emmanuel College), Francis Marsh (Fellow of Caius College 1651–1661) and John Wilkins (Master of Trinity College from the spring of 1659 to August 1660). Obviously alert to the hardships being experienced by Hartlib, Worsley reported to Lady Ranelagh:

> For our Unwearied Frind Mr Hartlib I am very glad to heare the Lord hath still preserved him. And indeed, his so miraculous or wonderfull preservation giveth me great hope, he will be at least continewed to that state of old Simeon even to see something of such a glory or publick good breake forth as to desire then to resigne up his soule in peace.³⁸

The Ireland of Worsley and Ranelagh had for long been a first line of defence for Hartlib, but after the Restoration, hitherto prosperous groups of Hartlib's supporters became impotent to help. Hence, the well-placed Myles Symner could only offer a small contribution, regretting this

---

36 Comenius to Hartlib, 10 August 1657, HP 7/111/23A-24B.
37 Figulus to Hartlib, 6 November 1658, HP 9/17/45A-B. For further on the Moriaen-de Geer episode see Young *Moriaen*, p. 231.
38 Worsley to Lady Ranelagh, 20 April 1659, HP 33/2/13B-14A (as edited by Hartlib!).

mean offering, but unable to do more owing to their hard times: 'the times have lately frowned upon him [Symner], as they have, or at least are like to do, upon most of the new English here in a great measure'.[39] In March, Wood scraped together some further small offerings, again apologising for the general state of deprivation in which he and his friends were subsisting: 'I shall send you the 18s which I received from Major Symner & shall make it up of my owne to be £3 which I desire you to accept from me: I having no Lands nor mony at use, nor publick employment; & that privat one I have to looke after my old Masters affaires here affords me only a bare subsistence, which yet in as much as I do desire or can expect from him in his reduced condition'.[40]

After the Restoration Dury led moves in the Netherlands to gain financial support for Hartlib. He complained that Hartlib's allies were handicapped by the lack of more forthright representations from Hartlib himself. In practice Dury fared no better than his Irish counterparts in his quest for funds from this source.[41]

Hartlib's financial situation continued to worsen and his pessimism mounted. Some indications of reassurance were forthcoming, but these had little relevance to Hartlib himself. From Petty's position of strength, he assured Robert Wood 'that we now have a Philosophical and mathematico-mechanical King, one that cared not for the vulgar exercises of the Body etc. etc.' [!] to which Wood responded sceptically. As his caustic remarks about Petty's knighthood and other elevations confirm, Hartlib was of the like opinion.[42] However, Worthington also detected some hope of amelioration. It seemed that Charles II was an admirer of Robert Boyle, while his brother Roger had become the Earl of Orrery. Worthington hoped that Katherine, their sister, might persuade her brothers to plead Hartlib's case at court.[43] Perhaps with such factors in mind, Hartlib penned a petition, which he contemplated presenting to both the new Parliament and to the king himself.[44] This was not a

---

39 Wood to Hartlib, 19 January 1661, HP 33/1/71A-B.
40 Wood to Hartlib, 23 March 1661, HP 33/1/23A.
41 Dury to Hartlib, 29 April 1661, HP 4/4/16A-B. Dury to Hartlib, 30 June 1661, HP 4/4/24A.
42 Wood to Hartlib, 26 March 1661, HP 33/1/73A.
43 Worthington to Hartlib [October 1660], Crossley I, pp. 217–18.
44 'Humble Petition' of Hartlib to the 'Commons in England assembled in Parliament', likely autumn 1660, White Kennett, *A Register and Chronicle* (1728), p. 872; also included in Henry Dircks, *A Biographical Memoir of Samuel Hartlib*

particularly convincing document. The text comprised a perfunctory resumé of his various activities, after which he pathetically concluded that:

> having continued in this Course of Life for the Space of Thirtie Yeares and upwards (without Partiality serving all publick and ingenuous Spirits indifferently) and in these great and strange Revolutions, being destitute of Support to continue this Kind of Negotiation, and in his sickly Age to maintain himself and his Family, for the Relief of which and of his Agency, he hath been forced to contract Debts, which in the Ende will sink him.

There is no evidence that these petitions were submitted, nor were they discussed among his friends. Worthington also came up with a list of openings that might yield an income, but Hartlib flatly rejected these as being beyond his capabilities.[45]

From the letters exchanged between Hartlib and Worthington, it is striking that Katherine Boyle was the lead player in the campaign to assist Hartlib. Notwithstanding her position of special privilege, Katherine sounded a strong note of realism about the new culture that was taking shape: 'I must assure you, that your straitned condition is not out of my thoughts or endeavours; but we live in a time that has upon it, besides many other marks of the last and worst, this also, that the love of many is waxed cold, and our excesses eat up our charity, which threatens that God's just judgment will sweep away the fuel of our excesses'.[46]

Notwithstanding such adverse auguries, Dorothy Dury focused on practical defensive measures, on this occasion identifying Arthur Annesley, now ennobled as the Earl of Anglesey, as a credible line of defence, even though appreciating that Katherine might not approve of this option, which was certainly the case given the long-standing animosity between the Annesley and Boyle families.[47]

(London: J.R. Smith, 1865), pp. 32–34. For a variant addressed to Charles II, HP 7/19A-B.
45 Hartlib to Worthington, 20 December 1660, Crossley I, p. 256.
46 Lady Ranelagh to Hartlib, c.15 December 1660, cited in a letter of Hartlib to Worthington, 20 December 1660, Crossley I, pp. 255–56.
47 Hartlib to Dorothy Dury, 4 January 1661, HP 7/5A; Dorothy Moore *Letters*, pp. 96–97; P. Little, *Lord Broghill and the Cromwellian Union with Ireland and Scotland* (Woodbridge: Boydell Press, 2004), p. 185.

Dorothy duly briefed Annesley concerning Hartlib's plight and elicited a positive response from the Earl.[48] Arthur Annesley may seem like an odd choice for this last-ditch attempt to bring comfort to Hartlib, but we should remember that in 1647 he was a key ally in securing his £300 payment from the public purse and that in the 1650s he had been supportive of Hartlib's schemes in Ireland.

Reflecting the desperation of his situation, Hartlib appealed to other potential patrons, including Henry, Lord Herbert, who was also one of the hopes of Martin Grundmann after he lost his benefice in Powys. Hartlib explained that he was making this approach on the advice of Arthur Annesley, who had indeed encouraged Hartlib to make his situation more generally known. To Herbert, he outlined his financial problems, indicating that his debts amounted to seven hundred pounds. He frankly admitted his desperate plight: 'I have nothing therefore left to keep me alive, with two Relations more, a Daughter and a Nephew... attending my sickly Condition'.[49]

In all likelihood, Hartlib was referring to aid given by Mary, his elder daughter, who also lived in Axe Yard. Also mentioned was Daniel Hartlib, Hartlib's nephew and son of his late brother Georg Hartlib. Daniel seems to have spent many years in England. In 1659/60 he lodged for at least a year with the physician Samuel Wartensky at Farnham. Wartensky was pleased that Daniel made progress with his piety; but at times his behaviour was wanting, and also, he seemed lacking in talent. Caring for Hartlib at this moment of terminal crisis must have been a hard test for Mary and Daniel. Their work was all the harder on account of a serious fire that broke out in Hartlib's study, just a few weeks before his death.

For Hartlib, one of the greatest anxieties of this final stage of his life was preventing his massive collection of papers from degenerating into a state of chaos. This fear was shared by his friends. Wartensky even suggested that Hartlib should evacuate from London and deposit all of his possessions in Farnham for safe-keeping and protection from

---

48 Dorothy Dury to Hartlib, 13 October 1661, HP 4/4/37A-B, Dorothy Moore *Letters*, p. 98, which seems to be the last known letter written by Dorothy Moore, who was herself to die in 1664 at the age of fifty-two.

49 Hartlib to Lord Herbert, 22 Nov/2 Dec 1661, White Kennett, *A Register and Chronicle, Ecclesiastical and Civil*, pp. 872–73.

general depredation (*omnius exposita rapinae*). Hartlib addressed this proposal seriously, in the course of which he took advice from Dury, who looked on the idea of 'going to the Country' with disfavour. Dury advised that Hartlib should stay in his current home, since this was his natural 'tabernacle' from where 'you may bee usefull to the public in a Cheerfull way of service & find support in your endevours'.[50]

Even in the eleventh hour, Worthington continued to fish around for practical advice to ameliorate Hartlib's condition, for instance suggesting that he might become master of one of the many Hospital charities that might become vacant. Most of these were virtual sinecures. Perhaps with Beale's futile attempt to redeem his place at St Katherine's Hospital Ledbury in mind, Hartlib politely declined this overture.[51]

5.4 'Not Without Dust and Heat'[52]

Given the multiple distresses experienced by Hartlib during the last five years of his life, it might be expected that the many initiatives with which he was associated would rapidly fade into extinction. There were of course many cases where the outcomes were disappointing, but Hartlib's effort remained relentless, almost unaffected by the mounting impediments that he experienced. From the testimony of his many adherents, it is evident that he remained a man worth knowing.

Naturally, none of his major missions were conducted alone. He relied on the continuing cooperation of many others, in particular his closest collaborators. He maintained his close identity of purpose with John Dury, his longest-standing associate, but also he maintained productive relationships with friends of more recent date, ranging from Benjamin Worsley and John Worthington to Dorothy Dury and Katherine Boyle. Then there were the new associates, among whom John Evelyn and John Winthrop were among the most notable. Evelyn was known to Hartlib by 1657, but their correspondence seems to have begun in August 1658; it lasted until November 1660. This association was important because

---

50 Wartensky to Hartlib, 23 July 1661, HP 32/3/40A; Dury to Hartlib, 23 June 1661, HP 4/4/21A.
51 Worthington to Hartlib [December 1660], Crossley I, p. 245; Hartlib to Worthington, 20 December 1660, Crossley I, p. 256.
52 Milton, *Areopagitica*, CPW, 2, p. 515.

it opened the door to Evelyn's correspondence with John Beale, which was of inestimable value to Evelyn.

Important among these later associates was John Winthrop, Jr., the first Governor of Connecticut and son of the first Governor of Massachusetts. The younger Winthrop's link with Hartlib was secured through his longstanding friend John Davenport who, as noted above, was actively assisted by Hartlib during his own early days in New England. As in earlier times, Hartlib went out of his way to cater for the specific interests of his clients.

Winthrop's introductory letter to Hartlib began by drawing attention to the 'fame of your Publique Spirit & worthy unwearied indeavours for the publique good', in particular his 'incouragement of learned & ingenious men & inventions excellent & usefull'. Specifically, Winthrop thanked Hartlib for the gift of his personal copy of Georgius Agricola's *De re metallica* (1556), a great classic, and at that date still a standard work of reference in the fields of mining and metallurgy.[53] In his next letter, Winthrop thanked Hartlib for his

> letter of the 16 of March last which came to my hand lately from our worthy Reverend friend Mr Davenport & not long after the box, & bookes & papers therein mentioned of which according to your intimation I send you a particular of every booke, & manuscript & paper (I thinke not one omitted) I thank you very much for your great paines in giving me so large & full & many intelligences in your letter, & for the favours of those usefull bookes and manuscripts.

Winthrop listed no fewer than fifty items contained in that box.[54] This was by no means an isolated gesture of generosity. In April 1659 Robert Wood in Ireland acknowledged a box of books comprising more than twenty items supplied by Hartlib.[55]

As the Restoration approached, figures like Robert Boyle faded into the background, but others of significant standing, like Nicolaus Mercator and John Ray, assumed his place. In this category William Brereton, later Lord Brereton, occupied an important place in Hartlib's affections and ultimately became the guardian of Hartlib's papers.

---

53 Winthrop to Hartlib, 16 December 1659, HP 32/1/3A-B.
54 HP 32/1/12.
55 Wood to Hartlib, 11 May 1659, HP 33/1/56A.

Like Boyle and Brereton, also destined for the Royal Society was Henry Oldenburg (c.1619–1677), the first secretary of that body, who was crucially important for its success. Oldenburg arrived in London in 1653 on a diplomatic mission representing Bremen, his home city. I suspect that he met Hartlib shortly after this date, but the first direct reference to him occurred in a letter from Dury to Hartlib, dated 17 May 1654.[56] Oldenburg's correspondence with Hartlib began in June 1656 and continued until February 1660. His last mention in Hartlib's papers dates from December 1661.

As noted above, in 1654 Dorothy gave birth to Dora Katherina, who was the only surviving child of the Durys. With the death of her mother in 1664 she became the ward and later the wife of Oldenburg, a factor that further entrenched Oldenburg in the Hartlib-Dury fraternity. In numerical terms, Hartlib was Oldenburg's main correspondent in the period 1656–1660. Because for most of this period Oldenburg was away in Europe touring with his charge, who was the son of Lady Ranelagh, this limited his familiarity with many of the projects that occupied Hartlib in London.

Most important among Hartlib's new European correspondents was Petr Figulus (1619–1670), who features prominently in this chapter and elsewhere in this study. His letters, from many perspectives, assumed particular importance for the period from 1657 to 1661. One aspect of his significance was his familiarity with all aspects of the affairs of Comenius, who was his father-in law. He was in general a key witness about Eastern European affairs, and subsequently about the Netherlands, after his arrival there as a refugee in the spring of 1658. He had been known to Hartlib since the 1630s. As noted above, Comenius introduced the fifteen-year-old Figulus to Hartlib in his very first letter to him of 9 January 1634. Soon after that he (as 'Peter') served as an amanuensis for John Dury, which was a form of slavery, but helpful in supplying him with a firm insight into Protestant ecclesiastical politics and also into Hartlib's activities in Britain. Figulus was graced with a charm and humane spirit which rendered him one of the most attractive figures in Hartlib's fraternity.

---

56   HP 4/3/9A.

5.5 From Pomiculture to the Good Old Cause

One of the most spectacular gains for Hartlib's group in the 1650s was John Beale, a Cambridge-educated scholar of great intellectual distinction, for whom the title polymath is an understatement.[57] Beale was deeply attached to his native Herefordshire where, in the course of the 1650s, he served as the vicar of the hamlet of Stretton Grandison. He fought relentlessly, but without success, to secure the Mastership of St Katherine's Hospital, Ledbury, which was no mean prize among such posts. In the contest for this office, despite being supported by his influential relatives, the Parliamentarian Mackworth family, Beale was outbid by a Baptist minister, the candidate of Major-General Thomas Harrison. In 1655 Harrison had been an ally of Hartlib with respect to a petition in favour of J.S. Kuffeler.

Following his customary habit, Hartlib spread the word about Worthington among his friends, including new ones like John Beale, who replied that 'I reioyce that Dr Worthington is the Man of Cambridge. I knowe his heart is for noble advancements in all kinds of sound literature. I can truely answere him that my Rural Plea is not deserted'.[58] Beale seems to have made contact with Hartlib in November 1656. By December they were in active communication. Thereafter Beale and Hartlib exchanged letters on an almost weekly basis until late 1661, after which Beale wrote intermittently to both Worthington and Hartlib until mid-February 1662, hence just a few weeks before Hartlib's death. At first, Beale's main mission was the promotion of fruit cultivation, especially with respect to orchards but, characteristic of this polymath, his final letters were largely about mnemonics.[59]

Among Beale's many-sided interests, at this date his main wish respecting Hartlib was to inject a fresh element into Hartlib's already substantial husbandry list, with special reference to the county of

---

57   Relevant here are *ODNB* John Beale (Patrick Woodland); H.M. Stubbs, 'John Beale, philosophical gardener of Herefordshire: part I, prelude to the Royal Society (1608–1663)', *Annals of Science*, 39 (1982), 463–89 and William Poole, 'Two Early Readers of Milton: John Beale and Abraham Hill', *Milton Quarterly*, 38:2 (2004), 76–99; Haffemeyer, *Les Lumières radicales*, pp. 89–91 et passim.

58   Beale to Hartlib, 18 January 1656, Royal Society, Boyle *Letters* 7.3,1A. Beale's 'Rural Plea' related to his commitment to an immersive rural way of life.

59   Lewis, *Language, Mind and Nature*, pp. 103–04.

Hereford, and specially the orchards of that county, upon which Beale possessed minute and accurate knowledge. Naturally this passion extended to cider production, which Beale aspired to consolidate and expand. The published result of this undertaking in February 1657 was his pithy short monograph, *Herefordshire Orchards, a Pattern for all England*.[60] Beale's monograph, like the rest of his writing was original, unusual and in places eccentric. This was by far the most advanced contribution yet published in the field of pomiculture. One striking point about this monograph is that the published version was a byproduct of a projected more expansive text that seems to have existed in draft form. Beale planned a further more general text, entitled 'Nurseries for Orchards. Encouraged and Directed: As well for other parts of Great Britain and Ireland, as for Herefordshire', which was also never published. Naturally Beale was disappointed at being thwarted in these wider ambitions, but his letters continued to outline his continuing efforts to publish more widely on cider and orchards.

Such indeterminate commitments might suggest that Beale's ardour was diminishing. But the evidence of his letters proves otherwise. In the gloomy atmosphere of 1659, Beale evolved a further ambitious project, this time a collective volume based upon a reprint of *The Commons Complaint* by Arthur Standish, dating from 1611. This addressed the issue of deforestation, a problem that had become ever more severe, which evoked a passionate response from Beale. Naturally, Hartlib was supportive and he had indeed made an entry about the *Commons Complaint* in his Ephemerides for 1639, where he opined that Standish trod 'experimentally', first 'concerning the decay of wood in England', and secondly 'the scarcity of victuals in respect of foule'. The Standish tract had been drawn to the notice of Hartlib by John Pell, who had lamented that the ideas of Standish had not been put into practice. In Beale's letters from this date, he affected reticence about direct political interventions, but felt this was unavoidable owing to the interests of 'peace, unity, & liberty of conscience'. He wished to publicly show solidarity with Brereton and Worsley, reflecting in turn Worsley's identification with Sir Henry Vane, whose *A Healing Question* (1656)

---

60 *Herefordshire Orchards, a pattern for all England… an Epistolary Address to Samuel Hartlib Esq.* (London: printed by Roger Daniel, 1657), text 62 pp. in the form of two letters dated 3 and 13 May 1656, Wing B155B.

had constituted the classic defence of the Good Old Cause republican argument, which the new Standish edition was overtly designed to reinforce. Beale must have known that this exercise had thrown Vane into prison and temporary disgrace, an outcome that Beale feared that he also was courting.

Throwing caution to the wind, the new edition was to be titled 'The True Interest of the Common-wealth of England'.[61] Beale recorded being busy on various fronts, but he adopted the Standish edition as his priority, since this was a necessary sacrifice for the public good by strengthening the cause of 'true Commonwealthsmen', which, he admitted, was under siege. Hence the urgent need for 'an argument in seasone For the consideration of true Comon-wealthes men. But I feare there are soe many counterfeite pretenders to Common-wealth, that you will hardly find their eares in seasone to receive republican advertisements'.[62]

The lengthy prospective title was to terminate: 'First undertaken by Arthur Standish, and further explicated & advanced by severall true-hearted Commonwealth-men in the way of their Epistolary Addresses to Samuel Hartlib Esqr.' The original address of Standish to King James I was discarded and replaced by an appeal to 'Noble Patriots' in the interests of the public weal and the public good, to be signed by Hartlib. Beale insisted that Hartlib should then outline the extent of his own direct contribution of service to the Commonwealth. Leaving nothing to chance, Beale sketched out the whole of Hartlib's Epistle to the Reader, including the ending which would assure the reader of 'his zeal for the Peace, Unity and Prosperity of these shaken Islands'.

Contrasting with the inflammatory preliminaries, the prospective contents, almost all of which were already in existence, were practical and uncontroversial. These included Beale's own 'discourse on Withies and Sallies' which has survived in Hartlib's papers. This essay, 'Of Withyes, Sallyes, willowes, & osiers', is a splendid exposition stretching over thirty-six paragraphs, worthy of comparison with the writing of Sir Thomas Browne. The penultimate section was to be a 'Large Treatise' by Dymock, while the concluding section would a further lengthy botanical

---

61 Turnbull *HDC*, p. 107, No. 63.
62 Untitled plan for an expanded Standish Edition, 19 March 1659, HP 51/82A-92B.

essay by Beale himself, the draft text of which was included in his book outline.

The concluding essay was to be devoted to his proposals for a series of reforms that would constitute his gift 'to all the Common people'. Naturally, the first of these was the wholesale development of orchards. Next, reinforcing the main message of Standish, since timber was a key resource for managing the interest of the Commonwealth in both the civil and military contexts, he outlined a programme of afforestation.

The volume was to end with an Epilogue, the material for which, Beale instructed, was to be drawn from their recent correspondence, but on the strict understanding that there should be no disclosure of Beale's name. The final lines were to read (as heavily edited by Hartlib for publication): 'Wee must beare it [the instability of the moment], because it seemes to bee the smiting of a Friend in love, &, such wounds are better than the flattery of an Enemy. And this I affirme from my heart & soule which suffereth noe small agonies at this time from a zeale for the Peace, Unity, & Prosperity of thiese shaken Islands'.[63]

At this point, on account of the lateness of the hour, further action on the Standish edition was aborted and the chance to strike a blow for the Good Old Cause was lost. This marked the end of Hartlib's original husbandry publications, but it is worth noting that in 1659 he reissued both the second and third editions of the *Legacie* under revised titles: the second edition as *The Compleat Husbandman* and the third edition as *Universal Husbandry Improved* (not 1670 as suggested by Wing). At this point Fussell's 'Age of Hartlib' in husbandry came to an end. Indeed, this 1659 trio of husbandry initiatives marked the conclusion of Hartlib's career as a publisher.[64]

5.6 Address: The Hartlibian Panacea

Arguably, Hartlib's most cherished specific project, and the one that occupied a great slice of his energies, was the Office of Address, an idea which was spun out into diverse manifestations, the narrowest of

---

63 HP 51/85A-B. For a list of contents of the Standish compilation, Turnbull *HDC*, No. 63, p. 107.
64 The enumeration of Hartlib's publications in Turnbull *HDC*, pp. 88–109, comprises sixty-five items.

which was a kind of labour exchange for humble classes of worker, a project that was realised in London for a short period around 1650 and later consciously reincarnated as the Labour Exchange of the twentieth century. The most labyrinthine incarnation of this concept envisaged a ramshackle administrative framework possessing almost boundless functionality. Of this, nothing was realised or was realisable.

Background

The more generalised address conception first found expression in John Dury's 'The Purpose and Platform of my Journy' (1631), a document preserved in the Sloane collection, which Kvačala published in 1902, and Turnbull in 1920.[65] Turnbull perspicaciously observed that 'one can almost fancy Dury and Hartlib writing it in conjunction, so closely do certain parts of it resemble schemes advocated by Hartlib'.[66] As outlined in the *Platform*, Dury's main object was to build up a 'Correspondency' between the different arms of the Protestant Churches. Sandwiched between his proposals regarding ecumenicalism was a lengthy statement declaring his broader aim to gather information relating to the general advancement of learning and innovations connected with economic development. For the purpose of evolving a 'Platform of Correspondency' he envisaged creating a 'Society and Corporation... to make a perfect corporation of the joint parts and uses of all sorts of persons skilled in all sorts of arts and industries Rationall and Mechanical'. In this somewhat clumsy manner, Dury was expressing his support for the establishment in the secular sphere of mechanisms for the more efficient integration of all manner of skilled labour. This aspiration persisted as an undertone in Dury's busy timetable of ecclesiastical negotiations during the 1630s. His Platform enthusiasms were reinvigorated by the prospect of a visit to England of Comenius, when he exclaimed to Hartlib 'O that it were God's will to frame the

---

[65] Turnbull *Hartlib*, pp. 10–13. This document does not feature in the Hartlib Papers. For a variant review of the Office of Address, Haffemeyer, *Les Lumières radicales*, pp. 310–38.

[66] Turnbull *Hartlib*, p. 13.

hearts of some able Christians in a correspondency of endeavours for the publick good of Religion and Learning!'[67]

As indicated in chapter 2, the visit of Comenius coincided with the beginnings of political instability which precluded any kind of planning for social amelioration, John Dury, writing shortly after his relocation to the Netherlands, soon returned his thoughts to the idea of improving intellectual coordination. In this context he produced a 'brief memoriall for the necessitie of Correspondency & how it should bee sette a foot', which he judged an interim measure pending production of 'a more ample discourse'. Dury intended to develop 'the generall notion of the usefulnesse & benefit of a correspondencye for all the endes which yow [Hartlib] have mentioned; for the multiplying of obiects in this nature will make men rather gaze at our vast conceptions, then persuade them to concurre with us in the worke; & so our endeavours shall always remaine in the Clouds & bee applauded by all', but in order to achieve full compliance, Dury felt that he needed to spell out the entire subject in detail.[68] Dury dispatched a copy of his promised Memorial on this subject to Hartlib in August 1643 but this was not followed through.[69]

One additionally relevant factor in planning the way forward was the issue of finding some kind of meaningful professional role for Samuel Hartlib. The problem of his perpetual insolvency has frequently featured in the pages of this study. His supporters found good reasons why he should be supported by the state, but on what basis? Dury insisted that he should search for a defined role, preferably on the basis of 'serving the public in those aimes which are most eminently profitable for the advancement of Pietie & learning'.[70]

At this point the Office of Address became the assigned vehicle for realising this broader objective. This idea had already vaguely occurred to Hartlib. For instance, in 1640 a letter from Amsterdam by Friedrich Heinrichson specifically described in some detail the mode of operation of the *Bureau d'Adresse* devised by Théophraste Renaudot, and mentioned that an account of these activities was available in print.[71] In 1643, on

---

67 Dury to Hartlib, 10 May 1639, HP 9/1/84B.
68 Dury to Hartlib, 9 October 1642, HP 2/9/37A-B.
69 Dury to Hartlib, 13 August 1643, HP 2/10/12A.
70 Dury to Hartlib, 28 July 1644, HP 3/2/45B.
71 Heinrichson to Hartlib, 24 September 1640, HP 27/27/1A-2B.

the basis of conversation with Gabriel Plattes, Hartlib recorded that the latter observed that: '1.A Lumbard. 2. An Office of Addresse. 3. A Freeschoole of Husbandry or a House of Experiments are greatly wanting in England.' [72] Next, Hartlib acquired through his French contacts some of the relevant Renaudot publications from the 1630s, which gave him an authentic insight into the range of functions of the original *Bureaux de Rencontre*.[73]

Launch

Work on the Office of Address concept in England began in earnest in 1646, when, following the decisive military defeat of the Royalists, conditions were sufficiently stabilised to allow more attention to be focused on civil contingencies. Culpeper was the first to join Hartlib in the more energetic pursuit of the Office of Address idea.

In February, Culpeper was heartened that Hartlib had resolved 'to persist with your office of address', which he believed represented an ideal manifestation of Hartlib's 'life of Faythe'. Culpeper's own distinctive contribution was the suggestion that the operation of the Office would be facilitated by application of the indexing system devised by Thomas Harrison, for which it was indeed highly appropriate. Culpeper was confident that the Office of Address could be an operational success and an asset to the economy.[74] Perhaps also dating from March 1646 was a draft 'Act for Erecting an Office for all Manner of Addresses', which was a lucid statement of a plan for a government-backed scheme for a comprehensive system of such offices, which, it was claimed, would be a catalyst for economic expansion and operate in the interests of all classes. There was no hint that these offices would serve anything but

---

72 Ephemerides 1643, HP 30/4/90B.
73 For a systematic assessment of Renaudot's work, Simone Mazauric, *Savoirs et philosophie à Paris dans la première moitié du XVIIe siècle: les conférences du bureau d'adresse de Théophraste Renaudot, 1633–1642* (Paris: Publications de la Sorbonne, 1997). For Renaudot and Hartlib, Haffemeyer, *Les Lumières radicales*, pp. 318–35.
74 Culpeper to Hartlib, 17 February, 4 March and 11 March 1646, Culpeper *Letters*, pp. 265, 269 and 272. See Noel Malcolm, 'Thomas Harrison and his 'Ark of Studies': An Episode in the History of the Organisation of Knowledge', *The Seventeenth Century*, 19:2 (2004), 196–232.

a practical function, which was also, at this date, the understanding of Culpeper.[75]

Partly on account of his immersion in the work of the Westminster Assembly, John Dury only reluctantly took notice of the Office of Address. Then, in August 1646, he appreciated that this scheme offered the means to find a niche for Hartlib, ease his financial problems and establish him as a valued servant of the state.

From August to December, Dury communicated with Hartlib on eight occasions concerning the Office of Address. As was often the case, Hartlib allowed Dury to become his spokesperson. However, at this time Dury was otherwise engaged, for instance in completing work on a new catechism, where he expected Hartlib to take over responsibility for the whole publishing operation. His other major priority at that moment was establishing a working relationship with the ascendant Independent political grouping within the Assembly. He was also immersed in what turned out to be futile campaigning on behalf of the colonial development schemes of the Huguenot refugees, Hugh L'Amy and Peter Le Pruvost.[76] This was an even lower priority for him than the Office of Address, but it unhelpfully diverted attention away from this issue of higher importance.

Notwithstanding these competing commitments, Dury agreed to write an apologia for the Office of Address. From the outset, he doctored the project to his own tastes. He split the Office in two sections, the first and more important relating to divinity and intellectual affairs, the second serving secular and practical functions. This was in reality a reversion to his proposals for the two parallel 'Platforms of Correspondences' outlined in his Platform document of 1631. Dury privately envisaged that the new Office would be headed by himself and Hartlib working in conjunction. In line with the inevitable precedence of spirituality, he favoured the religious correspondency Office being located in Oxford rather than London, even if a collegiate form of university was to be established in the capital.[77] Dury's bias became evident in the few

---

75 HP 63/7/8A-9B.
76 Thomas Leng, 'A "Potent Plantation well-armed and Policeed": Huguenots, the Hartlib Circle, and British Colonisation in the 1640s', *William and Mary Quarterly*, 3rd Series, 64:1 (2009), 173–94.
77 Dury to Hartlib, 4 August 1646, HP 3/3/22A-B. C.J. Minter, 'John Dury's Reformed Librarie-Keeper: Information and its Intellectual Contexts in Seventeenth-Century

remarks he made in his letters to Hartlib about progress with the memorandum. In late September he revealed that he was about to write the final section of the memorandum, which would be the only part specifically relating to the binary Office of Address.

Considerations Tending

Dury's tract was completed in November 1646 and published in the following May.[78] This badly executed fifty-nine-page document, even lacking in a proper title page, followed the plan that Dury had revealed to Hartlib. Only about ten pages of the pamphlet related specifically to the civil Office of Address as it was understood among Hartlib's experts. This diffuse publication accordingly achieved almost nothing in advancing the cause that it was calculated to support. It is difficult to find any reference to its reception. The only response that I have found is from Culpeper, who said almost nothing, but took exception to the idea that the Office should be split between London and Oxford.[79]

Almost everything we know about the Office of Address in the rest of 1647 relates mainly to the Accommodations civil function and derives from the letters of Culpeper. It is likely that the Accommodations Office was uppermost in their thoughts when Thomas Westrow, a friend of Cromwell, recalled that he had been discussing 'the business' with several persons, 'but none so apt to harken as Crumwell'.[80]

Further Discoverie

In response to such positive news, John Dury revised his thoughts and opted to produce two separate tracts, the first specifically on the civil Accommodations Office, and a second on the religious Communications Office. The draft of the former, this time with a distinct practical bias,

---

England', *Library & Information History*, 31:1 (2015), 18–34 discusses the links between the Office of Address and Dury's plan for reform of the Bodleian Library.

78 *Considerations tending to the happy accomplishment of Englands reformation in church and state. Humbly presented to the piety and wisdome of the High and Honourable Court of Parliament* (1647), Thomason E.389[4], Wing H381.

79 Culpeper *Letters*, pp. 286–87, undated letter, 1646/7.

80 Westrow to Culpeper, 29 February 1647, Culpeper *Letters*, p. 290. For Cromwell and Hartlib, Haffemeyer, *Les Lumières radicales*, pp. 406–33.

reached Hartlib in August 1647. Dury instructed him to convey the Accommodations draft to 'Cromwell by the hands of some other leading men'. In November this reached Culpeper and Boyle, after which, publication followed, it seems, in the spring of 1648.[81]

The major part of the text of the *Further Discoverie* was taken up with an outline of the four Registers or Books, which encapsulated the prime responsibilities of the new Office. These were: '1: One for the Accommodation of the Poore. 2. Another for the Accommodation of Trade, Commerce and Bargaines for profit. 3. A third for the Accommodation of all Actions which proceed from all relations of persons to each other in all Estates and conditions of Life. 4. A fourth for Ingenuities and matters of delight unto the mind in all Vertues and rare Objects.' All of this was executed with clarity by Dury and without the intrusion of his customary moralising interjections.[82] On this occasion Culpeper exclaimed that this tract 'dothe very muche please me'.

In January 1648 Culpeper was sure enough of his ground to recommend the establishment of a Parliamentary committee on the reward of ingenuities which, he envisaged, would remit these issues to the Office of Address. In March he assured Hartlib that he was acting as the 'sollicitor' on behalf of the project and already had the backing of Thomas Westrow, an influential Independent M.P., and the likely support of Robert Andrews, a lesser-known Independent M.P.[83] Culpeper was even willing to bear the salary of one of the clerks of the new office. If this was the case, it suggests that he was confident that Parliamentary action over the Office of Address was imminent. Finally, he was also heartened by the news that the influential Francis Rous, a good friend of

---

81   Respecting Cromwell, Dury to Hartlib, 17 August 1647, HP 4/1/6A; Hartlib to Culpeper, 3 November 1647, Culpeper *Letters*, p. 311; and Hartlib to Boyle, 16 November 1647, Boyle *Correspondence* I, p. 63. *A Further Discoverie of the Office of Addresse for Accommodations* (London: 1648), 30 pages. Wing H 957. The *Accommodations* tract was dispatched by Hartlib to Rawlin on 4 May 1648, Rawlin to Hartlib, 15 May 1648, HP 10/10/7A. The Communications *Further Discoverie*, a torrid 98-page draft, was never published; this document languishes in the Hartlib Papers, HP 47/10/2A-55B.

82   *A Further Discoverie*, pp. 09–10. With respect to the use of the term 'Accommodation' at that date: this referred to the reconciliation of agencies that have drifted into disharmony, to the general facilitation of transactions in fields such as employment, or to the achievement of innovation or efficiency.

83   For Westrow, Worden *Rump*, pp. 72, 136 et passim; for Andrews, pp. 99 and 113.

Hartlib, had agreed to intervene on the latter's behalf.[84] Alas, a few days later, Culpeper plunged back into pessimism, declaring that 'I have noe hope from the publicke concerning your office of Addresse'.[85] Only one further comment on this subject is recorded from Culpeper, which was made in September 1649, when he briefly wished Hartlib well with his Office of Address scheme.

Dymock, Robinson et al.

Even with the collapse of parliamentary interest in the Office of Address, the intrinsic idea was sufficiently plausible to provoke continuing lively interest. For instance, in about 1649 Cressy Dymock expanded at length and with striking verve on the sections of the *Further Discovery* relating to the role of the Office of Address with respect to the poorer classes and especially servants. This also provided him (a lawyer by training) with a platform to lament the collapse of legal protections of the poor, which he blamed on the 'crafty foxes' of the legal profession. This legal aspect of his presentation is reminiscent of John Hall's attacks on the universities and the medical profession, as outlined in the previous chapter.[86]

Also important for the poor was the proposal for an 'Office of Addresses and Encounters' proposed by Henry Robinson, which was the subject of a short pamphlet, announcing a self-financing version of this Office which was launched in Threadneedle Street in September 1650. This experiment may have been short-lived, but it proved that a scheme having a wide range of functions could be realised as a practicable concern.[87] Evidently, Robinson kept Hartlib's team informed about his plans and they were duly impressed:

> Mr. Robinson revealed his Addresse of Exchanges by the Banke both to Sir Cheney Culpeper and Mr Dury who judged it very practicable. And by it all the Money being commended it cannot bee otherwise but of

---

84 Culpeper to Hartlib, 18 January, 11 and 15 March, Culpeper *Letters*, 322–24.
85 Culpeper to Hartlib, 29 March 1648, Culpeper *Letters*, p. 330.
86 'Mr. Dymock's Advice concerning an Office of Address for Servants', HP 66/11/1A-B.
87 Henry Robinson, *The Office of Adresses and Encounters* (London: Matthew Simons, 1650), Thomason E.613[10], dated '29 September'; Wing R1677. See W.H. Beveridge, 'A Seventeenth-Century Labour Exchange', *The Economic Journal*, 24:95 (1914), 371–76.

mighty consequence. Mr Dury added "If an Office of Addresse wherby all the commodities come to bee known with the several carriages and transactions of men about them, hee could not see what more could bee desired for encrease of publick or privat riches." [88]

Building on Robinson's initiative, even offering to take him on as a partner, clearly with Hartlib's sanction, Cressy Dymock drew up a scheme for a whole system of Offices of Address serving all parts of London.[89]

Hartlib's correspondents continued to harbour confidence that the Office of Address would confront a whole range of social evils. One even argued that this institution would counteract 'this spreading infection of Quakers', or the unruly behaviour of the dissolute soldiery, groups who were seen as alien to the 'Methode, Order, Union' represented by Hartlib's agency. By affiliation with the Accommodations institution, these outcasts would experience a cultural transformation, and thereby contribute to the 'quickning & solliciting Trade, directing & advancing Literature & by great variety of helpes in Agriculture so multiplying the Riches of the Nation'.[90]

Between 1656 and 1660 the Hartlib Papers record about half a dozen attempts to establish Office of Address-type agencies in London, none of which seem to have succeeded. Only one of the schemes related to Hartlib. On the latter's persuasion, Robert Wood, when fresh to Ireland, attempted unsuccessfully to secure public funding for an Office of Address, but he was hopeful that a private individual would undertake such an operation. Wood was obviously monitoring the situation elsewhere, upon which he observed that 'The businesse of Publick Accommodations I conceive will prove not only very gainefull to the undertakers, but of great advantage to the Commonwealth; we shall consider of it here in relation to ours: Mr Nedham is a very able man, & like to master it'.[91] The reference to Nedham was indeed apposite. It seems that in London at this date, a sharp competition had opened up in which the formidable Marchamont Nedham teamed up with the printer and publisher Mathew Newcomb. The two were determined to break

---

88 Ephemerides, September 1649, HP 28/1/29B.
89 Dymock, 'A Proposition...', c.1650, HP 63/7/10A-13B.
90 Hartlib to Thurloe, BL Add.MS 4365, 269A-270A. Undated, c.1655.
91 Wood to Hartlib, 27 May 1657, HP 33/1/15A.

the office of address monopoly claimed by Oliver Williams who, it was rumoured, had the support of Cromwell himself. From the broadsheet warfare that this episode generated, it seems as if Williams was reviving the scheme engineered by Robinson. The free-for-all that was opening up was not welcome to Dury, which accounts for his strongly worded memorandum, stating 'Reasons why the State should not suffer the Office of Public Entries or Addresse to be in any other hand but, such as it shall appoint to have it'.[92]

It will be recalled that Dury's main reason for his positivity about the Office of Address was its relevance to improving the lot of Hartlib. At the outset of this later involvement, he unambiguously invoked the tragedy of Hartlib's destitution to a highly placed friend, probably Strickland, with the aim of 'craving your patronage'. The papers submitted along with this letter were in all probability about the Office of Address.[93] In the event, this proved to be yet another failed attempt to secure a stable position for Hartlib.

Petitioning Cromwell

Not to be deterred, Hartlib and Dury came up with a further idea which, in many respects, represented a repackaging of the Office of Address, but also harked back to Dury's aspirations during the 1630s. This next phase in the Office of Address saga began in the early months of 1656 in the form of a draft agreement, likely to have been composed by Dury, after which it was heavily edited by Hartlib.

This draft briefly set out the duties of Feoffees and a related Trust which would have been authorised by parliament to supervise the stated programme of work devised by Hartlib and Dury, which was to be executed by members of an 'Agency for Universal Arts and Learning'. The document was at this stage primarily designed for well-wishers who might offer interim payments to assist the work by the two authors, pending the formal agreement of Parliament to adopt the scheme. Somewhat ominously, and underlined in the text, trustees were warned that they must assent to 'the Aimes of those that set forward our National

---

92 HP 63/7/4A-5B anonymous, but clearly by Dury; undated, c.1650.
93 Undated draft of a letter from Dury, heavily edited by Hartlib, late 1646 at the earliest, HP 4/1/11A-B.

Reformation', a formula which is susceptible to various interpretations, but was likely to be offensive to many of Hartlib's patrons, including key figures such as Sir Cheney Culpeper. The nature of the intended intelligence operation was not spelled out in detail, but its intended workers would have been recruited from abroad and would be lodged in Hartlib's home.

Rather than spell out any further rationale for the agency, the draft referred readers to the works of Francis Bacon, and also half-a-dozen more directly relevant publications, mainly Hartlib-Dury tracts relating to the Office of Address, but also William Petty's *Advice for the Advancement of some particular Parts of Learning* (1648). The text of this agreement was followed by two further short items, first a 'memorial' mainly concerning the method of remuneration to be adopted for the agents; secondly, a list of eighteen areas of interest upon which the fund would be expended.[94]

After further drafting there emerged the final product, which contained many elements derived from the earlier version, but was more ambitious in its conception. The document was now a petition to the Lord Protector, dated 25 December 1656.[95] This was duly submitted under the names Mr Richard Eccleston and Mr James Rand, presumably chosen as representative and respected public figures. Unsurprisingly, both were already known to Hartlib, and in the case of James Rand, he was the prosperous elder brother of William Rand, one of Hartlib's most able younger recruits.[96]

The petition declared that the priority was the 'erection of a forreign Correspondency with learned men... for advancement & promotion generally of Learning and Religion'. However, these specialists were no longer specified as outsiders working from the home of Hartlib. As before, it was promised that this new agency would constitute a major asset to the 'publike service'. The means of financing was no longer to be voluntary subscriptions from miscellaneous well-wishers, but by the sale of Irish land debentures, a method that related to the compensation of indebted Irish Adventurers, or the military personnel requiring requital for arrears of pay. The petition even went as far as outlining the counties and towns

---

94   HP 47/15/1A-2B.
95   'To His Highnesse the Lord Protector', HP 47/4/1A-B.
96   Barnard, *Cromwellian Ireland*, pp. 229–34.

from which the funds would be derived.[97] The documents accompanying the petition are variants of those described above.[98]

Retreat to Ireland

At first in London the Eccleston-Rand petition was handled efficiently and in a constructive manner, but thereafter the process ground to a halt. Samuel Jr., who was well-connected in the higher realms of the administration, attempted to resolve the issue, but John Thurloe, although friendly with Hartlib personally, and whose influence was decisive, refused to take the petition seriously. In Ireland, the progress of their petition was hampered by inertia within the Irish Council system, the scepticism of key figures like Robert Wood, also the feud between Petty and Worsley, all of which hastened the blocking of the scheme by Lord Deputy Henry Cromwell. Even before the death of Oliver Cromwell in 1658, it was evident that the amorphous Agency for Learning, unlike its predecessor Office of Address, especially in the straitened and increasingly unstable circumstances of the time, would be judged as too impracticable and imprudent to merit serious consideration. For Hartlib, this was yet another setback, depriving him of an expected income of £250 p.a. Not only that, a secondary scheme to support him personally was estimated to yield only £5 p.a, adding to the prospect that his final days would be spent in poverty and insecurity.

5.7 Loose Ends

The above illustrations add to the pattern of evidence signifying that the final phase of Hartlib's life was darkened by persistent ill-health and a collapse in his sources of financial support. These dismal circumstances inevitably shook his confidence, but he confronted his many disappointments with stoical fortitude. As a consequence, his final years were not an anti-climax, but were characterised by remarkable resilience and ingenuity. Even in 1660 he received about eighty letters. A

---

97   For the details of the relevant financial arrangements, see Turnbull *HDC*, pp. 54–56.
98   See particularly 'Other Considerations humbly offerred to his Highness', also dated 25 December 1656, HP 47/4/1B-4B.

helpful indicator of his continuing ability to meet the expectations of his friends is the correspondence between Hartlib and Worthington, which occupies more than three-hundred pages in the Crossley edition, with a good proportion relating to Hartlib's last two years of life.

The sense of despair indicated by the *phosphore redde diem* entreaty that he shared with Robert Boyle was therefore an understandable cry of anguish, but it was not indicative of any systemic disruption of his relentless routine of activism. As on previous occasions, old associates faded away, but were amply compensated for by a cohort of young, capable and ambitious recruits. The scope of his associations therefore remained sufficiently buoyant to ensure that he remained thoroughly conversant with matters of the moment.

Scientific Organisation in Troubled Times

The foundation of the Royal Society constituted a notable element in the sphere of intense scientific activity that was evident throughout Europe at this date. One minor element in this story, attracting some notice among specialists, is the question of Hartlib's association with the founders of the Royal Society. In this sphere, George Turnbull's informative essay remains a main source of reference.[99] The following remarks are largely supportive of Turnbull, but adopt a different angle of approach.

Hartlib was evidently well-informed about the course of events during the formative phase of the Society's existence:

> Thus much is certain, that there is a meeting every week of the prime virtuosi, not only at Gresham College in term time, but also out of it, at Mr. Ball's chambers in the Temple. They desired his Majesty's leave that they might thus meet or assemble themselves at all times, which is certainly granted. Mr. Boyle, Dr. Wilkins, Sir Paul Neale, Viscount Brouncker, are some of the members. Mr. Wren is chosen Register.... His Majesty is sayd to profess himself one of those virtuosi.[100]

---

99 G.H. Turnbull, 'Samuel Hartlib's Influence on the Early History of the Royal Society', *Notes and Records of the Royal Society of London*, 10:2 (1953), 101–30. For Hartlib and the Royal Society, see also Haffemeyer, *Les Lumières radicales*, pp. 503–06.

100 Hartlib to Worthington, 17 December 1660, Crossley I, pp. 246–49. This group was known by various titles at this date, with the name 'Royal Society' becoming adopted in the first Royal Charter, which dates from July 1662.

Hartlib obviously possessed a detailed and accurate impression of the outcome of the meeting that had been held on 24 November, when twelve associates gathered together to formalise gatherings at Gresham College that had been taking place for some time.[101]

All now agree that this November date marked the beginning of the informal existence of the Royal Society. Of the official list of twelve, six were specifically mentioned in Hartlib's letter. As Turnbull points out, ten of these founders were personally known to Hartlib. I estimate that, by this date, five of these had been in touch with him for at least ten years. On account of his leading role in the Oxford experimental philosophy club when he was Warden of Wadham College, Wilkins held a position of special respect. Turnbull noted that the first reference to Wilkins in Hartlib's papers derived from the Ephemerides for 1650, an entry that I estimate dates from about September of that year. But there is also a prior reference to him in a letter from William Hamilton of All Souls College, dating from January 1649, which suggests that Wilkins was already at that date on familiar terms with Hartlib.[102]

The question remains, how was it that Hartlib became so well informed about the fledgling Royal Society? The letter of 17 December is the most important evidence of his curiosity, but he also recorded an antecedent meeting, which he described in a letter of 15 October 1660, and also a later meeting, noted in a letter of 1 January 1661.[103] Of those attending the November meeting, Boyle or Petty are possible sources of Hartlib's information. Of others close to these proceedings, William Brereton was identified by Hartlib on 1 January 1661 as one of the founding virtuosi, although this was not recognized as such by the official records. Given Brereton's long-standing and close friendship with both Hartlib and Worthington, he should perhaps be regarded as the most likely source of Hartlib's intelligence.

Of Hartlib's natural philosophical associates, many were admitted into the Royal Society: for instance, Ralph Cudworth and Henry More in 1662; John Beale, William Brereton, John Evelyn, Theodor Haak, Thomas Henshaw, Anthony Morgan, John Pell, Henry Oldenburg, Peter Pett,

---

101 The Journal Book of the Society records: 'The Lord Brouncker, Mr. Boyle, Mr. Bruce, Sir Robert Moray, Sir Paul Neile, Dr. Wilkins, Dr. Goddard, Dr. Petty, Mr. Ball, Mr. Rooke, Mr. Wren, Mr. Hill'.
102 Hamilton to Hartlib, 16 January 1649, HP 9/11/4A.
103 Crossley I, pp. 115, 257.

Robert Paston and Henry Slingsby, etc. during the general admission process of 22 April 1663; Nikolaus Mercator in 1666; but Robert Wood, not until 1681, while more humble or controversial figures such as Robert Anderson, Friedrick Clodius, J.S. Kuffeler, William Rand, Thomas Streete, John Webster and Benjamin Worsley, never! On the basis of the numerical analysis of attendance at meetings of the Royal Society up to 1663, of the sixteen most active participants, it is striking that only four of these were not particularly well-known to Hartlib.[104] Unavoidably, in view of the evidence from many quarters, it must therefore be contemplated that, as Turnbull suggested, a large section of the activist element in the early Royal Society was drawn from among the associates of Samuel Hartlib, who, as demonstrated above, constituted a coherent and evolving structure that extended back through the 1650s, with roots going back even further.

A further relevant issue that is often discussed and is difficult to avoid, is the failure of the Royal Society to engage directly with Hartlib or consider him as a candidate for membership. The usual response is that such a course was prohibited by political factors. There is no evidence to support this conclusion. In any case, the elite of the new society featured many who had been higher profile Parliamentarians than the humble Hartlib. The better response is to pay attention to Hartlib's personal situation. As noted above, since the mid-1650s he had been virtually housebound owing to ill-health. By the end of 1660 his health was considerably worse. His correspondence was sustained remarkably well, but he was completely incapable of attending informal meetings of the kind that constituted the backbone of the new society. Also, to Hartlib's experienced eye, the new group may have seemed like yet another instance in the teeming plethora of scientific and technical clubs that he had witnessed, but never joined, over the previous few decades. Hartlib even disregarded some of these groups and schemes, as for instance the returned Royalist exile Abraham Cowley's well-informed *Proposition for the Advancement of Learning* (1661). The existence of this source was known to Hartlib, but it seems was never read by him.[105] I

---

104 Webster *Instauration*, p. 92.
105 For Cowley, S. Malpas, 'In No One Thing, They Saw, Agreeing', *Restoration: Studies in English Literary Culture, 1660–1700*, 43:2 (2019), 49–74.

therefore conclude that with respect to the Royal Society, Hartlib took pleasure in this new venture, but had neither the ability nor the will to be more than a participant observer.

Antilia and Macaria

The turmoil that Hartlib was experiencing at the time of the genesis of the Royal Society is well-illustrated by his sudden outburst of references to Antilia and Macaria.[106] Both of these utopian tropes had been out of his vocabulary for almost twenty years. It is a curious coincidence that Hartlib's letters to Worthington of 15 October and 17 December 1660, which recorded the earliest meetings of the scientific virtuosi, also featured Macarian or Antilian points of reference. Generally, Hartlib cited Antilia or Mararia as some kind of agency that would assist with the achievement of difficult assignments, always on the horizon but never achieving any of their stated objectives. Worthington was irritated and puzzled by Hartlib's invocation of what he viewed as complete fictions. When he pressed Hartlib for explanations, these tended to be feeble and apologetic, as for instance, in the first of Hartlib's 'Royal Society' letters, when he admitted that: 'We were wont to call the desirable Society by the name of Antilia, and sometimes by the name of Macaria: but name & thing is as good as vanished'.[107] Similarly, in the very last reference to these entities Hartlib reluctantly conceded that: 'Of the Antilian society the smoke is over, but the fire is not altogether extinct'.[108] These two examples remind us that, for the years 1660 and 1661, apart from some citations in the Ephemerides, the main evidence concerning this late recycling of Antilia and Macaria derives from brief references contained in a handful of letters from Hartlib to Worthington. As noted below with respect to the Ephemerides, Antilia was apt to reappear in other contexts owing to the wider incidence of its appeal.

---

106 Dickson, *Tessera of Antilia*, pp. 223–35. The explanation for Hartlib's reawakening to Antilia lies in his correspondence with Joachim Polemann in 1659. The agile Polemann represented himself as belonging to the tradition of authentic Christian brotherhoods, including the 1620s Antilian experiment.
107 Hartlib to Worthington, 15 October 1660, Crossley I, p. 210.
108 Hartlib to Worthington, 26 June 1661, Crossley I, p. 342.

Skytte

A further illustration of the tendency for Hartlib's attentions to be distracted is provided by the above-mentioned letter of 17 December. Just prior to his account of the virtuosi, Hartlib devoted a few lines to Bengt Skytte, a Swedish nobleman, who is indeed a figure of unusual interest.[109] Skytte was a name already known to Hartlib. In 1655, he recorded that Skytte was 'one of the most versed in *omni Scibili* amongst all the Swedish Noble-men'.[110] Less favourable was a more recent letter which recalled that Skytte had employed an agent who had tried to trick Laurentius de Geer into making payments, which the agent intended secretly to transfer to Skytte in Sweden.[111]

Upon arriving in London in 1660 Skytte sought to make contact with Hartlib. In advance, Skytte submitted some papers, the purpose of which Hartlib could not understand. As is evident from an interesting document contained in Hartlib's papers, Skytte's main purpose was to further his scheme for a 'Universal College'.[112] Apparently, Hartlib and Skytte never met. In Hartlib's letters to Worthington, which are the only other specific references to Skytte in the Hartlib archive, the Swede was briefly mentioned on two further occasions, but mainly for the purpose of recounting that Skytte's approaches to the virtuosi had been rebutted. Unfortunately, Hartlib carelessly hinted that Skytte had become one of the 'virtuosi' which was never the case. Perhaps thinking that Skytte's scheme would be of interest to the new Irish Council for Trade, Hartlib dispatched Skytte's papers to Robert Wood, who dutifully circulated these among his colleagues, among whom, he recalled, they were met with some bewilderment.[113]

Among the many further distractions at the time of the birth of the Royal Society were some that affected Hartlib personally. This period of upheaval provoked alarmist phenomena, including a rash of apocalyptic

---

109 Jane Finucane, 'The Invisible Virtuoso: Bengt Skytte and the Royal Society', *History of Universities*, 26:1 (2012), 117–62; Dickson, *Tessera of Antilia*, pp. 228, 232–34, 259–63.
110 Ephemerides, c.April 1655, HP 19/5/28A.
111 Joachim Polemann to Hartlib, 19 December 1659, HP 60/4/169A.
112 HP 47/11/1A-7B. For a translation of the plan and Skytte's lengthy explanation, see Finucane, pp. 142–49.
113 Wood to Hartlib, 19 January 1661, HP 33/1/71A-B.

and millenarian writings, utopian and dystopian predictions and also impracticable schemes, of which Skytte's Universal College was one and Comenius's *Via Lucis* was another.

Olbia

Hartlib's attention was particularly attracted by one of these outpourings, which was perhaps the most eccentric of them all. This was a utopian work titled *Olbia*, which was announced as a Part I of no fewer than 380 pages, intended as the prelude to a further part which was entirely out of sight, but was intended to survey most of the topics listed on the title page of Part I, which read: *Olbia, the new i[s]land lately discovered with its religion and rites of worship, laws, customs, and government, characters and language: with education of their children in their sciences, arts and manufactures with other things remarkable* [London, 1660].

This prospectus attracted Hartlib's attention and aroused the expectation that the author had devised a treatise on education in the Comenian spirit. This connection might also have been aroused by the dedicatory note at the base of the title page: 'For Samuel Hartlib, in Ax-yard Westminster, and John Bartlet at the Guilt-Cup near Austins-Gate London: and in Westminster-Hall'. Hartlib had in fact known Bartlet for several decades and must have been familiar with some of his titles, for instance Hezekiah Woodward's *A Light to Grammar By M.F. for Iohn Bartlet, 1641*, which would have further suggested to him that *Olbia* would be educationally orientated.[114]

Olbia itself dashed all such expectations. It has foxed generations of readers. Even the infinitely patient James Crossley conceded that *Olbia* was 'one of the strangest of strange books'.[115] We owe to Richard Greaves a brave attempt to decipher *Olbia*: 'Couched as instructions from an elderly hermit to a shipwrecked voyager on a remote Atlantic isle, the book is an amalgam of theological discourse on law and grace; reflections on Christ's work, prayer, and spiritual counsel; an explication of the ten commandments; a discussion of the end times; and exhaustive, mind-numbing numerology'.[116]

---

114 For Bartlet and Hartlib, Haffemeyer, *Les Lumières radicales*, pp. 317, 532 (*Olbia*).
115 Crossley I, pp. 251–52.
116 *ODNB* John Sadler (R.L. Greaves).

Hartlib's first response was a feeling of humiliation: 'I confess I was not well pleased, seeing the book directed to my name as it is. They say it reflects upon me as if I were a refined Quaker, or a fanatick; insomuch that I was almost resolved to give public notice of my dissatisfaction, as for the addressing of it; for I never heard a word of it before, nor could I guess at the author'. At this point Hartlib discovered a further problem. On studying the text, he realised that the author was none other than his friend and patron, John Sadler, about whom, he admitted: 'I can suffer anything for his sake'.[117]

Hartlib dutifully dispatched *Olbia* to some of his best friends for comment. Worthington felt that the author was from a scholarly point of view somewhat out of his depth, but conceded 'there is much of imagination in it'.[118] By contrast, the more mystically inclined John Beale was entirely favourable in his response: 'I do in *Olbia* find many such profound rests for my spirit, as I will never obtain by other readings or studies'.[119] Beale's sensitive appreciation of Sadler's work suggests that its positive qualities were more evident to a greater segment of the informed readership than would be the case in later generations.

5.8 Extinction of the Ephemerides

One of the saddest losses during Hartlib's final years was the relentless decline in the content of his great daybook, the Ephemerides. This process of extinction exactly coincides with the crisis in his health. 1656 was the last of the expansive annual records, which extended to eighty-four sides. Thereafter the Ephemerides shrank steadily each year until 1660, when it occupied only fourteen sides. Just over six pages ran up to mid-March, three more until 2 April. After the remaining five, the Ephemerides terminated at a date shortly after 22 June.[120] This final section had much in common with the day book as whole. It comprised a miscellany of short and random notes, in the course of a single page ranging from titbits of gossip to serious issues of state. This fragment

---

117 Hartlib to Worthington, 17 December 1660, Crossley I, pp. 251–52.
118 Worthington to Hartlib, 11 March 1661, Crossley I, p. 276.
119 Letter from John Beale, cited in Hartlib to Worthington, 2 April 1661, Crossley I, p. 290.
120 Ephemerides 1660, HP 29/8/10A-16B.

from 1660 opened with methods of preserving rose petals and ended with a piece of crucial evidence relating to the last days of the famous Rota club.

The most striking statement in this final part of the Ephemerides occurs well before the half-way point, when Hartlib declared: 'N.B. For England is the royalists come in and the young king of Sweden'.[121] The date of this extract must be after 13 February, when Charles XI inherited his Swedish title, but likely before the formal declaration of the Restoration of Charles II on 14 May. With respect to the precise date, this might be around 13 March, when Parliament voted for its dissolution pending the return to monarchy. Whatever its date, this aside shows that Hartlib was not slow to bow to the inevitable on the political front.

A short entry early in 1660 features John Evelyn, which reminds us of Hartlib's long history working with ease with known opponents of the Commonwealth.[122] In 1660 Hartlib also noted that 'Mr. Evelyn is a gent. of great worth, well known unto me'.[123] The exact date of their acquaintance is difficult to ascertain, but 1657 is likely. In the autumn of 1659 Hartlib had supplied Evelyn with a series of extracts from letters, likely from Oldenburg, mainly relaying information about French botanical publications. In January 1660 Hartlib also remarked on Eyelyn's enthusiasm for a French method of producing marbled paper. Evelyn was invoked on further occasions in this last section of the Ephemerides, mainly with respect to the use of floral distillates, or botanical cures. In this context Hartlib added that Kuffeler, a major expert on distillation, also specialised in essences of this kind, including those generated from citrus fruits. As with Evelyn, Kuffeler also featured often in this last section of the Ephemerides. His distillation skills were again invoked by Hartlib in connection with his friend, Samuel Wartensky, who wrote from Farnham that he had access to the garden produce of his neighbour, Nathaniel Fiennes, the second son of Lord Say and Sele who, it seems, was celebrated for his displays of gilliflowers (carnations and pinks) in his garden at nearby Froyle.[124]

---

121 HP 29/8/13A.
122 HP 29/8/10A.
123 Hartlib to Worthington, 30 January 1660, Crossley I, p. 171.
124 For Robert Boyle's advocacy of essence of jasmine, HP 29/8/11B.

Robert Wood was another close associate of Hartlib who figured prominently in these pages. At this point he had just returned to London after the collapse of his career in Ireland. Wood's most striking reference related to yet another Royalist, William Backhouse (1593–1662), who appears, not by name, but as 'Sir John Bacchus's son'. Sir John (actually his elder brother) was yet another notable Royalist. William is praised by Wood for his collection of inventions and especially his thermometer and weather glass, all housed at his home, Swallowfield House in Berkshire. This was not news to Hartlib, who had detailed similarly in his Ephemerides for 1656.[125] As a notoriously reticent figure, it is not surprising that William Backhouse is not specifically mentioned elsewhere in the Ephemerides. Backhouse belonged to Henshaw's occult sciences group, which was well-known to Hartlib.[126] Wood's note about a manuscript on health and wealth 'from one of the Rosicrucians' may well refer to this same group. A further obscure reference to both Rosicrucians and Antilia is ascribed to 'Sir Brownlow of Lincolnshire'. Two knights of that name are possible candidates, but neither seems to have possessed any link with Hartlib or his friends.[127]

Clodius, who had featured prominently in the Ephemerides since the early '50s, accounts for most of the six references to Antilia that occur in these pages. This continuing awareness of Antilia is undoubtedly connected with the association of Hartlib with Joachim Polemann, which began in earnest in 1659 when Polemann was still in Germany and the Netherlands. His decision to settle in London was not a surprise. It is therefore not surprising that Polemann left his mark on the Ephemerides.[128] Inventions and chemical ingenuities, including alchemy, were yet a further area that, as throughout the Ephemerides, was well-represented in these final pages.

Further relevant to Hartlib's association with Royalists, he recalled that Friedrick Clodius was associated with Robert Paston, who was in

---

125 HP 29 /5/104B.
126 Dickson, *Tessara of Antilia*, pp. 186–207.
127 Perhaps Sir William Brownlow (c.1595–1666) of Humby in Lincolnshire, was educated at St Mary Hall, Oxford. He was a Parliamentarian during the Civil War and in 1653 was elected an M.P. for Lincolnshire.
128 HP 29/8/16A, early June 1660. A letter to Hartlib from Polemann, dated 13 July 1660, which transmits a recipe for stone, deriving from a member of the Royal household, was dispatched from Earl's Court, HP 26/73A.

turn also connected with Thomas Henshaw and his predominantly Royalist chemical club. Henshaw and Paston went on to join the Royal Society, after which they both became immersed in the search for the philosopher's stone. The first reference to Paston in this portion of the Ephemerides related to the advocacy of beer infused with saltpetre, which was championed as a cure for kidney and bladder stones in the first instance, but was also recommended as a general medicine for the poor. This treatment was credited to the Antilians, who were supposed to believe that this medicament possessed widespread powers. Paston and Clodius made a further appearance relating to saltpetre, which they were advocating as an air purifier.[129] Both Robert Paston (soon to become the first Earl of Yarmouth) and his father, Sir William Paston (both were ardent Royalists) were already known to Hartlib, who remembered that Sir William was wealthy and a 'promoter of ingenuities'.[130] Perhaps unnoticed by Hartlib, Sir William was most widely known as an art collector. Robert Paston was first mentioned by Hartlib in 1656, again in connection with Clodius.[131] Further on the subject of ales, Hartlib was so touched by the gift of a bottle of sassafras ale from Robert Wood that he entered the whole instruction to the brewer in his Ephemerides, which seems to be the only entry of this kind in whole journal.[132]

The very first entry in the 1660 Ephemerides is a notable reference to Thomas Streete and Robert Anderson, two relatively neglected mathematicians of humble origin: 'One Anderson (a ribband-weaver) a most excellent Mathematician or Astronomer, and an acquaintance of Streete who is now making ready against Easter his *Tabulas Planetarum*'.[133]

This entry, which emanates from Nikolaus Mercator (Kauffman), is a rare instance of documentary evidence relating to Anderson, which proves that he was well into his stride as a mathematician by this date. He went on, in collaboration with Streete, to play a pioneering role in the development of the science of ballistics. Largely through the enthusiasm expressed by Benjamin Worsley, Hartlib had known about Streete since 1657.[134] The similarly supportive Mercator was one of the most active

---

129 HP 29/8/11A-B and 15A.
130 Ephemerides 1651, HP 28/2/9B.
131 HP 29/5/67A; see also a letter from Robert Paston to Clodius, c.1659, HP 42/81A.
132 HP 29/8/10B.
133 HP 29/8/10A. Streete's important *Astronomia Carolina* was published in 1661.
134 For Hartlib's notes on Streete, HP 26/56/1A; 29/6/20A; 42/1/10B.

of Hartlib's later active correspondents and informants. The two had been in touch since the beginning of 1655; their correspondence began in September of that year and they remained in touch at least until December 1661.

A further entry, originating with Hartlib himself, or possibly Wood, relates to 'Potters Banco Designe'. The first part reads: 'The Friers. Major Morgan. Dr Petty. Mr Slingsby. Mr or Dr Pett. Mr Wood. These have met several times about it'.[135]

This summary constitutes convincing evidence that the elaborate exchanges of correspondence about economic policy, revolving around William Potter's Land Bank scheme, held during the last days of the Parliamentary regime, had not collapsed, but had continued thereafter, perhaps even under the auspices of the short-lived but vital Rota Club, in which William Petty played a prominent part.[136] Owing to its adverse political associations the Rota's meetings in all probability ended in February 1660. The above quotation, which derives from a slightly later date, provides evidence that its members continued to meet to discuss issues of mutual interest, in this case at 'The Friers', perhaps Austin Friars. The recorded discussants were an interesting group, all of them likely to be interested in Potter's scheme. Major Anthony Morgan (knighted in both 1656 and 1660), William Petty (knighted in 1660) and Robert Wood, had served in Ireland and had in some capacity worked under Henry Cromwell. All three, as well as Potter himself, had been on familiar terms with Hartlib for some years. The other two were probably unknown to Hartlib at this date. Henry Slingsby was employed at the Mint in the Tower of London and was soon to become the deputy to the Master Worker of the Mint, at which point he began to exercise major influence in the formulation of policy. Peter Pett (knighted in 1663) was an ambitious young Erastian and lawyer, close to Arthur Annesley, the first Earl of Anglesey, whose interests he served, including in Ireland during the 1660s.

Some further additional information relating to the Rota features in the very last paragraph of the 1660 Ephemerides. Here attention focused

---

135 HP 29/8/13B.
136 For a recent account of the Rota with special reference to William Petty, Rachel Hammersley, *James Harrington: An Intellectual Biography* (Oxford: Oxford University Press, 2019), chapter 14.

on Samuel Cradock on account of his propositions that promised to transform the whole British economy. In what turned out to be the concluding words of the whole Ephemerides, Hartlib concluded that Cradock's 'design may interfere with Potter's Designes except they reconcile'.[137]

Also relevant is an undated letter from Ezerel Tong to Hartlib, which must have originated at a similar date to the above Ephemerides entry and which covered similar ground. Tong disclosed that Samuel Cradock, in both written presentation and public discourse delivered at a Rota meeting, had promulgated proposals similar to Potter's ideas, which again suggests a connection with the Land Bank scheme.[138] Cradock, a rich gentleman from Suffolk, remains a shadowy figure: he was mentioned often in the exchanges between Hartlib and Worthington between May and July 1661, but he was misidentified by Worthington's editor.

Hartlib noted that the Cradock-Potter issue was just one of Tong's preoccupations at that date: 'Dr Ducket hath gotten a Patent and Dr Tongue made ready a Petition about Deanes and Chapters how they may bee improoved for Schooling et Learning. Etc'.[139]

The preamble to Tong's letter excuses his neglect of the Rota-related events on the grounds of his involvement in drafting patents, first for 'Dr. K', certainly his client Johann Sibertus Kuffeler, who at this point was creating a stir on account of his torpedo invention.[140] Secondly, he was acting on behalf of Thomas Ducket, an inveterate improver, whose activities can be traced in the Ephemerides from 1647 onwards.[141] Lastly, Tong admitted his preoccupation at this date with his own petition, the text of which was included with the letter. This, as Hartlib noted, on

---

137 Worthington-Hartlib exchanges between May and July 1661 regularly mentioned Cradock, who was a rich gentleman from Suffolk, widely travelled and keen on fostering improvement. Crossley, I, pp. 178–79, where Crossley, at length, conflates the layman Cradock with the well-known ejected Cambridge cleric of the same name.
138 [Tong to Hartlib] n.d., HP 10/4A-B. Tong notes that both he and Cradock were, at that date, like Hartlib and Grundmann, much involved with Sir Edward Harley, at that time Governor of Dunkirk etc.
139 HP 29/8/13B and 47/5/1A-2B.
140 Webster *Instauration*, pp. 390–91.
141 Webster *Instauration*, pp. 68, 426, 473: note the habit of Hartlib, as illustrated by both Ducket and Potter, of endowing such laymen with doctorates.

the basis of historical precedent, argued for diverting the proceeds of the estates of Deans and Chapters to the extension of secondary and tertiary education. This petition was an artfully adapted version of Tong's 'An abstract of a designe', probably prepared for submission to the Third Protectorate Parliament of 1659, which culminated with an inflammatory attack on the episcopacy.[142] As Tong's letter of 22 April 1660 shows, this rebellious spirit was slow to be extinguished. He recounted from Canterbury that there was a strong rumour that John Lambert had escaped from the Tower and was raising an army capable of occupying London, an outcome that Tong obviously found agreeable.[143] This story had an element of credibility. Lambert had indeed escaped from his imprisonment and set about raising an army of resistance. On this occasion his military genius was thwarted. He assembled a small force, but there was insufficient will to fight. As a result, on the day of Tong's letter, Lambert was again taken prisoner, after which he was doomed to permanent exile. These final incidents recounted in the Ephemerides and in associated documents are interesting curiosities in themselves, but they also provide significant evidence concerning responses to the challenges stemming from the unfolding political circumstances of the Restoration. Adaptation to this new situation created an especially arduous challenge to Hartlib at a time of his mounting hardship and rapidly declining health.

5.9 Being of the Spirit

In 1649 Hartlib pledged himself to be among those who, 'being of the spirit' and therefore compliant with the dictum 'of our Saviour Christ to his people, Not to fear them that can but kill the body, but are not able to destroy the soul'.[144] In the perilous circumstances of his final months, when his body was at its weakest, Hartlib displayed no sign of the weakening of his spirit. He was therefore able to maintain the momentum of his work and even embark on new and challenging ventures.

---

142 HP 53/28/1A-4B.
143 Tong to Hartlib, 22 April 1660, HP 10/7/1B.
144 Hartlib, Dedication to General Sir Thomas Fairfax, *Londons Charity Ingarged*, 1649, p. 5: from Matthew 10:28.

Indicative of Hartlib's fortitude, according to my estimate, in the year 1661, the last complete year of his life, he received 136 letters, which represented an increase of about seventy-five percent on the previous year. This total might well increase to about 150 if overlooked items, or those that are mentioned, but remain untraced, are taken into account.

The largest element in this increase is explained by the huge expansion of John Dury's input. Much of the year 1660 was lost to Dury owing to the crisis that he faced on account of the Restoration. In that year only four of his letters are recorded, with none to Hartlib. By 1661 Dury was back on the continent and again engrossed in his ecclesiastical peace mission. This was the main, but by no means the only topic upon which he reported to Hartlib in the course of no fewer than forty-six letters.

With the Restoration, Worthington also suffered a major setback, but this modest man absorbed his disappointments with commendable dignity. His contribution of letters to Hartlib was ten in 1660, which rose to eighteen in 1661. Next in line was Comenius, most of whose letters to Hartlib from that period are only preserved as fragments. His record was three letters to Hartlib in 1660, but seven in 1661. To the latter should be added four from Petr Figulus, his son-in-law. The letters of these four friends together constituted almost half the total. The other half comprised many small contributions, almost all of them much less than these same individuals had generated in previous years. This group still comprised a sizable cohort of some twenty correspondents, who remained in direct touch with Hartlib until a few months before his death. Of these eight were writing from the continent, or were exiles recently settled in England. As indicated by the total of eleven letters from seven correspondents for December 1661, there is little evidence of any tailing off with Hartlib's correspondence in the course of that year. Of these, as might be expected, Comenius, Beale, Dury and Worthington each contributed two. There was one from John Ray, a new associate, soon to become famous, particularly as a botanist, and one from Martin Grundmann, a Silesian exile, who had settled in Powys and by this date was intimate with Hartlib. The final letter derived from a newcomer, Albert Otto Faber (1612–1684) who, according to Hartlib, had arrived in England in about March 1661, apparently at the invitation of the King.

Hartlib described Faber as 'an excellent Helmontian physician'.[145] Faber was an artful self-publicist who rapidly shot into print and issued three iatrochemical tracts between 1661 and 1663.

Hartlib first mentioned Faber in 1653, apparently in response to favourable remarks received from Moriaen. Hartlib's particular interest in Faber was not as his own medical adviser, but because he was a witness to the religious experiences of an obscure Frieslander, who attracted widespread curiosity at that date. At this point the Hartlib team wanted to know whether the visiting angel possessed a grey or black beard. Faber is a late, although not the last, marginal figure to attract the attention of Hartlib during the last phase of his life.

In 1659 Petr Figulus had communicated an urgent plea for the recognition and support of Stephanus Keus, an obscure Amsterdam watchmaker, who had turned his hand to inventions in general, including optical instruments. In the course of supplying Hartlib with dozens of pieces of information demonstrating the inventive powers of Keus, Figulus pleaded: 'O that the Macaria might supply the Poore Man in these hard times, verily the Man would bee Instrumental to find out many other useful Engines and to perfect this [a lantern employing lenses instead of plain glass]'. True to form, both Hartlib and Comenius took Keus seriously and subjected several of his inventions to further investigation.[146]

Metamorphosis of the World

With respect to the higher priorities of Hartlib in these last years, we again benefit from the insight of Petr Figulus. Particularly significant is a short anonymous appraisal, which emanated from Amsterdam. This dates from mid-October 1659 and most definitely bears the stamp of Figulus. On account of the propitious nature of his message, Figulus again invoked Macaria:

---

145 Hartlib to Worthington, 20 August 1661, Crossley I, p. 356.
146 Figulus to Hartlib, 5 December 1659, HP 8/9/12A. For the eccentric Keus, see H.J. Zuidervaart, 'De Amsterdamse vernufteling Stephanus Pietersz Keus (c.1605–1679) en zijn contacten met de Hartlib Circle', *Studium. Tijdschrift voor Wetenschaps- en Universiteitsgeschiedenis*, 12:01–03 (2019), 110–22.

> Our secret intelligence concerning the Macaria shortly to breake forth in England doth continue. The whole Worke of God everywhere is yet but an Embryo, but I hope the time is now at hand that this Child shall soone bee borne and... revealed unto the World. There bee 2. things which doubtlesse will shortly bring a very strange Metamorphosis, first in England, then in Christendome, at last in the whole World.[147]

The two 'things' in the thoughts of Figulus are both more significant than they first appear. Firstly:

> In my former I told you of the Translation of the whole Bible into the Turkish Tongue by Levinus Warnerus a Man of excellent Intellectual Abilities for such a Worke. This is a true Propagation of the Gospel not by making an Independent a Presbyter or Presbyter Independent, but by converting those to Christianity that are either Enemies or Strangers to it.

Secondly:

> Wee are exceeding glad when you tell us there are the like endeavours in England and more Particularly that Mr Pocock (who is indeed very fit for such a Worke) hath translated Grotius Booke of the Truth of Christian Religion into Arabick, and that the Booke is partly printed at Oxford. Wee shal most gladly advise you how it may bee dispersed into several parts of the East to the greatest Advantage of the Designe which both you and wee pursue in it.[148]

Figulus left no doubt about the broader relevance of these specific publishing projects, including their significance for Hartlib's own priorities. Reflecting the emphasis in his letters from this period, Figulus took hope from what he judged as the consistent record of Protestant leadership that had been displayed by the Lord Protector and his 'Great Counsell', all of which was vital for lending authority to Hartlib personally in his mission to 'assist & bring about the great worke of the Lord, which without doubt hee will performe in these our dayes, to destroy the Beast in Christendome'. Thereby a powerful light was set to rise in the west that would destroy the kingdom of Antichrist and

---

147 HP 15/9/5B-6A.
148 The use by Figulus of the first-person plural suggests his close alliance with Laurentius de Geer on all of these propositions.

'kindle a light of a newe kingdome of Truth, which is the Gospell of Jesus Christ'.[149]

The specific publishing ventures outlined by Figulus were conceived as modest but positive contributions to the apocalyptic global transformation that he believed was on the verge of realisation. In expressing himself so unambiguously, Figulus must have assumed that Hartlib was similarly inclined. To the exiled community that had only recently arrived in Amsterdam, Cromwellian Britain seemed endowed with the natural leadership of embattled Protestantism. Even after the death of the Lord Protector, and the emergence of other impediments, Figulus's faith remained undimmed and was fortified by such factors as the sudden rash of initiatives relating in some way to the spread of the gospel. 'Thus we see God works on all sides towards some great change, and for the call of foreigners into the church'.[150]

To the best of his abilities Hartlib conscientiously assisted with the practical objectives that Figulus had set out and also with other cognate initiatives connected with spreading the word among strangers. At every point where Hartlib was directly involved, he encountered unforeseen obstacles, which inevitably impeded the ambitious goals that Figulus had so boldly proclaimed.

Turkish Bible

It is possible that, as Noel Malcolm suggests, the Turkish Bible initiative can be traced back to the spring of 1658, with the idea deriving from Comenius, in which case Figulus was likely to have been well-informed concerning this development. Once Hartlib became involved in the autumn of 1659, the word spread rapidly. Boyle, Oldenburg and Worthington quickly became immersed in the project.[151]

---

149 Figulus to Hartlib, 6 December 1658, HP 9/17/53A-B.
150 Figulus to Hartlib, c.mid-November 1659, cited in Hartlib to Boyle, 29 November 1659, Boyle *Correspondence* I, p. 392.
151 N. Malcolm, 'Comenius, Boyle, Oldenburg, and the Translation of the Bible into Turkish', *Church History and Religious Culture*, 87:3 (2007), 327–62; A. Ayşen, 'In-between Calvinism and Islam: Ali Bey's Transcultural Translation of the Bible into Turkish in the Time of Confessionalization', *The Biblical Annals*, 13:3 (2023), 439–61.

Figulus had good reason for selecting Levinus Warnerus (1619–1665) to take responsibility for translating the Bible into Turkish. He was a respected orientalist who, from 1655 to 1665, served as the Dutch Resident in Constantinople.[152] The omens for this project were favourable, particularly because Laurentius de Geer was its generous benefactor. All of this gave Figulus the confidence to inform Hartlib that in the next post he and de Geer would be writing to Warnerus 'to send it [the translation] over hither as soon as he can'.[153] At this point the patrons discovered that their aspirations were unrealistic, but they were satisfied that Warnerus was at least personally committed to their project and that he had evolved a realistic plan for its fulfilment. Henceforth Warnerus served as the organising agent, with local specialists being selected to undertake the main work of translation. At that date Constantinople was the ideal location for this operation. The initial translator was the Sephardic Jew, Yahya bin Ishak (Ahya ibn Haki), who worked on the project between mid-1658 and late 1661. He was succeeded by the brilliant and highly capable Albertus Bobovius (Wojciech Bobowski/Ali Ufkî Bey) (c.1610–1675), whose childhood was spent in Leopolis (now Lviv). He worked on the translation with amazing effect from February 1662 to December 1664.[154]

Although Ali Bey's achievement was remarkable, it should be noted that his work began only after the death of Hartlib. Yet further complications were in store. The adjudication by Jacobus Golius, professor of Oriental Languages at Leiden University, led to yet further revisions. Warnerus died in 1665, de Geer in 1666, Golius in 1667 and Comenius in 1670. The New Testament was not published until 1819, and the whole Turkish Bible followed in 1827.[155]

---

152 Figulus to Hartlib, mid-November 1659, cited in Hartlib to Boyle, 29 November 1659, Boyle *Correspondence* I, p. 392. For Warnerus, I. Tahan, ed., *The Ottoman Legacy of Levinus Warner* (Leiden: Brill, 2012).

153 Figulus, as note 152.

154 For Bobowski and his Turkish translation of Comenius's *Janua linguarum reserata*, see Blekastad *Comenius*, pp. 507, 631–32. In 1653, Bobowski was engaged by Isaac Basire (1607–1676), chaplain to the English Resident, to translate the Anglican Catechism into Turkish.

155 H. Neudecker, *The Turkish Bible Translation by Yahya Bin 'Ishak, Also called Haki* (Leiden: Oosters Instituut, 1994). For the Boyle-supported Lazarus Seaman Turkish New Testament published in 1666, the progress of which was much

Lithuanian and Armenian Bibles

The Warnerus Turkish Bible episode constituted a stark reminder of the hazards facing such ventures. Nevertheless, Hartlib and his friends were not deterred from engaging in further exploits of this kind. Each exhibited its own characteristic pitfall.

In the case of the Lithuanian language Bible, Hartlib sided with the embattled Bible translator, Samuel Bogusław Chyliński. They faced a campaign of obstruction mounted by Jan Krzysztof Kraiński, the official delegate in London of the Synod of the Lithuanian Reformed community. It will be remembered that Hartlib was well-informed about the Lithuanian Calvinist congregations through various of his correspondents in that region, including his brother, Georg Hartlib who, before his exile from Vilnius, was a senior figure in the Lithuanian Calvinist congregation.

Between December 1660 and December 1661 Hartlib and Worthington exchanged a dozen letters on the Chyliński affair, but neither they nor their allies, such as John Wallis, were successful in securing further funding for the printing operation. Chyliński's campaign collapsed and he died in poverty in London in 1668. The only surviving traces of Chyliński's heroic venture are a single copy of the printed version of the Old Testament Books from Genesis to Joshua, and the manuscript of his New Testament translation, both of which are now located in the British Library.[156]

At exactly the same period as their involvement with Chyliński, Hartlib and Worthington were concerned to discover the fate of the scheme in Amsterdam to edit and print a long-existing Armenian translation of the Bible. Hartlib was the direct intermediary, but clearly this was not a high priority, which disappointed Worthington. Also, Hartlib's correspondents in Amsterdam were strangely reticent. Hartlib was nearly out of time, but his last recorded remark indicated that he had at least found out that the assigned printer had died and

---

affected by the failing Warnerus project, see Malcolm, 'Comenius, Boyle, etc.', pp. 339–62.

156 G. Kavaliūnaitė, 'Historical Sources Bearing on Samuel Boguslaus Chylinski's Pursuits in England and the Netherlands and their Echoes in the Grand Duchy of Lithuania', *Lithuanian Historical Studies*, 16 (2011), 07–28.

that the arrival of a replacement was imminent.[157] The death of the first editor occurred in 1661, after which there was a hiatus until 1664, when there arrived the distinguished Vosgan (Ohan) Yerevantsi. After his hard work on the text, printing took place from March 1666 until October 1668. The resultant Oskaen Bible was in every respect successful.

Oriental Studies

When compared with the intractable field of Bible translation, Hartlib stood on safer ground when he negotiated the second main objective highlighted by Figulus, which was the production and distribution of an Arabic edition of *De veritate religionis christianae* by Hugo Grotius. This project had long interested Edward Pococke (1604–1691), who was the first Laudian Professor of Arabic at Oxford. He completed his translation by about 1640, but political factors in Oxford stood in the way of publication. The project was not resurrected until 1659 when Robert Boyle agreed to pay for completion of the printing and for arranging the distribution of the completed book. It is quite likely that Boyle's action over the Pococke Grotius edition was prompted by the Figulus memoir outlined above, which Hartlib would surely have made available to him. In his letter of 3 November, Boyle first commented favourably on the Warnerus Turkish Bible project and then immediately pledged his support for 'converting those to Christianity that are either enemies or strangers to it' and for demonstrating 'so Christian a commiseration of their souls, that yet sit as it were in darkness and in the shadow of death'. Boyle added that they in Oxford were not 'altogether regardless of such matter, for Mr. Pocock is at my request printing a translation of Grotius's Book of the Truth of the Christian Religion into Arabick'.[158] Boyle was to be greatly praised for helping to elevate the profile of Pococke, but he was straining the message of the Grotius edition if he thought that it would serve as a missionary tract. Completion of the printing operation

---

157 Hartlib to Worthington, 14 January 1662, Crossley II, Part 1, pp. 99–100. After this date it was only two months, and two further recorded exchanges between the two friends, before Hartlib's death.

158 Boyle to Hartlib, 3 November 1659, cited in Hartlib to Worthington, 7 November 1659, Crossley I, p. 161 and Boyle *Correspondence* I, p. 382.

in Oxford took a little time but the book was probably available by the spring of 1660. Hartlib and Worthington were pleased with this outcome, but they were concerned that insufficient interest was being shown by the author and his patrons in arrangements for distribution and promotion.

It is strikingly evident from their exchanges of letters that the above project had the effect of strengthening their interest in the further work of Pococke and in Arabic literature more generally. Hartlib pursued his enquiries in this field with his customary dogged perseverance.

His efforts were rewarded by the gathering of background information on every book published by Pococke between 1660 and 1663. In addition, particular interest attaches to the two correspondents' repeated references to Pococke's 'Arabic Philosophical Fiction' which, from January 1659 until Hartlib's death, they believed was on the verge of publication. Crossley identified this work as Ibn Tufayl's *Risalat Hayy ibn Yaqzān*, which was published only in 1671. Subsequent research has established beyond doubt that Pococke's edition was completed by about 1645, and therefore quite likely to have been known to the assiduous Hartlib and Worthington.[159]

After a long paragraph on Pococke, Worthington's letter of 24 February 1662 ended with a few lines regretting the continuing harsh circumstances of Edmund Castell, another orientalist, now mainly remembered as a lexicographer. For some time, the mounting tribulations of Castell had been followed by the two correspondents with alarm. In this letter, Worthington ended his further sympathetic remarks with the generalisation that 'I measure and value the excellency and worth of things by their respect and tendency to the best end,' a notion which Hartlib could hardly reject. As Crossley explains in his annotation: 'Here the correspondence between Worthington and Hartlib terminates, the latter's foreboding in the preceding letter, "this may be the last of mine," being, it appears, realised'.[160]

At this point Hartlib had just two weeks to live. We possess only one other letter addressed to him during these last days, which is a brief note

---

159 M. Nahas, 'A Translation of Hayy B. Yaqẓān by the Elder Edward Pococke (1604–1691)', *Journal of Arabic Literature*, 16 (1985), pp. 88–90.
160 Worthington to Hartlib, 24 February 1662, Crossley I, pp. 110–14.

from Comenius in the Netherlands, also dated 24 February.[161] This may not have reached Hartlib before his death. After a brief note of condolence to his sick correspondent, Comenius went on to outline the composition of a modest gift, the largest part of which derived from de Geer, with smaller additions from Comenius himself and from Serrarius, who had also at that date written directly to Hartlib. Comenius added that he had approached several of his correspondents concerning Hartlib, which undoubtedly implied that he was seeking financial support from them for the benefit of his sick friend. Comenius excused the brevity of his letter, which he attributed to his own ill-health.

Bible Translation Politics

The only other noteworthy remark in this letter of Comenius was a reference to the new edition of the *Gdańska Bible*. As might be expected, Hartlib already knew about this edition of the 'Polonian Bible', which he described as 'curiously reprinted', which was a reference to the octavo format, a pocket-book size, which was a cause of controversy.[162]

What would not have been anticipated by Hartlib was the request from Comenius for his assistance, which meant informing Kraiński that five copies of the new Bible edition had been dispatched to London for his use. As seen above, relations between Hartlib and Kraiński were strained and had never recovered. By 1662 it was self-evident that Kraiński, despite his claims to the contrary, was the main agent responsible for undermining the completion of the printing of Chyliński's Lithuanian Bible. Respecting Chyliński's many sympathisers such as Hartlib and his friends among the scientific elite, Kraiński was an unreformed reactionary. In their eyes, sending Kraiński the Polonian Bible would have confirmed that those of his persuasion were determined to preserve Polish as the *lingua franca* among the Lithuanian reformed community,

---

161 Comenius to Hartlib, 24 February 1662, HP 7/8/1A-B.
162 Hartlib to Worthington, 17 December 1660, Crossley I, p. 249. A revised edition of the Gdańska Bible had been commissioned jointly by the Polish Calvinists and Unitarians. This was published in November 1632 at the Andreas Hünefeld printing house in Danzig. The first major revision of this was *Biblia swięta: to jest, ksiegi pisma swietego starego y nowego przymierza* (Amsterdam: Christopher Cunrad, 1660) 8vo (187 x 119mm.), [16 (including an engraved title page)], 898, 219, 286, 10 pp.

thereby undermining Lithuanian aspirations to attain a unified national status.

Amen

If the above reading of his last correspondence is correct, Hartlib went to his death still in an undiminished state of excitement about his ever-expanding intellectual horizons, but also in a spirit of some despondency concerning the hazards affecting many of the ventures to which he had lent support. In that case he might well have uttered to himself the cry of *phosphore redde diem* that he had expressed to Robert Boyle in 1659.

Hartlib's death, perhaps occasioned by a further stroke that fatally overcame his weakened frame, therefore constituted a rude break in his productive life. This occurred during the morning of 10 March 1662. The record for this is a scrap of paper drafted by John Pell for his son. This note also records that Pell intended to accompany Hartlib's body to its grave. Samuel was buried, no doubt quietly, as he would have wished, at St Martin-in-the-Fields on Wednesday 12 March, the event being simply recorded in the parish register as '12. Samuel Hartlip vir'.[163] All in all, this was a fitting end for this notably unpretentious man who admitted to being 'a Stranger and no Free Denizon', albeit his 'Heart hath been truly Naturalized' so that 'as long as I have breathed in this aire' he dedicated himself to 'the advancement of all Designes for the general good of this Church and State'.[164]

---

163 Turnbull *Hartlib*, p. 72. For Pell's note, BL Add. MS. 4280, f.318, cited in Malcolm/Stedall *Pell*, p. 185.

164 From the anonymous draft petition to Houses of Parliament [c.January 1645], HP 7/30/3A.

Epilogue

> The zealous sollicitor of Christian peace Amongst all Nations, The constant Friend of distressed Strangers,... The sedulous advancer of Ingenuous Arts, and Profitable Sciences, And the Principall Contriver of Generall Accommodations... Your industrious endeavours for the benefit of all men, and particularly for the good of this Nation, hath well deserved the gratefull acknowledgement of all good men.[1]

When John Beale wrote this graceful acknowledgement, he had known Samuel Hartlib for only a few months, but he had already formed an acute understanding of the character and range of his dedicatee's activities. Once they were in direct contact, Beale was overcome by Hartlib's generosity and nobility of spirit, which seemed all the greater considering the serious ill-health of his new patron at that date.[2] Beale quickly became a settled and profuse correspondent of Hartlib, establishing a routine which lasted until shortly before Hartlib's death.[3] Beale soon became acquainted with many of Hartlib's leading coworkers and participated actively in their discussions, including on leading issues of the moment such as law reform. These new contacts included Lady Ranelagh, to whom he wrote intensively about religious experience. Chapter 5 features the extraordinary Standish publishing venture devised by Beale. Besides its ostensible purpose, Beale insisted on mobilising this venture to boost the fortunes of the republican party. The radical motivations of Beale at this date are revealed by his 'Philalethes from Eleutheropol. High Treasone' manifesto.[4] Thus, by the

---

1   John Beale, *Herefordshire Orchards*, February 1657, A1v.
2   Beale to Hartlib, 19 and 22 December 1656, HP 31/1/6A-8B.
3   Beale's letters to Hartlib amount to more than 120 for the period 1657–1661.
4   Dated 11 March 1659, HP 51/78A-79B—literally 'lover of truth from the city of the free'.

eve of the Restoration Beale had qualified himself as one of the most radical voices among the close associates of Hartlib.

John Beale's assessment of Hartlib touched upon some of the most important aspects of his work, but not all of them. Of the areas explored in this study, education is perhaps the most obvious omission, as is evident from the long review of this subject in chapter 4. Beale was certainly alert to this aspect of Hartlib's work and indeed at the date of his *Herefordshire Orchards* he was plying Hartlib with proposals for reform in this field. Interestingly, in his draft petitions to Parliament and Charles II, Hartlib listed his activities in very similar terms to the Beale dedication. The only evidence he cited for his involvement in education was the very first item in his list, which comprised a few words about his failed Chichester Academy project.

Beale rightly observed that Hartlib, with characteristic self-effacing humility, at the outset of his career had volunteered to act as John Dury's deputy in his friend's mission for ecclesiastical peace.[5] Almost oblivious of the mounting range of entirely different obligations assumed by his friend, for the rest of Hartlib's life Dury was relentless in his demands on the services of this humble deputy. On the other hand, Dury was not insensitive to the sacrifices imposed on his friend, and he reciprocated by seeking means of ameliorating Hartlib's perpetual financial problems. Also on the positive side, Dury's unrivalled experience in negotiation and communication was frequently placed at Hartlib's disposal, a very necessary service on account of his friend's congenital lack of confidence regarding any kind of literary expression. As noted often in this study, owing to his lack of direct engagement with Hartlib's secular projects and their authors, Dury's misplaced interventions as an apologist proved to be a very mixed blessing.

Beale also correctly drew attention to Hartlib's role as a host to strangers. From the date of his arrival in England, Hartlib's home, which was throughout his life also his workplace from which he only rarely emerged, was also home to visitors, mainly distressed Protestants of all ages driven away in exile from Eastern and Central Europe. The most

---

5   Soon after this commitment was made, Hartlib wrote that as the sole agent for this work in Britain and related countries, he valued this work almost as dearly as his salvation. Hartlib, letter to unnamed correspondent, 22 October 1632, *MGP* 26, p. 26.

famous of these was Comenius. These house guests were often young people nominated by Comenius and fellow seniors of the Bohemian Brethren. Many of these were recruited into the team of amanuenses upon whom Hartlib relied for his massive system of intelligence gathering and distribution. Others were important visitors and diplomats, some from as far away as Transylvania, for whom Hartlib, as their host, was also viewed as an indispensable guide to relevant intelligence sources and as a means of access to the highest ranks of the political establishment. As prominently indicated throughout this study, Hartlib's untiring generosity soon reduced his whole family to a state of ruin, from which, despite the best efforts of his well-wishers, they never recovered.[6]

Next in his list, Beale specifically, but obliquely, alluded to Hartlib's adoption of Renaudot's *Bureau d'adresse*, which became transmuted into the labyrinthine scheme for an Office of Address, within which the Accommodations part, as the most viable, attracted much contemporary curiosity. Appropriately, Hartlib's Accommodations plan was ultimately unearthed by William Beveridge and implemented as the British Labour Exchange system of the twentieth century. As the Office of Address issue demonstrated, Hartlib was capable of locating a worthwhile economic objective, and then bringing this through to realisation. In this process, he attracted the notice of a menagerie of entrepreneurs as well as some serious economists and social activists such as Henry Robinson. The Office of Address also immediately exposed the nightmarish dilemmas afflicting the world of innovators and projectors.[7] This was also a further case where the dominating influence of Dury deflected an eminently practicable scheme into a complete dead end.

A similar acuity regarding economic objectives was displayed by Hartlib in his identification of the Land Bank and related concepts as serious viable options for economic enhancement, all of which he then energetically pursued by means of well-engineered publicity and by coordinating high-level debates among a well-chosen body of experts in this field. These intercommunications through Hartlib's active agency proved to be of the utmost significance. With remarkable agility

---

[6] Perhaps, the first notification of this tragic situation was made by John Dury early in 1633: Dury to Lord Brooke, 12 April 1633, BL Sloane MS 654, f.250.

[7] Culpeper and the Office of Address briefly feature in Yamamotu's, 'Reformation and Distrust'.

Hartlib's eclectic working party evolved into an incipient school of new thinking that is now labelled the 'Hartlibian Political Economy'. These exchanges, it is believed, 'constituted England's first coherent discourse on political economy'.[8] This conclusion harmonises perfectly with G.E. Fussell's practice of entitling the period from 1641–1660 in the important economic arena of agriculture 'The Age of Hartlib'.[9]

Besides his superintendence of the discussions on political economy, Hartlib's special commitment to economic innovation serving the public interest was a notable attraction to those joining his team, as for instance Robert Wood, who became central to the political economy workshop. When Wood came forward with his plan for the decimalisation of currency, he declared: 'You being so known a Promotor of anything that lookes towards the public Good, and having made your inclinations to the carrying on of usefull Designes so universally appeare in your Communications to this whole Nation'.[10] Representative of the more humble level of innovator, Ralph Austen made contact with Hartlib, 'Having heard much of your unwearied labours and endeavours for Publique advantages and the Encouragements that you give to those who labour in profitable Designes, I am bound with you to crave your favourable assistance'.[11] Such examples could be multiplied. The sentiments expressed remind us that in the minds of the mostly young, ambitious figures who flocked to associate with Hartlib from the mid-1640s onwards, they were primarily attracted by his reputation as Beale's archetypal 'sedulous advancer of Ingenuous Arts, and Profitable Sciences'. Hence, Hartlib's adherents tended to regard him as the kind of rounded scientific intellectual that Francis Bacon sought to inspire and perpetuate.[12] Relevant here is an early expression of the young Robert Boyle's newly found passion for natural philosophy, mechanics and husbandry, according to the principle that 'values no knowledge, but as it hath a tendency to use'. When, a few months later, Hartlib

---

8   P. J. Stern and C. Wennerlind (eds.), *Mercantilism Reimagined: Political Economy in Early Modern England and its Empire* (Oxford: Oxford University Press, 2013), p. 74.
9   G.E. Fussell, *The Old English Farming Books from Fitzherbert to Tull, 1523 to 1730, Part V*, pp. 36–55.
10   Wood to Hartlib, 11 March 1655, HP 27/20/ 1A.
11   Ralph Austen to Hartlib, 8 April 1652, HP 41/1/4A.
12   Relevant to this argument is the case of John Evelyn, O. Matei, 'Merchants of Light and Lamps: John Evelyn's Transition from Descriptive to Experimental Natural Philosophy', *Perspectives in Science*, 32:5 (2024), 585–611.

sought news about this group, Boyle assured him that these objectives were 'highly concerned with all the accidents of your life'.[13] A few years later, John Ray, then a rising star of botany, described Hartlib as a successor of Bacon in the conduct of 'solid experiments', of which 'there are not any my genius more Inclines me to, then these kind of rurall Improvements, of which this fruitfull Iland of England is as capable as the Natives are careless'.[14] When the instances just described are added to many of the same kind outlined in this study, such as in the discussion of Hartlib's association with a substantial cohort which found its way into the Royal Society, it becomes essential to reevaluate his status within the scientific and technical community. He cannot be written off as a marginal eccentric. Rather, he was clearly perceived by scientifically inclined specialists among his contemporaries as a figure of authority and respect, who was recognised as playing a decisive role in mediating the adaptation of Baconianism to the conditions of the new age. It is too soon to expect acceptance of this construction, but one day it might be cogently contended that the 'Hartlibian Political Economy' was inextricably linked with a parallel 'Hartlibian Scientific Movement'.

Hartlib was only able to achieve and retain the position of leadership that he occupied in both the economic and scientific fields owing to his inexhaustible energy and relentless curiosity, which involved openness to knowledge deriving from any source. He assessed the character of his informants, but was all-inclusive. As often mentioned in this study, when it came to medical treatments and the peddling of cures, his ingenuity was indiscriminate, but such relentless inquisitiveness brought noticeable compensation in his many other fields of work.

For instance, the obscure John Shaw seems to be the first name that he came across when searching for substitutes for the recently deceased Gabriel Plattes. Shaw's defence of the scientific status of husbandry was valued and much exploited by Hartlib. Hartlib came across Shaw's now rare and rarely mentioned short and anonymous tract *Brief discoveries*

---

13 Boyle to Isaac Marcombes, 22 October 1646 and to Hartlib, 8 May 1647, Boyle *Correspondence* I, pp. 42 and 58.

14 John Ray to Hartlib, 9 March 1660, HP 33/5/57A; rejecting any doubt about the status of husbandry as a science, Hartlib's friend John Shaw insisted upon the supremacy of the science of husbandry. Indeed, 'no science was of greater antiquity, worth and excellence', *Brief discoveries of excellent wayes and means* (1646), A2r-v.

of excellent wayes and means, soon after it was published, early in 1646. He soon established that this was written by Shaw, located his address near Tower Street, opened up correspondence and introduced him to his friends, notably Cheney Culpeper, who quickly subjected Shaw's innovations to critical investigation. Shaw was soon lost in the pressing crowd of husbandry innovators, but he was still in touch with Culpeper and Hartlib in 1657.

A more important instance of the benefits derived from Hartlib's habitual curiosity relates to William Potter of Coventry, the economic theorist, who is crucial to the Hartlibian Political Economy. As noted in chapters 4 and 5, Hartlib played a leading role in the promotion of Potter's economic theories. This was by no means the limit of their association. His ODNB entry claims that virtually nothing is known about Potter, but this is not borne out by Hartlib's papers. Potter and Hartlib were close friends and correspondents. In the Hartlib Papers website their association is recorded in more than a hundred hits. As with the humble Shaw, Hartlib was in touch with Potter soon after *The Key to Wealth* was published. Potter's first recorded visit to Hartlib's home occurred on 1 January 1651, interestingly in the company of John Sparrow, Jr., best known as the leading translator of theosophist Jacob Boehme.[15]

Both Sparrow and his father were already well-known to Hartlib, and both were keen inventors. At this first recorded meeting, Potter mainly talked about a potentially lucrative scheme for fen drainage, the most prominent patron of which, he claimed, was Lord General Cromwell himself. Most of Hartlib's testimony about Potter relates to his activities as an inventor, mainly in the field of mine drainage, but also in the connected slippery territory of perpetual motion. Hartlib introduced Potter to Beale, Wood and Worsley, who collectively took care of Potter's interests and represented him during his spells of notoriously poor health. These exchanges prove that this group was alert, not only to Potter as an economic thinker, but also on account of his strongly

---

15   Ariel Hessayon, 'Jacob Böhme's Foremost Seventeenth-Century English Translator: John Sparrow (1615–1670) of Essex', in B. Andersson et al., *Jacob Böhme and his World* (Brill: Boston, 2018), pp. 329–57. Hessayon observes that 'Sparrow's obscurity is unmerited' (p. 330), a conclusion that equally applies to Potter himself.

expressed views on such issues as constitutional and law reform. These witnesses also confirm that Potter was still active around the time of Hartlib's death, which again is not generally appreciated.

Not only was Hartlib oblivious to social rankings. He also took little account of age. One of his many worthy attributes was his ease in relating to younger people. I note elsewhere that in developing his plans for the reform of the University of Oxford, he featured Robert Boyle, Elisha Bourne, Thomas Danson, Thomas Gilson and John Hall, all of whom were around the age of twenty when they first met or contacted him. Another Oxford link at this date was the slightly older William Petty, who was only 24 when in 1647 he came to Hartlib's attention, soon after which the young man dedicated to him, as one of the few 'that are Reall Friends to the Designe of Realities', his ambitious and pioneering *Advice to Mr. Samuel Hartlib*.[16]

The link with Potter and his friends also draws attention to Hartlib's liberality with respect to religious persuasion. To a much greater degree and earlier than John Dury, he moved comfortably among the ranks of Independents and separatists, and unselfconsciously exchanged ideas and embraced the partnership of figures under suspicion of being tainted by radical leanings on issues of belief, such as Socinians, philosemites, theosophists and radical mystics, even the Quaker Anthony Pearson. Such liberality excluded Hartlib from the good offices of the clerical establishment, but it greatly endeared him to Katherine, Lady Ranelagh, with whom he built up a most harmonious relationship which was maintained until the eve of his death.

Hartlib's conspicuous identification with such figures as John Pym and Philip Nye and their aristocratic patrons when they were an embattled minority, served him well during the Parliamentarian ascendancy, but his unambiguous identification with the insurrection inevitably contributed to his abrupt demise after the return to monarchy. This unexpected reversal was a shock, but despite the collapse of his health, he adapted to the new situation with remarkable assiduity and this buoyancy continued until it was interrupted by his death in 1662.

As evident from numerous episodes featured in this study, and underlined by the above account of the last months of the Ephemerides,

---

16   See my forthcoming, 'Samuel Hartlib, on Reforming Interregnum Oxford'.

Hartlib's deeply held reformist inclinations never stood in the way of association with allcomers displaying common interests. This liberality was particularly well-illustrated by his exchanges with Worthington during the months before his death. For instance, they both developed an admiration for Edward Pococke, the first Laudian Professor of Arabic, whose unrepentant Anglicanism and Royalism had plunged him into difficulties in interregnum Oxford. Through Pococke they developed an intense curiosity about middle eastern cultures and their literature, which they noticeably pursued without regard to missionary activity or indeed the propagation of the gospel.[17]

The ability of Hartlib to withstand countless setbacks and allow nothing to stand in the way of his intellectual and social commitments must be understood in the context of his lifelong experience. From the days of his youth Hartlib had lived in an environment of political and social disruption. Many of his closest associates had personally experienced the very worst of this instability and suffering, none more directly than Georg, his brother, or Comenius, his most esteemed friend. In addition to his own intimate experience of instability and strife in revolutionary Britain, through his multiple informants and correspondents Hartlib was familiarised, often in great detail, with the tragic events of war-torn Europe. These multiple tragedies, such as the incineration of Leszno and the Waldensian massacres, both he and Dury duly communicated to the political elite and relevant authorities, such as the Council of State, in their capacity as trusted agents. The unusually sensitive role that Hartlib occupied, fitted him to be valued, first as private informant, and later as an official news operative, and expert on the mutations of his times.

Mechanical record-keeping was just one aspect of Hartlib's mission. All of the turmoil that he experienced necessitated explanation which, in his day, necessitated referral to varieties of eschatological analysis and the construction of apocalyptic blueprints. Fundamental to these exercises was the expectation of a brighter future for the redeemed, but with the understanding that this would only come about via a convoluted pathway, inevitability involving a succession of false dawns. Hence, Hartlib's plea of *Phosphore redde* embodied the expectation that

---

17 For Pococke's problems at Oxford, Worden, *God's Instruments*, pp. 105–55.

acute disappointment was a necessary prelude to a better future. The universality of such assumptions is illustrated in chapter 3 in the context of the discussion of Hartlib's *Clavis apocalyptica* and Comenius's *Lux in tenebris*.

The impetus for the phenomenal effort on the part of Hartlib derived from many sources including the religious and metaphysical motivations just described, integral to which was the expectation that end times would be accompanied by the transformation in levels of human knowledge, including the power over nature. Such phenomena as the rise of new philosophies and their associated scientific movements seemed to represent the realisation of such biblical expectations.[18] In Hartlib's case, his motivation was clearly also associated with the general ethos of contemporary Protestantism, and Puritanism in particular, as is confirmed by his partnership with Dury and his associates, and his direct immersion in Puritan life and thinking. Relevant to this are the above discussions of the ethics of the Public Good and the Communion of Saints, as well as the preoccupation with eschatological themes such as millenarianism and apocalypticism.[19]

As noted at many points in this study, Hartlib's interventions were inevitably tied up with endemic preoccupations with economic self-interest, but the scramble for affluence was not his primary motivation, as was recognised by the many talented intellectuals and practitioners who flocked to enjoy association with the community of activists who coalesced under of his leadership. John Winthrop, Jr. was surely reflecting the consensus of opinion among his contemporaries when he linked Hartlib with John Davenport in New England, both of whom were judged to reflect 'that entire friendship and suitableness of spirit

---

18   For this argument, see for instance Webster *Great Instauration*, pp. 01–31; G.L. Miller, 'Beasts of the New Jerusalem: John Jonston's Natural History and the Launching of Millenarian Pedagogy in the Seventeenth Century', *History of Science*, 46:2 (2008), 203–43.

19   For a recent review of the Public Good in the context of Hartlib and his associates, see Slack, *From Reformation to Improvement*, pp. 77–101. For the mammoth Puritanism/Science debate, three representative items relevant to this current study: Robert K. Merton, *Science, Technology and Society in Seventeenth-Century England* (New York: Harper & Row, 1970), originally *Osiris* 1938; R.L. Greaves, 'Puritanism and Science: The Anatomy of a Controversy', *Journal of the History of Ideas*, 30:3 (1969), 345–68; D.C.R. Austen, 'Puritanism and Natural Philosophy Revisited: the Case of Ralph Austen (c.1612–1676)', *The Seventeenth Century*, 39:3 (2024), 359–99.

to favour all publick good both in religion, learning and industry, which is so eminently between you both'.[20] It was even urged that Hartlib's labours were divinely ordained: hence he was perceived as being at the 'Centre of Negotiations and Correspondencies involving all manner of persons and there was no Good Worke whether in Church, Schoole or Common-Wealth but hee hath a hand in it to helpe it forward and is by a Special Providence of God commonly the most profitable and Active Agent that goeth about it'.[21]

With respect to Hartlib's record as a whole Beale offered a most generous assessment, which is indisputably consistent with the case studies outlined in the above account. Beale obviously chose his final words with care, believing that Hartlib 'hath well deserved the gratefull acknowledgement of all good men', which was open to the interpretation that Hartlib deserved greater gratitude than he received. This was certainly the view of the eminent John Davenport, who had known Hartlib since about 1630: 'For myselfe, I looke at Yourselfe, & Mr Hartlib, & Mr Comenius as three witnesses against this unthankfull Age, by whom God hath offered singular advantages for Religion, Learning, & Universall Wellfare; yet neither have the Offers been thanckfully received, nor the offering Instruments honourably rewarded'.[22]

---

20 Winthrop to Hartlib, 16 March 1660, HP 7/7/1B.
21 Dury to 'Reverend Sir', late 1645, HP 7/26/1A.
22 Davenport to Dury, 25 June 1660, HP 6/5/1A. The witness of Davenport and Winthrop in these final paragraphs reminds us of the closeness of Hartlib's relations with New England, and therefore, through Davenport, with the foundation of Harvard College and the embryonic college that soon became Yale. Long may these institutions, without hindrance, continue to protect the values that Hartlib held dear.

Bibliography

Primary Sources: Publications by Samuel Hartlib

Comprises publications edited and/or published by Samuel Hartlib considered in this study. Chronologically arranged and with compression of many of the titles.

The digitised archive of the Hartlib Papers can be found here: https://www.dhi.ac.uk/hartlib/

[Comenius], *Conatuum Comenianorum Praeludia ex bibliotheca S.H.* (Oxoniae Excudebat Guilielmus Turnerus Academiae Typographus, 1637).

An Idea of Mathematics written by Mr Joh. Pell to Samuel Hartlib [untitled broadsheet; London, October 1638]. The title given here was adopted in the 1650 and 1651 editions.

[Comenius], *Pansophiae prodromus nova hac editone indicat praefatio S.H.* (London: printed by M.F. for L. Fawne and S. Gellibrand, 1639). Two separate issues.

[John Stoughton], *Felicitas Ultimi Sæculi: epistola in qua, inter alia, calamitosus ævi præsentis status serió deploratur, certa felicioris posthac spes ostenditur, & ad promovendum publicum Ecclesiæ & rei literariæ bonum omnes excitantur: publici juris facta à S.H.* (Londini: Typis Richardi Hodgkinson, impensis Danielis Frere, 1640).

[John Dury], *A briefe relation of that which hath been lately attempted to procure ecclesiastical peace amongst Protestants* (London: printed by I.R. for Andrew Crooke, 1641).

[John Dury], *Englands Thankfulnesse, or an Humble Remembrance Presented to the Committee for Religion in the High Court of Parliament* (London: Printed for Michael Sparke Senior, dwelling in Green-Arbour, at the signe of the blew Bible, 1642).

A motion tending to the publick good of this age and of posteritie, or, The coppies of certain letters written by Mr. John Dury (London: Printed by P.L. for Michael Sparke Senior, 1642).

[Comenius], *A reformation of schooles designed in two excellent treatises, the first whereof summarily sheweth, the great necessity of a generall reformation of common learning* (London: Printed for Michael Sparke, 1642).

A faithfvll and seasonable advice, or, The necessity of a correspondencie for the advancement of the Protestant cause humbly suggested to the great councell of England assembled in Parliament (London: printed by Iohn Hammond, 1643). Likely by Dury, but inscribed by Thomason '*Ex Dono Authoris* S.Hartlib feb 6 1642'.

A copy of Mr. John Duries letter presented in Sweden to the truly noble and religious Lord Forbes: briefely intimating, the necessity of a common, fundamentall confession of faith (London: Printed by G.M. for Thomas Underhill, 1643).

[John Milton] *Of Education. To Master Samuel Hartlib* ([London: for Thomas Underhill], 1644).

The Parliaments Reformation... the Education of all poore Children (London: printed for Thomas Bates, 1646).

A Brief Discourse Concerning the Accomplishment of our Reformation: Tending to shew, That by an Office of Publike Addresse in Spirituall and Temporall Matters, the Glory of God, and the Happinesse of this Nation may be highly advanced. Considerations tending to the happy accomplishment of Englands reformation in church and state: Humbly presented to the piety and wisdome of the High and Honourable Court of Parliament (London: s.n. 1647).

A Further Discoverie Of The Office Of Public Address For Accommodations (London: s.n., 1648).

[Cyprian Kinner] *A continuation of Mr. John-Amos-Comenius school-endeavours, or, A summary delineation of Dr.Cyprian Kinner Silesian, his thoughts concerning education... translated out of the original Latine, transmitted to Sam. Hartlib, and by him published* ([London]: Printed for R.L. [1648]).

Londons charity inlarged, stilling the orphans cry (London: Printed by Matth. Symmons, and Robert Ibbitson, 1650).

[Sir Richard Weston] *A discours of husbandrie used in Brabant and Flanders; shewing the wonderfull improvement of land there; and serving as a pattern for our practice in this common-wealth* (London: William Dugard, 1650). Later editions 1652 and 1654.

[Cressy Dymock] *The reformed husband-man, or, A brief treatise of the errors, defects,and inconveniences of our English husbandry in ploughing and sowing for corn* (London: printed by J.C., 1651).

— *An essay for the advancement of husbandry learning, or propositions for erecting [a] Colledge of Husbandry* (London: Printed by Henry Hills, 1651).

Samuel Hartlib his legacie: or An enlargement of the Discourse of husbandry used in Brabant and Flaunders (London: Printed by H. Hills,1651) [followed by second edition, 1652, and third edition, 1655].

Clavis apocalyptica, or, The revelation revealed. (London: Printed by W. D. for Tho. Matthewes,1651). At least 5 reissues in 1651, including a variant marked 'Second edition'.

Cornu copia, a miscellanium of lucriferous and most fructiferous experiments (London: s.n. 1652). Hartlib's association improbable.

A Designe for Plentie by an Universall Plantng of Fruit-Trees (London: Printed for Richard Wodenothe [1652]).

[Gerard Boate] *Irelands Naturall History. Being a True and Ample Description* (London: for John Wright at the Kings Head in the Old Bayley, 1652).

An interrogatorie relating more particularly to the Husbandry and Natural History of Ireland (London: Printed for Richard Wodenothe, 1652).

[Cressy Dymock] *A discoverie for division or setting out of land, as to the best form* (London: Printed for Richard Wodenothe, 1653).

The true and readie way to learne the Latine tongue (London: Printed by R. and W. Laybourn, 1655).

Chymical, medicinal, and chyrurgical addresses (London: Printed by G. Dawson for Giles Calvert, 1655).

The reformed Common-wealth of bees. Presented in severall letters and observations (London: Printed for Giles Calvert, 1655).

The compleat husband-man: or, A discourse of the whole art of husbandry; both forraign and domestick (London: printed and are to be sold by Edward Brewster [n.d., c.1659]).

Universal Husbandry Improved (London: Printed for R.H. and are to be sold in St. Pauls Church-yard [n.d., c.1659]).

Other Primary Sources

Ashmole, Elias, *Theatrum Chemicum Britannicum. Containing Severall Poetical Pieces of our Famous English Philosophers* (London, Printed by J. Grismond for Nath: Brooke, 1652).

Austen, Ralph, *A Treatise of Fruit-Trees, Shewing the manner of Grafting, Pruning, and Ordering of them in all respects* (Oxford, printed for Tho: Robinson, 1653).

Cheynell, Francis, *The divine trinunity or, The blessed doctrine of the three coessentiall subsistents in the eternall Godhead* (London: Printed by T.R. and E.M. for Samuel Gellibrand, 1650).

Collier, Jeremy, [Comenius] *A Patterne of Universal Knowledge* (London: T.H. for Thomas Collins, Northampton, 1651).

[Comenius], *Lesnae excidium anno 1656 in Aprili factum fide historica narratum* [Amsterdam, 1656].

[Comenius] *Opera Didactica Omnia* (Amsterdam: 1657).

[Comenius] *Lux in tenebris* (Amsterdam: 1657).

Crell, Johannes, *A learned vindication of liberty of religion* ([London, s.n.] 1646).

Dury, John, 'Meditatio de dissidio ecclesiastia', c.1630, HP 20/11/33A.

— *Israels call to march out of Babylon unto Jerusalem* (London: Printed by G.M. for Tho. Underhill, at the signe of the Bible in Wood-street, 1646).

— *The reformed school* (London: Printed by R.D. for Richard Wodenothe, [1650?]).

— *The unchanged, constant and single-hearted peace-maker drawn forth into the world* (London: Printed by J. Clowes, for Richard Wodenothe at the Starre under St Peters Church in Cornhill, 1650).

— *The Effect of Master Dury's Negotiations for the Uniting of Protestants* ([London], 1657).

Gauden, John, *The love of truth and peace. A sermon preached before the Honourable House of Commons assembled in Parliament. Novemb. 29. 1640* (London: Printed by T.C. for Andrew Crooke in Pauls Church-yard at the Greene Dragon, 1641).

Gilbert, Eleazar, *Newes from Poland wherein is declared the cruell practice of the popish clergie against the Protestants, and in particular against the ministers of the city of Vilna* (London: E.P. for Nathanael Butter, 1641).

Hall, John, *Horæ Vacivæ, or Essays. Some occasional Considerations* (London: Printed by E.G. for J. Rothwell, at the Sun and Fountaine in Pauls Church-yard, 1646).

— *A Modell of a Christian Society...The Right hand of Christian Love Offered* (Cambridge: Roger Daniel, 1647).

— *An Humble Motion To The Parliament of England Concerning The Advancement of Learning: And Reformation of the Universities* (London: Printed for John Walker, at the Starre in Popes-Head-Alley, 1649).

— *Chymiatrophilos, Mataeotechnia Medicinae Praxews. The Vanity of the Craft of Physick. Or, a New Dispensatory* (London: for Giles Calvert, 1651).

Jessey, Henry, *The exceeding riches of grace advanced by the spirit of grace, in an empty nothing creature viz. Mris. Sarah Wight* (London: Printed by Matthew Simmons for Henry Overton, and Hannah Allen, 1647).

Petty, William, *The advice of W.P. to Mr. Samuel Hartlib for the advancement of some particular parts of learning* (London: [s.n.], 1648).

[Plattes, Gabriel], *A Description of the Famous Kingdome of Macaria* (London: printed for Francis Constable, 1641).

Rand, William, [Iacopo Aconcio], *Satans stratagems, or The Devils cabinet-councel discovered* (London: Printed by John Macock, and sold by G. Calvert, 1648). Further edition with variant title, 1651.

— [Pierre Gassendi], *The mirror of true nobility and gentility being the life of the renowned Nicolaus Claudius Fabricius, Lord of Peiresk* (London: Printed by J. Streater for Humphrey Moseley, 1657).

Robinson, Henry, *Certain proposalls in order to the peoples freedome and accommodation in some particulars with the advancement of trade and navigation of this commonwealth in generall* (London: Printed by M. Simmons, 1652).

Shaw, John, *Brief discoveries of divers excellent wayes and means for the manuring and improving of land* (London: Printed for J.S., 1646).

Snel, George, *The Right Teaching of Useful Knowledg* (London: William Dugard, 1649).

Woodward, Hezekiah, *A childes patrimony laid out upon the good culture or tilling over his whole man. The first part, respecting a childe in his first and second age* (London: Printed by I. Legatt, 1640).

— *A light to grammar, and all other arts and sciences. Or, the rule of practise proceeding by the clue of nature, and conduct of right reason so opening the doore thereunto* (London: Printed by M. F. for John Bartlet, 1641).

Secondary Sources

Akkerman, N., *Elizabeth Stuart, Queen of Hearts* (Oxford: Oxford University Press, 2021).

Austen, D.C.R., 'Puritanism and Natural Philosophy Revisited: the Case of Ralph Austen (c.1612–1676)', *The Seventeenth Century*, 39:3 (2024), 359–99, https://doi.org/10.1080/0268117X.2024.2330088.

Ayşen, A., 'In-between Calvinism and Islam: Ali Bey's Transcultural Translation of the Bible into Turkish in the Time of Confessionalization', *The Biblical Annals*, 13:3 (2023), 439–61, https:doi.org/10.31743/biban.14599.

Barnett, P.R., *Theodore Haak F.R.S. The first German Translator of Paradise Lost* ('S Gravenhage: Mouton & Co., 1962).

Blekastad, M., *Comenius: Versuch eines Umrisses von Leben, Werk und Schicksal des Jan Amos Komenský* (Oslo: Universitetsforlaget/Prague: Academia, 1969).

Bömelburg, H.-J., 'Die Kontakte der schlesischen Reformierten zum polnischen und litauischen Adel in der ersten Hälfte des 17. Jahrhundert', in *Vom 16. Jahrhundert bis zur Altpreußischen Union von 1817*, ed. by J. Bahlcke and I. Dingel (Göttingen: Vandenhoeck & Rupecht, 2016), pp. 65–81, https://doi.org/10.13109/9783666101403.65.

Brecht, M., 'Joh. Val. Andreaes Versuch einer Erneuerung der württembergischen Kirche im 17. Jahrhundert', in *Kirchenordnung und Kirchenzucht in Württemberg vom 16. bis zum 18. Jahrhundert*, ed. by M. Brecht (Stuttgart: Calwer Verlag, 1967), pp. 53–82.

— 'Johann Valentin Andreae. Weg und Programm eines Reformers zwischen Reformation und Moderne', in *Theologen und Theologie an der Universität Tübingen*, ed. by M. Brecht (Tübingen: Mohr Siebeck, 1977), pp. 270–343.

Bremer, F. J., *Building a New Jerusalem: John Davenport, a Puritan in Three Worlds* (New Haven, Connecticut: Yale University Press, 2012), https://doi.org/10.12987/9780300188851.

Bromley, A., 'The Impact of Milton's *Of Education* on the Hartlib Circle's Understanding of Public and Private', *The Seventeenth Century*, 39:2 (2024), 241–60, https://doi.org/10.1080/0268117x.

Bucsay, M., *Geschichte des Protestantismus in Ungarn* (Stuttgart: Evangelisches Verlagswerk, 1959).

Burden, M., *A Biographical Dictionary of Tutors at the Dissenters' Private Academies, 1660–1729* (London: Dr. Williams's Centre for Dissenting Studies, 2013).

Cagnolati, A., *Il circolo di Hartlib: riforme educative e diffusione del sapere (1630–1660)* (Bologna: CLUEB, 2001).

Calafat, G., 'For a "Livorno-on-Thames": the Tuscan Model in the Writings of Henry Robinson (1604–1673?)', *The Seventeenth Century*, 37:4 (2022), 01–30, https://doi.org/10.1080/0268117x.2021.1975558.

Čapková, D., *Předškolní výchova v díle J. A. Komenského, jeho předchůdců a pokračovatelů* (Prague: Státní pedagogické nakladatelství, 1968).

— 'Comenius and His Ideals: Escape from the Labyrinth', in *Samuel Hartlib and Universal Reformation. Studies in Intellectual Communication*, ed. by M. Greengrass, M. Leslie and T. Raylor (Cambridge: Cambridge University Press, 1994), 75–91.

Čapková, D. and M. Kyralová, 'Unpublished Letters of J.A. Comenius', *Acta Comeniana*, 6 (1985), 166–68.

Capp, B., *The Fifth Monarchy Men: A Study in Seventeenth Century English Millenarianism* (London: Faber & Faber, 1972).

Caravale, G., *Censorship and Heresy in Revolutionary England and Counter-Reformation Rome* (London: Palgrave Macmillan, 2017).

Caricchio, M., 'John Dury, reformer of education against the radical challenge', *Les Dossiers du GRIHL (2009–2): Dissidence et Dissimulation*, https://doi.org/10.4000/dossiersgrihl.3787.

Čížek, J., *The Conception of Man in the Works of John Amos Comenius* (Frankfurt a.M: Peter Lang, 2016), https://doi.org/10.3726/978-3-653-07010-1.1.

Clucas, S., 'Samuel Hartlib's Ephemerides, 1635–59, and the Pursuit of Scientific and Philosophical Manuscripts: The Religious Ethos of an Intelligencer', *The Seventeenth Century*, 6:1 (1991), 33–55.

— 'The Correspondence of a Seventeenth-Century "Chymicall Gentleman"', *Ambix*, 40:3 (1993), 147–70.

— 'In search of 'The True Logick': Methodological Eclecticism among the Baconian Reformers', in Greengrass et al. (eds.), *Samuel Hartlib and Universal Reformation*, pp. 51–74.

— 'Samuel Hartlib, Intelligencing and Technology in Seventeenth Century Europe', in *Leonardo da Vinci und Heinrich Schickhardt: zum Transfer technischen Wissens im vormodernen Europa*, ed. by R. Kretzschmar, R. and S. Lorenz (Stuttgart: W. Kohlhammer, 2010), pp. 58–75.

Coffey, J., *John Goodwin and the Puritan Revolution* (Woodbridge: Boydell Press, 2006).

Cram, D.F. and J. Maat, 'Comenius, Dalgarno and the English Translations of the *Janua linguarum*', *Studia Comeniana et Historica*, 26 (1996), 148–60, https://hdl.handle.net/11245/1.349427.

Davies, E., 'Beyond the Jesuit College: the Role of Cambridge's 'Puritan' Colleges in European Politics and Diplomacy, 1603–1625', in *The Mind is its Own Place? Early Modern Intellectual History in an Institutional Context*, ed. by A. Beeton et al. (Oxford: Oxford University Press, 2023), pp. 25–43, https://doi.org/10.1093/oso/9780198901730.001.0001.

Deventer, J., 'Nicht in die Ferne—nicht in die Fremde? Konfessionsmigration im schlesisch-polnischen Grenzraum im 17. Jahrhundert', in *Glaubensflüchtlinge. Ursachen, Formen und Auswirkungen Frühneuzeitlicher Konfessionsmigration in Europa*, ed. by J. Bahlcke (Berlin: LIT Verlag, 2008), pp. 95–118.

Dickson, Donald R., *The Tessera of Antilia. Utopian Brotherhoods & Secret Societies in the Early Seventeenth Century* (Leiden: Brill, 1998), https://doi.org/10.33137/RR.V39I1.8881.

— 'Utopian Brotherhoods and Secret Societies in the Early Seventeenth Century', *Renaissance Quarterly*, 49:4 (1996), 760–802.

DiMeo, M., *Lady Ranelagh: the Incomparable Life of Robert Boyle's Sister* (Chicago, Illinois: University of Chicago Press, 2021), https://doi.org/10.7208/chicago/9780226731742.

Dircks, H., *A Biographical Memoir of Samuel Hartlib, Milton's familiar friend* (London: J.R. Smith, 1865).

Eckerle, J.S. and N. McAreavey (eds.), *Women's Life Writing & Early Modern Ireland* (Lincoln, Nebraska: University of Nebraska Press, 2021), https://doi.org/10.2307/j.ctvfxvbdk.

Eidghoffer, R., 'Johann Valentin Andreae vom Rosenkreuz zur Panoptie', *Daphnis*, 10:02–03 (1981), 211–39, https//doi.org/ 10.12775/klio2018.032.

Elmer, P. and O.P. Grell, *Health, Disease and Society in Europe, 1500–1800* (Manchester: Manchester University Press, 2003).

Fedorowics, J.K., *England's Baltic Trade in the Early Seventeenth Century* (Cambridge: Cambridge University Press, 2011).

Finucane, J., 'The Invisible Virtuoso: Bengt Skytte and the Royal Society', *History of Universities*, 26:1 (2012), 117–62, https://doi.org/10.1093/acprof:o sobl/9780199652068.003.0002.

Fussell, G.E., *The Old English Farming Books from Fitzherbert to Tull, 1523 to 1730* (London: Crosby Lockwood, 1947).

Gianoutsos, J., 'A New Discovery' of Charles Hoole: Method and Practice in Seventeenth-Century English Education', *History of Education*, 48:1 (2019), 01–18, https://doi.org/10.1080/0046760X.2018.1516810.

Gibson, K., 'John Dury's Apocalyptic Thought, a Reassessment', *The Journal of Ecclesiastical History*, 61:2 (2010), 299–313, https://doi.org/10.1017/ S0022046909008914.

Goris, W., M.A. Meyer and V. Urbánek (eds.), *Gewalt sei ferne den Dingen. Contemporary Perspectives on the Works of John Amos Comenius* (Wiesbaden: Springer, 2016).

Greaves, R.L., *The Puritan Revolution and Educational Thought* (New Brunswick, New Jersey: Rutgers University Press, 1969).

— 'Puritanism and Science: The Anatomy of a Controversy', *Journal of the History of Ideas*, 30:3 (1969), 345–68.

Greengrass, M., 'The Financing of a Seventeenth-Century Intellectual: Contributions for Comenius, 1637–1641', *Acta Comeniana*, 11 (1995), 71–87, 141–57.

— 'An "Intelligencer's Workshop": Samuel Hartlib's Ephemerides', *Studia Comeniana et Historica*, 26 (1996), 48–62.

— 'Samuel Hartlib and Scribal Communication', *Acta Comeniana*, 12 (1997), 47–62.

— 'Archive Refractions: Hartlib's Papers and the Workings of an Intelligencer' in *Archives of the Scientific Revolution: The Formation and Exchange of Ideas in Seventeenth-Century Europe*, ed. by M. Hunter (Woodbridge: Boydell Press, 1998), pp. 35–48.

— 'Samuel Hartlib and the Commonwealth of Learning', in *The Cambridge History of the Book in Britain*, vol. 4, ed. by J. Barnard et al. (Cambridge:

Cambridge University Press, 2002), pp. 304–22, https://doi.org/10.1017/CHOL9780521661829.015.

Greengrass, M., M. Leslie and T. Raylor (eds.), *Samuel Hartlib and Universal Reformation. Studies in Intellectual Communication* (Cambridge: Cambridge University Press, 1994).

Greengrass M., and L.T.I. Penman, 'L'Ombre des Archives dans les Cultures du Savoir du XVIIe Siècle: les Papiers de Samuel Hartlib (v. 1600–1662)', *Bibliothèque de l'École des Chartes*, 171:1 (2013), 51–64, https://doi.org/10.3406/bec.2013.464301.

Grell, O.P., *Dutch Calvinists in Early Stuart London: the Dutch Church in Austin Friars, 1603–1642* (Leiden: Brill, 1989), Publications of the Sir Thomas Browne Institute, 11.

Gribben, C., 'The Eschatology of the Puritan Confessions', *Scottish Bulletin of Evangelical Theology*, 20:1 (2002), 51–78.

Guibbory, A., 'Revolution and Reformation. Parliament 'Fast Sermons', the Elect Nation, and Biblical Israel', in his *Christian Identity: Jews and Israel in 17th Century England* (Oxford: Oxford University Press, 2010).

Haffemeyer, S., *Les Lumières Radicales de la Révolution Anglaise. Samuel Hartlib et les Réseaux de l'Intelligence (1600–1660)* (Paris: Classiques Garnier, 2018).

Hammersley, R., *James Harrington: An Intellectual Biography* (Oxford: Oxford University Press, 2019), https://doi.org/10.1080/23801883.2019.1703512.

Hedesan, G.D., *An Alchemical Quest for Universal Knowledge: The Christian Philosophy of Jan Baptist Van Helmont (1579–1644)* (London: Routledge, 2016).

Hessayon, A., 'Jacob Böhme's Foremost Seventeenth-Century English Translator: John Sparrow (1615–1670) of Essex', in *Jacob Böhme and his World*, ed. by B. Andersson et al. (Brill: Boston, 2018), pp. 329–57.

Hill, C., *Intellectual Origins of the English Revolution* (Oxford: Clarendon Press, 1964).

— *Antichrist in Seventeenth-Century England* (London: Oxford University Press, 1971).

Horsefield, J.K., 'The Origins of Blackwell's Model of a Bank', *The William and Mary Quarterly*, 23:1 (1966), 121–35, https://doi.org/10.2307/2936159.

Hotson, H., 'Philosophical Pedagogy in Reformed Central Europe Between Ramus and Comenius: A Survey of the Continental Background of the "Three Foreigners"', in Greengrass et al. (eds.), *Samuel Hartlib and Universal Reformation*, pp. 29–50.

— 'A Previously Unknown Early Work by Comenius: *Disputatio de S. Domini Coena, sive Eucharistia* under David Pareus, Heidelberg, 19 March 1614', *Studia Comeniana et Historica*, 24 (1994), 129–44.

— 'Irenicism and Dogmatics in the Confessional Age: Pareus and Comenius in Heidelberg', *The Journal of Ecclesiastical History*, 46:3 (1995), 432–56.

— *Johann Heinrich Alsted, 1588–1638: Between Renaissance, Reformation and Universal Reform* (Oxford: Oxford University Press, 2000), https://doi.org/10.1093/acprof:oso/9780198208280.001.0001.

— *Paradise Postponed: Johann Heinrich Alsted and the Birth of Calvinist Millenarianism* (Dordrecht: Kluwer Academic, 2001).

— 'The Ramist Roots of Comenian Pansophia. Ramus, Pedagogy and the Liberal Arts', in *Ramism in Britain and the Wider World*, ed. by S.J. Reid and E. Wilson (Farnham: Ashgate, 2011), pp. 227–52.

— *The Reformation of Common Learning. Post-Ramist Method and the Reception of the New Philosophy 1618–c.1670* (Oxford: Oxford University Press, 2020).

Houston, C., *The Renaissance Utopia. Dialogue, Travel and the Ideal Society* (Farnham: Ashgate, 2016).

Hunter, M., A. Clericuzio and L.M. Principe (eds.), *The Correspondence of Robert Boyle*, vol. 1 (London: Pickering & Chatto, 2001).

Hutton, S., 'Henry More and the Book of Revelation', *Studies in Church History*, 10 (1994), 131–40.

— 'The Appropriation of Joseph Mede: Millenarianism in the 1640s', in *Millenarianism and Messianism in Early Modern European Culture: The Millenarian Turn*, ed. by J.E. Force and R.H. Popkin (Dordrecht: Kluwer Academic Publishers, 2001), pp. 01–13.

— 'Mede, Milton, and More: Christ's College Millenarians', in *Milton and the Ends of Time*, ed. by J. Cummins (Cambridge: Cambridge University Press, 2003), pp. 29–41.

Iliffe, R., 'Hartlib's World', in *London and Beyond: Essays in Honour of Derek Keene*, ed. by M. Davies and J.A. Galloway (London: London University Press/Institute of Historical Research, 2012), pp. 103–22, https://doi.org/10.14296/117.9771909646445.

— 'Capitalizing Expertise: Philosophical and Artisanal Expertise in Early Modern London', in *Fields of Expertise: A Comparative History of Expert Procedures in Paris and London, 1600 to Present*, ed. by C. Rabier (Newcastle upon Tyne: Cambridge Scholars Publishing, 2021), pp. 55–84, https://doi.org/10.1086/657254.

Irving, S., *Natural Science and The Origins of The British Empire* (London: Pickering & Chatto, 2008).

James, M., *Social Policy and Problems during the Puritan Revolution, 1640–1660* (London: Routledge, 1930).

Josten, C.H., *Elias Ashmole: His Autobiographical and Historical Notes*, 5 vols. (Oxford: Oxford University Press, 1967).

Jue, J., *Heaven Upon Earth: Joseph Mede (1586–1638) and the Legacy of Millenarianism* (Dordrecht: Springer, 2006).

Karnitscher, T.B., *Der vergessene Spiritualist Johann Theodor von Tschesch (1595–1649). Untersuchungen und Spurensicherung zu Leben und Werk eines religiösen Nonkonformisten* (Göttingen: Vandenhoeck & Ruprecht, 2015).

Kavaliūnaitė, G., 'Historical Sources Bearing on Samuel Boguslaus Chylinski's Pursuits in England and the Netherlands and their Echoes in the Grand Duchy of Lithuania', *Lithuanian Historical Studies*, 16 (2011), 07–28, https://org/10.30965/25386565-01601002.

Keller, V. and L.T.I. Penman, 'From the Archives of Scientific Diplomacy: Science and the Shared Interests of Samuel Hartlib's London and Friedrich Clodius's Gottdorf', *Isis*, 106:1 (2015), 17–42.

Kempa, T., 'Religious Relations and the Issue of Religious Tolerance in Poland and Lithuania in the 16th and 17th Centuries', *Sarmatia Europaea. Polish Review of Early Modern History*, 1 (2010), 31–66.

Kennedy, C., 'Milton's Ethos, English Nationhood, and the Fast-Day Tradition in *Areopagitica*', *Studies in Philology*, 116:2 (2019), 375–400, https://dx.doi.org/10.1353/sip.2019.0015.

Kennett, W., *A Register and Chronicle Ecclesiastical and Civil: Containing Matters of Fact... Digested in Exact Order of Time. With Proper Notes and References Towards Discovering and Connecting the True History of England from the Restauration of King Charles II*, vol. 1 (London: R. Williamson, 1728).

Koch, B., and L. Ward, 'Johannes Althusius: Between Secular Federalism and the Religious State', in *Ashgate Research Companion to Federalism*, ed. by A. Ward (Farnham: Ashgate, 1996), pp. 75–99.

Lamont, W.M.L., *Godly Rule: Politics and Religion, 1603–60* (London: Macmillan, 1969).

Lausden, J.C., and R.H. Popkin (eds.), *Millenarianism and Messianism in Early Modern European Culture. Continental Millenarians, Protestants, Catholics* (Dordrecht: Kluwer Academic Publishers, 2001).

Léchot, P.-O., *Un christianisme 'sans partilitié' Irénisme et méthode chez John Dury (v.1600–1680)* (Paris: Honoré Champion Editeur, 2011).

Leng. T., *Benjamin Worsley (1618–1673): Trade, Interest and the Spirit in Revolutionary England* (Woodbridge: Royal Historical Society/Boydell & Brewer, 2008).

— '"A Potent Plantation well armed and policed": Huguenots, the Hartlib Circle, and British Colonization in the 1640s', *The William and Mary Quarterly*, 66:1 (2009), 173–94.

Lewis, R., *Language, Mind and Nature. Artificial Languages in England from Bacon to Locke* (Cambridge: Cambridge University Press, 2007), https://doi.org/10.1086/590289.

Little, P., *Lord Broghill and the Cromwellian Union with Ireland and Scotland* (Woodbridge: Boydell Press, 2004).

Malcolm, N., 'Thomas Harrison and his 'Ark of Studies': An Episode in the History of the Organisation of Knowledge', *The Seventeenth Century*, 19:2 (2004), 196–232, https://doi.org/10.1080/0268117X.2004.10555543.

— 'Comenius, Boyle, Oldenburg, and the Translation of the Bible into Turkish', *Church History and Religious Culture*, 87:3 (2007), 327–62, https://doi.org/10.1163/187124107X232453.

Malcolm, N. and J. Stedall, *John Pell (1611–1685) and his Correspondence with Sir Charles Cavendish* (Oxford: Oxford University Press, 2005).

Malpas, S., 'In No One Thing, They Saw, Agreeing', *Restoration: Studies in English Literary Culture, 1660–1700*, 43:2 (2019), 49–74, https://doi.org/109stable/e26911390.

Matei, O., 'Husbanding Creation and the Technology of Amelioration in the Works of Gabriel Plattes', *Society and Politics*, 7:1 (2003), 84–102.

— 'Macaria and the Puritan Ethics of Direct Participation in the Transformation of the World', *Society and Politics*, 5:2 (2011), 51–65.

— 'Gabriel Plattes, the Hartlib Circle and the Interest for Husbandry in the Seventeenth Century England', *Prolegomena*, 11:2 (2012), 207–24.

— 'Macaria, the Hartlib Circle, and Husbanding Creation', *Society and Politics*, 7:2 (2013), 07–33.

— 'Husbandry Tradition and the Emergence of Vegetable Philosophy in the Hartlib Circle', *Philosophia International Journal of Philosophy*, 16:1 (2015), 35–52.

— 'Experimenting with Matter in the Works of Gabriel Plattes', *Perspectives on Science*, 28:3 (2020), 398–420, https://doi.org/10.1162/posc_a_00345.

— 'Merchants of Light and Lamps: John Evelyn's Transition from Descriptive to Experimental Natural Philosophy', *Perspectives in Science*, 32:5 (2024), 585–611, https://doi.org/10.1162/posc_a_00616.

Mazauric, S., *Savoirs et philosophie à Paris dans la première moitié du XVIIe siècle: les conférences du bureau d'adresse de Théophraste Renaudot, 1633–1642* (Paris: Publications de la Sorbonne, 1997), https://doi.org/10.4000/books.psorbonne.15609

Maxwell, F.L., 'Calling for Collaboration: Women and Public Service in Dorothy Moore's Transnational Protestant Correspondence', *Literature Compass*, 2017, 14:4 (2017), https://doi.org/10.1111/lic3.12386.

McCormick, T., 'Food, Population and Empire in the Hartlib Circle, 1639–1660', *Osiris*, 35 (2020), 60–83, https://doi.org/10.1086/709104.

McGruer, A., *Educating the 'Unconstant Rabble': Arguments for Educational Advancement and Reform During the English Civil War and Interregnum* (Newcastle upon Tyne: Cambridge Scholars Publishing, 2010).

Miller, G.L., 'Beasts of the New Jerusalem: John Jonston's Natural History and the Launching of Millenarian Pedagogy in the Seventeenth Century', *History of Science*, 46:2 (2008), 203–43, https://doi.org/10.1177/007327530804600204.

Miller, T.E., 'Gold for Secrets: The Hartlib Circle and the Early English Empire, 1630–1660', Oxford University, D.Phil. Dissertation, 2020.

Milton, A., '"The Unchanged Peacemaker": John Dury and the Politics of Irenicism in England, 1628–1643', in Greengrass et al. (eds.), *Samuel Hartlib and Universal Reformation*, pp. 95–117.

— *England's Second Reformation. The Battle for the Church of England, 1625–1662* (Cambridge: Cambridge University Press, 2021).

Minter, C.J., 'John Dury's Reformed Librarie-Keeper: Information and its Intellectual Contexts in Seventeenth-Century England', *Library & Information History*, 31:1 (2015), 18–34, https://doi.org/10.1179/1758348914Z.00000000072.

Moore, K.A., 'The Blood that Nourishes the Body Politic', *Early American Studies*, 17:1 (2019), 01–36, https://www.jstor.org/stable/26554725.

Moran, B., *Distilling Knowledge: Alchemy, Chemistry, and the Scientific Revolution* (Cambridge, Massachusetts: Harvard University Press, 2005).

Mörhke, M., *Komenius und Andreä, ihre pädagogik und ihre Verhältnis zu einander* (Leipzig: Emil Glausck, 1904).

Morrill, J.(ed.), *Oliver Cromwell and the English Revolution* (Longman: Harlow, 1990).

Mulsow, M., 'Who was the Author of the *Clavis apocalyptica* of 1651? Millenarianism and Prophecy between Silesian Mysticism and the Hartlib Circle', in *Millenarianism and Messianism in Early Modern European Culture*, ed. by J.C. Laursen and R.H. Popkin (Dordrecht: Springer, 2001), pp. 57–76, https://doi.org/10.1007/978-94-010-0744-3_5.

Murdoch, S., *Scottish Kin, Commercial and Covert Associations in Northern Europe, 1603–1746* (Leiden: Brill, 2005).

Nahas, M., 'A Translation of Hayy B. Yaqzān by the Elder Edward Pococke (1604–1691)', *Journal of Arabic Literature*, 16 (1985), 88–90.

Newell, M.E., 'Robert Child and the Entrepreneurial Vision: Economy and Ideology in Early New England', *The New England Quarterly*, 68:2 (1995), 223–56, https://doi.org/10.2307/366257.

Newman, W., *Gehennical Fire: The Lives of George Starkey, An American Alchemist in the Scientific Revolution* (Cambridge, Massachusetts: Harvard University Press, 1994).

Nordtröm, S.G. and W. Sjöstrand (eds.), 'Comenius' självbiografi. Comenius about himself', Årsböcker i svensk undervisningshistoria, 131:54 (1974) (Stockholm: 1975).

North, M., 'Elbings Außen- und Binnenhandel im 16. und 17. Jahrhundert', in *Elbing 1237–1987: Beiträge zum Elbing-Kolloquium im November 1987 in Berlin*, ed. by B. Jähnig and H.-J. Schuch (Münster, Westf.: Nicolaus-Copernicus Verlag, 1991), pp. 129–44.

O'Day, R., *Education and Society 1500–1800* (Harlow: Longman, 1982).

Pal, C., 'The Early Modern Information Factory: How Samuel Hartlib Turned Correspondence into Knowledge', in *Empires of Knowledge. Scientific Networks in the Early Modern World*, ed. by P. Finden (London: Routledge, 2018), pp. 166–58, https://doi.org/10.4324/9780429461842.

Parr, A., 'The Laws of Nature and the Nature of Law: Insights from an English Rebel, 1641–57', *History of European Ideas*, 50:3 (2023). 370–91. https://doi.org/10.1080/01916599.2023.2267056

Peacey, J.T., 'Seasonable Treatises: A Godly Project of the 1630s', *English Historical Review*, 113:452 (1998), 667–99, https://www.jstor.org/stable/578033.

Penman, L.T.I., 'Areopagitica, Freedom of the Press, and Heterodox Religion in the Holy Roman Empire', *The Seventeenth Century*, 33:1 (2018), 45–61, https://doi.org/10.1080/0268117X.2017.1316515.

—— '"Ein Liebhaber des Mysterii, und ein großer Verwandter desselben." Toward the Life of Balthasar Walther: Kabbalist, Alchemist and Wandering Paracelsian Physician', *Sudhoffs Archiv*, 94:1 (2010), 73–99, https://doi.org/10.25162/sudhoff-2010-0004.

Pietrzak, E., 'Das Brieger Gymnasium und seine Rektoren in den Jahren 1604–1633', *Germanica Wratislaviensia*, 87 (1989), 29–46, https://doi.org/10.1515/9783050095752-011.

—— *Literatur für den Hof: Die Piastenhöfe als kulturelle Zentren Schlesiens im 17. Jahrhundert* (Heidelberg: Universitätsverlag Winter, 2021).

Pincus, S.C.A., *Protestantism and Patriotism: Ideologies and the Making of English Foreign Policy, 1650–1668* (Cambridge: Cambridge University Press, 1996), https://doi.org/10.1017/CBO9780511560781.

Pomata, G. and N.G. Siraisi (eds.), *Historia: Empiricism and Erudition in Early Modern Europe* (Cambridge, Massachusetts: MIT Press, 2005), https://doi.org/10.7551/mitpress/3521.001.0001.

Poole, W., 'Two Early Readers of Milton: John Beale and Abraham Hill', *Milton Quarterly*, 38:2 (2004), 76–99, https://www.jstor.org/stable/24465232.

Powak, M., *Jan Mylius (1557–1630), rektor Gimnazjum Elbląskiego w. Zasłużeni ludzie dawnego Elbląga* (Wrocław: Narodowy im. Ossolińskich, 1987).

— 'Die Geschichte des Elbinger Gymnasiums in den Jahren 1535–1772', in *Kulturgeschichte Preußens königlich polnischen Anteils in der Frühen Neuzeit*, ed. by S. Beckmann and K. Garber (Tübingen: Niemeyer, 2005), pp. 371–94.

Ptaszyński, M., 'Was a Confessional Agreement in Early Modern Europe Possible? On the Role of the Sandomir Consensus in the European Debates', *Religions*, 13:10 (2022), 1–16, https://doi.org/10.3390/rel13100994.

Quatrini, F., *Adam Boreel (1602–1665): A Collegiant's Attempt to Reform Christianity* (Leiden: Brill, 2021), https//doi.org/10.1017/S0009640723001257.

Raylor, T., 'Samuel Hartlib and the Commonwealth of Bees. Culture and Cultivation in Early Modern England' in *Writing and the Land*, ed. by M. Leslie and T. Raylor (Leicester: Leicester University Press, 1992), pp. 91–129.

— 'New Light on Milton and Hartlib', *Milton Quarterly*, 27 (1993): 19–31, https://doi.org/10.1111/j.1094-348X.1993.tb00807.

— 'Milton, the Hartlib Circle, and the Education of the Aristocracy', in *The Oxford Handbook of Milton*, ed. by N. McDowell and N. Smith (Oxford: Oxford University Press, 2011), pp. 382–406, https://doi.org/10.1093/oxfordhb/9780199697885.013.0021.

Riches, D., *Protestant Cosmopolitanism and Diplomatic Culture: Brandenburg-Swedish Relations in the Seventeenth-Century* (Leiden: Brill, 2012) https://doi.org/10.1080/0268117X.2014.893410.

Röhrs, H., 'Die Studentzeit des Comenius in Heidelberg', in *Semper Apertus*, ed. by W. Doerr and P.A. Riedl (Berlin: Springer Verlag, 1985), pp. 399–413.

Ruellet, A., *La Maison de Salomon, Histoire du patronage scientifique et technique en France et en Angleterre au XVIIe siècle* (Rennes: Presses Universitaires de Rennes, 2016), https://doi.org/10.4000/artefact.3721.

Salmon, V., 'Joseph Webbe: Some Seventeenth-Century Views on Language Teaching', *Bibliothèque d'humanisme et Renaissance*, 3:2 (1961), 324–40.

— 'Problems of Language Teaching: A Discussion among Hartlib's Friends', *The Modern Language Review*, 59:4 (1964), 13–24.

— *The Study of Language in 17th-Century England* (Amsterdam: Benjamins, 1988).

Siedel, R., *Späthumanismus in Schlesien: Caspar Dornau (1577–1631). Leben und Werk* (Tübingen: Max Niemeyer Verlag, 1994).

Sierhuis, F., 'Transnational Networks and Radical Religion: Johannes Rothe and the Construction of Prophetic Charisma', *Renaissance Studies*, 36:1 (2021), 142–62.

Slack, P., *The Invention of Improvement. Information and Material Progress in Seventeenth-Century England* (Oxford: Oxford University Press, 2015), https://doi.org/10.1111/ehr.12390.

Slaughter, M., *Universal Languages and Scientific Taxonomy in the Seventeenth Century* (Cambridge: Cambridge University Press, 1982).

Smoluk, M., 'Hezekiah Woodward. Views on Teaching the Young in England', 1st Annual International Interdisciplinary Conference, AIIC 2013, Proceedings, pp. 584–88.

Sprunger, K.L., *The Learned Doctor William Ames: Dutch Backgrounds of English and American Puritanism* (Urbana: University of Illinois Press, 1972).

Steiner, M. and V. Urbánek, 'Otevřená brána tvého přátelství: Nová evidence o počátcích korespondence Jana Amose Komenského a Samuela Hartliba', in *Justus et Bonus: Ad honorem Jiří Beneš: křesťanská kultura a vzdělanost v českých zemích od středověku po Komenského*, ed. by O. Podavka (Prague: Filosofia, 2020), pp. 251–71.

Stern, P.J. and C. Wenderlind (eds.), *Mercantilism Reimagined: Political Economy in Early Modern England and its Empire* (Oxford: Oxford University Press, 2013).

Strasser, G., 'Closed and Open Languages: Samuel Hartlib's Involvement with Cryptology and Universal Languages', in Greengrass et al. (eds.), *Samuel Hartlib and Universal Reformation*, pp. 151–61.

Strazzoni, A., 'Samuel Hartlib', in *Encyclopedia of Renaissance Philosophy*, ed. by M. Sgarbi (Cham: Springer, 2022), pp. 1485–89, https://doi.org/10.1007/978-3-319-14169-5_503.

Stubbs, H.M., 'John Beale, Philosophical Gardener of Herefordshire: Part I, Prelude to the Royal Society (1608–1663)', *Annals of Science*, 39:5 (1982), 463–89, https://doi.org/10.1080/00033798200200361.

Tahan, I. (ed.), *The Ottoman Legacy of Levinus Warner* (Leiden: Brill, 2012), http://www.brill.com/publications/online-resources/middle-eastern-manuscripts-online-2-ottoman-legacy-levinus-warner.

Thirsk, J., 'Plough and Pen: Agricultural Writers in the Seventeenth Century' in *Social Relations and Ideas: Essays in Honour of R.H. Hilton*, ed. by T.H. Aston et al. (Cambridge: Cambridge University Press, 1983), pp. 295–318.

— *Economic Policy and Progress; the Development of a Consumer Society in Early Modern England* (Oxford: Oxford University Press, 1978).

Tode, S., 'Bildung Wissenskultur der Geistlichkeit im Danzig der Frühen Neuzeit', in *Bildung und Konfession: Theologenausbildung im Zeitalter der Konfessionalisierung*, ed. by H.J. Selderhuis and M. Wriedt (Tübingen: Mohr Siebeck, 2006), pp. 71–101.

Toon, P. (ed.), *Puritans, the Millennium and the Future of Israel: Puritan Eschatology 1600–1660* (Cambridge/London: James Clarke Co., Ltd., 1970).

Turnbull, G.H., *Samuel Hartlib: A Sketch of his Life and his Relations to J.A. Comenius* (London: Oxford University Press/Humphrey Milford, 1920).

— 'The Summoning of Comenius to England by Parliament', *The Central European Observer*, 5:2 (1927).

— *Hartlib, Dury and Comenius. Gleanings from Hartlib's Papers* (London: University Press of Liverpool/Hodder & Stoughton, 1947).

—'Robert Child', *Publications of the Colonial Society of Massachusetts*, 38 (1947), 21–53.

— 'J. A. Komenského Dva spisy vševědné—Two Pansophical Works by John Amos Comenius', Prague: Česká akademie věd a umění, 1951, pp. 07–18.

— 'The Visit of Comenius to England in 1641', *Notes and Queries*, 17 (1951), 37–42.

— 'Oliver Cromwell's College at Durham', *Durham Research Review*, 3 (1952), 01–07.

— 'Samuel Hartlib's Influence on the Early History of the Royal Society', *Notes and Records of the Royal Society*, 10:2 (1953), 101–30.

— 'An Incomplete Orbis Pictus of Comenius printed in 1653', *Acta Comeniana*, 1:2 (1957), 35–52.

— 'Plans of Comenius for his Stay in England', *Acta Comeniana*, 17 (1958), 07–28.

Turner, J., 'Ralph Austen, an Oxford Horticulturist of the Seventeenth Century', *Garden History*, 6:2 (1978), 39–45.

van Duinen, J., '"Pym's Junto" in the Ante-Bellum Long Parliament: Radical or Not?', in M. Cariccio and G. Tarantino (eds.), *Cromohs Virtual Seminars. Recent Historiographical Trends of the British Studies (17th–18th Centuries)*, 2006–07.

van Dülmen, R., *Die Utopie einer christlichen Gesellschaft. Johann Valentin Andreae (1586–1654)*, vol. 1 (Stuttgart: Frommann-Holzboog, 1978).

van Stekelenberg, D., *Michael Albinus 'Dantscanus' (1610–1653)* (Amsterdam: Rodolpi, 1987).

Vincent, W.A.L., *The State and School Education 1640–1660 in England and Wales* (London: S.P.C.K, 1950).

Wąs, G., 'Calvinismus und Modernisierung. Ein Fallstudie zur politisch-konfessionellen Entwicklung der schesischen Fürstentümer Liegnitz und Brieg im 16. und 17. Jahrhundert', in *Die Reformierten in Schlesien. Vom.16 Jahrhundert bis zur Altpreußischen Union von 1817*, ed. by J. Bahlcke and I. Dingel (Göttingen: Vandenhoeck & Ruprecht, 2016), pp. 189–204, https://doi.org/10.13109/9783666101403.189.

Webster, C., 'English Medical Reformers: a Background to the Society of Chymical Physitians', *Ambix*, 14:1 (1967), 16–41, https://doi.org/10.1179/amb.1967.14.1.16.

— (ed.) *Samuel Hartlib and the Advancement of Learning* (Cambridge: Cambridge University Press, 1970).

— *The Great Instauration. Science, Medicine and Reform 1626–1660* (London: Duckworth, 1975).

— *Utopian Planning and the Puritan Revolution: Gabriel Plattes* (Oxford: Wellcome Unit for the History of Medicine, 1979).

— *In Times of Strife* (Oxford: Taylor Institution Library, 2023).

— 'Samuel Hartlib, his associates and his Corpus Allies on Reforming Interregnum Oxford' (forthcoming), *Pelican Record*, 21(2025).

Webster, T., *Godly Clergy in Early Stuart England. The Caroline Puritan Movement, c.1620–1643* (Cambridge: Cambridge University Press, 1997).

Wenderlind, C.C., *Casualties of Credit: The English Financial Revolution, 1620–1672* (Cambridge, Massachusetts: Harvard University Press, 2011).

— 'Money: Hartlibian Political Economy and the New Culture of Credit', in *Mercantilism Reimagined: Political Economy in Early Modern Britain and its Empire*, ed. by P.J. Stern and C. Wenderlind (Oxford: Oxford University Press, 2014), pp. 74–94, https://doi.org/:10.1353/ecs.2015.0036.

Wollgast, S., 'Morphologie schlesischer Religiosität in der Frühen Neuzeit' in *Kulturgeschichte Schlesiens in der Frühen Neuzeit*, vol. 1, ed. by K. Garber (Tübingen: Niemeyer, 2005), pp. 113–90.

Worden, B., 'Cromwellian Oxford' in *The History of the University of Oxford: Volume 4, Seventeenth Century*, ed. by N. Tyacke (Oxford: Oxford University Press, 1997), pp. 732–72.

— *The Rump Parliament 1648–1653* (Cambridge: Cambridge University Press, 1974).

— *God's Instruments: Political Conduct in the England of Oliver Cromwell* (Oxford: Oxford University Press, 2012).

Wotschke, T., 'Der posener Kirchenpfleger Georg Hartlieb', *Historische Monatsblätter für die Provinz Posen*, 11:1 (1910), 1–5.

— *Die Reformation in Lande Posen* (Leszno: Oskar Gulitz, 1913).

Yamamoto, K., 'Reformation and Distrust of the Projector in the Hartlib Circle', *The Historical Journal*, 55:2 (2012), 375–97.

— *Taming Capitalism before its Triumph* (Oxford: Oxford University Press, 2018).

Yeo, R., 'Between Memory and Paperbooks: Baconianism and Natural History in Seventeenth-Century England', *History of Science*, 45:1 (2007), 01–46.

— 'Memory and Empirical Information: Samuel Hartlib, John Beale and Robert Boyle', in *The Body as Object and Instrument of Knowledge: Embodied Empiricism in Early Modern Science*, ed. by C.T. Wolfe and O. Gal (Dordrecht: Springer, 2010), pp. 185–210.

Young, J.T., *Faith, Medical Alchemy and Natural Philosophy: Johann Moriaen, Reformed Intelligencer and the Hartlib Circle* (Farnham: Ashgate, 1998).

Young, R.F., *Comenius in England: The Visit of Jan Amos Komenský (Comenius)... to London in 1641–1642* (London: Oxford University Press/Humphrey Milford, 1932).

Zins, H.R., *England and the Baltic in the Elizabethan Age*, trans. by H.C. Stevens (Manchester: Manchester University Press, 1972).

Zuidervaart, H.J., 'De Amsterdamse vernufteling Stephanus Pietersz Keus (c.1605–1679) en zijn contacten met de Hartlib Circle', *Studium. Tijdschrift voor Wetenschaps- en Universiteitsgeschiedenis*, 12:01–03 (2019), 110–22, https://doi.org/10.18352/studium.10192.

Index

academies and gymnasia 6, 13–17, 19, 30, 32–33, 41, 46, 89–91, 98, 103, 107, 134, 146–147, 160, 164, 195, 250
Aconcio, Iacopo (Acontius) 3, 107–111
Adderley, William 86
Agricola, Georgius 209
agriculture. *See* husbandry
Ahya ibn Haki (Yahya bin Ishak) 243
alchemy 169–171, 186, 203, 234
Aldenham School 140
Aldrich, William 106
Ali Ufkî Bey. *See* Bobowski, Wojciech
Alsted, Johann Heinrich 117–118
Ames, William 26, 73, 77, 118
Amsterdam 51, 66, 80–81, 91–92, 105, 107, 109, 111, 113, 157, 173, 177, 192, 203–204, 216, 240, 242, 244
Anchoran, Jean 40, 43, 144–145
Anderson, Robert 228, 235
Andreae, Johann Valentin 22–25, 68, 97–99
   Christianopolis 97–98
   Modell of a Christian Society 97
Andrews, Robert 220
Annesley, Arthur, First Earl of Anglesey 88, 201, 206–207, 236
Antilia 22–23, 29–30, 51, 115, 137, 229–230, 234
apocalypticism 5, 75, 115, 118, 127, 257
Appelius, Heinrich 81, 86, 92, 149, 173–177
Archer, Ferdinand 143
Aristotle 103, 108, 171, 173
Armenian Bible 244
Arnold, Johannes 49–50, 55
artisans 5, 153, 156, 165–166, 169

Ashmole, Elias 170–171
Assche, Justinus van 26, 90–91
Austen, Ralph 182, 252, 257

Backhouse, William 234
Bacon, Francis 40, 59, 61, 65, 68, 89, 93, 117–118, 173, 224, 252–253
Ball, Thomas 19–20, 142
Baptists 85, 211
Barnard, T.C. 163
Barrington, Lady Joan 38, 171
Barrington, Sir Thomas 82, 171
Bartlet, John 231
Barton, John 49
Basire, Isaac 243
Basnett, Edward 183–184
Bastwick, John 31
Bathe, William 144
   Janua linguarum (1611); English translation 1634 39–43, 45, 144, 243
Bathurst, Dr. John 154–155
Beale, John 86, 126, 164, 171, 182, 197, 201, 208–209, 211–214, 227, 232, 239, 249–252, 254, 258
   Herefordshire Orchards (1657) 200, 212, 250
   'Withies and Sallies' 213
Bedell, William 36
Beuthen 16
Beveridge, William 221, 251
Bible translation politics 242–245, 247–248
Biggs, Noah 101
Billingsley, Francis 49
Bisterfeld, Johann Heinrich 52, 55, 117
Blith, Walter 8, 181–182, 184–185
   The English Improver (1649) 181
Blount, Colonel Thomas 133

Boate, Arnold 186, 189–190
Boate, Gerard 84, 86, 90, 187
Boate, Katherine (née Manning, wife of Gerard Boate) 84
Bobowski, Wojciech (Ali Ufkî Bey) 243
Boehme, Jacob 17–18, 52, 124, 254
Bohemian Brethren (Unitas Fratrum) 8, 11–12, 17, 40, 47, 53, 70, 251
Bonde, Christopher 125
Boreel, Adam 76–77, 90–92
Boston, Lincolnshire 20
botany 190, 253
Bourne, Elisha 19, 255
Boyle, Katherine (Jones, Viscountess Ranelagh) 5, 7, 84–86, 94–95, 104, 127, 152–153, 156, 161–162, 204, 206, 208, 210, 249, 255
Boyle, Robert 1, 7, 85, 90, 92, 94–95, 97–98, 114, 137, 174, 178, 181, 183, 187, 189–190, 203, 205, 209, 226, 233, 245, 248, 252, 255
  Sceptical Chymist 1661 174
Boyle, Roger, Lord Broghill and First Earl of Orrery 205
Brabant 3, 31, 183, 185–186
Braddick, M.J. 83
Bradshaw, Richard 188
Brandenburg 11, 27, 121, 134
Bremen 44, 210
Brereton, William 181, 209–210, 212, 227
Brieg 6, 13–19, 121, 146
Brightman, Thomas 116
Broghill. *See* Boyle, Roger
Broniewski, Hieronim 52
Brooke, Lord. *See* Greville, Robert, 2nd Lord Brooke
Brookes, William 6, 34, 36, 47, 143
Brouncker, William, 2nd Viscount Brouncker 226–227
Browne, Sir Thomas 8, 106, 213
Burningham, Mary. *See* Hartlib, Mary

Caius College, Cambridge 204

Calafat, G. 145
Cambridge 19–20, 66, 97
Cambridge Platonists 119, 127, 136, 204
Cambridge, University of 3, 6, 19–21, 30, 35, 43–44, 83, 87, 96, 98–99, 104–105, 115–116, 127, 136, 140, 147, 154–155, 157–158, 163, 204, 211, 237
Campanella, Tommaso 51, 97, 107
  Civitas Solis 97
Capp, B. 120
Castell, Edmund 246
Cavendish, Sir Charles 58
Charles XI, King of Sweden 233
Charles X, King of Sweden 125, 135
Charleton, Walter 175
Chelsea College 69–70
Cheynell, Francis 110
Chichester 6, 32–34, 146, 250
Child, Robert 169–171, 180, 182, 185–187, 190
  'Large Letter...Defects and Remedies of English Husbandry' (*1650*) 185
Christ's College, Cambridge 105, 115
Chyliński, Samuel Bogusław 244
Clavis apocalyptica, or, The revelation revealed (1651 etc) 115–116, 120–122, 124–125, 133, 257
Clodius, Friedrick 170, 198
Clotworthy, Lady Margaret (Margaret Jones) 84–86
Clotworthy, Sir John, First Viscount Massereene 82, 85
clover husbandry 185
Coffey, J. 4, 116–117
College of Physicians (London) 113, 132, 158, 175
Collier, Jeremy 98–99, 140, 147, 155
Cologne 25–26
Comenian Movement in England 139
Comenius (Komenský, Jan Amos) 2–3, 8, 11, 13, 23, 33–34, 39–71, 75, 79–83, 92, 98, 107, 117–118,

122, 124–128, 134, 137, 139–142, 144–145, 153, 169, 173, 188, 203–204, 210, 215, 231, 239–240, 242–244, 247, 251, 256–258. *See also* Komenský, Jan Amos
Comenian 46, 56, 68, 139, 231
Conatuum Comeniorum praeludia (Pansophiae prodromus: Reformation of Schooles) 49–50
Didactica magna 40, 42, 46, 53–55, 63, 141
first links with Hartlib 6, 40–41, 44, 46
Informatorium maternum, Der Mutterschule 42, 63
Janua linguarum reserata 39–41, 45, 144, 243
later influence 122, 125–128, 142, 231, 240, 242–247
Lux in tenebris 125–126, 257
Methodus linguarum novissima 140
Pansophiae diatyposis (Pattern of Universal Knowledge, 1651) 140
prelude to English visit 46, 49, 56
Vestibulum 40
visit to London 6, 31, 51, 59–72, 79, 216
Committee of Both Kingdoms 85–87
Communion of Saints 6, 29, 37–38, 77, 257
Connecticut 201, 209
Constantinople 91, 243
Cotton, John 20, 35
Council for Schooling (Hartlib) 140, 151, 154–155
Council of State 132–133, 135, 182, 184, 188, 197, 256
Covent Garden 85
Cowley, Abraham 228
Coxe, Dr. Thomas 89–90
Coyet, Peter Julius 135
Cradock, Samuel (Cambridge) 237
Cradock, Samuel (Suffolk) 237
Crell, Johannes 107–109

Vindiciae pro religionis libertate 107
Cromwell, Henry, Lord Deputy of Ireland 162, 225, 236
Cromwell, Oliver, Lieutenant-General, Lord Protector 7, 35, 74, 88, 100–102, 109, 117, 120, 125–127, 133, 135, 154, 157–158, 182, 188, 203, 219–220, 223, 225, 254
Cudworth, Ralph 162, 204, 227
Culpeper, Sir Cheney 2, 5, 31, 62–63, 67, 69, 81, 83, 87, 90, 92–95, 97, 133, 146, 168, 177, 192–193, 217–221, 224, 254
Currar, William 170
Czepko, Daniel 18

Danson, Thomas 255
Danzig 12–15, 19, 21, 23, 30, 40–41, 44, 144, 196, 247
Davenant, Bishop John 36, 57
Davenport, John 31, 35, 77, 82, 139, 157, 209, 257–258
dead palsey (stroke) 202
decimalisation 252
Dee, John 171
Dell, William 158
Designe for Plentie by Universall Planting of Fruit-Trees (1652) 182
Dickson, D.R. 22–23
Discours of husbandrie used in Brabant and Flanders (1650) 183
Discoverie for division or setting out of land (1653) 190, 192
distillation chemistry 178, 233
Dornau, Caspar 16, 18
Drabik, Mikuláš 126–127
drainage innovations 81, 165, 168, 254
Drebbel, Cornelius 166
Dublin, New College 162
Ducket, Thomas 237
Dugard, William 183–184
Dunbar, Battle of 100, 158
Durham, New College 157, 160–162
Durie family 25

Dury, Dorothy. *See* Moore, Dorothy (1644, Mrs John Dury)
Dury, John 2–3, 5–7, 9, 14, 19–21, 23–27, 29–33, 35, 37–39, 43–44, 48–49, 51, 55–58, 61, 63–77, 79–82, 84–92, 100, 102, 106–111, 117, 119, 122–125, 132–135, 137–139, 141, 145–151, 155–157, 163, 178, 181, 188, 191, 197–200, 205–208, 210, 215–216, 218–224, 239, 250–251, 255–258
   ecclesiastical peace mission 239
   Elbing 25–27, 29–30
   Israels call to march out of Babylon unto Jerusalem (1646) 71
   Office of Address 139, 216, 218–219, 223–224, 251
   On Education 24, 30, 32–33, 67, 75–76, 138–139, 147–150, 156–157
   'Some Proposalls towards the Advancement of Learning' (1653) 149
   The Reformed School (1850) 58, 138–139, 147–149
   Westminster Assembly 88–89, 110, 218
Dymock, Cressy 155–156, 168–169, 180–181, 190, 192, 213, 221–222
   Discovery for Division or Setting out of Land (1653) 190, 192

ecclesiastical peace. *See* reconciliation of the churches
Eccleston, Richard 224
economic debate 41–44, 136, 150–151, 165–166, 191–193, 251–252, 254–255
education administration 54–68, 89–91, 98–99, 149–150, 153–155
education and training 3–4, 6–7, 13–14, 23, 26, 30, 33–34, 39, 41, 43, 45–48, 53–54, 56, 61, 63–65, 67–68, 72, 75, 82, 89, 94–95, 99–100, 106, 132, 137–139, 141–150, 152–157, 160, 163–164, 197, 221, 231, 238, 250
   administration 64, 99, 138
   artisans 5, 153, 156, 165–166, 169
   poor 152, 160, 164
   Scholasticism, critique of 72
   schools 42, 46, 50, 64, 67–68, 73, 81, 139–142, 145, 147, 149, 153–155, 160, 252
   universities 14, 20, 72, 99–100, 103, 106, 132, 146, 151, 153, 163–164, 221, 230
   women and girls 145, 148, 197
Elbing 6, 11–14, 21, 24–27, 29, 73, 82, 137
Emmanuel College, Cambridge 20, 204
enclosure debate 180, 184
England as a haven for scholarship 43, 55–56
Englands Thankfulnesse, to the Committee for Religion in the High Court of Parliament (1642) 64, 66, 71, 75
episcopacy 238
Erbery, William 158
Eure, George, 6th Baron Eure 159
Evelyn, John 112, 114, 170, 201, 208–209, 227, 233
Evenius, Sigismund 45

Fabel, Hans 175–176
Faber, Albert Otto 239–240
Felicitas Ultimi Sæculi (1640) 116–118
Field, Thomas 187
Fiennes, Colonel Nathaniel 233
Fifth Monarchists 120, 127
Figulus, Petr 43, 92, 124, 127, 134, 196, 201, 203–204, 210, 239–243, 245
Flanders 183, 185, 189
Fleetwood, Lieutenant-General Charles 188
Franckenberg, Abraham von 16–18, 121
Frankland, Richard 160, 164
   Rathmell Academy 164
French, John 173, 176
Fridwald, Johann 21, 23–24

Frost, Gualter Sen. 86, 133
Froyle, East Hampshire 233

Galen 103, 106, 132
Galileo Galilei 112
Gassendi, Pierre 105, 112
Gauden, John 61, 65
Geer, Laurentius de 92, 198, 203, 230, 241, 243
Geer, Ludovicus de 62, 70
Georg II, Duke of Brieg 15
Georg Rudolf, Duke of Legnica 15, 17
Gerbier, Balthazar 146
Gilson, Thomas 255
Glauber, Johann Rudolf 81, 173, 175–178
  Furni novi philosophici (*1646-1649*) 175–176
Glaum, Phillip 23
Gloucestershire 152
Goddard, Jonathan 133
Godemann, Caspar 38, 79, 90
Godemann, Jacob 27
Golius, Jacobus 243
Good Old Cause 124, 213–214, 249
Goodwin, John 109
Goodwin, Thomas 20
Górka, Stanisław 12
Görlitz 17
Gray's Inn 96
Great Queen Street 85
Greengrass, M. 83, 143
Gresham College 67, 226–227
Greville, Robert, 2nd Lord Brooke 33, 81
Groningen 106
Grotius, Hugo 241, 245
Grundmann, Martin 203, 207, 237, 239
Gryphius, Andreas 17
Gühler, Michael 121–124
Gustavus Adolphus, King of Sweden 116

Haak, Theodore 20, 50, 58, 63, 68, 80, 90, 227
Hackney 6, 33, 36, 195
Hall, Bishop Joseph 57
Hall, John 7, 36, 94, 96–104, 113–114, 131–133, 140, 146–147, 155, 157–158, 175, 186, 221, 231, 255
  Humble motion concerning the advancement of learning, and reformation of the universities (1649) 99–103, 132–133, 146, 158
  Mataeotechnia medicinae praxeōs: with an humble motion for the reformation of the universities (1652) 101–104
Hamilton, William 68, 106, 149, 195, 227
Harding, John 172
Harley, Sir Edward 201, 237
Harmar, Samuel 7, 152–153
Harrison, Major-General Thomas 74, 211
Harrison, Thomas (inventor) 90, 217
Hartlib, Anne (Nan) (younger daughter of Samuel) 197, 199
Hartlibian Political Economy 252–254
Hartlibian Scientific Movement 253
Hartlib, Mary (elder daughter of Samuel) 197–199, 207
Hartlib, Mary (née Burningham, wife of Samuel) 32, 196
Hartlib, Samuel
  academies, failed 32–35
  communications system 36–39
  coworkers 4–5, 7–8, 249. *See also* Katherine Boyle, Robert Boyle, Comenius, John Dury, John Hall, Dorothy Moore, William Petty, William
  early life and education 11–28
  economic innovation 4, 7, 57, 93, 136, 160, 165, 168, 191, 193, 215, 217, 236, 251–254, 257
  educational change 13–15, 32–34, 39–42, 45–47, 63–64, 68, 89, 95, 99–100, 137–139, 237–238
  family life 11–13, 32, 195–199
  housing exiles 37, 41, 92, 134, 196, 250–251

ill-health 2, 8, 93, 199–202, 225, 228, 249
political associations 2, 43, 61–62, 83–84, 91, 96, 100, 102, 125, 131–135, 137, 212, 218, 236, 251–252, 256
poverty 31, 33, 37, 81–82, 86, 88, 203–208, 216, 225
Puritan affiliations 6, 20, 23, 35–37, 73, 116, 118, 170–171, 257
relations with age and social groups 166, 226, 253–255
terminal illness 200–202, 207, 232, 238–239, 246–248
writing block 64, 186, 188–189, 213–214, 218–219, 250
Hartlib, Samuel Jr. (son of Samuel) 195, 197–198, 225
Hartlieb, Daniel (son of Georg, brother of Samuel) 207
Hartlieb, Elizabeth (mother of Samuel) 30
Hartlieb, Georg brother of Samuel) 12–14, 19, 40–41, 196, 207, 244, 256
Hartlieb, Georg (father of Samuel) 11–12
Haslmayr, Adam 115
Hayy ibn Yaqzān. *See Risalat*
Hebraic studies 76, 91
Heidelberg University 13, 41
Hein, Heinrich 22–23
Heinrichson, Friedrich 216
Helmontians 102, 132, 174–175, 240
Helmont, Jan Baptist van 81, 102, 106–107, 113, 171–176
  Ortus medicinae (1648) 173–176
Henshaw, Thomas 170–171, 227, 234–235
Herbert, Edward, Lord Herbert 46
Herbert, Edward, Lord Herbert of Cherbury 114, 207
  De Veritate (1624) 114
Herbert, Philip, Earl of Pembroke 82
Herefordshire 153, 200–201, 211–212, 250

Hill, Joseph 159
History of Trades 95, 151
Hitchin 147, 153
Hobbes, Thomas 107, 111
  Leviathan (1651) 107, 111
Hofmann, Christian von Hofmannswaldau 18
Holbeck, Martin 153
Hoole, Charles 142–143
Horne, Thomas 34, 43, 45, 144–145
Horn, Georg 155
Horrocks, Jeremiah 137
Hübner, Joachim 50–54, 59–60, 63–64, 79, 105
Hünefeld, Andreas 247
Hunton, Philip 159
husbandry 3–4, 7–8, 31, 105, 154–156, 165, 170, 179, 181, 183–187, 189–192, 211, 214, 217, 222, 252–254
Huser, Johannes 172

Ibn Tufayl 246
Idea of Mathematics written by Mr Joh. Pell to Samuel Hartlib (1638) 58
Independents 83, 87, 94, 109, 132, 218, 220, 241, 255
international Puritanism 118
Invisible College 95
Ireland 7, 79, 84–85, 93, 95, 134, 161–162, 187–189, 193, 204, 206–207, 209, 212, 222, 225, 234, 236
Irelands Naturall History (1652) 186–187
  interrogatories 186–189
Israel 71, 73–74, 77, 101, 117, 119, 128, 131
Israel, Menasseh ben
  Hope of Israel (1650) 119

Jessey, Henry 85–86, 124
Jesus Christ 67, 76, 116, 119, 242
Jesus College, Cambridge 136
Jews 74–77, 91, 116, 119–120, 122
  Conversion of 91, 116, 119

Joachim Friedrich, Duke of Brieg 15
Johann Christian, Duke of Brieg
    15–17, 121
Jones, Katherine, Lady Ranelagh.
    See Boyle, Katherine (Jones,
    Viscountess Ranelagh)
Jones, Margaret, Lady Clotworthy 84
Jonston, John 40, 46

Kabbalah 21
Kalthoff, Caspar 156, 167–168
Karaism 91
Karl Ludwig, Prince Elector Palatine
    39, 79–80
Kempe, Joseph 147–148, 150, 153
Keus, Stephanus 240
kidney stones 93
King, Edward 83
King, Sir John 83
King, Sir Robert 133–135, 151
Kinner, Cyprian 16–18, 141, 148
Kinner, Samuel 18
Komenský, Jan Amos 39, 60
Königsberg University 13–14
Koy, Johannes 24
Kraiński, Jan Krzysztof 244, 247–248
Küffeler, Johann Sibertus 160, 166,
    237
Kvačala, Ján Radomil 215
Kynaston, Sir Francis 98, 146

Lambert, Major-General John 159,
    238
L'Amy, Hugh 90, 93, 218
Land Bank concept 145, 191–193,
    236–237, 251
Langley, Henry 88
Langton, Elizabeth (mother of
    Samuel Hartlib) 12
Langton, John (grandfather of
    Samuel Hartlib) 12
language teaching methods 34, 140
Lauban, Melchior 15–16, 146–147
Laurin, Jiří 41, 43
Lawrence, Henry, Lord President of
    the Council of State 133, 135

Leiden 14, 25, 31, 91, 243
Lenthall, William, Speaker of the
    House of Commons 102, 158
Leszczyński, Rafal 42–43
Leszno (Lissa) 8, 11, 40–41, 43–44,
    49–50, 52, 54, 60, 63, 70, 134, 142,
    144, 256
liberty of conscience 16, 107–108, 212
Lilburne, Colonel Robert 159
Lincoln College, Oxford 161–162
Lithuanian Bible 244, 247
Liu, Tai 117
Llwyd, Morgan 124
Logau, Friedrich von 14, 16, 18
London 6, 9, 11, 23–24, 30, 32–34, 39,
    41, 43, 48, 52, 59, 62, 67–68, 70, 76,
    79–80, 82–84, 87–88, 91–93, 97,
    104, 106, 109, 111, 113, 118, 125,
    132–134, 139–145, 153–154, 158,
    162, 164–166, 169, 195–196, 198,
    204, 207, 210, 215, 218–219, 222,
    225, 230–231, 234, 236, 238, 244,
    247
London Corporation for the Poor
    152
projected college for inventions and
    experiments 59, 93
projected university 75–76, 91, 163
Lord Protector 126, 134, 168, 224,
    241–242
Louvain 106

Macaria 59, 229, 240–241
    Description of the Famous Kingdome of
    Macaria (1641) 59
Malcolm, N. 242
Marshal, Alexander 166
Marshall, William 96
Marsh, Francis 204
Martini, Johannes 16
Massachusetts Bay Company 35
Mede, Joseph 20, 115–116, 120–123
Mercator (Kauffman), Nikolaus 169,
    209, 228, 235
Merchant Adventurers Company 25
Mercurius Britannicus 131

Mercurius Politicus 131
Merton, R.K. 257
Metcalfe, Anthony 196
Millenarianism 75, 116, 118–119, 121, 257. *See also* Fifth Monarchists
Milton, John 1, 7, 72, 98, 100, 102, 109, 118–119, 145–146, 155
  Areopagitica 51, 72, 100, 118
  Of Education 72, 100, 145–148
mnemonics 211
Mochinger, Johann 40
Montagu, Edward, Viscount Mandeville, 2nd Earl of Manchester 38
Montanus, Johannes 172
Moore, Dorothy (1644, Mrs John Dury) 3–5, 7, 83–85, 92, 133, 148, 151, 197, 206–208, 210
Moray, Sir Robert 227
More, Henry 136, 204, 227
Morgan, Edward 166
Morgan, Sir Anthony 227, 236
Moriaen, Johann 2, 26, 50–51, 166, 190
Morsius, Joachim 18
Mortalism 114
Morton, Bishop Thomas 36
Motion tending to the publick good of this age (1642) 66–69
Mulsow, Martin 121
Mylius, Jan 13

Navigation Acts 93
Nedham, Marchamont 131, 155, 222
Neile, Sir Paul 227
Neomenius, Johannes 16–17
Netherlands 4, 23, 26, 55, 60, 70, 80, 84, 87, 105–106, 110, 116, 118–119, 177, 198, 205, 210, 216, 234, 247
Nevil, John 187
New England 23, 29, 35, 82, 139, 157, 193, 209, 257–258
New Haven 82, 139, 157
New Jerusalem 6, 71, 77, 117
Newton, Isaac 127

Nominated Assembly (1653) 74, 133, 149
  Committee for the Advancement of Learning 133, 149
Northampton 143
Northampton Free School 143
Nüssler, Bernhard Wilhelm 18
Nye, Philip 35, 255

Of Education. To Master Samuel Hartlib (1644) 72, 145–148
Office of Address 5, 8, 37, 94–95, 98, 105, 133, 139, 145, 150, 164, 214–225, 251
Oldenburg, Henry 210, 227, 233, 242
Olearius, Adam 198
Opitz, Martin 18
Oriental Studies 8, 91, 155, 243, 245–246
Oxenstierna, Axel 12
Oxford 51–52, 79–80, 107, 133, 148, 151, 182–183, 218–219, 241
Oxford, University of 87–88, 90, 99, 148, 157–158, 161–163, 171, 183, 234, 245–246, 255–256
  Bodleian Library 80, 87, 97, 99, 148, 219
    Library Keeper 87–88, 148
  experimental philosophy club 227
  Parliamentary Visitation (1647-1652) 183

Palissy, Bernard 58
Palmer, Herbert 30, 87
Palmer, Thomas 86
Paracelsus (Theophrastus von Hohenheim) 18, 115, 172
Pareus, David 13
Parliament 30–31, 61–62, 64–66, 68–69, 71–72, 74, 79–81, 86–88, 94, 99–103, 111, 117, 119–120, 131–133, 138, 140, 149, 151, 158–159, 162, 182, 205, 219, 223, 233, 238, 248, 250
Paston, Robert, First Earl of Yarmouth 228, 234–235

Paston, Sir William 235
Peake, Mrs (aunt of Samuel Hartlib) 30
Pearson, Anthony 255
Peiresc, Nicolas-Claude Fabri de 105, 112
Pell, John 1, 32, 45, 50, 56–58, 63–64, 80, 87, 89–90, 92, 126, 147, 155, 157, 184, 198, 200, 212, 227, 248
  Idea of Mathematicks (1639) 147
Pennington, Isaac 38, 80
Pennoyer, William 152–153
Pepys, Samuel 196, 198–199
Pereira, Gómez 106–107
Pergens, Jacob 91
perpetual motion 169, 254
Pett, Peter 227, 236
Petty, William 7, 89, 92, 94–96, 100, 106, 133, 147, 150–151, 154–156, 167, 181, 184, 205, 224–225, 227, 236, 255
  Advice of W.P. to Mr. Samuel Hartlib for the advancement of some particular parts of learning (1648) 95, 100, 133, 147, 150–151, 154, 224, 255
Philosemitism 75
Philosopher's stone. *See* alchemy
Pinnel, Henry 172
Piscator, Johannes 118
plague 12, 16, 24
Plattes, Gabriel 7, 58–59, 80, 117, 165, 179–180, 190, 217, 253
Pococke, Edward 245–246, 256
Poehmer, Joachim Abraham 22, 24–25, 50–51, 55
Polemann, Joachim 229, 234
Polesworth, Warwickshire, Free School 155
Posnań (Posen) 11–12
Potter, William 156, 168–169, 191–193, 236–237, 254–255
  The Key to Wealth (1650) 191, 254
Potts, Charles 38
Powell, Vavasor 124

Presbyterians 25, 102–103, 110, 170. *See also* Scottish Presbyterians
Preston, John 19
Privy Council Committee on Durham College 159, 200
Protector. *See* Lord Protector
Protestant exiles 8, 196
Protestant societies and pacts 21–24, 68–69, 98–99, 167, 169, 198–199, 229, 234–235
Protestant state alliances 125, 134–135
Providence Island Company 35
Pruvost, Pierre le 90, 93, 218
public good 25, 33, 37, 48, 57, 68–69, 73–74, 86, 102, 132, 201, 203–204, 213, 252, 257–258
Pulham St Mary, Norfolk 153
Puritanism 4, 6, 8, 19–20, 23, 26, 35–37, 48, 59, 73–74, 77, 100, 110, 116–118, 137–138, 170–172, 183, 257
Pym, John 1, 36, 38, 48, 64, 79, 81, 132, 255

Quarles, Francis 195

Rákóczi, Prince György (of Transylvania) 118
Rand family 104–106, 111, 224
Rand, William 3, 7, 92, 96, 104–107, 109–114, 149, 155, 164, 175, 190, 224–225, 228
Ranelagh, Viscountess. *See* Boyle, Katherine (Jones, Viscountess Ranelagh)
Rave, Christian 155
Rawlin, Joshua 106, 153–155
Ray, John 166, 209, 239, 253
reconciliation of the churches 26, 47, 65–66, 72–73, 86, 91, 98, 118, 123–124, 134–135, 215–216, 240–243, 250
Reformation of schooles (1642) 53, 141–142
Renaudot, Théophraste 37, 216–217, 251

republicanism 100, 107. *See also* Good Old Cause
Revelation, Book of 116–117, 121, 123–124
Richardson, John, Bishop of Ardagh 36
Rich, Robert, Earl of Warwick 38
Rich, Sir Nathaniel (cousin of Robert Rich) 82
Risalat Hayy ibn Yaqzān 246
Ritschel, Georg 80–81, 160
Rittangel, Johann Stephan 66, 71, 75, 90–91
Robartes, John, Baron Robartes, later First Earl of Radnor 38, 58
Robinson, Henry 108, 145, 181, 191–192, 221–223, 251
Roe, Sir Thomas 38, 57, 81
Rosicrucians 52, 234
Rostock University 22
Rota Club 193, 233, 236
Rothe, Johannes (Sir John Rode) 199
Rotterdam 71, 84, 86, 197
Rous, Francis 91, 106, 132–133, 149, 220
Royal Society 59, 166, 210, 226–230, 235, 253
Rulice, Johann 20, 92
Rump Parliament 99, 102, 119–120, 138
Rusdorf, Johann Joachim von 39

Sadler, John 83, 89–91, 106, 133, 171, 181, 232
Saltonstall, Sir Richard 124
Samuel Hartlib his legacie: or An enlargement of the Discourse of husbandry used in Brabant and Flaunders (1651 etc) 185–187, 189–193
Sárospatak 118, 142
Sarson, Laurence 66
sassafras 235
Schaum, Constantin 134
Scherfer, Wencel v.Scherferstein 18
Schickfus, Jakob 15

Schlezer, Johann Friedrich 127, 134
Schwenckfeld, Capar v., Schweckfeldians 18
Scottish Presbyterians 25
Seaman, Lazarus 243
Second Coming 116
seed drill experiments 181
Serrarius, Petrus 26, 92, 128, 247
Shaw, John 253–254
  Brief Discours of Excellent Wayes and Means (1646) 253–254
Sibbes, Richard 20
Sidney, Robert, 2nd Earl of Leicester 84
Silesia 6, 13–18, 30, 41, 121–122, 124, 146, 172, 239
  cultural diversity 6, 15, 17
  religious tensions 17
Skytte, Bengt 230–231
Slingsby, Henry 228, 236
Smart, John 148
Smith, Thomas 105
Snel, George 7, 154–156
Society of Graduate Physicians 104, 112–114, 164
Socinianism 45, 52, 107–109, 114, 255
Somerset, Edward, 2nd Marquess of Worcester 156, 167
Sparrow, John 171, 254
Speede, William 32, 34
Spenser, William 183–184
spiritualism and mysticism 17, 29, 72, 77, 86, 108, 121, 232, 255
Sprigg, William 159–161
St Amand, John 81
Standish, Arthur 212–214, 249
Stanley, Thomas 96, 98
Starkey, George 170
St Catharine's College, Cambridge 20, 105
steam power 167–168
St John, Oliver 82, 87–88, 91, 120, 132–133
St John's College, Cambridge 44, 96, 98, 140, 154

St Katherine's Hospital. Ledbury 201, 208, 211
St Martin-in-the-Fields 202, 248
St Mary's, Aldermanbury 20
Stoughton, John 20, 48, 60, 117
Stoughton, Nicholas 62, 65, 81
Streete, Thomas 171, 228, 235
Streso, Caspar 20, 43–44, 46
Stretton Grandison, Herefordshire 211
Strickland, Sir William 159
St Stephen's, Coleman Street 31, 35, 109
Stuart, Elizabeth, Queen of Bohemia, Electress Palatiine 79
Summary delineation of Dr. Cyprian Kinner Silesian, his thoughts concerning education (1648) 141
Sweden 13, 23, 62, 70, 79, 125, 127, 135, 230, 233
Sweeting, John 106
Switzerland 134, 188
Sybilista, Wendelius 198
Sydenham, Colonel William 83, 89, 133
Sydenham, Thomas 89
Symner, Myles 133–134, 151, 188, 204–205
Szprotawa (Sprottau) 11

Tassius, Johann Adolf 52, 54, 57
Tauler, Johannes 18
technical innovation 1, 7, 165–166, 179
Temple, John 84
The Hague 69, 112, 200
Third Protectorate Parliament 238
Thirty-Years War 116
Thurloe, John 87, 133, 197, 225
Tolnai Dali János 118
Tong, Ezerel 7, 127, 158–161, 164, 167, 170, 237–238
Tradescant, John, Jr. 106
Trenchard, John 83, 133, 156
Trevor-Roper, H. 60, 68

Trinity College, Cambridge 204
Tschesch, Johann Theodor von 16–18
Turkish Bible 242–245
Turnbull, G.H. 1, 13–14, 19, 24–25, 27, 30–33, 39–40, 56, 60–63, 68–69, 84, 88, 97–98, 142, 148, 152, 157, 185, 198, 202, 213–215, 225–228, 248

Underhill, Thomas 146
universities. *See* education and training
Upsala 135
Ussher, James, Archbishop of Armagh 36, 38, 57, 162
    Library to Dublin 162
Utrecht 106

Vane, Sir Henry the younger 117, 212–213
Vaughan, Thomas (chemist) 170
Vaughan, Thomas (Durham College) 159–160
Vauxhall house 156
Vechner, David 41, 43
Vechner, Georg 15, 41, 43
Venner, Thomas 125
Verulamian College 93–94
Vindication of Liberty of Religion (1646) 107–108
Vosgan Yerevantsi 245

Waldensian massacres 134, 256
Waller, Sir William 38, 49, 88–89
Wallington, Nehemiah 117
Wallis, John 244
Walloon College, Leiden 25
Walther, Balthasar 18
Ward, Nathaniel 21
Ward, Samuel 20–21
Warner, Levinus 90–91, 241, 243
Wartensky, Samuel 207, 233
Warwick, Earl of. *See* Rich, Robert
Watson, F. 138
Webbe, Francis 170
Webbe, Joseph 34, 143
Webster, John 158, 228

Węgierski, Andrzej 40
Weigel, Valentin 18
Welles, Walter 32, 35
Westminster Assembly 82, 87–89, 110, 218
Weston, Sir Richard 31, 183–184
Westrow, Thomas 133, 219–220
Wheare, Degory 99
Whichcote, Benjamin 204
Whitehall Conference (1655) 120
Whiting, Chares Edward 157
Wight, Sarah 85–86
Wilkins, John 168, 204, 226–227
Williams, Bishop John 33, 64
Winchester 7, 49, 82, 88–90, 92
Winthrop, John Jr. 169, 201, 208–209, 257–258
Wodenothe, Richard 185, 189
Wood, Robert 151, 160, 162, 184, 188, 192–193, 205, 209, 222, 225, 228, 230, 234–236, 252, 254

Woodward, Hezekiah 34, 143–144, 231
Worsley, Benjamin 2–3, 7, 76, 86, 89–96, 98, 105–109, 111, 119, 126–127, 150, 156, 165, 167, 171–172, 177–178, 181, 190–192, 200, 204, 208, 212, 225, 228, 235, 254
  Phytological Letter 190
  'Proffits humbly presented' 3, 76, 93–94, 150, 165, 192
  Vindication of liberty of religion (1646) (vid Johannes Crell) 107–108
Worthington, John 1–2, 5, 20, 76–77, 111, 127–128, 136, 163, 199, 202, 204–206, 208, 211, 226–227, 229–230, 232, 237, 239, 242, 244, 246, 256

Zeller, Michael 24
Zürich 156

About the Team

Alessandra Tosi was the managing editor for this book.

Lucy Barnes proof-read this manuscript.

Hannah Shakespeare and Lucy Barnes indexed this book.

Jeevanjot Kaur Nagpal designed the cover. The cover was produced in InDesign using the Fontin font.

Annie Hine typeset the book in InDesign. The main text font is Tex Gyre Pagella and the heading font is Californian FB.

The conversion to the PDF and HTML editions was performed with open-source software and other tools freely available on our GitHub page at https://github.com/OpenBookPublishers.

Jeremy Bowman created the EPUB.

Hannah Shakespeare was in charge of marketing.

This book was peer-reviewed by three anonymous referees. Experts in their field, these readers donated their time to help ensure the academic rigour of our books. We are grateful for their generous and invaluable contributions.

This book need not end here...

Share

All our books — including the one you have just read — are free to access online so that students, researchers and members of the public who can't afford a printed edition will have access to the same ideas. This title will be accessed online by hundreds of readers each month across the globe: why not share the link so that someone you know is one of them?

This book and additional content is available at
https://doi.org/10.11647/OBP.0486

Donate

Open Book Publishers is an award-winning, scholar-led, not-for-profit press making knowledge freely available one book at a time. We don't charge authors to publish with us: instead, our work is supported by our library members and by donations from people who believe that research shouldn't be locked behind paywalls.

Join the effort to free knowledge by supporting us at
https://www.openbookpublishers.com/support-us

We invite you to connect with us on our socials!

BLUESKY	MASTODON	LINKEDIN
@openbookpublish.bsky.social	@OpenBookPublish@hcommons.social	open-book-publishers

Read more at the Open Book Publishers Blog

https://blogs.openbookpublishers.com

You may also be interested in:

Pietro Giannone (1676–1748): The Tragedy of a Historian and the Inquisition
His Autobiography, translated with commentary by Therese Ridley
Thérèse Ridley
https://doi.org/10.11647/OBP.0483

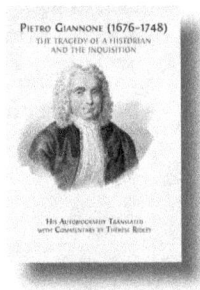

Science in the Salon: Atoms and Animals in Madeleine de Scudéry's 'Conversations' (1680–92)
An Essay and Translation
Helena Taylor
https://doi.org/10.11647/OBP.0465

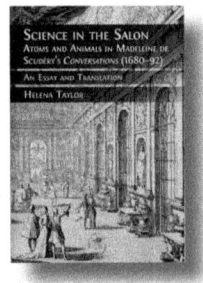

The European Experience
A Multi-Perspective History of Modern Europe, 1500–2000
Edited by Jan Hansen, Jochen Hung, Jaroslav Ira, et al.
https://doi.org/10.11647/OBP.0323

www.ingramcontent.com/pod-product-compliance
Lightning Source LLC
Chambersburg PA
CBHW050204240426
43671CB00013B/2240